HARVARD HISTORICAL STUDIES, 154

Published under the auspices
of the Department of History
from the income of the
Paul Revere Frothingham Bequest
Robert Louis Stroock Fund
Henry Warren Torrey Fund

The Demands of Liberty

*Civil Society in France
since the Revolution*

Pierre Rosanvallon

Translated by Arthur Goldhammer

Harvard University Press
Cambridge, Massachusetts
London, England
2007

0911852

Originally published as *Le Modèle politique français:
La société civile contre le jacobinisme de 1789 à nos jours*
© Editions du Seuil, 2004

Library of Congress Cataloging-in-Publication Data

Rosanvallon, Pierre, 1948–

[Modèle politique français. English]

The demands of liberty: civil society in France since the
Revolution/ Pierre Rosanvallon; translated by Arthur Goldhammer.

p.   cm—(Harvard historical studies; 154)

Includes biographical references and index.

ISBN-13: 978-0-674-02496-0 (alk. paper)
ISBN-10: 0-674-02496-6 (alk. paper)

1. France—Politics and government.   2. France—History—Revolution,
1789–1799—Influence.   3. Representative government and
representation—France.   4. Democracy—France.   I. Title.

DC252.R6413 2007

320.944—dc22   200605078

Contents

The Demands of Liberty

Introduction

Democratic Pathways and the French Case

At the dawn of the twenty-first century, democracy is at once triumphant and uncertain. While the principles on which it is based are now universally held to be self-evident, there is growing perplexity regarding its nature and ultimate form. Questions proliferate at all latitudes even as globalization blurs the boundaries of democracy's territory. Democracy today seems to suffer from an inherent contradiction. On the one hand, men and women aspire to take ever more direct charge of their own lives, and to that end they see the constitution of a strong and autonomous civil society as a prerequisite of their emancipation. On the other hand, they are asking more and more of politics in order to enhance their ability to manage their shared destiny. So on the one hand we find an aspiration to ever greater pluralism and decentralization, broader counterpowers, and closer scrutiny of institutions at the grassroots level, while on the other hand we see a search for a central location where an effective common will can take shape and find expression in order to ward off the danger of "governance without government." This contradiction is today the source of numerous conflicts bearing on the legitimacy and representativeness of public and political institutions on the one hand and civil society on the other.

These tensions have been exacerbated by recent changes on the international scene. In themselves, however, there is nothing novel about them. They stand as a permanent backdrop to contemporary history. The gap between "civil" democracy and "political" democracy has manifested itself continually over the past two centuries. Related to this, the definition of the general interest has always been controversial, ranging from the notion that the general interest is somehow merely a composite of particular interests to the idea that it encompasses a more general view transcending all

1

particular interests. Indeed, the problem of defining the general interest has revealed the fundamental tensions of democracy in their most radical form, most especially the confrontation between the particular and the general, between civil society and the state. Hence this issue offers an ideal vantage point. The aim of this book is twofold: to retrace the history of this question, about which, paradoxically, little has been written and much has been obscured by clichés; and to use this study as a way of gaining a broader view of what conditions might favor the development of a more vibrant democracy today.

The Two Histories of France

France has long stood out as a country in which government has assumed a paramount role in organizing collective existence. But that role has often been presented in a reductive fashion, exemplified by Alexis de Tocqueville's description of an omnipotent state, unchecked by any opposing forces, dominating an atomized, unorganized, and subjugated civil society. *L'Ancien Régime et la Révolution* inscribed the canonical verses of this vulgate in the marble of conventional wisdom. Since Tocqueville's time there have been any number of negative accounts of a central government that "managed to destroy all intermediary powers" to become "the ultimate driving force of the social machine and sole and necessary agent of public life," having ensured "that between it and private individuals nothing remained but a vast and empty space." It became common to refer to this inveterate failing of French political organization as the embodiment of the "Jacobin tradition," and "Jacobinism" was taken to be synonymous with the demon of centralization. This diagnosis was rephrased in every imaginable idiom, from journalistic essays to learned tomes and political broadsides, to say nothing of party platforms and stump speeches. There is no shortage of facts that can be marshaled in support of this analysis; a prosecutor would have no difficulty drawing up a list of institutions and laws, bureaucratic practices, and political statements to be included in an indictment of Jacobinism. But such a procedure will not take us to the heart of the matter. There is in fact another history that needs to be taken into account if we wish to achieve a fuller portrait, namely, the history of the powerful forms that resistance to this very Jacobinism has taken. Indeed, the Jacobin model was vigorously denounced and criticized even as it was widely asserted to be dominant. Furthermore, the model has not remained fixed in its original form; indeed, it has been extensively modified. For instance, it was necessary to make room for trade unions and civil associations, although these were initially rejected as superfluous or illegitimate. If we are to appreciate France for what it really is, we must take this essential tension into account.

My purpose is to grasp both horns of the dilemma in order to propose a broad new interpretation of what has been called "the French model." For quite some time now there have existed two opposed and mutually exclusive types of French history, from which emerge two very different pictures of France. On the one hand there is the history of ideas, which focuses primarily on institutional discourse and legal forms and emphasizes the centralizing tradition as well as the permanent antiliberal temptation stemming from the "absolutization" of popular sovereignty and the state's claim to institute and instruct society. On the other hand there is social history, which focuses on social movements and the actual functioning of institutions, points up the autonomy of social agents and their ability to alter the programmed course of events, and reveals conflicts and ways in which proclaimed principles need to be compromised and tailored to fit social realities. To a certain extent this distinction is one between representation and reality. Against the conventional image of a situation in which the state supposedly confronts society directly, without intermediaries, we are forced to recognize the concrete existence of "intermediary bodies" denied by theory.[1] Thus there is a "general" political or intellectual history, which is contradicted in practice by a whole set of "specific" histories of various aspects of institutional and social life. The goal, however, is not to separate these two approaches in order to compare or juxtapose them in the hope of arriving at a more adequate description. It is rather to weave them together, to write a dynamic history of representations by incorporating the tensions and contradictions that beset them, and in so doing to offer a reflective history of the social in which the perceptions and projects of the social agents play a directly active role.

In this regard, methodological problems are inextricably intertwined with epistemological issues. Could France have functioned if Tocqueville's frozen description had really been accurate? There is no escaping the conclusion that France is far more distinctive in the ways in which it represents itself than in its actual conduct. The history of France is the history of an attraction and a resistance that together constitute a system. For that very reason it is a vibrant history, whereas the Tocquevillean vulgate assumes a

static France, devoid of history and straitjacketed by the radical character
of its fundamental principles. My purpose is not to deny the power of illiberal political culture in France.[2] That culture, however, needs to be seen in
its dynamic context, in relation to the difficulties and obstacles it has continually faced.

From Jacobinism to the Political Culture of Generality

Jacobinism is a reference as evocative as it is imprecise; it produces a convenient image, but it also serves as a screen, by focusing attention on a particular revolutionary faction as defining the essential character of the French
model. Our first order of business must be to deconstruct this overly vague
idea, with its unduly narrow connotation, and to replace it with another:
the political culture of generality.[3] The first part of the book is devoted to a
methodical characterization of this idea. The three principal dimensions of
this political culture are examined at the moment of their inception in the
French Revolution. Thus we look at the political culture of generality as a
social form (the celebration of the "great national whole"), as a political
quality (faith in the virtues of immediacy), and as a regulatory procedure
(the cult of the law). Significantly, this approach has the virtue of making
comparison easier. Whereas the customary term "Jacobinism" tends to
make the French case exceptional and peculiar, the idea of a political culture of generality embeds it in the broader and more complex context of
democratic modernity.

Generality must first be understood as a *social form*. Its defining characteristics from 1789 on were the rejection of intermediary bodies and the
aspiration to achieve a single, unified society. "There is no longer any corporation within the state; henceforth there is only the particular interest of
each individual and the general interest. No person is permitted to inspire
any intermediate interest in citizens or to alienate them from the public
good by inspiring a corporatist spirit." These celebrated words of Isaac-
René-Guy Le Chapelier clearly expressed the type of preoccupation that
animated the members of the Constituent Assembly. The rejection of a society of orders and corporations stemmed from this vision. With it arose a
novel representation of communal existence, of "being together" *(l'être ensemble)*. In order to throw off the weight of the past, the nation asserted itself in the Revolution as a totality, a whole that could not be reduced to any
of its intermediate components. The concept of *polarization* can be intro-

duced at this stage to describe a vision of a society arrayed between two poles, the individual on the one hand and the "whole" on the other, with all intermediary structures suspected a priori of either impeding access to the generality or profiting from it. The elimination of intermediary bodies also led to a realignment of social affects. The "corporate bond" that lent practical substance to communal existence and structured each individual's representations of his relation to others could not simply be replaced by an assertion of belonging to some larger whole, even when that whole was magnified and sublimated in festival and thereby given legible form. The inevitably more abstract character of the new "general" social bond thus all but required some sort of tangible token. This requirement explains the importance that the issue of friendship and fraternity assumed in the Revolution: warmth of private affection was called upon to compensate for the abstract nature of the bond of citizenship.

Generality is also a *political quality*. The rejection of intermediary bodies discussed in the preceding paragraph, sociological in nature, was extended into the realm of politics proper: any authority capable of competing with the legal expression of the general will was open to challenge. Thus the role of clubs and popular societies was vigorously debated. "Political intermediary bodies" were regarded as an intolerable threat to the fundamental principle of representative government: monopoly of collective expression. They were also suspected of sapping the efficacy of the state by impeding its unity of action. Any intermediary political body was suspected of corrupting the general will by insidiously influencing the way in which it was formed. This suspicion was soon compounded by criticism of representatives as the equivalent of a new aristocracy bent on confiscating the people's voice. An important distinction should be kept in mind, however. Linked to the attack on the entropy of representative government, calls for *direct democracy* harked back to the utopian vision of the people as continually active in the role of both legislator and magistrate. The idea of *immediate democracy* referred to something else. It implied that the people were capable of expressing themselves as a body, as a unit able to speak with a clear voice and to stake out an unambiguous position. Direct democracy rejected *delegation*, the principle that one person can act and speak for others. Immediate democracy dismissed any form of *interface*, that is, any form of institution or procedure that functionally contributed to the structuring of collective expression.

Lastly, the generality has a *procedural* dimension. This relates to the role of law, which is granted paramount status. It is customary to stress the explicitly liberal implications of such "nomophilia" by contrasting the rule of law to the unpredictable exercise of arbitrary power. Of course the celebration of the law was closely related to recognition of the sovereignty of the general will from which the law was now said to emanate. Another aspect of this also deserves close attention, however: this is the argument, historically associated with the Physiocrats, that what constitutes good government is not the procedural but the rational basis of government action. From Cesare Beccaria's *On Crimes and Punishments* to Jeremy Bentham's proposed *pannomion* we find the same utopian ideal of the legislator as society's generalizer and instructor. This image of the legislator as teacher is closely related to the idea that government should be capable of at once comprehending society as a whole and guiding its operation in detail. Revolutionary philosophy of law draws heavily on this source. The power of generality it envisions is thus not exclusively procedural. For the men of 1789, the law was not only an effective and legitimate norm but also a *political agent*. In a sense it summoned men to reconstruct reality itself. Viewed through the prism of generality, the rough edges of the world disappeared, leaving only the pure concept in its crystalline transparency. By excluding all forms of particularity, the law enacted an imaginary world. One of the significant consequences of this notion was the distrust of executive power, which was seen as a particularized form of action. This has weighed heavily on the French political system ever since.

The Forms of History

After examining the debates around the origins of this "utopian generality" (notably in connection with the respective roles of the absolutist heritage and of revolutionary abstraction in its constitution), I turn in the second part of the book to a description of the resistances and challenges that this political culture has faced since the first half of the nineteenth century— particularly the ways in which the three imperatives of governability, socialization, and liberty led to a relegitimation of the very intermediary bodies that had previously been condemned.

Attention was again focused on intermediary bodies during the Consulate (1799–1804), when a proposal to reinstate *corporations* (trade associations) caused considerable agitation. To many people, the market and the law by themselves seemed inadequate to regulate economy and society, and specifically to put an end to what was seen as renewed labor market disarray. The issue persisted during the Restoration (1815–1830) and the July Monarchy (1830–1848), becoming linked to an increasingly steadfast opposition to the market society that was beginning to emerge. The specter of social collapse, an obsession of so many early nineteenth-century writers, contributed to reviving the issue of intermediary bodies. The advent of an individualistic society was seen as an inevitable consequence of the construction of an overarching unit or "great whole" *(un grand tout)* and as a symptom of the flaws inherent in the degraded collectivity. Pierre Leroux, describing a transformation that was at once moral and social, wrote that "society is no longer anything but a 'bunch of selfish individuals' and therefore no longer a body. The limbs have been severed from the cadaver." Similar sentiments were widely expressed. Hence numerous voices called for restoring or reinventing intermediary bodies to overcome the difficulties caused by the crumbling of the social bond. An end to utopian generality was therefore perceived as a radical solution by those who called above all for the creation of true local authorities (the term "decentralization" was first used in this context in 1829 and quickly gained currency).

A third imperative contributing to the critique of utopian generality was that of liberty. For instance, liberals and ultras under the Restoration argued that the existence of autonomous intermediary bodies helped to keep liberty alive. When they defended the principle of association and local liberties, they hoped to create protective interfaces between government and citizens. In the 1830s, association was seen by workers as both a means of action and a form of resistance, as a cooperative ethos was combined with the needs of collective action. The Revolution's anticorporatist strictures were all the more subject to criticism because the workers' philosophy of solidarity fed on memories of close bonds among craftsmen. The political culture of generality was thus challenged in three different dimensions, so that what was once taken for granted now became a problem.

These early nineteenth-century resistances and critiques shook the French model but did not cause it to collapse. Under pressure, the original "Jacobinism" changed its nature and established itself on new foundations. Initially the need for order played a crucial role in curbing civil society's ability to organize itself. Throughout the century repressive legislation subjected associations to strict public control. The political culture of generality burnished new arguments, emphasizing administrative necessities as the foundation of its legitimacy while wrapping itself in the banner of democracy. Even more crucial, however, was the *liberal recasting of Jacobinism*. Louis Adolphe Thiers and François Guizot exemplify to perfection the purging of Jacobinism of all revolutionary ideas and images. This development proved decisive for implanting it firmly in the culture.

The major change in direction came in the 1880s at the behest not of liberals but of republicans. The third part of this book examines that turning point, symbolized by the law of 1884 on trade unions and the law of 1901 on associations, which marked the end of restrictions associated with Le Chapelier. Many factors contributed to making this shift possible. First, the fear of socialism and the specter of the welfare state helped to rehabilitate intermediary bodies, which were seen as forces of restraint. The intellectual revolution that followed the emergence of sociology as a discipline also played a key role by fostering new and more objective criticism of Jacobinism's individualist-statist vision. Sociology saw the work of the Revolution in a new light and distinguished sharply between the general political import of the revolutionary project and the theory of society on which it had been based. Associations and other "secondary" groups thus came to be perceived in a more positive way.

From this time forward there would be change in the French model but not rejection of it. The laws of 1884 and 1901 by no means marked a real break with the system, though it is essential to note that the unions were dealt with in a distinctive way, establishing a truly novel form of social regulation. By contrast, the right of association was conceived far more narrowly, in such a way as to structure the freedom of association without actually acknowledging the social function of the resulting institution. The final chapters of the book are devoted to describing this altered model. They are organized around two images: that of a *polarized democracy* and that of a network state. Polarized democracy allows for the coexistence of social pluralism (in which civil society is granted a certain autonomy) with the general interest as fundamental constitutional principle *(intégrisme constitutionnel de l'intérêt général)*. It is a more flexible and open version of the illiberal democracy that was established under the Second Empire (1852–1871). Men like Pierre Waldeck-Rousseau and Léon Bourgeois are typical representatives of this dualism. The network state, for its part, is no longer organized on monist principles like the original Jacobin state. To some extent it incorporates the associative dynamic and relies on a certain network of secondary bodies. A vast range of associations and quasi-intermediary bodies serve as buttresses and props of the generality, forming what Bourgeois called an "internal armature within the state." Thus the revised French model that came into being at the turn of the twentieth century was characterized by political concentration and administrative pragmatism. Though it soon faced harsh challenges of its own, it retained this twofold character.

An Open-Ended Book

The goals of this work are at once ambitious and modest. The book proposes a broad new interpretation of the French model based on a historical analysis of active tensions between the monist principles of revolutionary democracy and the social aspirations of a certain kind of pluralism. In this way it leads to a revision of what is commonly and all too lazily summed up by the term "Jacobinism." But much more remains to be done. Although research in a variety of areas has begun to show the way, many mountains of archives must be explored before anyone can claim to offer a comprehensive and careful account of the model sketched here. This book will have served its purpose if it can offer a set of concepts and an analytical framework useful as a guide for further research.

— Part I —

Utopian Generality

— 1 —

Generality as Social Form

Hatred of Corporate Bodies and the Sense of the Common Good

The aspiration to unity that mobilized hearts and minds in the summer of 1789 set the tone for the period. Union was perceived simultaneously as a quality and as the form of something new and near at hand that corresponded to everyone's desires. "We have but one desire: to lose ourselves in *le grand tout,* the great whole." This manifesto issued by the Commune of Paris symbolized the nascent spirit of the new French regime, as Michelet strongly emphasized; whence the obsession with eliminating old barriers and putting an end to the differences that kept people apart. The desire for unity manifested itself in the very first meetings of the Estates General with the passionate refusal of the Third Estate to assent to separate verification of mandates and separate deliberations of each of the three estates as envisioned by Louis XVI. Thus unity and equality were seen as inseparable imperatives from the outset of the revolutionary process. The new egalitarian imagination reflected a profound change of sensibility, a change of almost anthropological proportions. The society of identical individuals that everyone desired was understood as something that was bound to establish a novel type of bond among men. This is the content of the idea of citizenship (designating membership in a society of peers), and it is what the principle of universal suffrage symbolizes.[1]

The rejection of the society of orders and *corps,* or corporations, stemmed from this vision. It did not arise solely out of the economic and juridical demands that may have been superimposed upon it. It was above all an outgrowth of the new collective imagery, of the novel representation of "being together." The old corporatist spirit was the chief culprit: "Everyone today feels the need to establish social unity upon the destruction of orders

13

and of all the great corporations."[2] The words came from the pen of the abbé Emmanuel Joseph Sieyès, but the idea was everywhere. The meaning of the word "corporation" was broadened as a result. Previously it had referred to a productive institution (such as a trade guild), but now it came to denote any organization that walled individuals off from one another. The "corporatist spirit" was widely compared—in a riot of medical metaphors—to a source of gangrene, a rotting of the social bond. The aspiration of the age was to bring forth the "pure nature" of the social, breaking sharply with all previous organic representations. "Fundamentally, and in the nature of things, there is but one body, which is the nation," observed Rabaut Saint-Etienne in summing up the sentiments of the members of the Constituent Assembly in 1789.[3]

In order to free itself from the "Gothic" weight of the past and the dangers of division, the nation was thus obliged to assert itself as a homogeneous and self-sufficient totality, irreducible to any intermediate component whatsoever. Although it was Sieyès who became the most tireless and uncompromising champion of the nation as "One," it was a young political writer named Toussaint Guiraudet who found the most striking formula for the change: in his lapidary phrase, "the French nation is a society of roughly twenty-five million individuals."[4] In place of the palpable society composed of various *corps*, the Revolution envisioned a new society consisting of a "vast association that enumerates heads and not classes, that counts and does not weigh."[5] For the men of 1789, the nation was not a composite of *corps* and *ordres;* it was an immediate totality. Sieyès would go so far as to say that "one ought to think of nations on earth as individuals outside the social bond" in order to capture this aspiration to a novel form radical in its conception of collective existence.[6] André Chénier called for its advent with a warmth that perfectly conveyed his meaning. "Imprudent and unfortunate is the state in which a variety of associations are formed," he wrote. "Happy is the country in which there is no association but the state, no *corps* but the fatherland, and no interest but the common good."[7]

In this context, the common interest invoked by Chénier takes on a meaning never before formulated. It can in fact be distinguished in two ways from the usual understandings of "common" as a mode of participation and a form of sharing. "Common as participation" designates a configuration in which it is the articulation of differences recognized as complementary that expresses the meaning of "generality." "Common as sharing" refers to an "overlapping community" in which human beings form a society on the basis of shared values or material similarities, so that "generality" means a sharing of particularities. The idea of the nation championed by Chénier, Guiraudet, and Sieyès suggested a third perspective: that of a general interest defined as equally distant from all singularities. The idea was thus one of "common as difference," which gained approval because it was deemed to be the most radical and therefore invulnerable definition of the general interest. In this spirit Sieyès observed that "the public welfare [*salut public*] requires that the common interest of society be maintained somewhere, pure and unadulterated."[8] For him, the general interest was not just different from a mere addition or overlapping of particular interests. It was constructed *in opposition* to those interests, so as to make certain that there was no inadvertent admixture of the particular with the general, and therefore completely independent of any process of integration. This perspective can be explained to some extent by the course that the Revolution took in its social dimension. "All classes of the Third Estate are bound by a common interest against the oppression of privileges," commented the author of *Qu'est-ce que le tiers état?*[9] But it also has philosophical roots, which one finds in Rousseau when he looks to the establishment of an insuperable distance between the public and the private as an essential condition for maintaining the former. In this perspective, the rejection of intermediary bodies is more radical than a mere denunciation of corporatist loyalties as particular interests. It is based on a certain absolutization of the general interest, which can be conceived only in the form of a necessary abstraction. The critical sociology of the Old Regime was thus linked to a novel political philosophy of the common good.

For the men of 1789, the exaltation of the nation's indivisibility arose out of this vision. Sieyès insisted on this notion repeatedly: "France is and must be a single whole."[10] Representing society in unified form made it possible to express the difference between the new society and the Old Regime. The *form* of communal existence defined the new social power that the Revolution was creating. Popular sovereignty was inextricably intertwined with the novel representation of the social on which it was based.[11] The nation could thus be understood as a community redeemed from its outward appearances by the abolition of all contingent categories and forced into conformity with the abstract principles on which it was founded. It was a "regenerated" society, to borrow an expression that was repeatedly invoked during the Revolution. Capping this regeneration were the processes first of *assimilation* and, later and even more important, *adunation* (union or combination into one).[12]

To be sure, the revolutionary obsession with unity also had a banally circumstantial dimension. It reflected a quasi-military imperative in a France threatened on its borders by the old powers of Europe. Unity was in fact a primary requirement for protection and security against peril from without. Yet the essential thing was to break with the Old Regime while at the same time marking the advent of a new world. In this instance, words and images were summoned to justify the people's impatience and to make the wheel of history turn faster.

The Forms of Unity

The rejection of intermediary bodies and the aspiration to a unified society were thus the principal features of revolutionary political culture from the beginning. "Henceforth there are no corporations within the state. There is only the particular interest of each individual and the general interest. No person is permitted to inspire in citizens any intermediate interest or to alienate them from the common good by fostering a corporatist spirit."[13] These vivid sentences were formulated by Le Chapelier in the summer of 1791, when corporations were officially abolished.[14] For us they symbolize the direct encounter between individuals and the state that the revolutionaries of 1789 earnestly desired. For contemporaries, however, the episode passed almost unnoticed: the old corporatist system was already tottering, and only part of the economy was still subject to its regulation.[15] Hence they focused their attention on other areas.

While the abolition of guilds and corporations gave rise to little discussion, a proposal to abolish religious congregations was subjected to lengthy debate, even though the two issues were framed in very similar terms.[16] In both cases it was the existence of intermediary bodies that was at issue. Indeed, for many people the clergy, more than any other institution, symbolized the essence of the corporatist phenomenon. No one emphasized this more than Pierre Athanase Torné, the constitutional bishop from the Cher, who delivered a report on the issue to the Legislative Assembly. "Before the Revolution," he pointed out, "the kingdom's clergy, taken as a whole, was an important corporation in three respects. In its relation to the state regime, it was one of the three orders, indeed the first of the three. In its relation to society, it constituted a unified whole, which was isolated from society by its mode of government. In its relation to divine worship, it formed a mystical whole, whose members were assigned places in an entirely spiritual hierarchy. In the first respect, the clergy was a political corporation; in the second, a civil corporation; in the third, a religious corporation."[17] The creation of the National Assembly, with its concomitant abolition of the three orders, eliminated the clergy as a political corporation. Its existence as a spiritual community was exempt from legal scrutiny.[18] That left only one dimension: the "civil corporation," which was vigorously debated in the autumn of 1789.

That fall the National Assembly received a first report on the legal status of the religious orders from its ecclesiastical committee.[19] Significantly, Le Chapelier played a very active role in its examination,[20] which led to the decree of 13 February 1790 abolishing the regular congregations (cloistered orders). There was nothing antireligious about this decision, which at this stage of the Revolution should not be imputed to the anticlerical movement that arose later. Many voices were raised in the Assembly to insist that the question of orders be kept separate from any judgment of religion as such. Indeed, we find some of the speakers proclaiming themselves "convinced that the Catholic religion is the national religion," while others publicly declared themselves to be inspired by "sentiments of piety" even as they argued fervently for the abolition of the congregations.[21] The February 1790 text was characterized in these terms by Jean-Baptiste Treilhard, acting as spokesman for the committee that considered it: "What are the intentions of this law? There are just two: the congregations should no longer be collective, and vows should henceforth constitute only a bond of conscience, not a legal bond."[22] What the law abolished, therefore, was the congregations as *institutions* that constrained their members (monastic vows previously having had legal force implying permanent "civil death") rather than mere spiritual *associations* (monks who wished to remain cloistered were free to do so).

Although the abolition of the regular congregations partook of a general climate of suspicion in regard to orders and *corps,* it was essentially a legal device related to the defense of individual rights. The goal was to allow the religious personnel covered by the law to become genuine individuals, free to modify their lifestyle if they chose, whereas previously they had existed legally solely as members of a group.[23] By contrast, the anticorporatist aspect was crucial in the decision to abolish the secular congregations, which was not taken until 18 August 1792. The goal clearly stated by the spokesman for the committee that examined the bill was to allow "members of separate societies" to rejoin "the larger society," given that the charitable, educational, and medical functions of the congregations were destined to be taken over by the state.[24] Again it was Torné who most forcefully expressed this position in the debate on the issue that began in the spring of 1792. A number of his comments were particularly striking and therefore made a greater impression on his contemporaries than Le Chapelier's remarks had done a few months earlier. For that reason it is worth quoting him at length. "Sound policy," he argued,

> compels you to dissolve the secular congregations as well as the religious orders. What an obstruction is to the human body, a corporation of citizens is to a political body. *(Applause)* The members of each corporation live in I know not what commonality of interests, opinions, and sentiments that goes by the name *esprit de corps,* and this particular spirit is ordinarily a diversion of the public spirit. The more individuals are attached to the smaller whole of which they are members, the less attached they are to the fatherland. *(Applause)* . . . Let us therefore abolish all that remains of corporations in the Empire. Each *esprit de corps* that is snuffed out inflames the public spirit all the more, and the members of the dissolved societies become so many conquests for the general society.[25]

Significantly, Torné, in pursuing his anticorporatist position, went so far as to advocate a ban on religious costumes, which he suspected of interfering with the drive toward greater equality and unity. His arguments are again worth attending to carefully, for they offer a striking illustration of the anticorporatist sensibility and of a whole philosophy of collective existence.

> No good constitution, particularly ours, tolerates any particular corporation. It regards all of them as possessing to a greater or lesser degree an *esprit de corps* damaging to the public spirit. A well-organized state recognizes free associations of individuals joined together in accordance with the law and under its eyes, but it recognizes no corporation other than the general corporation of citizens . . . Every particular association that adopts distinctive signs without the approval of the law presages a kind of political schism. A particular society is then formed within the larger society, a particular society that isolates itself and gives the appearance of a dismemberment of the social body. This is the symbol of a particular

spirit that severs itself from the public spirit . . . In view of these principles, which must not be diluted in any way, what are we to think of the
secular clergy or of some class of religious who persist in distinguishing
themselves from the national mass by wearing a total or partial costume
not established by the nation? Would not such a costume, adopted by the
private authority of those wearing it, constitute an attack on the unity of
the social contract and on the equality of those who have sworn to up-
hold it? . . . Having abolished all the bodies with which religion encum-
bered the state, should we allow symbols of those bodies to remain?[26]

The decree of 18 August 1792 followed this advice.[27] In contrast to this
aversion for distinctions and particularisms, the issue of whether the representatives of the people ought to adopt a distinctive costume came up at
several points during the Revolution, reflecting a desire for equality and a
wish to make the National Assembly a visibly homogeneous body and as
such the living embodiment of the newly unified society. As finally approved in Year IV of the Revolution (1796), the costume of members of the
legislative body was supposed to translate republican principles into a representation understood as a microcosm of the nation. (In 1848 the provisional government stated that "equality implies uniformity of costume for
all citizens called upon to perform similar functions.")[28]

The determination to make the nation the ultimate unit, subsuming all
previous identities, again made itself felt in unmistakable fashion in the fall
of 1789 in the important debate on dividing the territory of France, which
led ultimately to the creation of the *départements.* Although carving up the
territory into smaller units had proven to be an administrative necessity,
the hope was that the new division would in no way recall the old one involving provinces, *bailliages, généralités,* and dioceses.[29] The new map, it
was argued, "should yield the incalculable benefit of melding the local and
particular spirit into a national and public spirit. It should make Frenchmen of all the inhabitants of this empire, who until now have been only
Provençaux, Normans, Parisians, and Lorrainers."[30] From this came the
idea of basing the subdivision on the most abstract of criteria, namely,
population, coupled with a coldly geometric approach to geography.[31] The
goal was to create a purely functional division, one that would avoid reference to any social, political, or cultural reality—in other words, to borrow
Mona Ozouf's quip, "a nondivisive division" that would take no account of
the traditions and habits of the past. As Bertrand Barère emphasized, "ev-

ery trace of history must be erased, every prejudice resulting from community of interests or origins. Everything must be new in France, and we want
time to be counted only from today."[32] At this point the members of the
Constituent Assembly were searching for a way to transform reality completely, to reinterpret it in a novel way. "I have long felt the need to divide
French soil in a new way," Sieyès wrote. "If we allow this opportunity to
pass, it will never come again, and the provinces will retain forever their
corporatist spirit, their privileges, their pretensions, and their jealousies.
France will never achieve the political *adunation* so necessary to create a
great people governed by identical laws and subject to identical forms of
administration."[33] The goal was to find a purely mechanical way of slicing
up the territory that would avoid all actual oppositions and distinctions,
which meant proceeding on the basis of a totally artificial plan derived
from a quasi-mathematical principle. The intention was to eliminate all
shackles on thinking so as to approach the problem in a totally new way.
Indeed, the true objective was even more ambitious, not to say utopian: it
was to make the whole of society interchangeable with the parts, to achieve
something utterly without precedent, namely, a purely instrumental and
totally neutral division.[34] This goal was clearly stated: "To meld the local
and particular spirit into a national and public spirit."[35]

Hence the vast majority of the Constituent Assembly remained completely impervious to the arguments of Honoré de Mirabeau, who called
for compromise with established habits and realities so as to "bring the administration of men and of things closer" to the people and who criticized
"a mathematical, almost idealized, division, the execution of which seems
impractical."[36] Indeed, it was precisely this idealization that was expected to
bring about the regeneration of the body politic in the form of a "nation
one and indivisible." Sieyès's forceful formulations set the tone: "France
should not be a congeries of little nations that govern themselves separately as democracies. It is not a collection of states. It is a unique *whole*,
composed of subsidiary parts. Separately, these parts must not exist as
complete entities, because they are not simply united wholes but parts
forming but a single whole."[37] Jacques-Guillaume Thouret, who reported
to the Assembly on the proposed law governing the new division of the
kingdom, made the same point repeatedly: "To establish the Constitution
is to reconstruct and regenerate the state . . . It is to introduce the supreme
law that ties the various parts of the state together and subordinates one to
another."[38] The first maxims of a good constitution, he added, "are those

providing for the political union of all members of the state in a single body, and for the subordination of all the parts to the great national whole."[39]

The "whole," the "great whole," the "national whole": the men of 1789 repeated these formulas obsessively, as if they were almost enough in and of themselves to sum up the spirit and purpose of their enterprise. For them, "particularity" was the enemy—particularity in its multiple forms and denominations: privilege, *esprit de corps*, corporatist sentiment, local sentiment, provincial sentiment ("which is only an individual spirit in the state," said Thouret, hence "an enemy of the true national spirit"). Thus they set the particular spirit in opposition to the spirit of generality. In practice, of course, they were obliged to compromise. For instance, the division of France would take into account certain geographical realities and practical constraints. A certain diversity came to be accepted of necessity, and Jacques Revel was right to point out that "the Revolution was that paradoxical moment when the will to unity was combined with the discovery of regional differences, each driving the other."[40] Yet this tension remained largely unconceptualized (it was not until the end of the nineteenth century that the bonds between the republic and the *petites patries* were made explicit and formulated in the language of national unity). That is why words dominated realities in 1789; they called for a transformation of those realities while at the same time hiding them from view.

The Work of the Imagination

"One must take hold of man's imagination and govern it": Fabre d'Eglantine's imperative formula clearly suggests that the constitution of the "great whole" could not be accomplished merely by overturning institutions and laws. It also took place in hearts and minds. One of the major functions of the revolutionary festivals was to celebrate in an active and therefore immediately perceptible way the *union-fusion* that the men of 1789 hoped to achieve. The festivals were thus seen as direct means of production, whose product was society itself. Indeed, the Constitution of 1791 ascribed this role to them in its Title I: "National holidays shall be established to preserve the memory of the French Revolution, to maintain fraternity among citizens, and to associate them with the Constitution, the fatherland, and the law." Though their immediate objects were varied and their contexts diverse, the festivals of the revolutionary era all shared the function of "bringing men together in the single and indivisible space of civic ardor and transparency of the heart."[41] They sought to create a palpable sense of social unity as well as to foster a certain way of being equal by incorporating individuals into an indistinct mass, visibly absorbing them as mere numerical constituents. The festivals thus fulfilled three purposes: they allowed people to experience a transfigured space; they staged a scene of social harmony; and they offered society a glimpse of itself as spectacle.

The festival was first of all an "experiment in space."[42] It organized gatherings in the open in order to demonstrate the contrast between the new world and the old, defined by compartmentalization and by the many barriers formerly established between men and women. It expanded all horizons, bringing people out of their own narrow universes. No one described this process better than Louis Blanc, who spoke of the experience of the *fédérés* who traveled the highways and byways of France to converge on a single destination: "Twelve hundred inner frontiers disappeared. Mountain peaks seemed to shrink; rivers became nothing but moving conveyor belts linking populations that had too long been kept apart. The fatherland became conscious of its own existence and announced its presence."[43] The Festival of the Federation was meant to exalt this newly leveled world and to stage a veritable "drama of national unity," to borrow Mona Ozouf's characterization.[44] That is why the only conceivable venue for it was out of doors, in an absolutely plastic space without limits or constraints of any kind. "National festivals cannot be held in any enclosure with smaller bounds than heaven's vault, since the sovereign, which is to say, the people, can never be contained in any circumscribed or covered space," was the way one contemporary put it.[45] That is why the Champ-de-Mars in Paris became the preferred site for national celebrations. Revolutionary processions often chose this as their destination rather than any of the capital's more important sites, thus demonstrating that "they were less concerned with a geographical center than with a metaphysical one."[46] Indeed, Michelet went so far as to say that the Champ-de-Mars was therefore "the only monument left by the Revolution." He had his own magnificent phrase for it: "The Revolution has the void as its monument," he wrote, thereby emphasizing the contrast with other regimes that had left numerous edifices as their mark on the capital.[47]

The purpose of the festival was to stage a harmonious society in which all differences were temporarily suspended. It instituted a sort of sacrament of social unity, melding bodies and hearts into a unanimous ensemble. As a commentator noted at the time, "it was the festivals that impressed a single unique character on the social mass and gave it a single and unique spirit . . . which thus molded all the members of the state into a single and unique whole."[48] They rooted the "one and indivisible" character of the Republic in the sensibility of each individual, thereby acting as a powerful force for moral and social transformation, turning dispersed individuals into citizens no longer subject to corporate ties of any kind. They made the advent of a collective visible, a collective that could no longer be represented in the usual ways because its structure no longer reflected differences known and recognized by all. The festivals created "*electric commotions*, which impress a single thought of virtue on an entire people and lead all citizens to identify with one another by way of the fraternal spirit."[49]

Thus the true object of any festival was not its immediate pretext, whether it was the commemoration of an event, the celebration of an institution, or the invocation of a great principle. It was rather society itself. One observer stressed that the revolutionary festival was supposed to be a "general celebration" in which the stage was everywhere and everyone was an actor; the explicit goal was to mobilize all the people from one end of the nation to the other.[50] It was to this assimilationist utopia that readers of an article in *La Bouche de fer* on civic and fraternal festivals were summoned: "Make a spectacle of the spectators. Make them the actors. Let each participant see and love himself in the others, the better to unite them all."[51] In expressing himself in this way the writer was merely following in the footsteps of Rousseau, who, in his *Letter to d'Alembert on Spectacles*, had written that in any festival there was, strictly speaking, nothing to show: "Plant a post crowned with flowers in the middle of a square, bring people together there, and you have a festival."[52] Hence the festival was in its way both the sacrament and the academy of *le grand tout*.[53] Along with laws and institutions it contributed to the revolutionary enterprise of regeneration and transfiguration.

The Social Contract and the Sentimental Contract

The elimination of intermediary bodies gave rise to a simultaneous redistribution of social affects. The "corporate bond" that gave practical substance to "being together" and structure to the representation of social relations could not simply be replaced by assertion of membership in a "great whole," even when that whole was magnified and sublimated in the festival, wherein it acquired an intelligible form. Because the new "general" social bond was inevitably more abstract, it virtually required a tangible counterpart. This circumstance accounts for the importance that the issue of friendship and fraternity assumed in the Revolution. The new social contract was linked to a kind of "sentimental contract," in which the warmth of private affections was called upon to compensate for the abstract nature of citizenship ties. If we are to understand fully the consequences of abolishing intermediary bodies, we must therefore consider the *general economy* of the social bond.

In this connection Rousseau became the universal reference. It was because he was the author of *both* the *Social Contract* and the *New Eloise* that he struck everyone as so obviously the author of the moment. His work provided the men of 1789 with a way of "humanizing" the rather frigid character of the totality. His *Letter to d'Alembert* shows, moreover, how acutely aware Rousseau was of the need to see the political question in the context of a more general economy of bonds and affects. In that text he pointed out that the solidity of a state could not rest solely on its institutions because a whole range of *customs* also contributed to its well-being. Among these he included the sociability of circles and cafés, the celebration of military holidays, and the shared pleasures of the hunt. Taking Geneva as his example, he cited all customs that afforded citizens "the opportunity to form societies around the dinner table, excursions to the country, and ties of friendship."[54] He also denounced the risks to the polity of having too large a theater, for then, he believed, instead of a diversity of social activities and private ties, the danger was that sociability and playfulness might become concentrated in a single place and "absorb everything." "The moment there is a Comédie," he warned, "goodbye to circles, farewell to societies!"[55] The *grand tout* of citizenship was not enough in Rousseau's eyes to give substance to collective existence, which had to be made flesh through various possible forms of local sociability. Although Rousseau was an implacable critic of intermediary bodies, which he accused of being a "sickness in the state," he thus presented himself as an apostle of recreational associations. There was no contradiction, because these circles and societies were purely private in nature. They had no function that could rival public action or threaten the expression of the general interest. They bore no resemblance to a corporation. Like certain kinds of festivals but on a different scale, their true object was the social bond itself. For Rousseau, conviviality was a complement or prop of the social contract.

No one understood this better than the abbé Claude Fauchet, the indefatigable leader of the Cercle Social and the Confédération des Amis de la

Vérité, who discussed the Genevan social theorist's work in the fall of 1790 before an enthusiastic audience that included the marquis de Condorcet and Sieyès. He began by pointing out that "the general laws have forgotten the friendship that associates everything and concern themselves only with the discord that divides everything. None of those laws has yet taken as the basis of society the fact that man is a loving creature, and none has tried to turn public institutions in this conciliatory direction. On the contrary, all have assumed that man is selfish and the adversary of his fellow man."[56] In these terms Rousseau's enthusiastic disciple followed the master in urging his contemporaries to back up the social contract with a sentimental one. Only then, he insisted, would it be possible to "overturn this horrible system from top to bottom, by which I mean not society, but the *insociation* that keeps men disunited."[57] While he thus joined all his peers in condemning the partial associations that threatened to form within the state, he nevertheless celebrated in ringing terms "the associative principle that is the source of all good."[58] Thus the idea of association was either completely privatized or else reduced simply to the expression of an affect, thereby fulfilling much the same function as, for example, the notion of sympathy in Adam Smith.[59] For that very reason, however, Fauchet was able to give the associative principle a centrality *equivalent* to that which it had had in the old corporatist society, only now it was seen as a concomitant of the "great association" constituted by the nation as a whole.

Historians of the Revolution have not often accentuated this aspect of it, essential though it is. If we consider revolutionary aesthetics and sensibility, for instance, it is striking to find Jacques Louis David's militant compositions coexisting apparently peacefully with ubiquitous celebration of domestic cheer and the joys of friendship. To see this difference as the indication of a sharp contrast between the worlds of men and women, as some interpreters have suggested, is not satisfactory.[60] The family was indeed celebrated as never before in novels and plays as well as music and painting. The virtues of intimacy and closeness, the pleasures of the home, and the warmth of friendship took on unprecedented importance in this period.[61] Public and private spheres were redefined even as they were becoming in a sense increasingly autonomous.

The celebration of friendship was further accentuated as the revolutionary process turned more radical, as if the increasingly combative abstraction of the political made it all the more necessary. It is telling that Robespierre called for the erection of altars to "divine friendship."[62] Although the theme was omnipresent after 1793, it was Louis Antoine Saint-

Just who expressed it most strikingly. "You must build a city, which is to say, citizens who are friends, who are hosts and brothers," he said as the Terror widened, as if there were no contradiction between citizenship and friendship.[63] This understanding of the relationship between the two registers, civic and affective, was set forth in particularly striking fashion in Saint-Just's *Fragments d'institutions républicaines* (in the chapter titled "Des affections"): "Every man above the age of twenty-one is required to declare in the temple who his friends are, and that declaration must be repeated every year."[64] Friendship was placed at the center of social life, and Saint-Just deemed it to be the most complete and necessary form of the social bond. Friendship thus ceased to belong exclusively to the realm of private affections and took on a collective dimension that called for a pledge and implied a responsibility to all members of the society. "If a man gives up a friend," Saint-Just insisted, "he is required to explain to the people, in the temple, his reasons for doing so . . . If a man has no friends, he is banished."[65] Saint-Just thus radicalized his vision of the social bond: on one side he placed the realm of *general friendship*, on the other that of the *general will*. In his eyes, citizenship and friendship thus characterized two types of relations that abolished differences among individuals. He construed friendship in a way that paid no attention to the inequalities or peculiarities that might separate one person from another, that is, in parallel with citizenship, which also abstracted from anything that might differentiate individuals. In order to flesh out the social and deal with the threat of abstraction stemming from the rejection of all intermediary bodies, Saint-Just was thus led to what one might call an absolutization of private affects. The totalitarian naiveté of his vision attests to the kinds of paradox and confusion to which the revolutionary celebration of the "great whole" could lead. Indeed, the exacerbation of the political ultimately led to a confusion of politics with ethics.

Without going to such extremes, it is worth pointing out explicitly that the principle of benevolence (of proximity) continually served to check and balance the tendency to absolutize the (abstract) general interest in the revolutionary political culture. This phenomenon is striking in connection with the issue of combating poverty. At first, to be sure, there was a movement to denounce foundations and entrust all poor relief to the state, which was to take charge of all institutions responsible for indigent assistance. In this regard, Barère's celebrated report on how to put a stop to begging may be taken as emblematic of a kind of sacralization of the welfare state.[66] Yet Barère himself was not averse to philanthropy or charitable action by individuals. He did not hesitate to write that "society is a daily exchange of reciprocal assistance, and the man whose soul does not take heart from an opportunity to help his fellow man is not a good citizen. To husband happiness for oneself is to cut oneself off from civic association; it is to limit one's own pleasures by renouncing the most pleasant of sensations, of beneficence, of gratitude, and even of friendship."[67] Such an approach was by no means exceptional. The men of 1793 and 1794 insisted all the more on friendship and benevolence because they had given themselves over so fully to the fantasy of the republic one and indivisible. Even the far more sober *constituants* (deputies to the Constituent Assembly) of Year III did not hesitate to write in the Declaration of Rights and Duties that "no man is a good citizen if he is not a good son, good father, good brother, good friend, and good husband."

The importance of the theme of *fraternity* in the Revolution needs to be understood in this context. Like friendship, fraternity formed the basis of a noncontractual bond. It rested on a moral imperative, not a legal obligation, yet played a role judged to be essential in the constitution of the social.[68] We cannot delve more deeply into this complex question here. In fact the very term *fraternité* has deep roots in the old corporatist universe.[69] It was in any case this link to the past that allowed the word to fulfill its primary function, namely, to introduce an organic dimension into a society of individuals. As early as 1789, fraternity was seen as both a *quality* and a *metaphor* for unity and equality: the fraternal pact reinforced and supported the social contract. Social fraternity was an extension of and complement to the general will, which is why people like Fauchet often spoke of "general fraternity." The ambiguity of the term is obvious, for what is distinctive about society is precisely the fact that it cannot be conceived as a family or a band of brothers. Yet it attests to contemporaries' acute awareness of the need to expand the formalism that they had initially set out to create.

Standing as a kind of negative of an overwhelmingly powerful image, the celebration of friendship and fraternity thus offers proof of how important the symbolism of belonging to a "great whole" was in the collective imagination of the period.

Polarized Society

The critique of corporations that we have just examined figured within a vision of society defined by two poles, the individual and the *"grand tout."*

The various intermediary structures were suspected in advance either of thwarting access to the generality or of living off of it as parasites. This polarization had profound consequences. To begin with, it discredited the very idea of the "social," in the sense the word has had since the end of the nineteenth century. We see this clearly in the way in which the members of the Constituent Assembly treated the issues of ownership of ecclesiastical properties and communal lands. The men of 1789 wanted to recognize only two types of property, private and public, and rejected any notion of what we would today characterize as social property. When they abolished corporations, they therefore sought to nationalize or privatize all properties in mortmain. Hence the debate on the ownership of ecclesiastical properties took on, in parallel with the debate on abolition of the corporations, particular importance.

It was again Thouret who reported on the question to the Assembly. If corporations existed, he argued, they could not own property.[70] Unlike individuals, who had rights stemming from their nature and their innate faculties—rights that the law did not create but merely recognized—corporations had no essential nature; they existed only by virtue of the law and therefore could not claim the possibility of perpetuity implicit in the concept of ownership. "Corporations are merely instruments fabricated by the law for the greatest possible good," Thouret summarized.[71] Hence they could not claim to be performing a public service mission (such as education, hospital administration, poor relief) in order to justify their possession of real estate of which they regarded themselves merely as trustees or administrators.[72] To be sure, passions ran high in this debate, which revived old grievances against the Catholic Church. Interests also played a part, since the nationalization of clerical possessions raised the prospect of a vast and much-desired expansion of private property. But the essential question was philosophical: corporate ownership inherently raised the prospect of a rival to public authority. The corporations in a sense threatened the state's claim to a "monopoly on perpetuity," perpetuity being in the order of temporality the equivalent of generality in the order of social forms.

In defending this position, the *constituants* were by no means innovating. In a sense, they were simply taking up arguments previously put forward by Anne Robert Jacques Turgot, who had attacked property in mortmain with energy comparable to that which he expended on combating corporations. He, too, had seen the two battles as logically connected and complementary. He had set forth his critique in a celebrated article titled "Fondation" in the *Encyclopédie*. "A founder," he wrote, "is a man who seeks to extend the effect of his will to all eternity." That, for him, was precisely the problem. "Founders are seriously deluded if they imagine that their zeal is transmitted through the centuries to the people charged with perpetuating its effects . . . There is no *corps* that has not lost the spirit of its origins in the long run." As he saw it, no corporate body and no individual should be allowed to mortgage the future in this way. "Public utility is the supreme law and must not be weighed against superstitious respect for what is called 'the founders' intention,' as if ignorant and blind individuals had the right to shackle still nonexistent generations to their capricious wills." Only the state could assert mastery over time and express a truly general will. And just as no individual or corporation could claim sovereignty, none could claim to impress its indelible mark upon time. Hence mortmain and corporations were equally harmful.[73] The state was in fact as wary of allowing durable enterprises not under its auspices as it was of tolerating collective interests whose organization and expression it did not control.

The issue of *communal properties* raised similar problems later on. In England as well as France, eighteenth-century economists had vigorously denounced the negative consequences of too much communal real estate. In the *Traité politique et économique des communes*, which appeared in several editions starting in 1770, Jean-François Essuile showed that communal property was relatively unproductive and often barren for want of enclosures and maintenance.[74] For Essuile, as for the Physiocrats, any revision of property rights should be aimed at increasing agricultural productivity. Essuile and many others had championed the idea of an egalitarian division of communal fields as a way of redistributing land, increasing agricultural production, and encouraging marriage by increasing the number of smallholders. Such ideas were widely shared in 1789, and the issue was often raised in *cahiers de doléances* (books of grievances).[75] Although the Constituent Assembly took up the question many times, it remained for the Legislative Assembly to deal with it in a methodical way. That body's agricultural committee undertook a broad survey of *départements* in the fall of 1791.[76] All the debates of previous decades reemerged, but what interests us in the present context is that the problem of communal properties was now reinterpreted in keeping with the new project of creating a France "one and indivisible."

There is no better indicator of the new state of mind than the response of the Montpellier district. In his report to the Assembly on the committee's proposed new law, the district's chairman, Claude-Dominique Fabre, stated: "The constitution recognizes only one corporation, that consisting of all the French; it concerns itself with only one interest, that of the nation, which comprises the combined interests of all citizens. In its eyes, only two types of property can exist: national property and individual property. Nothing is more contrary to these principles than the existence of nontransmissible communal properties. These destroy unity of administration. They isolate the citizen from the larger community by substituting local and partial interests for the general interest."[77] Similar formulas can be found in countless memoranda received by the agricultural committee. "The only true community is the national community" was the sentiment often repeated, and this was coupled with strictures against those who "might conceive the notion of separating themselves from the great commune." Although the initial decree that communal lands be divided was later modified, the basic idea remained.[78] Once again, it was the local spirit and the existence of particular societies that were denounced. In reporting on the final bill on the subject, Fabre reverted to language that had been hammered home repeatedly since 1789: "All customs must bow before the law. It must be the same for all Frenchmen. They have the same rights, and the revolting mishmash of Roman, Gothic, and Saxon laws must no longer be allowed to soil the body of a Republic one and indivisible."[79]

The issue of the division of communal goods points up in striking fashion the *double polarization* that took place during the Revolution. While the critique of intermediary bodies led to an exaltation of the public sphere as the *grand tout,* it also led, in a parallel and inextricably related development, to an extension of the private sphere. The expansion of state-administered forests and of areas subject to public surveillance (such as marshlands) went hand in hand with the consolidation and expansion of individual property. In other words, the revolutionary process led to a generalized polarization of all institutions.

The effects of this polarization can be seen in many other areas as well. One notable consequence was to shape the perception of male-female relations by precluding consideration of sexual difference as fundamental to the constitution of the social. French revolutionaries coupled exclusion of women from citizenship with feverish celebration of a great national whole that was supposed to abolish any number of differences. How can we explain why the hope of achieving unity and eliminating all divisions did not lead to an end of sexual discrimination in politics? In other words, why did sexual difference remain when so many other distinctions were erased in the new definition of citizenship? How are we to understand the strange contrast between the terms in which the general conditions of social emancipation (equality, unity) were couched and the categories in which family issues and relations between the sexes were formulated? These questions become all the more urgent when we recognize that the gulf between the sexes widened during the Revolution. For example, the expulsion of women from the political sphere was particularly thoroughgoing in 1793–94, the very period in which the citizenship imperative was most enthusiastically exalted. Here we touch on the heart of a very French contradiction: even though the radical goal of "universal" male suffrage was achieved quite early, recognition of the political rights of women was a long time coming.

Many works have been devoted to the interpretation of this revolutionary paradox. The majority of these have proposed a social analysis of this "masculine monopoly of the universal," an analysis based on contemporary prejudices and fears regarding the nature of women.[80] I would like to suggest a different explanation in keeping with the argument I have been developing in regard to the political culture of generality. Succinctly stated, it runs like this: the resistance to granting political rights to women in France derives its specific character from the fact that sexual difference, institutionalized in the family, could not be seen as constituting the equivalent of an "intermediary body." In other words, the gendered condition of men and women could not be recognized in the public sphere, for to do so would have been to concede that the public sphere did not transcend all differences. Hence there were only two ways of looking at the gendered condition. Either it was subsumed by a form of radical individualism, thus in a sense positing that sexual difference was merely one social construct among others; or it was "privatized" and "functionalized," by which I mean that the family was posited as the only true cell of society, so that the social individual consisted of a man *and* a woman.

This key point is worth pursuing. If the gendered condition could not be subsumed in an absolute individualism, then the political exclusion of women in the revolutionary period can be understood as a reaction to the unprecedented upheaval that such absolute individualism would have implied. In *Le Sacre du citoyen* I pointed out that the "ordinary" individualism of revolutionary political culture was accepted by late eighteenth-century society only because it was counterbalanced by the erection of a very rigid barrier between the contractualist space of civil society and the organic universe of the family. The very strict maintenance of a "family community," with its implicit confinement of women to the domestic sphere, was the historical and cultural prerequisite of, and price to be paid for, the advent of a masculine society of equal individuals. The situation in which women were placed was a way of dispelling or "compensating" for the fear of entering a world without qualities, an atomized world that the elimination of intermediary bodies had deprived of any visible structure, and for which the creation of a great national whole did not really serve as a substitute. Hence the political situation of women needs to be understood in the context of the "general economy" of the individualist revolution. If negation of sexual difference was seen as one of the consequences of individualism, the fears that individualism aroused could only have been increased. There was no room to grant equivalent political recognition to both "individual man" and "individual woman" while simultaneously respecting the difference between them. In America and Britain, by contrast, this could be done relatively easily, although it was initially difference alone that was acknowledged as justifying the inclusion of women in the political sphere (in other words, women were seen as having their own distinctive spheres of action and expertise—in, for instance, the domestic and educational areas—which justified their representation on the grounds that they were different from men).

If the gendered condition is regarded as decisive for the structure of the social, then it is the union of the sexes—hence in practice the family—that becomes the true political subject. During the Revolution, many political writers took this path to explain why the political exclusion of women was not incompatible with the principle of equality. "Just as in mathematics a point is an element of a line," Guiraudet explained, "the family is the elementary social point, which, when multiplied many times over, constitutes all political associations . . . No other division can be elementary or natural. Thus the one that considers man at first isolated and then in society viewed as a combination of men accomplishes a kind of division in which the final term is not an integer. *Man so considered falls within the purview of physics or morality;* but the sole element of society is *man in the family.*"[81] Thus Guiraudet could vehemently denounce "Gothic, servile, and humiliating classifications" while at the same time regarding sexual difference as somehow positively encompassed by the family. Later Pierre-Louis Roederer would rehearse the same argument, opposing a structure in which "union or aggregation exists only by virtue of differences" to a purely conventional entity such as society, which was "founded on the perfect resemblance" of those who constituted it.[82] In a related vein, a writer close to Sieyès put the point this way: "Husband and wife are but a single political person and can never be anything else, although they may be two civil persons."[83] If women did not vote, he went on to explain, it was "for the simple reason that no one wants to count the same vote twice. One vote counts for two: the woman's vote is virtually included in her husband's vote."[84] Thus, *in practice*, the representation of the wife by the husband was legitimated without raising a philosophical challenge to the idea of a universal right to suffrage.

The principle of abolishing differences in the public sphere could thus be respected under this approach to the citizen family. The political exclusion of women was not seen as a consequence of any individual incapacity; it was solely functional. As a result, however, the prospect of their *personal* political emancipation was paradoxically rendered much more uncertain.[85] In different ways, the impossibility of regarding sexual difference as the equivalent of an "intermediary structure" in the constitution of the social thus led to an accentuation of the difficulty of achieving political emancipation for women, who were caught between the dizzying prospect of absolute individualism and the trap of the citizen-family. In effect, the world envisioned by these revolutionary principles restored the ancient Greek contrast between the free and egalitarian world of the city and the closed "despotic" world of the household, a contrast that the process of civilization had continually sought to reduce by expanding the space accorded to an intermediary social sphere.[86]

— 2 —

Generality as Democratic Quality

The Principle of Immediacy

The Critique of Political Intermediary Bodies

The repudiation of intermediary bodies was not limited to the abolition of corporations. Equally rejected were all the various symbols of the collective capable of hindering the constitution of a *grand tout,* or overarching whole. Only the nation was permitted to constitute itself as a body and signify a "we" for the men of 1789. This rejection, which one might call rejection *of a sociological type,* was extended into the political realm itself. Any organism capable of challenging the legal expression of the general will was also contested. Thus the role of clubs and popular societies—it is still too early to speak of political parties—was vigorously debated. The Constituent Assembly's final decree on 30 September 1791 subjected their activities to strict regulation. The terms of its preamble were particularly firm: "No society, club, or association of citizens can have a political existence in any form or exercise any influence or supervisory function with respect to the actions of the constituted powers and legal authorities. In no case may citizens represent themselves by a collective name, whether to circulate petitions, dispatch deputations, participate in public ceremonies, or for any other purpose."[1] Political "intermediary bodies" were seen as an intolerable threat to representative government, which depended on a monopoly of collective expression. They were also suspected of hindering effective rule by making unified state action difficult.

It is worth noting that the rapporteur on this bill was Le Chapelier, who in condemning clubs used arguments similar to those elaborated three months earlier in the drive to end corporations. "The popular societies have assumed a political role they should not be playing," he argued.

34

No powers exist that have not been constituted by the will of the people as expressed by their representatives. No authorities exist that have not been delegated by the people. No action is permitted unless mandated by the people in the delegation of public functions. To defend this principle in all its purity, the Constitution banished corporations throughout the Empire, and, from that day on, only the social body and individuals were recognized . . . The state takes no notice of societies, peaceful gatherings of citizens, or clubs. Should they venture outside the private sphere in which the Constitution has placed them, they stand in opposition to that Constitution; they destroy rather than defend it.[2]

Le Chapelier's critique was radical. It denied that the clubs were mere translations into the political order of what corporations represented in the social and economic order. The decree we are analyzing here is by no means an isolated detail of revolutionary history. Laws regulating petitions and political signs were also based on a refusal to allow groups of "private" citizens to express themselves collectively in the public space. The assumption was that parliament and the ballot box allowed sufficient scope for the two legitimate forms of democratic expression: deliberation and election.

The criticism of popular societies thus figured as one aspect of the culture of generality we began to explore in the previous chapter, taking generality to be a *democratic quality*. In this context, "generality" refers to the idea that state institutions are perfectly adequate, ideally suited to their purpose, so that the existence of intermediary bodies is rejected as an intolerable interference with their operation.

Revolutionary political culture remained remarkably constant in this respect, as the great debate on popular societies in the fall of 1794 reveals.[3] Like most debates in this period, this one can be deciphered only if seen in context. Three months after Thermidor, many Conventionnels hoped to dismantle the network of societies affiliated with the Jacobin Club, which they were quick to blame for all the evils of the Terror. Speakers delivered fanatical diatribes against these "inquisitorial societies" and their bloodthirsty members.[4] Despite the vengeful obsession with the Jacobins, the arguments advanced by the club's adversaries are a good indicator of what contemporaries regarded as self-evident standards that had to be met if political representation was to be considered legitimate.

These were well summed up in a speech by François-Louis Bourdon, a deputy from the Oise, who developed two main arguments in his attack on what he considered the popular societies' threat to the "representative republic" of which he proclaimed himself the ardent defender. The first argument was sociopolitical, the second institutional. "The popular societies," he began, "are a group of men who, like monks, choose one another. In all the world I know of no aristocracy more constant or better constituted than that."[5] In his mind, the opposition aristocracy/democracy was an opposition between elitist separatism (with selection by co-optation) and overt universalism (governed by the electoral principle): "We are a democratic republic. Our government is representative. It is composed of men chosen by the people. But what are the popular societies? Associations of men who have selected themselves." By this logic, every association was aristocratic! If the primary offense was the violation of universality, Bourdon saw a lesser offense in the form of misrepresentation. "I see the people only in the primary assemblies," he noted. "But I see a second sovereign arising beside representative government . . . To the people I say, 'Choose between the men you have appointed to represent you and those who have risen up alongside them. Take either one, provided you choose one and only one representation.'"[6]

This critique of the popular societies was at the heart of revolutionary political culture, but it was rarely stated in such radically concise form because powerful historical circumstances tended to undermine principles, leading *in practice* to praise for the positive role of the clubs in establishing and defending the new France. Le Chapelier himself emphasized the importance of these circumstances in the fall of 1791. In "stormy times," he acknowledged, the popular societies contributed to a show of force that intimidated those nostalgic for the past and shaped public opinion. "While the Revolution was still going on," he felt,

> this arrangement was almost always more useful than harmful. When a nation changes its form of government, each citizen is a magistrate. All deliberate, and should deliberate, on public affairs. And whatever promotes, ensures, or hastens the revolution must be pressed into service. This temporary ferment must be encouraged and even intensified . . . But when the Revolution is over, when the Constitution of the Empire is fixed, when all public powers have been delegated and all authorities summoned, then, for the sake of preserving that Constitution, the most perfect order must be reestablished everywhere.[7]

In any event, those who opposed his proposal refrained from arguing the basic principles at issue and limited themselves to opportunistic sniping.

For instance, Robespierre, in justifying his opposition to imposing restrictions on the actions of the clubs, said, "I do not believe that the Revolution is over."[8] In the face of rampant intrigue and grasping ambition, the clubs had something to add that the regular operation of governing institutions could not provide. Thus in most people's minds, principled suspicion of popular societies readily coexisted with pragmatic acceptance.

Thus the whole question of popular societies was incorporated into a broader context, *a general economy of revolutionary action*. During the winter of 1792, when the disorder that the clubs had helped to create began to arouse opposition, their utility was again justified as a necessary *compensation*. Granted that the existence of the clubs led to a certain political dualism, though reprehensible in itself this dualism could be seen as an instrument made necessary for the time being by a situation in which the forces of the present had to overcome resistances associated with the past. Institutions, confined within their normal spheres of action, lacked the means to intervene effectively. Thus the popular societies introduced a kind of *corrective dualism*. This implicit division of labor between institutions and clubs was consolidated in the winter of 1792–93, when the first "committees of surveillance" and "revolutionary committees" were established to enforce measures of "public safety" with all the vigor required.

This led ultimately to a purely political judgment of the usefulness of popular societies, which varied according to the needs of the moment. After 1793 the Convention lurched back and forth between ardently defending and vehemently denouncing them. Intermediary political bodies were feared as *rival bodies* but also celebrated as *auxiliaries*. In July 1793 a law was passed stipulating the harshest of penalties for "any authority or individual" attempting to dissolve the popular societies or prevent them from meeting.[9] The Convention thus protected and encouraged those political associations that facilitated its actions by shaping public opinion in accordance with its objectives.[10] By the end of the summer, however, the goal had changed. Now the objective was to centralize revolutionary action, and Robespierre angrily attacked "the so-called popular societies." At this point he could find no words harsh enough to denounce "the conspirators who join them," and he described the organizations themselves as "a host of private societies organized by agents of foreign powers for their own purposes" rather than as representatives of the people, who were said to be absent from their ranks.[11] "The great popular society is the French people," was the way the Incorruptible summed up his argument, using words that might have been written by Le Chapelier. At the time, of course, there was an internal struggle among these groups, with the Jacobins (who formed "popular societies") clashing violently with "sectional societies" that had been created in the fall of 1793 to protest the persistence of sectional assemblies.[12] A short while earlier, similar questions had arisen when a number of societies had banded together to form "congresses."[13]

What stands out starkly in all these conflicts and debates is that the real issue was the representation of the people. Where were the people? Who were the people? These were the questions of the hour. What had to be resolved was a problem of representation. The Jacobins waged an energetic battle against the sectional societies, which they unsurprisingly accused of harboring aristocrats and counterrevolutionaries. When the conflict was at its height in the spring of 1794, Marc-Antoine Jullien expressed the extraordinary opinion that "the Jacobins are a living body of public opinion," while a member of the Committee of Public Safety railed against sectionnaires, whom he characterized as "unnatural children."[14] Significantly, proposals were heard in this period to dissolve the primary assemblies into the popular societies on the grounds that the "active" people, those engaged in militant activities, were sufficiently representative of the "passive" people, those who merely cast their ballots.[15]

Does all this mean simply that principles were swept away by circumstances? To be sure, the dynamic character of revolutionary events tended to create a situation in which controversies were constantly being resolved by the relative strength of the parties in conflict, and in this respect the Jacobins can be seen more as calculating strategists than as jealous guardians of a doctrine. Yet by setting forth the broad outline of a rhetorical argument, the critique of political corporations left an indelible imprint.

The Rejection of Interfaces

The critique of popular societies can thus be seen as part of a "sociological" rejection of intermediary bodies, but that is not all it was. It also derived in part from a certain view of democratic decision-making in which there was no room for the type of interface that political associations represent. These forerunners of modern political parties derived their structural justification from their ability to encourage deliberation and to organize elections. During the Revolution, this created a problem. Every intermediary political body was suspected of corrupting the general will by introducing an insidious bias into the process that shaped it. Doubts about political association on this score were soon linked to criticism of representatives as tantamount to a new aristocracy that claimed to speak for the people.[16] The two lines of attack should be kept distinct, however. Associated with the attack on representative entropy, the idea of *direct democracy* derives from the utopian ideal of a continually active people serving as both legislator and magistrate. The idea of *immediate democracy,* on the other hand, reflects a belief that the people are capable of expressing themselves as a body, as a unit that speaks with a clear voice and assumes a distinct presence. Direct democracy rejects *delegation,* the principle that one person can act and speak for others. Immediate democracy rejects *interfaces,* that is, institutions or procedures that shape collective expression. Direct democracy aims to eliminate mechanisms of *substitution,* whereby the representative takes the place of the represented. Immediate democracy rejects all *reflexivity* of the social, by which I mean that it rejects the assumption that the expression of the social requires a reflective agent to structure or focus intervention. Immediacy pertains to the figurative dimension of representation, whereas directness pertains to the procedural dimension. It can therefore coexist, paradoxically enough, with a quite archaic concept of popular expression, in which the voice of the collectivity is more a matter of consent than of deliberative choice.[17]

On this basis some rather obscure bonds were formed during the Revolution between the archaic and the radical. Nothing illustrates this more clearly than the words used by Abbé Fauchet, the great commentator on Rousseau whom we encountered earlier, to describe his ideal democratic regime. In the autumn of 1789 he could find no criticisms harsh enough to attack the insidious influences he believed to be at work in the Commune of Paris, where he feared that "the rights of the people [would be] immolated to representative aristocracy," "the arbitrary power of representation" would reign supreme, and a "caste of representatives" would transform itself into a "company of conquerors of the right to represent."[18] Does this mean that the radical abbé believed in the necessity of direct democracy? Apparently. Yet he by no means envisioned anything resembling self-government. Although he called for the people to act directly, he warned that "I have not spoken of discussion, but of consent."[19] He boldly envisioned the passage of laws by voting in primary assemblies, yet the conditions under which he stipulated that this exercise should be conducted are surprising: "The law should simply be heard," he wrote,

and then each man must say yes or no according to his soul and his conscience. Some may say that my system is a violation of liberty because it
deprives the people of freedom of discussion. This is no violation of liberty but rather assurance of its perfection. It prevents the local prosecutor, the village magistrate, the priest, or the man of established wealth
from violating it. The people in general will not insist on the right to read
the law, because they do not know how to read. They will not insist on
the right to debate the law, because they do not know how to debate. The
readers and the debaters can read and debate at their leisure, in their
homes, among their families and neighbors. But the people as a whole
have neither the time nor the ability to listen to the refined and absurd
politics of the fine minds of the canton. They have nothing to do with all
that, they want nothing to do with it, and they cannot want anything to
do with it. The president of the Assembly will clearly state each article of
the law and count the yeas and nays. The plurality will carry.[20]

Although Fauchet angrily rejected the suggestion that the people were but
a "vaporous sovereign" and popular sovereignty "merely a vague, limp, and
altogether chimerical generality,"[21] he did not really see the people as a veritable political actor.

One finds the same ambiguity in circles close to the Club des Cordeliers,
which in the summer of 1791 favored a bill calling for popular ratification
of all legislation. Louis de Lavicomterie, René-Louis de Girardin, and other
political commentators published a number of texts on the subject in Paris
and the provinces, and La Bouche de fer presented a synthesis of their
views. The idea was to organize annual gatherings in which the people
would be encouraged to exercise their sovereignty in a concrete way.[22] But
these meetings, to be held over a period of three days around July 14, were
by no means envisioned as deliberative assemblies. They were conceived
rather as festivals taken up primarily with "fraternal festivities," dances, and
games. What is more, the actual sanctioning of the laws was envisioned
more in terms of staging a liturgy than in terms of organizing an election.
The assembly was to be deployed in the form of a circle, "to represent eternal equality." There was to be no stage or platform, only a simple stone in
the center of the circle to signify that the place of power was empty. Still
more surprising, individuals were to be chosen to read the laws by acclamation in a unanimous and vibrant outpouring of emotion, and no one
was expected to submit his candidacy in advance. All further voting was

also to be by acclamation ("no discussion" was formally specified). This is what the goal of immediacy meant: the procedural aspect of democracy was totally absent. Democracy was thus apprehended as a social form: that of a unified and indivisible group. The critique of intermediary bodies was thereby associated with an archaic, prepluralist political culture.

The celebration of immediacy as a political characteristic of generality played a very important role by making it possible to represent generality in its pure state, untainted by even a formal element of particularity. Hence the importance of festivals, which gave perceptible form to the totality without an interface of any kind. More than a school, the festival was a sacrament of unity. "All of society's dissociative pretensions" could be "banished."[23] As we have seen, festivals served to erase differences and to represent the unity of the regenerated people, but they also allowed for an immediate form of collective expression: a common opinion could arise from their midst without the need for any representative mechanism. Thus immediacy as a characteristic of generality was opposed in this context to the idea of a representative process intended to reveal identities and preferences by way of differentiation and reflective distance (bearing in mind that representation is not just delegation and symbolization but also has an intrinsically epistemological dimension).

Political societies were not totally excluded from this approach, but they were conceived primarily as pedagogical instruments. François-Xavier Lanthenas, one of the leaders of the Cercle Social, championed this view. In his mind the popular societies were not "parties" at all. They made sense only if seen as one of the two branches of the national educational system (the public schools being the other). Thus he hoped that every primary assembly would establish a *society* open to all citizens for the purpose of organizing readings and lectures and enhancing the cohesion of the group.[24] What he hoped for was a veritable conversion of the "clubs" into "peaceful and philosophical general associations devoted from this point on exclusively to instruction and good works."[25] Primary assemblies and popular societies could thus ultimately merge, since they would merely be two distinct phases of the same social and political reality. The goal should therefore be to universalize the popular societies. To that end, Lanthenas envisioned patriotic organizations of two kinds. Organizations of the first type were familiar from the Revolution: "They consist mainly of citizens separated from their more numerous brethren by wealth, enlightenment, and habit."[26] Hence they could not claim to represent the people faithfully. For

Lanthenas, the solution was not to ban these organizations, as Le Chapelier had urged, although Lanthenas, too, was quite wary of these unrepresentative groups ("Truth disdains the support of men organized and classified," he wrote).[27] Instead, he proposed to resolve the difficulty by increasing the number of patriotic societies, in the plural, until they coincided exactly with society itself, in the singular, "becoming nothing other than the French people themselves."[28]

Thus, although Lanthenas went as far as anyone in acknowledging that the popular societies might play a positive role, he was by no means a pluralist. He, too, dreamed of a general will that would manifest itself as it had done on the Fourteenth of July 1789, "in an awesome, spontaneous, and unanimous manner."[29] Like nearly all his contemporaries, he rejected pluralism for two reasons, one sociological, the other functional. The *sociological rejection of pluralism* was associated with the critique of intermediary bodies, on the grounds that they interposed a screen between the individual and the "great whole." The *functional rejection of pluralism* was linked to a conception of the immediate expression of the general will, which takes shape without the need for any reflective interface. In order to understand the antipluralism of French political culture, both reasons for rejecting pluralism should be taken into account. Does the fact that Lanthenas, like Jacques-Pierre Brissot, celebrated the freedom of the press undermine this reading? No, because for both men freedom of the press was a way of allowing a *generalized reflection,* a reflection therefore exempt from the reproach of introducing a bias into the formation of the common opinion (as the popular societies did by allowing *polarized reflection*). As they saw it, freedom of the press thus offered a universalized and diffracted mode of representation and could therefore be accommodated within a globally antipluralist culture.

The same suspicion of intermediary bodies and aspiration to a certain democratic immediacy can also be found in the way in which the revolutionaries conceived of that palpable symbol of public space, the form of political assemblies themselves. The newly elected representatives of the people found the hall reserved for the Estates General at Versailles too majestic as well as acoustically inappropriate, and they subsequently devoted a good deal of thought to the question of what sort of parliamentary architecture accorded best with their political philosophy. They wanted an arrangement that would reflect the unity of the assembly and adopted the hemicycle rather than a rectangular chamber, which seemed to lend itself more easily to divisions (the English House of Commons was the model they wished to avoid on the grounds that it encouraged adversarial debate).[30] The French were looking for a way to indicate that their goal was unanimity. In a properly designed chamber, it was believed, the general will would emerge almost spontaneously. "We no longer need speeches or correspondence, only silent sessions in which each deputy divines in the eyes of the others what he needs to do," as one Jacobin put it.[31] The deputies were thus supposed to form, without mediation, one single body, physically and intellectually. To be sure, this utopian vision was quite remote from the tumultuous reality, yet it has long been taken as something worth aiming for.

The Impossible Middle Term

The rejection of interfaces to some extent overlaps the critique of intermediary bodies, despite the distinctions we have explored thus far. But the quest for immediacy also led to the rejection of a third type of mediation, of a purely procedural order. The best example of this involves elections and the way in which candidacies were conceived. Candidacies were seen as part of the electoral process, but they were not associated with any institution. Candidates simply appeared when needed, then disappeared. Candidacies thus exemplify what I call the "structuring middle term" *(tiers organisateur)*, the purpose of which is to reduce the many (the voters) to one (the elected official). The middle term is merely a kind of procedural accelerator and concentrator, thus the least constraining and most neutral form of mediation that one can imagine. Yet even this was rejected. Throughout much of the revolutionary period, declared candidacies were banned. The consequences were serious. To begin with, the electoral process itself was greatly complicated. Without a focusing framework, votes were inevitably scattered among numerous people. Hence it took many rounds of voting for the preferences of citizens to emerge. Maneuvering behind the scenes was encouraged, and obscure conspiracies inevitably filled the void left by the absence of official procedures.[32] Understanding the reasons for the ban will deepen our analysis of the principle of immediacy in the revolutionary political culture.

One reason for rejecting candidacies might be characterized as democratic. To put oneself forward was to offend the principle of equality by asserting one's superiority to others. It was to introduce an undeniable sign of distinction. "According to our customs, the man who carries immodesty to the point of deliberately soliciting the votes of the people thereby makes himself unworthy of their favor," Beugnot observed in 1791, giving concise form to a widely shared sentiment.[33] Declarations of candidacy were also suspected of fomenting intrigue and encouraging base conspiracies among the wretched sort of people who went "begging for votes," thereby degrading the process of civic choice. Condemnation of the practice was not merely moral and philosophical, however. It also stemmed from a feeling that the existence of a structuring middle term distorted the process, especially since people were convinced that the "voice of the ballot" should arise spontaneously from the assembled voters.

People at the time were strongly wedded to the idea that the right choice should appear to be self-evident. "Form a crowd," the abbé de Mably said, "and common sense will soon permeate it."[34] Inherited from the Physiocrats, this understanding of choice as assent to an obvious truth was embraced by the men of 1789. No one imagined that merit and virtue might not be universally and spontaneously recognizable. "The desire to single out the man worthy of election and bestow high office upon him through one's vote is only a seed, as it were, in the soul of each voter," a contemporary observed. "It is in meetings and great assemblies that that seed develops and blossoms. There, by way of I know not what moral electricity compounded of elements of all sorts, the majority experiences a shock against which it is helpless. A common thought occurs to it, and it strikes a blow for justice that none of its members could have struck on his own."[35] Benjamin Constant would later borrow this notion of "moral electricity" to praise its ability to "temporarily subjugate individual ambition and the parochial spirit."[36] In order to generate the electricity in question, a law of Year VI (1798) stipulated that primary and communal assemblies should be preceded by celebrations of popular sovereignty. "The effects of the previous night's festival will influence the day's voting," the law noted.[37]

The issue of candidacies remained alive throughout the Directory (1795–1799). In reaction to the increased prevalence of intrigue and manipulation during the Terror, the ban on candidacies was temporarily lifted for the elections of Year III: the law stipulated that an official list of candidates should be drawn up and that any citizen could nominate himself or anyone else.[38] In Year V a directive institutionalized this procedure for a time.[39] But the interval was brief, and lists were again prohibited in Year VI.[40] Throughout the various phases of the Revolution, its institutions remained opposed in spirit to elections based on declared candidacies. As one political commentator noted, "the true list of candidates is the one favored by public opinion, the only one acceptable to our form of government and our mores. It likes to generalize what others particularize. It seeks the enlightenment of theory and the assistance of reasoning."[41] Despite the urgent practical necessity, the idea of declared candidacies periodically resurfaced but never took hold.[42] Hence during this period Brissot was quite isolated in his thinking about pluralist elections, his approval of declared candidacies, and his belief in the virtue of holding a separate preliminary or screening election before the final ballot.[43]

Between Freedom and Institutions

"Citizens have the right to assemble peacefully and to form free societies." This edict of 19 November 1790 was unequivocal: it recognized the right of association, thus giving backbone to Article 11 of the Declaration of Rights of 1789, which stated that "free communication of thoughts and opinions is one of man's most precious rights." The Constitution of 1791 confirmed this right as one of its basic principles, using a formula that would be used again in 1793. But what was the significance of this right if intermediary bodies were simultaneously outlawed?

This contradiction runs through the whole history of the Revolution. In effect, political societies occupied a place on the border between two worlds: one in which freedom (to assemble or to speak) could be exercised in a positive way, and another in which institutions operated. *Freedom-societies* were authorized, but *institution-societies* were banned. Le Chapelier himself made clear use of this distinction in 1791. "All citizens are allowed to assemble peacefully," he acknowledged, adding that there was a need to foster interest among citizens in discussing public affairs. "But," he went on to warn, "alongside this general interest and warm affection to which the existence of a homeland and free enjoyment of the rights of the citizen give rise, we have the maxims of public order and the principles of representative government." He therefore denounced the various factors (such as affiliation of societies and regular correspondence) that encouraged societies "to assume a public existence" that could interfere with operation of institutions.[44]

This duality is at the heart of revolutionary political culture. One finds its expression everywhere. Roederer, who wrote abundantly on the question, was one of the first to reflect on and attempt to give grounds for the distinction between individual rights and political rights that underlies it. In an important pamphlet published in Year III, he began by stating that it was "an inalienable right of man to assemble in popular societies," but he went on to attack the *political* activity of those societies in the most vehement of terms.[45] The distinction between the legitimate exercise of the right to assemble and its objectionable derivative was linked in Roederer's mind to the type of activity that each exemplified. The purpose of the freedom-society was to encourage interaction *among individuals:* Roederer emphasized friendship and instruction as two means of forging social bonds and thus achieving the ends for which societies were created (the principles involved being the principle of communication and the principle of perfection). The purposes of institution-societies were different. Generally they sought to "oversee, inspect, censure, denounce, or enlighten the constituted authorities . . . [and] to serve as organs of the people with their representatives and of the representatives with the people." Thus their goal was to interact *with public institutions.* Roederer deemed this unacceptable, because it meant that the societies were no longer exercising the faculties of individuals but performing *public functions* and *official acts.* How should the line dividing one type of society from the other be drawn? The question was asked repeatedly, because the criteria for making the distinction were always open to debate.

Nevertheless, the Constitution of Year III set out to give substance to the right of assembly.[46] It did so in two ways. First, it banned the use of the term "popular society," which was deemed to be dangerously ambiguous. Second, it imposed strict regulations on the activities of all authorized societies: public meetings were banned, as were the wearing of distinctive insignia, correspondence with other societies, and affiliation among different societies. It was further stipulated that political rights—that is, the right to deliberate in common and express collective wishes—could be exercised only in primary and communal assemblies. Still, these regulations did not cover everything. To be sure, the attributes of a public role were broadly prohibited, and those obsessed with a possible Jacobin comeback could take this threat as grounds for a very strict interpretation of the ban on political corporations. They could even go so far as to maintain that only recreational and literary societies were authorized.[47] Nevertheless, another, less restrictive interpretation of the Constitution was still possible.[48] Thus the question remained open.

In the Directory period, which was punctuated by a series of violent episodes and electoral surprises, the issue came up regularly. Various measures intended to restore order were adopted one after another, but their
legal basis was never clearly established. In the spring of 1796, a period of
some confusion, the clubs were again shut down by fiat. Then, in the fall of
1797, a new law went so far as to ban certain newspapers.[49] As a result, attempts were again made to clarify the legal status of the popular societies.
Earlier ambiguities were not eliminated, however, and the great debate
about legislative reform initiated by the Council of Five Hundred seems to
have rehashed many old controversies. The only "advance" in this period
involved a search for criteria on the basis of which freedom of the press
could be distinguished from freedom for the clubs. Brissot had been the
first to associate the two: "The clubs and the newspapers are freedom's two
stoutest columns," as he put it.[50] But since then no one had developed the
theme. Now it became crucial, however, to justify the differentiation of
these two types of liberty. Reporting to the Council of Five Hundred on a
new proposal to regulate the popular societies, Jean-Baptiste Mailhe in
1796 proposed a functional distinction:

> The relation between the press and the clubs is analogous to the relation
> between written thought and spoken thought. Yet there are enormous
> differences in the character and above all the rapidity of their respective
> efforts. Thought spoken to a club or a large audience influences an as-
> sembled mass of citizens simultaneously. Written thought affects only
> one reader at a time or at most a small number of people at a reading. If
> the number were to swell at some point, whether periodically or unex-
> pectedly, it would thereby take on the character of a club or mob that
> would need to be dispersed.[51]

A book or newspaper mediates a series of dialogues or "conversations" between author and reader, and each of these is singular, whereas a club has
an *immediate* collective influence. Thus the difference between the two institutions is a question not only of audience (individual versus mass)[52]
but also of reception (mediate versus immediate; spontaneous versus reflective; rapid versus slow). Hence the nature of the two freedoms was different.[53] One clearly involved the organization of individual rights, while
the other had a *political function* and therefore needed to be incorporated
as an element of a larger structure. The press had a role to play in the process of representative government by helping to shape common opinion

and facilitating communication between representatives and those they represented, while clubs tended to create a dual representation.

These distinctions were not enough to end debate, however. It was by no means simply a matter of legal definitions. Various political tensions found their expression in this controversy. One sees this clearly in Year VII, a few weeks before Brumaire, when the waning of the royalist threat and the specter of a kind of anarchy brought moderates and neo-Jacobins closer together. After the events of 30 Prairial, which gave rise to a broad coalition opposed to the executive Directory, the consensus that was achieved led to the assertion of a constitutional right to form political societies, though subject to regulation.[54] This agreement settled nothing, however, because it was in part a product of circumstances and lacked the support of a coherent theory of democratic politics. Between the more restrictive view of the clubs as entirely apolitical (still championed by Roederer)[55] and the view favored by some that the popular societies, seen as a *mere phase* of the existence of primary assemblies,[56] ought to be quasi-institutionalized, the various proposals for structuring the right of assembly were based on nothing more than a concern for order or other practical considerations. There were suggestions to limit the size of popular societies, to restrict the geographical area from which they could recruit members, to regulate the hours at which they could meet, to require them to make regular declarations to the authorities, and to ban affiliations and correspondence.[57] Thus it was simply a question of regulating behavior or authorizing certain practices, not a change of outlook or the introduction of a new legal principle, and lurking suspicions remained. As the revolutionary period drew to a close, the political culture of generality thus remained extraordinarily persistent, as we see here in connection with the principle of immediacy.

— 3 —

Generality as Mode of Regulation

The Cult of Law

The Revolution and the Passion for Law

The men of 1789 never tired of celebrating the law. "Nation, Law, King": among these three powers, which in their eyes formed a trinity, law occupied the central place. Coins struck in 1791 bore the inscription "Rule of Law." The iconography of the period magnified the three imperious letters of the word "law" in any number of ways. A grammarian of the period even proposed that France henceforth be considered a *loyaume* (a "law"-dom).[1] Although this nomomania irritated a few people on the margins of society, little attention was paid to them. So it comes as no surprise to find one Parisian patriotic society taking the name Society of Friends of the Law and Humanity in 1791, while another adopted the more erudite title Society of Nomophiles.[2] Early in 1790, when the Society of Friends of the Constitution (the future Jacobin Club) was taking its first timid steps, the deputy Gilbert Romme had already successfully launched the Society of Friends of the Law with meetings at the home of Théroigne de Méricourt.[3] In the spring of 1792, a "Festival of the Law" (one of the first festivals to be held after the Festival of the Federation) was staged with great ceremony in the streets of Paris, featuring forests of banners bearing inscriptions such as "The Law," "Respect for the Law," and "Die to Defend the Law."[4] Enthusiastic approval of the rule of law is evident in the spontaneous and fervent cries of "Vive la loi!" that could be heard at countless public meetings.

The law was repeatedly invoked in debate as well as in celebration.[5] Of the seventeen articles of the Declaration of Rights of 1789, seven referred to the functions of law and thus established its centrality. When Maximin Isnard, in the fall of 1791, advocated severe treatment of refractory priests, he justified himself by saying, "my God is the law. I have no other."[6] Even

49

Saint-Just, who set little store by formalities, was spontaneously moved to remark that "apart from the law, everything is sterile and lifeless."[7] Thus Jules Michelet had good reason to characterize the first phase of the Revolution as an "advent of law." But we need to delve into the matter more deeply. Behind the apparent unanimity there were in fact three different approaches to law in 1789. The first, which might be characterized as "liberal," banally opposed the virtues of a state governed by fixed rules to the caprices of arbitrary power. But for the men of 1789, the idea of a "rule of law" also referred to the Physiocratic view that a good government was defined by the rational basis of its actions and not by the procedures it uses. Finally, the celebration of the law derived in part from recognition of the commanding role of the general will, of which the law was seen as an emanation. The problem is that these three visions of the law—the liberal, the rationalist, and the democratic, to put it simply—are by no means equivalent.

The rule of law of which the revolutionaries of 1789 dreamed had a clearly liberal dimension. The law was seen as "the guarantor of liberty," to use an expression that cropped up in any number of speeches to the National Assembly. "The law," Talleyrand said, "should just be liberty itself and nothing else."[8] For everyone the rule of law was the antithesis of arbitrary rule. Montesquieu's canonical phrases were on everyone's mind, and it was natural to attack despotism as a regime in which "one man's will and caprice decides everything, unencumbered by law or rules." In other words, despotic power was private or particular power (the arbitrary will of the prince), whereas general rules guaranteed liberty. The law embodied generality in three ways: by its origin (because parliament made it); by its form (impersonal norms); and by its mode of administration (the state). From this threefold generality the law derived its prestige. It was not only a *principle of order,* allowing the "transformation of an infinite number of men . . . into a single body" and thus making the law "to the republic what the soul is to the body,"[9] but also a *principle of justice,* because in its generality it knew no particular person, thus allowing the law to rule as "intelligence without passion."[10] So it is not surprising that Abbé Barthélemy's *Voyage du jeune Anacharsis en Grèce,* which recounts the amazement occasioned by the discovery of Lycurgus's laws, scored a great publishing success in 1788 and influenced the thinking of an entire generation.

Such reverence for the law could not arise solely from philosophical reflection, however. It was also the fruit of a slow institutional maturation connected with the history of the *parlements* in the Old Regime. Indeed, the magistrates sought to contain the power of the sovereign by highlighting the administrative and social functions of the law, exhausting themselves in the effort to carve out a "kingdom of law" within the kingdom of the prince. The political and moral virtues of the law were thus rooted in a powerful professional culture, of which, in the eighteenth century, Chancellor Henri François d'Aguesseau was the incontestable champion and most brilliant interpreter. In his eyes, the magistrates constituted a "great body of enlightenment" that provided society with certain reference points and safeguards,[11] and law was a science based on the experience of the ages. Jurists gave expression not only to the power of norms but also to "the reason of all the legislators who speak with its voice and pronounce through its mouth oracles of eternal truth."[12]

The *constituants* of 1789 belonged to this liberal tradition, especially since many of them had had legal training and were lawyers by profession. For these men, law was not just a normative power; its purpose was also to tether liberty to reason. The formal generality of law was thus supposed to be rooted in the substantial generality of reason. On this view, positive laws can yield benefits only if conceived as "laws for handling the natural order [*lois de manutention relatives à l'ordre naturel*]" (the phrase is François Quesnay's)—that is, only if they are derived from natural laws for instrumental purposes. The revolutionary passion for the law was thus linked to a broadly rationalist political culture. This was the work of the Physiocrats, who were the most powerful embodiment of that culture in the mid-eighteenth century. Although the revolutionaries paid little heed to Quesnay's views concerning the citizen-landowner or to his economic theory of the net product, they shared much of his philosophical inspiration.[13] What they had in common was reverence for generality.

For Quesnay and his disciples, men did not need to invent anything in order to be free. They had only to observe and abide by the laws of nature. "The law," wrote Guillaume François Le Trosne in *De l'ordre social,* "is written in perceptible characters in the great book of nature."[14] Politics was thus both an observational art and a deductive science; it created nothing new and instituted nothing novel. Quesnay made this point in his *Maximes:* "Neither men nor their governments make laws, nor can they make them. They recognize laws as being compatible with supreme reason, which governs the universe. They pronounce the laws. They *present* the laws to society . . . That is why they are called bearers of law, *legislators,* and collectors of the laws thus presented, whereas no one has ever dared call them makers of law, *legisfactors*."[15] The book that most strikingly captured this vision of politics was Pierre Le Mercier de la Rivière's *L'Ordre naturel et essentiel des sociétés politiques* (1767). Legislative power, Le Mercier explained, is not the same as the power to invent laws. "Making bad laws is a misfortune, an accident of humanity," he wrote, "and in no sense a *right* or prerogative of authority . . . Legislative power is not the power to make obviously bad laws arbitrarily."[16] In other words, liberty lies in conformity with nature, whereas oppression arises only when human will goes astray. This conception of the relation between liberty and law is based on an epistemology centered on the notion of *self-evidence*. This point is fundamental. It is the crux of what distinguishes French liberalism, conceived as political rationalism, from the radically different English liberalism.

For the Physiocrats, self-evidence was the true guarantor of liberty. Generality expressed itself as self-evidence, thus transcending all discord, ambiguity, uncertainty, and particularity. "When men are unfortunately deprived of evidence," Le Mercier wrote, "opinion in the narrow sense is the only source of moral force. Then we can neither understand nor count on any force. The result is inevitably a state of disorder, in which the idea of establishing any kind of counterforce to prevent the arbitrary abuse of sovereign authority is obviously illusory. The opposite of the arbitrary is the self-evident. Only the irresistible force of self-evidence can serve as a counterforce to the force of arbitrariness and opinion."[17] On this point the Physiocrats were disciples of Nicolas Malebranche.[18] They read and meditated on *De la recherche de la vérité* and invoked its author to discredit will and opinion. In the face of self-evidence, necessity and will fused: "Self-evidence should be the source of all authority, because it is what unites all wills," Le Mercier said.[19] It was equivalent to the principle of unanimity, a form of universal reason.

In adopting this heritage, the men of 1789 were led to link reverence for the law to enthusiasm for the rationalizing state in a very particular way; the same can be said for the way they linked the notion of a government of laws to the idea of administrative authority. In their view, the advent of a rational state was a prerequisite of liberty: eventually law, state, and general rule came to overlap. In the second half of the eighteenth century, this political rationalism was not only established as a doctrine but reinforced and implemented in various concrete transformations of the administrative apparatus. After 1750, the old world of *officiers* (owners of venal offices) began to decline as *commissaires* (functionaries serving at the pleasure of the monarch) came into their own, marking a decisive turn in the evolution of the monarchical administration toward a modern bureaucracy. Enlightened despotism and French-style "liberalism" forged an ambiguous new relationship in this rationalization of the state apparatus. This configuration was quite distinct from the world envisioned by English liberals.

Of course the invocation of law in 1789 also had a democratic dimension. "Law is the expression of the general will," according to Article 6 of the Declaration of Rights. The character of generality thus derived from its origin: "law" meant any decision of the legislative body.[20] The Constitution of 1791 stressed this point: "Edicts of the legislative body have the force of law and bear the name and title of law."[21] The celebration of law thus merged with the celebration of the people (in its representatives). Thus the three dimensions of generality, contradictory as well as complementary, combined in the revolutionary political culture to form the basis of French "legicentrism."

Codifying Ardor

The revolutionary celebration of law at first confirmed and later helped to further the process of legal rationalization that had begun in the eighteenth century. Rationalization attacked the thicket of customary law and the accumulation of ad hoc regulations. "The law is like an old building," d'Aguesseau complained, summing up the general feeling.[22] This perspective explains the Enlightenment's nostalgic admiration for the work of Lycurgus, the great mythical lawgiver of Sparta. "Lacedemonia," the chancellor noted, "is perhaps the only republic that had a true body of legislation composed of a small number of laws but all pertinent to the common good, effective, and enforced."[23] The *Encyclopédie* summed up the feeling of the period well when it asserted that "all other things being equal, the proliferation of laws proves that a government is poorly constituted."[24] Rousseau was even more scathing: "If I were asked which nation is most defective, I would straightaway answer, the one with the most laws."[25]

For contemporaries, the goal of rationalizing and simplifying to reduce the number of laws was first of all a pragmatic issue. Everyone agreed on the need to put an end to conflicts and controversies stemming from ambiguous and overlapping regulations. In the preamble to a 1731 ordinance on gifts, d'Aguesseau put these words in the mouth of Louis XV: "Justice should be as uniform in its judgments as the law in its provisions, and it should not vary with time and place, just as it derives glory from ignoring differences between persons. All legislators share this spirit, and there is no law that does not aim for perpetuity and uniformity. The principal object of the law is to prevent litigation, even more than to end it."[26] The abbé Castel de Saint-Pierre explained in his *Mémoire pour diminuer le nombre des procès* how this concern led to an idea of parsimonious generality in the law. Litigation, he argued, usually arose when ambiguities in the law or incompatible customary regulations led to divergent interpretations. Hence he held that rationalization of the state and improvement of the law went hand in hand. The good law was one that left no uncertainty as to its application: "Laws should be so clear that anyone reading them should be able to see the decision of the case that concerns them and, more than that, to see it if possible in a way that needs no interpretation. Thus a good legislator should seek to reduce the need for legal scholars."[27] In other words, the law should be the expression of general reason, intimately weaving together the two principles of rationality and generality. "It is appropriate for the number of specific laws to be equal, insofar as possible, to the number of specific kinds of cases to be decided; or, rather, it is appropriate for each law to be stated in such generality that it includes and encompasses all special cases without exception, as the only good way of reducing the number of laws is to generalize them."[28] To that end, he called for the creation of a French Academy of Law as well as a "perpetual company" to examine the laws.

The desire to codify the law translated this theory into action. The very term "code" is suggestive of the reformist impulse to replace the old patchwork of customary laws with a uniform and rational legal system.[29] The Constitution of 1791 explicitly stipulated that "a common Civil Code shall be established for the entire kingdom."[30] For the *constituants*, codification was truly therapy, as much intellectual as political. It was not merely a technical affair (as was an earlier proposal to reduce customary laws to written texts so as to establish their content once and for all). The first fruits of this labor were presented by Jean-Jacques Régis de Cambacérès in the summer of 1793. Unsurprisingly, he argued for a "simple structure" and insisted that the lawmakers should leave few questions unresolved.[31] His proposal was rejected on the grounds that it "was too highly developed in its detail and not philosophical enough overall." The same imperative would govern work on the Code of Commerce that began several years later. Once again the goal was to achieve "absolute uniformity" by way of "absolute principles."[32]

Although French jurists were the first zealous champions of this effort, it was an Englishman, Jeremy Bentham, who expressed a more radical version of the same utopian ideal.[33] In January 1789 he proposed a *pannomion,* which was to legal reform what the Panopticon would become some years later to prison reform. At that point, just a few months before the Revolution, Bentham dreamed that Louis XVI and the Estates General would seize upon his idea to overhaul the social and political order in France.[34] A little later he wrote to James Madison with a similar goal in mind.[35] If Bentham aroused the enthusiasm of many reformers around the world at the turn of the nineteenth century, it was surely with the French experience that his work resonated most clearly.

The Power of Generality

The idea of the "rule of law" relates in various ways to an assertion of the power of generality. There are both procedural and substantial aspects to this relation: the law is both norm and form. The intention here is not narrowly technical, however. It is closely associated with two kinds of political utopia: it draws implicitly on the image of the legislator as demiurge, the unacknowledged teacher and sovereign of the world order; and it is informed by the prospect of exerting total regulatory control over society.

With the passion for law comes an exaltation of the role of the legislator, seen as the sculptor of the human race. Rousseau, for example, shared this exalted view of the role of the true legislator, whom he painted as a towering figure surveying human experience from on high. As he famously put it, the legislator was one who "dares to institute an entire people," with the goal "of transforming each individual, who by himself is a perfect and solitary whole, into part of a greater whole."[36] For him, the legislator was a *teacher-generalizer.* Nor was Rousseau exceptional in this respect. From Fénelon to Condorcet a long line of French thinkers had related the celebration of law to a pedagogical ambition. Many who wrote about politics and the law also wrote about the theory of education. Mably, for example, came from a family of tutors (Condillac was his brother). Le Mercier de la Rivière did not confine himself to writing about politics but was also the author of one of the first treatises on public education. In that book he asked, "Should a government be the principal instructor of its subjects?"[37] The Revolution would afford such ambitions ample opportunity.

This vision of the legislator as teacher is intertwined with a second utopian vision: that of a power capable of grasping every detail of a society and controlling everything that happens in it. This was a powerful element in the revolutionary philosophy of law. The power of generality envisioned here was thus not simply procedural. For the men of 1789, the law was not merely an effective and legitimate norm. It was also a *political force*. In a sense, it summoned men to reconstruct reality itself as an abstract truth. The prism of generality smoothed the world's sharp edges and made everything fit together in a clear design, a transparent concept. The law, by excluding all specificity, painted an imaginary world. No one put this better than Merlin de Douai, one of the period's leading legal scholars: "In order for the object of the law to be presumed general, it is enough for law to treat abstractly the persons and things of which it speaks."[38] In other words, the procedure was reflected onto the object and shaped that object. The application of generality became a process of *dematerialization*.

Rousseau illustrates this displacement-cum-reversal to perfection. To be sure, he shared his contemporaries' view of the law as a neutral power, and hence as a structural guarantee of liberty. For him, the law's impersonality was foremost among its virtues.[39] But he did not stop there. His originality lay in conflating the form and substance of the law: for him these were only two ways of expressing social generality. "It is this twofold universality that defines the true character of law," he wrote.[40] If the law was to combine generality of the object with generality of the will, it could do so only by eliminating the peculiarities of the world and retaining only the common residue. Just as the general will is defined in a sense in opposition to particular wills, social generality is constructed *in opposition to reality*, which is always particular. Think of the classic statement of this point in the *Social Contract*: "When I say that the province of the law is always general, I mean that the law considers all subjects collectively and all actions in the abstract; it does not consider any individual man or any specific vision."[41] Hence generality not only has a methodological or procedural dimension; it is also a social construct. It is a *fiction*, in the legal sense of the term, a fiction that is a necessary condition for the law to be effective (for otherwise legal language has no universalizing virtue). The problem is that the construction of this fiction, which is a technical prerequisite of law,[42] ends up being confused with political reality, as is clear from the line of argument of the *Social Contract*. To love the law, then, means to distance oneself from reality. Saint-Just offers a fine illustration of this perverse turn. "The legislator commands the future," he proclaimed in a famous speech. "There is no point in his being weak. It is up to him to will the good and to perpetuate it. It is up to him to make men what he wants them to be. Depending on how the law animates the social body, *which is inert in itself,* the result is either virtue or crime, good morals or ferocity."[43]

Underlying the ardor to codify we thus find a veritable utopia: to govern the world flawlessly by remaking it through abstraction so as to achieve absolute comprehensibility. No one has described better than Jean Carbonnier the link that was to be created between what he calls "a phenomenon of legal psychology" and a certain political vision: "To legislate is a more exquisite pleasure than to command. It is no longer the crude order that the master barks to the slave or the commander to the soldier, the immediate imperative that ends as soon as it is carried out. No, it is the *law,* the faceless order, which aims to be universal and eternal, like divinity and equivalent to it—an order projected into space and time to meet an anonymous multitude and unseen generations to come."[44] This, too, was a part of what the men of the Revolution cherished in the power of generality. That is why they would offer the most frighteningly literal translation of Abbé Raynal's definition: "The law is a sword that must impartially cut off anything that would raise itself up above it."[45]

Total Law

This totalizing vision of generality encourages thinking of the law as absolutely adequate to reality in all its diversity. In other words, what the law says is supposed to have the ability to encompass the plurality of possibilities, the infinite range of particularities. The fabrication of the law thus figures as part of an effort to rationalize the world, extending the political rationalism of the Physiocratic project as well as the Rousseauian perspective we have just explored. Hence in this case the sovereignty of the law signifies not only a government of laws but also the legislator's ambition to assume all political functions, including those of the executive and judiciary.

Cesare Beccaria was the first to conceive of the role of law in these terms in his great opus *On Crimes and Punishments* (1764), which his contemporaries hailed as a major work. Beccaria's point of departure can certainly be characterized as classically liberal. His first objective was of course to propose a remedy for a system of justice so incoherent as to assign widely varying penalties for identical crimes. Like many eighteenth-century philosophers, he was haunted by the specter of judicial error and revolted by the arbitrariness of punishment. For him, the root of all these evils was the power of judges to interpret the law. Hence he fought for a more objective legal system that would make the law less ambiguous in the face of a diversity of offenses. True justice—impersonal and therefore not arbitrary—meant that the letter of the law should be perfectly clear. Indeed, Beccaria went so far as to comment ironically that "the spirit of tyranny goes hand in hand with the taste for reading."[46] Logically summing up his argument, he wrote: "There is nothing more dangerous than the common axiom which holds that the spirit of the law must be taken into consideration."[47] In considering a crime, the judge should "form a perfect syllogism," thereby closing the door to uncertainty. For that outcome to be possible, the general law should coincide precisely with the facts. Thus for many men of the Enlightenment, love of the law and distrust of judges went hand in hand. Diderot, for example, urged Catherine II to get rid of commentators on the code,[48] while Voltaire had this to say in his *Dictionnaire philosophique:* "Let every law be clear, uniform, and precise. To interpret the law is almost always to corrupt it."[49]

The political culture of the Revolution drew on this current. We see its influence clearly in the great debate on judicial reform in 1790, which occupied the Constituent Assembly for several months.[50] It is worth briefly recalling the terms in which the Cour de Cassation (appellate court) was conceived by the law of 27 November 1790.[51] Although the law agreed with Barère that a provision for appeal "was unfortunate but necessary,"[52] the *constituants* were thoroughly aware of the danger of allowing an autonomous power to interpret the law. Although they also believed that an appellate court could serve, as Antoine Barnave put it, "to maintain the unity of the law,"[53] they nevertheless feared that a tribunal charged with safeguarding and protecting the law might in some insidious way become its master. Hence they decided that there should be only one court of appeal, and that it should sit *alongside the legislature,* so that the court's pronouncements would simply clarify the meaning of the law and not establish an independent jurisprudence.[54] "The word 'jurisprudence' . . . should be erased from our language," Robespierre said, encapsulating the general sentiment on this point. "The jurisprudence of the courts is nothing other than the law."[55] In practice, moreover, the activity of the Cour de Cassation in this period was limited to nullifying ordinances deemed to be in "formal contravention" of a law or to derive from an "incorrect application of the law." In this respect, the court scrupulously obeyed the letter of an edict of 17 November 1790, Article 3 of which stipulated that appeals should be allowed only where there was "*express* contravention of the text of the law."[56]

This obsession with the idea that interpretation of the law might dena-
ture it seemed to vanish for a time, however.[57] In his celebrated *Discours
préliminaire sur le projet de Code civil,* Portalis exhibited a modesty at odds
with the statements cited above.[58] To be sure, he deemed it "desirable that
all matters be capable of being settled by law," but he immediately moderated that ambition. "We have protected ourselves against the dangerous
ambition of seeking to regulate and anticipate everything," he emphasized.

> Try as one might, positive laws can never entirely replace the use of natu-
> ral reason in the affairs of life. The needs of society are so varied . . . that
> it is impossible for the legislator to foresee them all. Even in those matters
> to which he devotes particular attention, a host of details will escape him
> . . . However complete a code may appear to be, no sooner is it finished
> than a thousand unexpected questions vie for the attention of the magis-
> trate. For laws, once drafted, remain as they were written. By contrast,
> men never rest. They are always active; and this ceaseless activity, the ef-
> fects of which are modified in various ways by circumstances, constantly
> yields new combinations, new facts, and new results.[59]

Far from sharing the triumphalist views of the great legal scholars of the
revolutionary period, the father of the Civil Code recognized that it was to
some extent utopian to believe that a small number of simple laws could
ever be enough, and he was careful to distinguish the *science of the legislator* from the *science of the magistrate,* which he deemed complementary. A
short while later, the great Locré put it more bluntly: "We are no longer living in that time of fantasy and ignorance, when revolutionary philosophers wanted the law to provide for every case, and the office of the judge
was limited to opening his law book, looking up the case before him, and
converting the law's provisions into a judgment."[60] Yet these blunt statements should not be allowed to mislead. They do not indicate that a step
backward had been taken. Indeed, Locré denounced "judicial arbitrariness" in the harshest of terms.[61] Both authors were in fact guided by practical political considerations. It was Robespierre whom they feared, not a
philosophy of generality that they rejected. Their primary aim was to protect against the danger to public order that would result from a gap in the
law. Evidence of this can be seen in the central importance they ascribed to
the celebrated Article 4 of the Civil Code,[62] which required the judge to
render a decision in all cases or be liable to prosecution himself for "denial
of justice" (even if dealing with a case in which the law was obscure). This

article was among the most bitterly debated because it was seen as contrary to the very notion of a legal code, and some said that it would resurrect "the awesome power to interpret the law."[63] Yet its drafters saw its sole purpose as ensuring that the institution functioned in a regular manner. They were by no means advocates of common law, however.

It is worth noting that French liberals were almost entirely silent on the question of the status of the law. Benjamin Constant was alone in arguing that "to extend the competence of the law to all matters is to set the stage for tyranny."[64] His attack on the likes of Gaetano Filangieri and Mably for conferring almost limitless power over human existence upon the legislator was not echoed by other leading voices normally prompt to worry about the abuse of power.

The Discrediting of Executive Power

The totalizing vision of generality led to a sacralization of legislative power, which consequently became identified with sovereignty. Executive power was sharply distinguished from legislative power because the former, by its very essence, engages only in particular acts. Hence executive power was said to be dangerous, since particularity corrupts the legislative by definition. In this vein, Rousseau wrote: "Executive power cannot belong to the generality as legislative or sovereign, since executive power is exercised only in particular acts that are outside the province of law and therefore outside the province of the sovereign, which can act only to make law."[65] In other words, although he recognized the role of the executive, he regarded it solely as subordinate or derivative. Hence if it became too active, it would constitute a menace. What made this problem even more important in Rousseau's eyes was the existence of a structural asymmetry between the legislative and the executive: the former was intermittent, the latter permanent. Since the rule of law was identified with the sovereignty of the people, executive power had to be narrowly focused and constrained and, ideally, reduced to a bare minimum.[66]

The men of 1789 shared Rousseau's depreciation of executive power. Their intellectual doubts were even stronger because they were rooted in vehement rejection of ministerial power in the Old Regime. Although the king himself was still untouchable in 1789, resentment and discontent focused on his ministers. The *cahiers de doléances* were filled with recriminations against the crimes of the ministers. From the very earliest days of the Revolution, a host of books and pamphlets fleshed out the charges against the royal minions. In *Révolutions de Paris,* for example, we read that "from the very beginning of the monarchy we groaned first under feudal despotism and then under ministerial despotism."[67] Jean-Nicolas Billaud-Varenne made a name for himself by publishing three stout volumes on ministerial despotism.[68] This was a way of criticizing executive power while absolving the monarch himself by resorting to what Mirabeau called a "pious fiction."[69] At first, some critics took the precaution of arguing that ministerial power "degrades executive power" (as Talleyrand put it), but soon executive power itself was indicted on the grounds that it could not avoid the crime of *lèse-nation,* as is clear from the constitutional debates of 1791.

The *constituants* firmly rejected the idea of allowing the king or his ministers to initiate legislation, and at the time Barère noted that "the executive power will always be the enemy of the legislative power and will injure it in any way it can. In all political systems this battle rages."[70] This blunt statement fairly summarizes the general sentiment. It is worth noting that some sought to eliminate the very term "power" from the name attached to the executive. The hope was to downgrade it by attaching a more modest label such as "function" or "authority."[71] Sieyès, who was always in the forefront when it came to semantic imagination, ventured expressions such as "executive commission," "combining and regulatory thought," "overseer of the public establishment," and "intermediary commission of the powers."[72] "Execution" was thus used in its narrowest and most mechanical sense so as to limit its ability to interfere with the power of the law as expression of generality. Condorcet even went so far as to imagine a "mechanical king," which would put the wonders of the new science of automata to work in the political realm.[73] At this point Necker was totally isolated in his intellectual and political defense of the executive power as a specific entity in need of a certain autonomy to perform its function. His remarkable magisterial opus *Du pouvoir exécutif dans les grands états,* which methodically takes up the views of Rousseau, Mably, and the majority of *constituants,* was given short shrift by his contemporaries.

This depreciation of executive power stemmed from more than just the culture of generality. It also drew on the widespread notion that government was essentially a simple affair and that a small number of laws should suffice to regulate the activity of society. The liberal utopia of cheap government thus played a major role in reinforcing the attitude of the *constituants.* Most of them sincerely believed that the administrative hypertrophy of the executive was merely an outgrowth of absolutism. Just as they opposed the division of powers and maintained that all power resided in the legislature, so, too, did they imagine that the law could be implemented in the political realm as directly and mechanically as it could be enforced by the judiciary.[74] When the Convention defined the prerogatives of its direct agent, the Committee of Public Safety, Barère remarked as if it were self-evident that "the ministry is merely an executive council charged with details of execution and strenuously supervised, and its heads come every day at specified times to receive the committee's orders and decrees."[75] In 1791, Roederer, speaking in a similar vein, had proposed renaming all ministries "Ministry of the Law of . . ." in order to make their subordinate character clear.[76]

The denial of executive power reached a climax on 1 April 1794 (12 Germinal, Year II), when the executive council (and therefore the post of minister) was eliminated and replaced by twelve commissions under the direct authority of the Committee of Public Safety.[77] In the process leading up to this radical decision, Saint-Just expressed his opinion that "all the enemies of the Republic are in its government" and "the bureaus have replaced monarchism," adding that "it is impossible to govern without laconism."[78] A few months later Billaud-Varenne issued a warning along similar lines: "The moment legislative centrality ceases to be the axis of the government, the edifice loses its principal foundation and inevitably crumbles."[79]

To be sure, executive power regained substance after Thermidor, and the Constitution of Year III enshrined it. Yet there was no real rupture of continuity. The same can be said of the simultaneous introduction of bicameralism and of the recognition that some degree of division of powers could play a positive role. These various changes in attitude reflect a new caution and were pragmatic in nature. The principle of legislative centrality was not truly abandoned but only modified. The idea that "the Legislative Body must be liberated from its oppression by the Executive" remained dominant.[80] For example, Barère in Year V stressed that "the spirit of the government of the laws is the political measuring stick that ministers must take away from meetings of the Directory so that later they can measure in detailed executive analyses the public administrative operations to be undertaken in response."[81] This constituted the third cornerstone of the political culture of generality.

— 4 —

The Question of Origins

The figure of utopian generality, in the three dimensions we have just examined, defined the French political model as it sought to establish itself during the revolutionary period. But how are we to understand what drove it and where it came from? The ritual reference to Jacobinism actually obscures the significance of the model by suggesting that it was a system logically derived from a coherent doctrine of some sort. Yet as we have seen, it is questionable whether such a doctrine ever existed, and in any case invoking this supposed doctrine tells us nothing about its underpinnings. If the analysis is to proceed, therefore, we must set this nominalist incantation to one side, not least because it assumes that an ahistorical model emerged fully formed from a great historical event. Hence we need to dig deeper. In touching on the legal and political rationalism of the eighteenth century in the previous chapter, we have already begun to broaden our approach. In this chapter we will push that exploration still further. For this purpose, Burke and Tocqueville are two excellent guides. Both men loom large in this context, each having proposed an influential interpretation of the hexagonal model. Later we will broaden the analysis still more by looking at the French case in the context of a more general history of democratic modernity.

The French Exception, from Burke to Tocqueville

Burke's *Reflections on the Revolution in France* was published in London in 1790 and quickly translated into French. The book proved to be a bestseller and was widely commented on, drawing both harsh condemnation and warm applause. It offered the first comprehensive interpretation of the

63

French revolutionary phenomenon—at a time when the word "Jacobin" did not yet exist in the French vocabulary. Burke grasped the power of the event, which he understood as a radical break with the past that would lead to a novel political regime—a regime that already, in the fall of 1789, he believed would be fundamentally illiberal. His analysis is sufficiently well known that there is no need for a systematic recapitulation. For the sake of the subsequent exposition, however, I shall point out a few of its more striking features.

Topping Burke's indictment of 1789 was of course the charge that it had established a kind of "speculative republic." His whole argument was directed to identifying the effects of abstraction in politics, and he contrasted the emerging French model point by point with the government of England. On the one hand, a geometric and arithmetic constitution; on the other, respect for tradition and for the natural order. On the one hand, a utopian vision of a simple government based on a mechanistic understanding of society; on the other, a pragmatic approach based on prudence and recognition of complexity. On the one hand, an arrogant political metaphysics that treated the world as a "vast gaming table"; on the other, a modest politics based on experience. For Burke, these two distinct visions of governmental action captured what was novel about the French Revolution. From the first, the Revolution had made it clear that two antagonistic conceptions of society were at issue. The new world of 1789 was ruled by hatred of particularism and the aspiration to unity, and ultimately this led to treating men as "isolated tokens." By contrast, the English "attach great value to dividing men into different classes," each individual deriving his identity from membership in a body. For Burke, "abstraction" was the word that best summed up the essence of the emerging French model. This formed the basis of his famous critique of the French understanding of human rights, which according to Burke failed to take account of palpable diversity. "It is boasted that the geometrical policy has been adopted, that all local ideas should be sunk, and that the people should no longer be Gascons, Picards, Bretons, Normans; but Frenchmen, with one country, one heart, and one Assembly. But instead of being all Frenchmen, the greater likelihood is, that the inhabitants of that region will shortly have no country."[1]

This analysis is still a long way from the frankly reactionary views of men like Louis Bonald and Joseph de Maistre. Burke was a liberal conservative with no feelings of charity for the Old Regime.[2] Nevertheless, a whole generation of opponents of the Revolution drew on Burke's storehouse of critical formulas and arguments. His attack on modern reason's claim to govern politics was amplified by criticism of 1793, including criticism that sought to distinguish sharply between 1789 and 1793. Burke fortified both the liberal thought of the nineteenth century and the thought of those nostalgic for the past. Although he methodically described the French demon of abstraction and all its consequences, he did not deal with the question of its origins. A host of others would do this for him, attacking various eighteenth-century writers as the root of the evil. If we leave aside the feverish diatribes of Abbé Barruel and various others against Freemasons and *illuminés*,[3] it was the emblematic figure of the *philosophe* that came in for the brunt of the criticism. The hatred of Descartes in "ultra" (conservative royalist) circles originated here, for it was in Descartes that the cult of reason and the presumptuousness of philosophy were supposed to have converged.[4] But the "disparagement of men of letters," to borrow Paul Bénichou's expression,[5] came from others besides the prophets of counterrevolution, Joseph de Maistre foremost among them. From Jean-François de La Harpe to Jean Etienne Marie Portalis, authors associated with liberalism also linked the distinctiveness of French political culture to the preponderant role of men of letters.[6] Portalis, in particular, developed arguments in this vein that would later exert a considerable influence on Tocqueville.[7] The "cruel mania to generalize everything" and the permanent tendency to "abstract away from all details" became political faults, according to Portalis, because in France the *philosophes* constituted a "particular and dominant class."[8] Toward the end of the nineteenth century, Augustin Cochin would apply this approach to understanding the dynamics of the revolutionary phenomenon itself, showing how "men of words" *(gens de parole)* gradually took power, forcing out men of action *(gens d'oeuvre)* and thereby reproducing and exacerbating a tendency that had already developed earlier in the eighteenth century.[9] This sociological "law of triage" led, Cochin argued, to a growing divorce from reality. The process "eliminated the real from the mind instead of reducing what was unintelligible in the object."[10]

On this view, the reign of abstraction and the subjugation of the imagination combined in France to create a political culture of generality. This "philosophical" analysis has its sociological counterpart: the authors we have been discussing saw abstract thought and rejection of intermediary bodies as two sides of the same coin. This understanding, which owes so

much to Burke's pioneering *Reflections,* yielded the first notable interpretation of what is distinctive about France. Nearly a century later, Hippolyte
Taine would draw heavily on it, thereby demonstrating its influence among
conservatives. It would not be difficult to compile a sampling of quotations
from Taine's *Origines de la France contemporaine* that might seem to have
been taken directly from Burke.[11]

Writing in the middle of the nineteenth century, Tocqueville would propose the second major new interpretation of "Jacobinism." In well-known
passages of *Democracy in America* he followed in the footsteps of Pierre
Paul Royer-Collard in calling attention to the link between the omnipotence of the state and the advent of a society of individuals and between
the increase in social power stemming from the leveling of conditions and
the destruction of intermediary bodies. There will be more to say about
this sociological analysis in the next chapter. Here I want simply to recall
Tocqueville's explanation of the origins of the French model as it emerged
from the revolutionary maelstrom. In *L'Ancien Régime et la Révolution* he
developed a sociological argument that traced the most important features
of the revolutionary regime to the absolute monarchy.

Of course Tocqueville was not the first to suggest such a filiation. During
the Restoration, François-Dominique de Montlosier had pointed out that
Jacobinism was merely the developed stage of a political pathology already
visible in absolutism.[12] François Guizot, in his *Histoire de la civilisation en
Europe* (1828), had also shown the importance of absolutism in the genesis
of modern France. But Tocqueville strengthened the argument by presenting it in the form of a sociological law. In this approach he differed from
Burke, for whom the revolutionary utopia of the *tabula rasa* was merely an
intellectual illusion that had resulted in defective constitutional principles.[13] For Tocqueville, the problem was in effect one of the *prefiguration* of
the major features of the Jacobin model in absolutist France. He argued
that it was the Old Regime that had begun to destroy secondary powers,
destabilize the corporatist system, and establish an implacable administrative centralization. In one of his most celebrated passages he wrote: "In the
eighteenth century, the central power in France had not yet acquired the
healthy and vigorous constitution that we have since seen. Nevertheless,
since it had already succeeded in destroying all intermediary powers, and
since nothing remained between it and individuals but a vast empty space,
each person already saw it from afar as the only source of energy in the social machine, the sole necessary agent of public life."[14] Many equally force-

ful expressions struck Tocqueville's contemporaries as they read *L'Ancien Régime,* thus giving canonical form to this second major interpretation of utopian generality as the culmination of absolutism.

Tocqueville's genius was to place the Revolution in the context of a longer history. One virtue of that history was that it made some ruptures seem less important than others. With regard to the question of central concern to us, that of intermediary bodies, it is indeed enlightening to recall the terms of Turgot's battle against corporations. "Only sovereign authority can form a body within the state," a writer close to Turgot pointed out.[15] The great d'Aguesseau accurately reflected the feeling of many magistrates and officials of the time with his blunt observation that "any association within a state, of any type whatsoever, is always dangerous."[16] Numerous remarks of this sort were available to provide grist for Tocqueville's mill. Thus what the state had to say about itself and society largely corroborates the argument of *L'Ancien Régime.* But did Tocqueville perhaps take for reality what was more in the nature of a fantasy, project, or ambition? Recall one of his best-known formulations:

> The effects of the French Revolution are frequently exaggerated. Surely no revolution was more powerful, more rapid, more destructive, or more creative than the French Revolution. Nevertheless, it would be strangely misleading to think . . . that the foundations of the edifice it erected did not exist previously. The French Revolution created a host of minor and secondary things, but it only nurtured the seed of the main things. These existed before it . . . In France, the central power had already taken charge of local administration to a greater extent than anywhere else in the world. The Revolution only made that power shrewder, stronger, and more enterprising.[17]

Any number of facts can be adduced to weaken or even refute this hypothesis. For example, Tocqueville spends a good deal of time insisting that the *intendants* (agents of royal power) are like the *préfets* (prefects, agents of republican power), each being taken as a symbol of the relations between state and society in their respective periods. But detailed research has cast serious doubt on the identification of these two emblematic figures.[18] Appealing though Tocqueville's argument is, it needs to be subjected to careful scrutiny. Its essential weakness lies in its reduction of the various modalities of the state to the all too vague notion of *centralization.* The more general the description of the state, the easier it is to point out continuities. That is why categories such as "Colbertism," "Jacobinism," and the "Napoleonic heritage" prove to be so ambiguous when used to characterize the phenomenon of the French state. They are so sweeping that they end up telling us very little.

To understand the history and the inner strength of the French model, we need to complicate the picture and draw a careful line between the state as bureaucratic and administrative apparatus and the state as political form. When we do this, the history of the state can be seen in the first instance to be the history of a *process of rationalization*. Max Weber described its principal characteristics: constitution of a corps of stable, competent functionaries; institution of regular managerial procedures; definition of a clear hierarchy of responsibilities. But the history is also that of an *effort of democratization:* institution of representative government, administration subjected to guidance by the general will, transparent exercise of authority. The two processes do not necessarily coincide, and the relation between them varies from country to country in western Europe. In Great Britain, the democratization process preceded rationalization, whereas the reverse was true in Germany. In France, things were more complex, mainly because of the contradictory character of the upheavals that accompanied the Revolution. This both accelerated and distorted the rationalization of the administration while at the same time marking the abrupt transition to democracy.

Both Burke and Tocqueville treat the French case as an exception. Hence their analyses make it difficult to include France in a broader comparative perspective. Their work has contributed to a static picture of France by branding the French state with the curse of its origin.

The Tension between Generality and Particularity

The French model cannot be understood solely in terms of its own history, regardless of whether that history is understood as one of continuity between Old Regime and Revolution or as one of radical rupture in the revolutionary moment. For its distinctive features to be grasped, the model has to be seen in a broader context, in relation to the various antinomies that constitute democratic modernity. Three of these played a central role in the dynamic process of social change as societies began in the late seventeenth century to reorganize themselves on the basis of some sort of social contract. Schematically, we may characterize these as involving tensions between generality and particularity, fiction and reality, and law and government. As we shall see, we are really dealing with one contradiction in three specific spheres: values, social forms, and modes of political management.

Hegel was the first to propose an interpretation of the contradictions of modernity in terms of the dialectic of particularity and generality. For him, the distinctive feature of modernity is the "liberation of the powers of particularity,"[19] or, in other words, the assertion of individual freedom and autonomy. He identifies this "moment of subjectivity" with the development of *civil society* as a sphere for various private activities. Here what men have in common is purely formal. Hegel speaks of an *"external universality"*:[20] administrative procedures and legal norms establish a regulatory framework for civil society. This move gives rise to a lack, which is reflected in the aspiration toward a more substantive universality. Out of this comes an "objective moment," instituting a society of communion and participation, that is, a *political society*, founded on a requirement of generality. But how can the two contrary tendencies of generality and particularity be combined? For Hegel, this is the problem of the modern world. The French Revolution had brought this contradiction to full maturity by taking the view that the community was a totality incapable of disaggregation and rejecting any particularizing differentiation. Conversely, England had built a political model based entirely on valuing and protecting particularity.[21] "The Constitution of England," Hegel wrote, "is a complex of mere particular rights and particular privileges . . . This is the leading feature of what the Englishmen call their Liberty, and it is the very antithesis of such a centralized administration as exists in France."[22] He thus contrasted two visions of freedom: on the one hand, freedom as participation, which presupposes a homogeneous body politic in which everyone can take part; on the other hand, freedom as autonomy, based on the pursuit of self-interest, which leads to social differentiation.

Using these concepts, Hegel developed an analysis that had many points in common with Burke's. He, too, attacked the Revolution's consecration of "abstract individuality" and the resulting "society built in the air, as it were." He did not idealize the English model in reaction, however. Instead, he suggested that France and England represented two extremes of a modernization that was not yet complete, two consequences of an impasse of modernity. The French Revolution had been able to destroy the Old Regime but not to construct a political community based on something other than abstract universalism. Conversely, England had been able to find value in concrete commonality, but the price of this was that it had been obliged to retain some of the old world of privileges. Hence the opposition of the two models was not merely a reflection of the opposition between democracy and liberalism. Instead, both models exhibited pathological forms of both systems. The Revolution had exacerbated the abstraction and generality of democracy to the point of denying all the practical wisdom of the community and making government impossible, because the polarization of the political precluded recognition of the need for functional differentiation (among the executive, legislative, and judicial branches, for instance). England, meanwhile, remained the prisoner of a liberalism of particularity and thus failed to conceive a true community, that is, a community in which individuals shared sovereignty and were not merely rights-bearing subjects. For Hegel, then, a response to the tensions of modernity required attending to both the limitations of the English model and the perversions of the French.

Hegel's questions can be compared to those that Tocqueville would ask a short while later. By focusing on the differences stemming from the ways in which the French freed themselves from the Old Regime and the English remained attached to their old liberties and privileges, Hegel was able to point out how the dilemma of modernity, exemplified by the tension between generality and particularity, *in practice* centered upon the issue of intermediary bodies. Tocqueville shared this point of view. The author of *Democracy in America* and *The Old Regime and the Revolution* never ceased to believe in the value of small, vital, decentralized communities as a bulwark against the egalitarian and homogenizing pressures of democracy. Thus both Hegel and Tocqueville asked what conditions were necessary to guarantee liberty and participation in modern society.[23] Despite this similarity, the difference between their two philosophies of history is striking. Tocqueville believed that the democratic revolution was the seed of modernity. It was for him an irresistible tendency of civilization, even if he looked upon it with a certain melancholy in keeping with his almost tragic view of the world. By contrast, Hegel believed that the democratic utopia of a society of direct and total participation was but a fleeting vision of human possibility and that there would come a time when people rediscovered the virtues of concrete differentiation and membership in specific communities, outside of which freedom and identity have no reality.

Hegel went further than Burke and Tocqueville because he did not dwell on the problems and obstacles associated with the histories of particular nations. He saw the English and French cases in the context of a view of modernity in which the tension between particularity and generality structured the modern world. Thus he did not stop at treating France as an "exceptional case" in contrast to England. He paved the way for a truly comparative history of the two countries by taking each as virtually an ideal type. He thus ascribed general philosophical importance to the question of intermediary bodies.

For Hegel, then, the great issue of modern times was to organize the "interpenetration of the substantive and the particular."[24] This task fell to the state. It was up to the state to reconcile the particularity of nature with the universality of mind; to allow the principle of subjectivity to mature so that each individual could express his own individuality and yet at the same time embody some form of objective unity. But if generality and particularity were to be reconciled in the state, Hegel argued, some form of mediation was necessary. By participating in the realm of corporations and municipalities, individuals could begin to partake of generality in a concrete way. For him, in other words, the diversity of civil society and organizations was a prerequisite of access to the universal.[25]

Paths of Abstraction

In their different ways, Burke and Tocqueville thus both arraigned the French passion for abstraction, which they saw as the source of all error and perversion. From Benjamin Constant to Hippolyte Taine, nineteenth-century liberals and conservatives would maintain this accusation in a number of variants. Here again, however, the problem of France comes into clearer focus if seen in a broader context. The abstraction that is so characteristic of France actually reflects a tendency that affected all democracies. The insistence on equality, which was necessary if each individual was to be granted rights and full-fledged citizenship, meant that all distinguishing characteristics had to be set aside. Only one quality was essential and common to all, namely, that of being an autonomous subject. Put slightly differently, it was the juridical anointment of the individual that led to the rejection of any substantive incorporation of the social as archaic and intolerable. Hence democratic society rejected any concept of organicity along with all particular bodies. The requirements of equality and the prerequisites of autonomy combined to define an artificial relationship between individuals from which all natural qualities and historical background were inevitably eliminated. The project of modernity thus drained the social of its substance and reduced it to a mere share in common rights defining the conditions of equivalence and commensurability among independent individuals. The solidity of the social vanished, giving way to a formal principle of legal construction. One might say that substance and procedure became one.[26]

Since then, modern society has continued to exacerbate the conventional and abstract character of the social bond. The development of legal conventions and fictions is of course related to the wish to ensure equal treatment of naturally diverse individuals, to institute a common sphere in which very different men and women can interact. In this respect, the legal fiction is a necessary condition for integrating a society of individuals, in contrast to traditional societies, where differences serve the purpose of integration (in hierarchical systems, particularities are conceived as complementary). Democracy is thus a regime of fiction in two senses: first, sociologically, because the people are symbolically conceived as constituting a body; but also technically, because the rule of law implies "generalizing the social," or, if you prefer, abstracting it, so as to make it possible to govern society by universal rules. Formalism thus serves as a positive principle of social construction in a democracy ruled by law. By the same token, however, formalism makes it more difficult to see how a palpable "people" can be constituted.

In democracy, "the people" has no form. The body politic has no density; it is simply *number*, that is, a force composed of equals, of individuals equivalent before the law. This is the radical meaning of universal suffrage: it marks the advent of a serial order. The citizen, considered as *homo suffragans*, is a deliberately abstract individual, a simple numerical component of the national unity. The voter can fulfill his role in the ideal sense only if he identifies with what is general in him, only if he can strip himself of his particular characteristics and immediate interests to become a sort of functionary of national unity.[27] Society then consists only of identical voices, substitutable one for the other, and reduced in the fundamental moment of voting to mere units of account collected in a ballot box: it becomes a purely arithmetical fact. Substance is completely hidden by number, reinforcing the effects of the abstraction associated with the purely procedural constitution of the social.

In this measurement process, people and nation cease to have palpable flesh. Both need to be constructed with the aid of political vision on the one hand and intellectual elaboration on the other. In the nineteenth century, this need gave rise to a certain sociological stupefaction in the face of universal suffrage, as the inception of such a radically desubstantialized world left even its most ardent champions anxiously disoriented. Indeed, number meant not just the crowd, that anonymous and uncontrollable power, the mere thought of which provoked countless fantasies in government officials and property owners alike. Implicit in the concept of number was also an idea of what could be neither named nor described, of something shapeless and literally unrepresentable, something that posed the deepest of threats to identity. Serialization was thus both a prerequisite of equality and a problem for identity. Hence throughout the nineteenth century the promise of a new equality went hand in hand with an obsessive fear of disintegration, inviting permanent questions about the possibility of separating the political principle of democracy from the sociological principle.

Abstraction is thus in general a consequence of the democratic imperative.[28] The conditions surrounding the advent of democracy turn out to be crucial for differentiating the various national models. In the English case, democracy took hold only very slowly and gradually, and for a long time representative government served merely to guarantee certain liberties and privileges. That is why the old corporate bodies persisted there.[29] By contrast, the French Revolution required a violent disincorporation of the social in order to achieve liberty through equality (whereas in England liberty signified conquest and preservation of particularities). The revolutionary process thus destroyed not only all the lesser bodies to which individuals belonged but also, and simultaneously, the "great imaginary body" of the king,[30] which established order among all the lesser bodies and gave them meaning. To combat the "Gothic colossus" of the old world, it was necessary to find a new and "invincible colossus" to replace it, namely, the nation.[31] Before the nation could assert itself as such a colossus, it had in a sense to absorb all the vitality of society so as to constitute a single great body. The abstraction of the social thus became a fundamental condition of collective power, which in turn became a fundamental condition of equality.

Nomocratic Utopia

The cult of the law, that is, of government by general rule, played an important role in the constitution of the French model, as we have seen.

Though it was celebrated in the eighteenth century, this cult has much older roots. The functional utopia of the law, of an effective power of generality, is a modern conception. Beyond it lies the more prosaic claim of the prince to exert complete mastery over the public order, to subject everything to his domination. Underlying this is a kind of pride inherent in the very notion of power over men and things. Plato was the first to call attention to this in his *Statesman*. In an extraordinary passage in that dialogue, he marvels at the illusion of thinking that the law alone can suffice to govern.[32]

> Law can never issue an injunction binding on all which really embodies what is best for each; it cannot prescribe with perfect accuracy what is good and right for each member of the community at any one time. The differences of human personality, the variety of men's activities, and the inevitable unsettlement attending all human experience make it impossible for any art whatsoever to issue unqualified rules holding good on all questions at all times.[33]

Yet all power aspires to some type of abstract universalism, some form of "simplicity," because such simplicity presumably signifies an ability to exert absolute control over things and to rule others unerringly. Plato attacks power's claim to generality in dealing with a reality constituted only of particularities. The world, he argues, is constantly changing, constantly in flux. In essence it is pure diversity, owing not only to its complexity but even more perhaps to its historical character. The nomocratic illusion that Plato criticizes ultimately derives, he says, from a combination of (political) presumption with (cognitive) ignorance. If we are to banish this dangerous and deceptive view, must we not revert to a more modest art of government, based on the pragmatic wisdom of a "royal person" aware of the variety of situations and diversity of circumstances?[34] Plato rejects this answer as well. No such royal person can exist: to believe otherwise would be to imagine a physician stationed permanently at the bedside of every patient. Against this illusion, too, we must be on our guard.

Seen in this way, politics is torn between two illusions: rigorous nomocracy on the one hand and the pure art of management on the other. The modern world has inherited this tension but in a more radical form. The democratic imperatives of equality and equity have in fact intensified the nomocratic temptation, to a degree we have measured in an earlier chapter. Seen in this light, the French case seems tailor-made to illustrate the nomocratic aspiration, while the English case might be taken to represent an overtly pragmatic view of government.[35]

In this respect as well as others that we have considered previously, there is thus nothing exceptional about the French model. It is not an outlier among liberal democracies. Indeed, it is fully implicated in the antinomies that define the structure of modernity. Comparative study can reveal the *specificity* rather than the eccentricity of the French case. In each instance that specificity involves an element of radicalism, which makes the study of France particularly illuminating.

— Part II —

Trials and Recompositions

— 5 —

The Imperative of Governability

Proposals to Restore the Corporations

The prohibition of corporations, guilds, and *maîtrises* (organizations of master craftsmen) during the Revolution was, as we have seen, scarcely debated, as if it had been no more than a natural and unexceptionable extension of the imperatives of equality and liberty. That everyone should have access to the various trades upon payment of the requisite *patente*, or license fee, and that monopolies should be strictly prohibited, seemed a self-evident principle. In practice, however, complications soon arose. The question of reinstating corporations was broached early in the nineteenth century, barely ten years after the Allarde and Le Chapelier laws, marking the first fundamental debate about intermediary bodies in the economic realm. There had been no such debate during the Revolution, because the imperative of 4 August 1789 seemed to render any discussion useless in advance. Nor had there been any real debate before the Revolution. Vehement attacks on the corporatist system in the middle of the eighteenth century by Abbé Coyer, Cliquot de Blervache, and Bigot de Sainte-Croix had been directed mainly against its abuses and inconsistencies.[1] It was in the same spirit that Turgot had taken his decision to abolish the system in 1776. Necker's reform of the system after Turgot's edict was withdrawn had also been carried out in a rather pragmatic spirit, seeking compromise between contradictory demands. To be sure, the economists had vituperated against monopoly and overly burdensome regulation in the name of "natural liberty," but there was definitely a wide gap between their rather abstract and somewhat repetitive theoretical writings and the dynamic conflicts of interest swirling around the issue of corporations.

Toward the end of the revolutionary period, by contrast, various people

79

immersed in the realities of the day began to contemplate the possibility of reinstating corporations. All the proposals formulated at the time began with a straightforward recognition of fact: absolute freedom of commerce and access to the trades was an untenable system. By the early 1800s, the practice of various professions was already regulated by a variety of legal measures. For instance, an ordinance of 11 October 1801 stipulated that in Paris "no one may exercise the profession of baker without authorization by the prefect of police." In addition to requiring authorization, the law imposed standards of quality, specified how the profession should be organized (including nomination of syndics and collection of dues), and limited the number of master bakers in Paris to 641, the number practicing the trade at that time.[2] The meat business was subjected to similarly strict regulation on 30 March 1800,[3] and a statute of 30 September 1802 imposed tight restrictions on the trade of butcher.[4] It was almost a return to the old corporatist system. In another sector, the profession of money changer was reorganized in 1802: it became a closed, regulated activity.[5] In this case the First Consul took a pragmatic stance: "I do not shrink from borrowing examples and rules from times gone by. While preserving all the useful innovations of the Revolution, I will not give up the good institutions it mistakenly destroyed . . . There are professions that must not be left vulnerable to every caprice; the profession of money changer is one of them."[6] The high principles of the revolutionary period were all but forgotten. Lawmakers intervened in many other sectors to restrict and regulate freedom of commerce and industry. For instance, the professions of physician, pharmacist, herbalist, and midwife were subjected to strict regulation by the law of 21 Germinal, Year XI. The government also regulated the building trades (establishing an office of carpentry contractors in 1803). It was also proposed that notaries, lawyers, and bailiffs *(huissiers)* be required to obtain a license to practice.

It was not just a matter of regulating special cases. Many people were asking whether the elimination of certain economic and social institutions during the Revolution had been justified. The movement thrived for a variety of reasons. The most obvious of these had to do with the traditional government function of overseeing commerce to ensure the health and safety of the public. The need to monitor workers judged to be dangerously unruly also played an important role. This was the reason for some very restrictive legislation, which stands out in sharp contrast to the "liberal" principles proclaimed earlier. A case in point is the well-known law of 22 Germinal, Year XI (12 April 1803), which required every worker to carry a passbook and imposed regulations on factories, workshops, and studios.

In these circumstances, proposals to reinstate corporations soon made themselves heard. Louis-Nicolas Dubois, who was prefect of police at the time, mentioned in several of his daily reports that more and more merchants and wholesalers were expressing a desire to return to the old system.[7] Certain occupations became the subject of administrative inquiries.[8] After the professions of baker and butcher were reorganized, the First Consul himself acknowledged that he was "besieged with confidential messages of all sorts proposing the restoration of this or that part of the Old Regime."[9] Regnault de Saint-Jean-d'Angély, who prepared a report on these issues for the Corps Législatif in preparation for the law of 22 Germinal, Year XI, dealt with the matter at length. Although he recognized the abuses committed by the old arts and trade guilds, he called for the establishment of "regulatory" mechanisms to control private interests, on the grounds that since 1791 manufacturers had enjoyed "the most absolute freedom but must also be held responsible for many disorders and abuses."[10] The Conseil d'Etat also considered the issue on several occasions, as did the recently restored Paris Chamber of Commerce.[11] All this activity shows that this was not a marginal question. Nor was debate limited to Paris: similar demands arose in any number of provincial cities, and several departmental councils considered matters pertaining to the oversight of factories and the organization of the professions.[12]

The movement assumed more obvious importance early in 1805, however, when Paris winesellers petitioned for reinstatement of the corporatist system in their profession.[13] Whereas the problem had previously been approached obliquely, the winesellers' petition served as the first opportunity for detailed, in-depth debate of the issues. Vital-Roux, a merchant who later became regent of the Bank of France and one of the principal drafters of the Code of Commerce, was appointed rapporteur on the bill by the Paris Chamber of Commerce, to which it was referred. In January 1805 he drafted a very dense report rejecting the proposal but in a way that ratified its topical importance by approaching the issue in general terms.[14] Almost simultaneously Claude-Anthelme Costaz, head of the Bureau of Arts and Manufacturing in the Ministry of the Interior, drafted a report for his superior in a similar spirit. In it he examined the problems associated with the illegal reinstitutions of bakers' corporations in Lyons and Bordeaux.[15] Shortly thereafter Toussaint-Bernard Emeric-David, a member of the Corps Législatif who was more open to corporatist ideas, wrote an "essay on *maîtrises* in the arts and trades."[16]

This debate actually continued behind the scenes,[17] only to flare up again during the Restoration, first in 1817 and then again in 1821. In October 1817 the merchants and artisans of Paris petitioned the king concerning the "need to reinstate the *corps de marchands* and the *communautés des arts et métiers.*" Antoine Levacher-Duplessis, the attorney representing the signers of this petition, claimed that they numbered around 2,000. The affair caused quite a stir. The minister of the interior received some of the petitioners, and the Board of Trade took up the case, as did the Board of Textiles and Manufactures. The Paris Chamber of Commerce also became involved. For three months the affair elicited a series of critical reports, administrative notes, explanatory memoranda, and articles in newspapers and magazines. The debate was more public than it had been in the previous period. More people participated, and still more were attracted by the publicity. Numerous additional petitions were addressed to the legislature. Though their demands were rejected, the petitioners did not back down. When the direction of policy changed in 1820, they renewed their campaign in the spring of 1821, triggering a new round of interventions and reactions by the administration and by the various consulting bodies mentioned above.

Thus the issue of reinstating corporatist forms of organization cannot be regarded as having been marginal during the period of the Empire and Restoration. Nor was it limited to agitation in a few Parisian circles, as is evident from the fact that a number of departmental regional councils took up the issue after 1818.[18] The movement continued to gain strength until 1821, when seven departments explicitly urged the government to reinstate *maîtrises* and corporations. During this brief period, nearly a quarter of the departments expressed similar wishes, in addition to which there were demands from nearly everywhere to protect local production and to obtain tax exemptions for, and stricter regulation of, fairs and markets. The issue remained alive until the final years of the Restoration, as is evident from both minutes of the regional councils and correspondence between the prefects and the minister of the interior.[19] Clearly, then, the upheavals that the Revolution had caused in the economic and social order were a long way from being regarded as positive achievements that could not be tampered with.

The Old and the New

How are we to interpret this movement to reinstate corporations in the first quarter of the nineteenth century? Was it an archaic, anachronistic wish, a product of misplaced nostalgia? That was the way it used to be described, when it wasn't simply overlooked. Thus a leading student of the history of corporations had this to say about these various proposals: "They addressed the public in a language it no longer understood. To a society already dressed in the somber garb of the nineteenth century, they presented themselves in powdered wigs, doublets, and breeches."[20] Of course the temptation to think in these terms is strong when the period under consideration is the Restoration. The prospect of a corporatist reorganization can indeed be seen, particularly after 1820, in the context of numerous texts and rituals expressing a nostalgia for the past. Joseph de Villèle and his friends appreciated the traditionalist, religious ethos that the memory of the old workers' corporations evoked. Thus they invited strapping warehousemen and hodcarriers to parade at the baptism of the duc de Bordeaux. Ultra circles were of course more broadly interested in any movement that might seem to resonate with the idea of reverting to a more corporatist society, and they were indeed very active in this whole affair. Levacher-Duplessis, the lawyer who orchestrated the movement in 1817 and 1821, was one of them. The first deputy to defend the idea before the Chamber of Deputies in 1816 explicitly evoked "the benefits of reinstating eminently monarchical institutions,"[21] while a publicist friend noted that "restoring these wise institutions will help turn people's thoughts back to monarchical ideas."[22]

This strictly political analysis is insufficient, however. The issue of reinstating the corporations arose initially in the realm of labor itself. The first demands emerged from small and medium-sized businesses and artisans' workshops during the Consulate, before there were any utopian dreams of partially restoring the Old Regime. Employers and workers shared the same idea, each group with an inflection of its own.[23] Even if we confine our attention to the political realm, however, it is important to note the ambivalence of the movement. Not surprisingly, on the ultra side, a prerepublican tendency took shape around this issue. As early as 1791, the reactionary voice of *L'Ami du roi* had joined Marat in *L'Ami du peuple* to blast the Allarde law and attack the elimination of intermediary bodies, which were said to safeguard the liberties and interests of workers.[24]

Thus far we have used the terms "restoration" and "reinstitution" for the sake of convenience, but these should not be allowed to create a false impression. During the period in question, no one actually called for a plain and simple *return* to the old system. Indeed, what was meant by "the old system" was not always clear: it is generally impossible to tell whether the reference was to the system that existed before 1776 or that which emerged from Necker's 1779 reforms. In some vague but urgent way, the term "corporation" was pregnant with many possibilities mingled with various expectations and fears. "The times are too fraught to reinstate the corporations, but I will say loudly and clearly that we desperately need something in their place . . . Let us not reinstate the six corps but rather invent something to replace them and give us back the good things they produced," wrote an associate of Levacher-Duplessis.[25] Indeed, when Napoleon considered a proposal to reinstate the corporations, he observed that "people are opposed to the corporations as they existed, but they want them if the system is modified."[26]

The Saint-Simonian approach to the issue is typical of the perplexities and questions that it raised even in those circles most hostile on principle to everything associated with the Old Regime. Restoring the old system of regulation was out of the question, Prosper Enfantin noted, "*but* we think it is useful to point out the futility of the vague principle of liberty."[27] Meanwhile one of the most fervent worker propagandists for the movement wrote: "It's all well and good to reject the *maîtrises* and *jurandes* [regulated trades], *but* is no happy medium possible between unlimited competition and regulation?"[28] The economic and social institutions of the past were rejected, but the rhetorical caution indicates clearly that the wall of certitudes and automatic responses had been breached. Among those who energetically rejected the idea of "reinstituting" the corporations, some spoke out to say that what was needed was an *equivalent.* For example, Jean Charles Simonde de Sismondi wrote that "we must look to the *effects of the guilds* for lessons on ways to combat the calamity that afflicts society today."[29] Some also spoke of "rejuvenating" the corporations or sought to "reconcile" them with freedom of trade and industry.[30] The terms of these arguments reflect the nature of the preoccupation with economic and social regulation.

The Disorder of the Professions

The corporatist question arose in connection with a general rethinking of the relation between state and society and between individuals and the law at a time when the coming market society was still only a vague threat. Well before the basic texts of socialism arrived on the scene, we witness a proliferation of petitions attacking a new type of "capitalist monopoly" said to be driving artisans into bankruptcy.[31] The advent of what one pamphlet writer called the "Gargantuas of commerce" was also deplored.[32] The revolutionary regime had in effect allowed "merchants of novelties" to emerge as powerful competitors of traditional small business. It had also encouraged the construction of factories capable of unlimited large-scale production. What was resented by many as a more immediate menace, however, was peddling by itinerant vendors. The growth of this "vagabond and mobile commerce," accessible to anyone who paid the required license fee, symbolized the advent of a new world whose anomie many people feared: the resulting "disorder of the professions" was perceived as a threat.

How well founded were these recriminations? It is not always easy to distinguish fantasy from reality in this regard. Yet there is no denying that many people were affected by the sense that a new economic and social order had arrived, and the fact that it was difficult to characterize and evaluate made it all the more menacing. Indeed, society seemed harder to represent and more opaque. No longer organized in terms of generally established and regulated economic principles, the new order was difficult to interpret. Those who denounced this pessimism and criticized what they saw as the "fable of disorder"[33] may or may not have been accurate in their judgment, but they failed to grasp what at least amounted to a dramatic shift in representations.

This obsession with social disorganization was not new. Earlier, in the wake of the Turgot edicts, any number of voices had spoken out against "the disorder and mingling of estates." "Anarchy," "subversion," "confusion," "chaos," "pell-mell," "carnival"—these words recurred as leitmotifs in 1776 to express the anger tinged with panic that had gripped numerous professions.[34] "To demolish *corps,* to reduce the world of commerce to a vast sphere in which every individual who sells or labors will be mixed up with all the others, is to revert to primordial disorder," said one spokesman for the leading corporations.[35] Although the corporatist system had an economic function, it was really rooted in a sociopolitical representation. This fact is quite clear in the "remonstrance" that advocate-general Antoine-Louis Séguier directed against Turgot's decision. Séguier spoke of the "precious chain" of *corps,* characterizing these communities as "small republics concerned solely with the general interest of all their members," and he deplored the new world in which "each manufacturer, each artist, and each worker will see himself as an isolated individual."[36] Nobody proposed restoring the corporatist society of old in 1805 or 1817, but the actual advent of a market society was perceived as a danger whose effects needed to be contained. For many, the somber predictions of 1776 had indeed become a reality.

The question of reinstating the corporations must be seen in the context of these changes. It pointed as much to a problem as to a solution of a certain kind. It was an expression of fear and doubt as much as a proposal for reform. It became the nucleus around which deep perplexities concerning the *sociological* implications and effects of the French Revolution were first formulated. By "deep perplexities" I mean that the questions involved did not merely reflect reactionary nostalgia but suggested puzzlement as to what the essence of the revolutionary project had been. For instance, Emeric-David, in his efforts to pinpoint the negative aspects of the new society—such as its "perpetual unrest" and "upheavals"—sought to distinguish between what could be classified as "disorders of revolution" (implicitly understood as fleeting and therefore not associated with its essentially positive accomplishments) and what could be seen as a structural problem and therefore likely to be persistent, namely, "unlimited liberty."[37] Levacher-Duplessis raised a similar question: "Make no mistake. The system that is tending to dissolve a nation into individuals is one of the saddest errors of the Revolution. It is the greatest obstacle to a return to order and consolidation of true liberty. Consult history. It teaches us that wherever despotism would establish itself, it isolates men in their individual weakness and leaves them to face the all-powerful government on their own."[38] What was at stake, then, was not just an economic institution but the very shape of society itself.

For everyone involved, the problem was one of a society "abandoned to a blind, mechanical process."[39] What this unstable new world urgently needed was fixed landmarks. The goal was to make society representable and governable by establishing "a sound system for classifying human beings."[40] Against the anonymous "great whole," the hard-to-grasp society in which the only social bonds were bonds of abstract equivalence and impersonal rules, critics offered the visible solidity of a collection of groups. Instead of a modern "administrative science" that dealt only with numbers, they preferred a government of men embedded in self-organizing natural and professional groups.[41] In a sense, the goal was to "re-internalize" what the market and law had sought to externalize, to re-embed politics and law in the social.

At the root of the new corporatist demands was thus an anxious vision of a world seen as fundamentally disordered. This was not just a vague fear, and at times it crystallized around certain specific issues. The professional tax, or *patente* (a license fee required for the exercise of any profession), which had been seen as a measure of equality and emancipation, thus became a symbol in the neocorporatist literature for a disaggregated society in which people and jobs were indiscriminately mingled. The disintegration of the traditional apprenticeship system was also seen as unfortunate. Apprenticeship was said to have been a "producer of order," serving both to regulate the quality of products and to promote stability in the various trades. Hence its disappearance was said to be catastrophic.[42] Proposals to establish a legal and social framework for apprenticeship were therefore vigorously debated in this period. Although some writers, such as Louis Costaz, envisioned a system of "apprenticeship contracts" backed by legal guarantees,[43] many others argued that only organized professions were in a position to regulate apprenticeships in the manner required for maintaining a well-ordered society.

At stake here was a whole way of thinking about the social. Recent historical research has examined this question in sufficient depth that there is no need to go into further detail here.[44] Note, however, that the language itself was changing. In the eighteenth century the word "corporation" had denoted an *institution* whose constitution and function could be precisely described. In the nineteenth century it referred to a *social form*. It now belonged to the sociological and cultural vocabulary rather than the legal. We shall have more to say about this later. Further evidence of this can be seen in the fact that the adjective *corporatif* (corporate) and the adverb *corporativement* (corporately) did not appear until about 1820.[45]

Mirages of Regulation and Codification

The prospect of reinstating the corporations was linked both to employers' fears of a new type of social disorder and to workers' concerns with establishing new types of protective organization. The issue should therefore be seen in the context of a far broader search for responses to the danger of social dissolution—a nineteenth-century obsession (manifestations of which we shall examine in the next chapter). But it was also related to the search for new forms of regulation, for alternatives to both state regulation and market regulation, each of which had aroused resentment. Advocates of corporatism accordingly directed their initial arguments to traditional concerns with *la police,* or public order. A text by Soufflot de Merey published in 1805 rehearses all these arguments.[46] He begins by rejecting the idea that when it comes to ensuring quality production, "the best and most impartial inspector is the consumer" (as Vital-Roux put it). "You say that the consumer is the sovereign judge, but what recourse will he have if the merchant or artisan has speculated on his credulity? Syndics and journeymen who can go unannounced to inspect merchandise placed on sale inspire a salutary fear. Thus *corporate regulation* [la police du corps] *offers both the government and the public a much more useful surveillance than even state regulation.*"[47] For Soufflot de Merey, the oversight conducted by the intermediary body was preferable because economic control was exerted in the more immediately effective form of *social control.* Through the mediation of the *corps* the social was reincorporated in the economic, where it served to regulate the economic sphere.

Such a defense of a moral economy of trust based on corporatist social control was by no means novel, but now that the possibility of social dissolution had become an obsessive concern, the theme acquired a new resonance. That it was taken up by any number of writers therefore comes as no surprise. Evidence of this can be seen in the fact that critics of corporations justified their opposition on the grounds that modern society was different from traditional society in that it was based on anonymity rather than face-to-face relations. For the defenders of corporations, however, this very anonymity justified their existence. For them, corporatist organization was not a legacy of traditional society but a response to the most urgent problems of the modern world. One of them put it this way: "In small towns, where everyone knows everyone else, the merchant and artisan have the greatest interest in doing their duty, but when they work amid a huge population and can escape general surveillance, they begin to see only their personal interest and to believe that any means are permissible provided they lead to success. Hence it was to remedy all these problems, which not only harm the consumer but also are prejudicial to the general interest and the interests of government, that a real need for corporations and *maîtrises* was felt."[48] The idea of a "mutual surveillance"—at once economic, social, and moral—was thus contrasted with the idea of market regulation. The *corps* was here cast in the role of "sociological compensator" for the logic of depersonalization at work in the modern world.

Furthermore, decentralized monitoring by the *corps* was said to be more effective than general oversight. Listen once again to Soufflot de Merey:

> I have proved that regular oversight was insufficient in a host of professions; that, if we are to do better, oversight must always be unobtrusive; and that we can obtain, without cost or overhead, from the syndics and *jurés* of the corporations themselves, a more active oversight and more enlightened guarantee. Furthermore, this oversight turns out to be of benefit to both society and the government that is inseparable from it: [decentralized oversight] diminishes the number of paid agents [of the government]; it substitutes a mild, unobjectionable authority for the invariably draconian and frightening measures of the police. Finally, this oversight has the great art of preventing evil, while the police can and should only punish and do not know how to do anything else, for they see only crimes.[49]

Thus the defenders of corporations turned their adversaries' argument on its head. For them, corporations had the ability to penetrate the social, to govern society better by knowing it more intimately. In response to the charge that the corporations represented particular interests, they offered an argument based on efficiency, which they understood as a consequence of particularity. They believed that decentralized oversight made for more effective governance. To those who argued that "since the communities were banned, an excellent system of oversight has been established,"[50] they replied that this oversight was superficial. Henrion de Pansey, one of the leading jurists of the day, pointed out that "the sometimes hairsplitting but always diligent and enlightened oversight of the *jurés* and syndics is today entrusted to functionaries, who have neither their experience nor their knowledge."[51] The corporation as an institution between state and market was thus implicitly seen in the quite modern context of a general economy of information. In effect, the partisans of intermediary bodies based their support for corporations on their intuitive grasp of the idea of transaction and information costs.[52]

Reinstating the corporations was an idea that drew the interest of people looking for new forms of "governability" in the early nineteenth century. Two different avenues were explored. Guizot and other so-called *doctrinaire* liberals (a group of conservative liberals first organized under the Restoration) sought to define a new type of state that would be able to steer society from within[53] even as the establishment of intermediary bodies gave rise to new sources of information and new means of action. To a degree, these two perspectives overlapped, as we shall see, and the advent in this period of the new word "governability" reflected the concern with developing techniques suited to related new arts of corporate and political governance.[54]

Understanding economic regulation in terms of obtaining and processing information was not in itself new. In the eighteenth century, this was how market theorists explained the superiority of laissez-faire over a regime of prohibitions and controls. The best-known account was that of Turgot in his *Lettre à l'abbé Terray sur la marque des fers* (1773). "In order to guide the course of nature without disturbing it or doing harm to oneself, one would need the ability to trace every variation in the needs, interests, and industry of men. One would have to know these in a detail that is physically impossible to obtain, about which even the most active and diligent government would risk being wrong at least half the time."[55] Yet advocates of corporations did not limit themselves to economic and political arguments; moral and sociological considerations were equally important to them.

Proponents also used the informational argument to suggest that reinstituting corporations could yield tax advantages. Corporations with information about their members would in effect be in a position to assess taxes efficiently and equitably. "The administration cannot keep track of everything and oversee everyone by itself,"[56] and the tax authorities in particular encountered social resistance from taxpayers less than eager to pay their due. With corporations, by contrast, "the tax authorities can also turn to central agents, making their surveillance easier and more economical and less cumbersome for taxpayers. It can, if it chooses, free itself from a multitude of burdensome and at times confusing details."[57] This argument was ubiquitous; we even find it coming up in budget debates in the Chamber of Deputies.[58]

In a related development, the informational argument was raised against proposals to regulate industry. "The laws are powerless," Levacher-Duplessis argued.[59] It was deemed impossible for a "great organizer" to gather the data needed to support centralized action at a reasonable cost. Legal regulation of firms was also suspect for structural reasons: the range of situations was too wide to be encompassed under a small number of general principles. Soufflot de Merey perceptively described this aspect of the problem: "I can imagine a Dictionary of Arts and Crafts," he wrote. "I can imagine a patent on an invention. I can imagine a copyright on a dramatic work. But an industrial code! . . . Industry is the daughter of invention, and, like inventiveness, it knows no limits. Each day will add something to or subtract something from this changing code, and no code can be exposed to all the variations that a lucky discovery or straightforward improvement may necessitate."[60]

Soufflot did not reject the idea of an industrial code. Indeed, he expressed unreserved approval for the Commercial Code that was being drafted at the time. Like the Civil Code, this was to incorporate principles and procedures deemed sufficient a priori to describe and govern reality. Any future disparity between the general framework and particular situations would indicate a problem of *interpretation.* Yet, Soufflot insisted, things were very different in the industrial domain, where each situation was irreducibly and structurally distinct. In this realm of human action, in other words, generality was inconceivable. Every factory was unique, and its development was necessarily singular. This did not mean that no laws could be promulgated in this realm, but these would always be *regulatory laws (lois de police)* linked to a specific problem or situation (such as a health or safety issue associated with a specific product). Hence in this area, legality was not the same thing as law, and still less could a compilation of regulatory measures be regarded as a legal code.

From Theory to Practice

Those who advocated a return to the corporatist model had always been aware of the difficulty of mounting their critique on economic grounds. Although the *sociological* attack on the "disorder" stemming from a mobile society of individuals undeniably evoked a response, the actual *economic* superiority of an organized professional system was less easy to prove. How could one explain why a system that appeared to yield *theoretical* benefits led in *practice* to destructive measures? There was of course nothing original in this contrast between theoretical promises and practical results. It had figured centrally in the thinking of all who had criticized the "perversions" of the Revolution as consequences of abstract thought. From Burke to Portalis, the theme recurred in any number of works, as we have seen. Between 1805 and 1821 this approach was naturally applied to the corporatist question by all who lamented the fact that a positive mode of professional organization had been destroyed even as unjust privileges were being eliminated. "In administration as in commerce," Soufflot de Merey pointed out, "the imaginary best is truly the enemy of the real good."[61] Levacher-Duplessis also blamed various economic and social errors on "abstractions," "idle theories," and "speculative opinions."[62] One observer of the organization of commerce summed it up as follows: "People allowed themselves to be seduced by the logic of a general theory without studying the more certain results of practice, and evil inevitably followed from the good they had sought to do."[63]

The sharp contrast between theory and practice was seen as fundamental, yet the reasons for it remained mysterious. Sismondi was the first to propose a real analysis. His remarks are particularly interesting given that he went in a few years from a zealous champion of Adam Smith to a defender of professional organizations. In his first major work, *De la richesse commerciale* (1803), he had harshly attacked *maîtrises*, condemned apprenticeship statutes, and expressed the view that corporations constituted "a league against the consumer and society."[64] At that time he saw only virtues in absolute freedom of commerce and industry. By 1819, when he published *Nouveaux Principes d'économie politique,* he had almost completely reversed his views. In the later work he called for "giving the trades a corporate interest," even if he refused to "revive the privileges of old" or return to the "dues of the *jurandes.*"[65] He rehearsed the history of corporations in a far more measured way, acknowledging their benefits while hiding none of their errors. How are we to explain this conversion? The premonitory signs of the coming pauperism, about which we shall have more to say later, surely played a part in his change of heart, turning his attention to concrete protections for labor as opposed to formal guarantees of equal access to various occupations. But Sismondi's evolution also stemmed from thinking about the significance and status of his discipline. "No science is in greater need of being guided by experience than political economy," he wrote. "Nowhere else is theory more deceptive, because it is so difficult to take into account so many apparently independent but in fact mutually interacting circumstances and hence to predict the unintended consequences of the changes one is seeking to bring about."[66] This epistemological observation underscores the importance of the informational aspect of the problem. If practice can prove theory wrong, it is because theory rests on too narrow a base. This is the source as well as the justification of the critique of the state by civil society and of the question of the actual power of generality of various legal texts. Generality is not always a quality but often merely a pretense: all who stressed the positive role that intermediary bodies might play in the regulation of the economy repeatedly hammered this point.

— 6 —

The Sociological Trial

After Thermidor, critical thinking about the tortured history of the Revolution was essentially political and constitutional. From Benjamin Constant and Mme. de Staël to the Ideologues, a new generation sought to rethink republican forms so as to anchor them durably in the waters of liberty. From Year III on, this movement led to a proliferation of ideas about modes of election, the meaning of representation, further division of powers, the nature of protected rights, the neutrality of government, and so on. With the coming of empire, this critical and innovative thinking was obliged to recede into the shadows or to seek refuge in exile, but this withdrawal only compounded the need to redefine the foundations of the French polity so as to wed democracy permanently to liberty. It was in this context that some of the great classics of French political liberalism were conceived, among them *De l'esprit de conquête et de l'usurpation* and the *Considérations sur la Révolution française*.

The ideal regime to which many aspired failed to emerge from the Restoration. The new Charter did, however, establish a parliamentary government that turned its back on the errors, tragedies, and betrayals of the past. Debate continued to swirl around this evolving new regime, debate made all the fiercer by the continued resistance of the ultras. The focus of anxiety had shifted, however. The chief concern was now postrevolutionary *society*. One young commentator summed up the general feeling this way: "The Revolution gave us not only a new government but also a new society, nothing like the one that preceded it and perhaps like no other in the world."[1] The very term "new society" was taken up in this period by any number of writers to hint at a new perplexity. Novel words such as "numbers" and "masses" also gained currency, suggesting the advent of a new social form whose contours were difficult to make out. "Society is proceeding down novel paths," wrote Pierre Simon Ballanche. Benjamin Constant said that it had been "revolutionized," while Charles de Rémusat remarked that "French society is an enigma," and Alphonse de Lamartine spoke of the emergence of "large intangible number." All agreed that the goal was to constitute a society as well as a government.[2] The era ended, moreover, with the publication of a great work, Tocqueville's *Democracy in America,* whose primary goal was to describe the new world just then emerging.

It was on this second front, that of sociological anxiety, that the issue of intermediary bodies was once again raised. The discussion proceeded on three distinct levels, though all three related to the same basic anxiety: these were fear of social dissolution, critique of individualism, and disorganization of the professions. This sociological anxiety was also reflected in persistent efforts to describe and decipher a society that had suddenly become baffling to interpreters.

Society Reduced to Dust

The specter of social dissolution haunted most observers of the French scene in the early nineteenth century. France, one of them noted, "was then a body without unity, without harmony, all of whose members were seeking mutually to dissolve one another."[3] Another was blunter still: "Society no longer exists."[4] Such lapidary judgments, repeated countless times, were uttered in a variety of accents. Some came draped in aristocratic nostalgia for a society that revolved around certain *grandes existences,* which were supposed to give relief to the whole of society. Others pointed to worries of a spiritual sort having to do with the simultaneous decomposition of the social and the moral order. Thus Chateaubriand took fright at "the great and universal malady of a world in dissolution" and a "decomposed civilization."[5] "Society has been reduced to dust," Pierre Leroux noted with alarm, "because men are dissociated, no bond unites them, and man is stranger to man."[6] In poetry as in life, all talk was of debris, ravaged cities, somber cemeteries. Constantin-François Volney's *Les Ruines* went through several editions and enjoyed a prominent place on many bookshelves. Anxiety took many forms but invariably rested on a sociological perception: that society had become atomized and no longer enjoyed the structure that came from intermediary bodies.

"The classification system of earlier societies has vanished."[7] The assertion is Guizot's, but many other writers, from Ballanche to Constant to Bonald, made similar observations. The old science of social distinctions, which for Rémusat constituted "virtually all the science of the world," suddenly seemed unable to shed any light on anything.[8] Thus we find everywhere a need to decipher. Everyone used whatever means were available to make sense of a society for which no a priori system of classification existed. Even before Auguste Comte formulated his ambitious program of "social physics" to explain the new world in gestation, we find glimmerings of a new sociology in the work of both Bonald and Saint-Simon. The same concern can be detected in much of the literature of the period. Balzac's *Comédie humaine* is the very type of a literary effort to grasp the "sociological moment" and identify the new categories just then emerging. To observe humanity in the throes of a profound transformation was indeed a ubiquitous ambition of the time. A veritable "fever of self-analysis" gripped France in the first decades of the nineteenth century.[9] People wanted to understand the enigmatic postrevolutionary society even as they denounced it.

A disaggregated, atomized society—in other words, a society of individuals. "We cannot avert our eyes from the fact that our long civil troubles have given rise not to a new nation but to a collection of individuals." These words belong to Joseph de Villèle, but the same idea can be found in a thousand pamphlets.[10] The advent of a society of individuals was seen both as a predictable consequence of the creation of a *grand tout* subsuming all intermediary bodies and as a sign of the defective structure of a degraded collectivity. Again it was Pierre Leroux who hit on the most striking description of a transformation that was at once social and moral: "Society," he wrote, "is no longer anything more than a bundle of egoisms; hence it is no longer a body. It consists of the severed members of a corpse."[11] It was in this context that the term "individualism" was coined. This cannot be understood simply as one more "ism" of the sort that had lately burst upon the French language with so much fanfare. In fact it was more the reflection of a diffuse anxiety and perplexity than a harbinger of some new ideology.

As is often the case, the earliest uses of the word did not establish its ultimate meaning. Joseph de Maistre seems to have been the first to use it. For him, though, it had a philosophical and religious rather than a sociological meaning. For the author of *Considérations sur la France*, "individualism" referred to a fragmentation of ideas and division of the mind reflecting what he called "political Protestantism pushed to the point of absolute individualism."[12] At about the same time, the young members of the so-called Société des Individualistes seem to have used the word in a positive sense.[13] Other positive references to the "doctrine of individualism" can be found in *Le Globe*, which was at the time the intellectual organ of the new liberal generation.[14] It was in Saint-Simonian circles in the mid-1820s that the term was first used in a truly systematic way, however. It was taken up by writers such as Pierre Leroux and Prosper Enfantin, as well as by Laurent in the columns of the journal *Le Producteur*.[15] These authors used the term to denounce the advent of a fragmented, divided society, in which each man's will was juxtaposed with the will of others and particular interests were anarchically intertwined. Individualism was seen as the general social form corresponding to what was called competition in economics and egoism in ethics. One observer did not hesitate to speak of "that dreadful sentiment which the language has thought worthy of a savage word, individualism."[16]

The society "dedicated to egoism and anarchy" that the Saint-Simonian literature hammered on so mercilessly was also the society that novelists were attempting to describe. In *César Birotteau*, for example, Balzac deplored the fact that the nation was dissolved, "because it is held together now by nothing more than the ignoble bonds of material interest, by the commandments of the cult created by Egoism properly understood."[17] The term "individualism" was then an adjective whose moral and sociological connotations were closely intertwined.[18] Accordingly, we find it being used by writers of ultra and, later, legitimist stripe as well as by Saint-Simonians. For instance, Ferdinand Béchard noted that "the old social order is now nothing more than a heap of ruins. Upon its smoking debris only one thing remains standing, namely, individualism."[19] Yet the "reign of individualism," though condemned by nearly everyone, was scarcely analyzed. The problem was merely perceived in general terms, as evidenced by its very broad and largely indiscriminate usage. One contemporary observer described it as "a new word invented by politico-social hygiene, a word that is nowadays at home everywhere, in philosophy, in ethics, in political economy, in salons, and above all on the rostrum. Yes, the dreaded *individualism* is all around us, somber and menacing."[20] Tocqueville was alone at the time in his attempt to distinguish in a more rigorous way between the old "egoism" and the new "individualism" and thus to explore the complexity of the emerging democratic society.[21] (To be sure, Tocqueville's analysis appeared somewhat later, since it is found in the second part of *Democracy in America*, not published until 1840.) This very comprehensive and vague vision explains why many people found it so difficult to distinguish between the *spirit of individuality*, which was seen as a positive achievement of the modern era, and individualism, which was attacked as a malady. Thus Benjamin Constant boasted of the "triumph of individuality" as a moral and juridical fact consecrating the principle of individual autonomy and the establishment of the rule of law, even as others were expressing alarm about individualism.[22]

To be sure, there were other voices stating loud and clear that there was nothing to deplore in this new social order and urging their contemporaries to take a less dramatic view of the problem. Thus Guizot, in his 1828–29 course on the history of French civilization, issued this stern challenge to his students at the Sorbonne: "I hope that you are not misled by the words 'dissolved society' and 'dying society' and that you can perceive their real meaning. A society dissolves only when a new society is fermenting and forming within it. A hidden process tends to separate the elements of the society, causing them to enter into new combinations."[23] This appeal to relativism deserves to be mentioned, but it should not be overestimated. Those who saw growing individualism as merely a transitory evil necessary to dismantle the Old Regime but destined to wither away *naturally*, were few in number. These optimistic voices remained a small minority, and the vague prospect of a radiant future for the middle classes was hardly enough to swell their ranks.

The Spirit of Association

The question of intermediary bodies presented itself forcefully in this context, which was dominated by the specter of social dissolution and chaos in the professions. The expression itself cropped up both in the formulation of a diagnosis—that a harmful void had opened up between the state and individuals, threatening to undo the social bond—and in the suggestion of a remedy. Many called for a restoration or reinvention of intermediary powers as a way of countering the disintegration of the social. No one put this better than Hercule de Serre, one of the great orators in the liberal camp, in a memorable speech. "The dissolving system of individual isolation must be abandoned," he said. "We must return to the life principle of every durable free government, namely, the association of distinct interests. Are recent examples of the power of the associative principle needed? I shall take them from ages of dissolution. It was associations that delivered Germany; association shaped a moral force that destroyed physical force ... Let us cease to be slaves to the word 'unity.' Unity is not always an absolute rule. The rule of unity is not that of the creator himself: if it were, the elements would have to be returned to their original chaos ... Government can be strong only if it relies on associations and not on isolated individuals, strangers to one another."[24] The break with utopian generality here seems radical.[25] It was as much pragmatic as it was philosophical. De Serre was a statesman. It was above all to cope with the reduction of the social state to "powder" that he championed intermediary bodies. Against the "principle of individual isolation," on which he laid primary blame for dissolution, he invoked its opposite: the principle of association.

"The salvation of France will come from the principle of association. This will deliver France from individualism, the greatest of her woes and primary cause of her suffering." These words are taken from *L'Avenir*, Félicité Robert de Lamennais's newspaper, but similar sentiments were ubiquitous.[26] The "spirit of association" was invoked by Saint-Simonians as well as ultras and liberals of nearly every stripe. Its prophets and theorists were legion. Numerous books and articles about it appeared from the very earliest days of the Restoration. Alexandre Laborde's weighty treatise *De l'esprit d'association dans tous les intérêts de la communauté* (1818) found many readers,[27] who shared its methodical celebration of the principle of association in the various realms of social activity. Rémusat, meanwhile, lauded the spirit of association and the division of labor as "the two great forms of human industry."[28] Then at the beginning of his career, the young writer on public affairs was one of the first to treat the spirit of association as the mark of modernity. Long before Tocqueville, he contrasted France with England and the United States, deploring the fact that France was a country in which the spirit of association had been "so slow to become naturalized." He called upon his contemporaries to abandon a statist tradition, which he judged archaic:

Among enlightened peoples, the most liberal of religions (Protestantism) has generally accredited the idea that government should leave it to society to do what society can do as well as government. Hence the sphere of government intervention shrinks as society gains in resources, talent, and enlightenment. The more society can do, the less government should do.

The isolated or combined forces of individuals remove that much of the burden from the public force . . . It is therefore advantageous and politic to extend the spirit of association.[29]

Writing in a different philosophical tradition, Pierre Leroux reached the same conclusion. "Liberty, equality, association" was the slogan he placed on the cover of his *Revue encyclopédique*.[30] For him, association was the response to the "disassociation" of the modern world.[31] In yet another universe, that of legitimism, Ferdinand Béchard made himself the apostle of the law of association, which he said was "to the moral order what the law of attraction is to the material order."[32] "Association" was indeed one of the key words of the time. The various intellectual and political families of the period, though divided on every other issue, were virtually unanimous on this one.

The praise of association and denunciation of individualism were not limited to reconstituting a true social fabric, however. (The "social fabric" metaphor was all the rage, though organic metaphors also abounded.) The threat of social decomposition extended beyond the realm of institutions and the organization of work. It was seen as far more radical, bearing on the very nature of human life. Evidence for this perspective can be seen in the fact that the same critics denounced the "bachelor spirit" as a primary form of individualism.[33] Some writers even described the bachelor as a sort of "cheater on the social contract." That is why so many in this period spoke out forcefully in favor of consolidation of the family as the basic cell of the social body. This also explains why the issue of divorce suddenly became central in the early years of the nineteenth century. Beyond the obvious religious obsession with erasing what many resented as one of the most reprehensible pieces of revolutionary legislation, the concern with divorce also represented a sociological worry. If the ultras were naturally the most ardent backers of Bonald's antidivorce campaign, the issue mobilized a much broader coalition because it was linked to the specter of social disintegration. The debates leading up to the law of 1816 are significant in this regard.[34] Even outspoken proponents of divorce granted that the law "is foolish and destructive of all virtue and all social order when it makes divorce too easy."[35] Quite apart from moral and religious concerns, the problem of legal separation of married couples was indeed related to the more general question of social dissolution. Still more generally, as Mona Ozouf has shown, this set of issues included the whole question of male-female relations. Women were thus considered by many writers

(Tocqueville foremost among them) as essentially "bound" creatures, guarantors of a modicum of stability in a world that had become incomprehensible.[36]

At the opposite extreme from this "intimate" view of social order, a powerful need was felt to see society in a new, comprehensive framework. In this connection, the appearance of the word "socialism" is an important sign. Credit for inventing the word is generally given to Pierre Leroux, who used it in his 1834 article "De l'individualisme et du socialisme."[37] At the time, however, the word did not have the ideological valence it later acquired. Its meaning was primarily *sociological*. This is clear from the fact that Lamartine used it at precisely the same time in an obviously nonpolitical sense in predicting that the proletarian class "will stir up society until socialism has replaced the odious individualism."[38] Earlier still, the author of *Harmonies* referred to the "social party" to indicate the significance of something that needed to be done[39] and spoke of "our flag, that of sociability."[40]

The Invention of Decentralization

Decentralization: the word did not appear until 1829, but the aspirations and projects with which it came to be associated were ubiquitous as early as 1815. Calls to reinstate or organize intermediary bodies in order to ward off social dissolution were associated at that time with criticism of Napoleonic centralization and demands for the creation of true local communities. A young deputy with a brilliant future ahead of him, Villèle, initiated the debate in the Chamber of Deputies. "Breaking the bonds that tie us to our village, our town, and our *département* and killing our interest in our secondary administrations . . . destroys the public spirit, disunites and demoralizes the nation, and isolates Frenchmen from one another."[41] In creating "secondary administrations," he suggested, the goal should be to "reconstitute" a disoriented country as "a *corps de peuple*."[42] The ultras would make this one of the principal battle cries in the early years of the Restoration. For them, the goal was to restore a seriously cracked social edifice by shoring up its foundations: the family and the village *(commune)*. Bonald and his friends continually hammered home these themes in speeches and publications. The literature on the subject is as vast as it is repetitive. From the pages of *Le Conservateur* to the columns of *L'Avenir*, the same formulas occur again and again. "The village is to the political system what the franc is to the monetary system, the primary, basic unit," observed the author of the *Théorie du pouvoir politique et religieux* in summing up his vehement critique of "the dominant ideas of personal individuality."[43] Thus the outcry against centralization was set in motion, combining the obsession with disorder, the fear of a society of individuals, and the critique of bureaucracy. Of course the ultras' immediate political objectives also played a part in their position. They favored decentralization all the more in that they were out of power and displeased with the new France they saw taking shape before their eyes. The struggle against centralization and its abuses was also a theme to which provincial notables were particularly sensitive, and they constituted the bulk of the electorate in this period of *censitaire* suffrage.[44]

So narrow an interpretation is not acceptable, however. Although the ultras did have a way of celebrating family and village together in a style that mingled sentimental attachment to the old provinces with nostalgia for corporatist society,[45] the concerns they expressed were much more widely shared. Centralization was also attacked by liberals, who feared what might happen if society grew too anemic. Early in the century, they were the first to develop what would later become a major Tocquevillean topos: the idea of a historical link between the construction of an omnipotent state and the dissolution of society. The canonical formulation of the problem can be found in the work of Pierre Paul Royer-Collard. Because it left such a durable imprint on liberal thought, it is worth looking at a little more closely. "We have seen the old society perish," Royer-Collard proclaimed,

and with it the host of domestic institutions and independent magistracies it included . . . Not one has survived, and no new ones have arisen in their place. The revolution left standing only individuals. The dictatorship that ended it consummated its work in this respect. It dissolved even the, as it were, physical association of the village. It dispelled even the shadow of those magistracies in which rights were vested and by which they were defended. Nothing like it had ever been seen! Only in the books of the philosophers had anyone ever seen a nation decomposed in this manner and reduced to the least of its elements. Out of a society reduced to dust came centralization. There is no need to look elsewhere for its origin. Unlike any number of no less pernicious doctrines, centralization did not arrive with its head held high, with the authority of a principle. It insinuated itself modestly, as a consequence, a necessity. Indeed, where only individuals exist, all affairs that are not individual matters are public affairs, affairs of state. Where no independent magistrates exist, there are only agents of government. That is how we became a people of administrative subjects, under the thumb of irresponsible functionaries, themselves centralized in the government of which they are the ministers.[46]

Contemporaries would quote, plagiarize, and mimic these famous lines, which remained fresh in everyone's mind at the end of the nineteenth century, as the example of Durkheim makes clear. It would not be difficult to compile a long list of echoes of Royer-Collard's sentiments from the writings of Benjamin Constant, Prosper de Barante, Jouffroy, and Rémusat or from the pages of the *Archives philosophiques, politiques, et littéraires, La Minerve,* and *Le Globe.* How did these voices differ from those of the ultras? The difference had to do with the "objective," sociological character of the analysis, which in the case of the liberals was not tinged by reactionary passions. This feature only made it stronger and more impressive.

Thus all voices in the 1820s seemed to converge on the idea of decentralization as a symbol of needed reforms, a way of giving substance to the new spirit of association that was expected to remedy the disintegration of society. The issue of municipal and departmental reform remained omnipresent, especially at the beginning and end of the period. After the fall of Charles X, it was seen as one of the areas to which the new July Monarchy most urgently needed to turn its attention. As the reign of Louis-Philippe wore on, however, the issue lost some of its centrality. To be sure, the legitimists, led on this issue by Béchard, continued to view decentralization as essential to the revitalization of society. In 1832 *La Gazette nationale* published a program that devoted considerable attention to the emancipation of the provinces and enfranchisement of villages.[47] Some writers, including Tocqueville, made decentralization a primary concern. By this point, however, intermediary bodies were no longer the only remedy proposed for the atomization of society. References to association assumed growing importance, especially among workers and other milieus where the persistence of terms such as "corporatism" and "corporations" also reflected the aspiration to a reintegrated society.

The World of Workers' Societies

That the nascent workers' movement of the early 1830s rallied beneath the banner of association almost goes without saying. This history is well enough known that there is no need to dwell on it here, despite its importance. A brief review will suffice for our purposes. Although a few mutual aid societies were established during the Restoration, often continuing old cooperative forms of solidarity, "association" did not really become a watchword until the July Monarchy.[48] It was a difficult time for industry, and memories of glorious collective action were still fresh: "Three days were enough to change our role in the economy and society."[49] The combination sufficed to give rise to a spate of new workers' societies. At first these were intended to aid the unemployed members of this or that occupational group, as well as to set rules and rates and to monitor the system of employment.[50] Yet it was in this same period, 1830–1834, that the search for a more radical alternative to the workers' current condition began in earnest. Theorists like Philippe Joseph Benjamin Buchez, joined by countless anonymous militants, proposed that workers band together "in association" to set up workshops in which the means of production would be owned in common.[51] This type of association was conceived as a remedy to the exploitation that the isolation of workers made possible. It offered a solution to the egoism and individualism that had fragmented industry as well as society in general. Workers in Lyons summed up the situation this way: "In the current state of civilization, egoism . . . leads men little by little to a degree of isolation and cruelty . . . approaching the state of savages and threatens society with dissolution."[52] The cooperative project associated with this diagnosis thus shared the same concerns expressed by those who called for the establishment of intermediary powers as a way of giving perceptible structure to a disintegrated society.

No one understood this state of mind better than a modest cobbler, Zael Efrahem, the author of a short pamphlet that can be taken as one of the fundamental texts of the French workers' movement, *De l'association des ouvriers de tous les corps d'état* (1833). "Association," he noted, "yields a twofold advantage, bringing all forces together and imparting a direction to the whole." The goal, as he saw it, was to enable all workers sharing the same condition "to form a *corps*." Labor could thus prevent the disintegration and dissipation of its strength and avoid "plunging into the individualism and egoism of isolation." He also saw a loftier ambition beyond bringing people of various walks of life into association with one another, namely, to form "an association of all the different occupational groups [*corps d'état*]" and "to give this great body of workers [*corps ouvrier*] a central committee consisting of delegates representing the particular associations." He concluded with the hope that "to this association of our interests, our rights, and our courage we will provide a thinking head, a firm and intelligent will, to set a course for action and direct the movement. We will set one central power at the summit of this grouping: this thinking head, the powerful, ruling will, this strong administrative power, will come from our association's central committee." The remedy to the dissolution of society was thus to *constitute* a population of isolated workers *as a class*. Jules Leroux, a typographer who was the brother of Pierre and a tireless militant, summed up the same state of mind in the following formula: "Our class does not exist; there are only individuals."[53]

"To form a *corps*": the search for a remedy to social disintegration led these early working-class advocates of association to revert to the old language of corporatism. Some, moreover, openly deplored what they experienced as a loss. For example, one noted that "we have no syndical chamber or corporation of the sort we had before the Revolution."[54] In a classic work, William Sewell analyzed the way in which the nineteenth-century working class reappropriated the corporatist language.[55] Although terms such as *jurandes, maîtrises,* and *communautés* had gone out of use, the word "corporation" remained quite common. In addition to Efrahem, who conceived of the union of working men like himself in terms of a *grand corps ouvrier,* there were many proposals for workers' societies and savings unions *(caisses)* that instinctively used the word "corporation" to characterize the occupational group whose solidarity was invoked as the basis for the project. The list of early workers' associations reflects the remarkable persistence of the old vocabulary of labor.[56] But more was involved than nostalgia for a naively reenchanted world. Everyone involved in workers' emancipation in the 1830s recognized that the new world of labor was different from the old. In 1833 *Le National* published an unambiguous assessment under the title "Des anciennes corporations et des nouvelles coalitions d'ouvriers": "beyond the names 'coalition,' 'philanthropic association,' and 'corporation,' the workers have, if you will, but one goal . . . to resist a social organization that oppresses them . . . Hence it is ridiculous to reject the new corporations by invoking the memory of the old ones. The corporations that the Constituent Assembly dissolved once and for all were hostile to liberty, whereas the new ones are reconstituting themselves in the name of liberty."[57] Despite this clear delineation of a substantive difference between the old and the new, the persistence of the eighteenth-century vocabulary indicates how difficult it was to conceive of a *modern* alternative to the society of individuals.

The use of the word "corporation" to characterize the whole world of labor would persist throughout the nineteenth century. One of the texts that marked the rebirth of the workers' movement in the 1860s, under the Second Empire, was significantly titled *L'Organisation des travailleurs par les corporations nouvelles*.[58] Still later the first trade union congresses called themselves "corporatist congresses," a usage that the Confédération Générale des Travailleurs officially maintained until 1923.[59] In a magisterial work titled *La Coutume ouvrière*, published early in the twentieth century, Maxime Leroy gave an excellent analysis of the slow transition from the "corporatist spirit" to the "class spirit," and it would not be difficult to find significant traces of the former persisting well into the century.[60] The important point is that this language had a primarily *sociological valence* in the world of labor: it indicated a desire to break with the society of individuals. This was the way in which labor exhibited the tensions of modernity. Out of it came two attempts to overcome the ordeal of social disintegration: by conceiving of society as a new kind of *corps*, or by imagining a new entity, the working *class*, conceived as a separate, regenerated nation within the nation. Proudhon combined both visions: the part redeemed from its limitations on the one hand, the whole truly keeping its promises of unity and homogeneity on the other. The question of intermediary bodies in the world of labor was always intimately intertwined with this fraught quest.

— 7 —

The Requirement of Liberty

Intermediary Powers and Counterforces

If liberty was to be kept alive, intermediary bodies had to be encouraged: this imperative was clearly recognized during the Restoration in both ultra milieus and certain liberal circles. For the ultras, the idea of liberty was still linked culturally to the idea of the independence and autonomy of the various *corps* constituting society. Thus it harked back to a comprehensive pre-absolutist conception of the social (in contrast to the conception of Louis XIV, who of course liked to say that he tolerated no intermediary power). This conception of the social was inherited from the eighteenth century, during which it was still firmly rooted in many minds despite the attraction of the new political rationalism of the Physiocrats. For example, a figure representative of this aristocratic liberalism, Marc Marie René de Voyer d'Argenson, wrote in his *Considérations sur le gouvernement ancien et présent de la France* (1764) that "the venality of offices is the great stumbling block to despotism's designs . . . The progress of aristocracy must always be taken as a sure sign of despotism's weakness."[1] Even Paul Henri d'Holbach, despite being one of the most vehement adversaries of privileged corporations, held that in the absence of other forms of representation they constituted "an always essential rampart between supreme authority and the liberty of subjects."[2] This sensibility, embodied most prominently by Montesquieu and spearheaded as an active force by the *parlementaires,* also reflected, albeit in muted terms, a distinctive conception of privilege as service as well as a positive guarantee against encroachments by government. In many countries in Europe, moreover, struggles for liberty had often been linked to struggles for the granting or preservation of privileges representing legal forms of individual or group autonomy. This competition for privilege was well established in England and the Netherlands.[3] The history of France was different, but these examples and recollections constituted a sort of "aristocratic memory" of liberty, which persisted in ultra and later legitimist circles.

Their celebration of communal liberties under the Restoration must be seen against this background. "We must have powers between the general administration and the administered. Otherwise there will never be liberty or stability in France," according to Joseph Fievée, a leading public intellectual of the right.[4] "Our misfortunes," he continued, "stem particularly from the fundamental error of believing that liberty resides in houses of representatives, when in fact it can only manifest itself there. It must exist in all primary institutions. The monarchy needs intermediary bodies, and where can they be found now if not in the provincial administrations, which are alone capable of halting the overly uniform action of the [central] administration?"[5] Meanwhile, for Béchard, whose work we encountered earlier, the great merit of intermediary bodies was that "they serve as barriers to anarchy and despotism."[6] One finds these same themes in Tocqueville, who was supremely sensitive to the question of how modern liberty related to traditional forms of autonomy.[7] Here, the intermediary body was an *intermediary power,* a protective interface. "Local institutions are to liberty what elementary schools are to knowledge," according to the author of *Democracy in America.*[8]

A range of liberals took basically the same approach, even if "aristocratic memory" naturally played a much less central role in their thinking. What took its place was an emphasis on the separation of powers as a prerequisite of constitutional government. Benjamin Constant regularly insisted on the "protective" aspect of intermediary bodies, especially at the most basic local level. For him, local bodies were useful not simply because they were institutions but because they extended a certain *culture* of liberty as lived experience. "The interests and memories that stem from local habits," he noted, "contain a germ of resistance, which authority tolerates only with misgivings and hastens to uproot. It deals with individuals more easily. Its enormous weight rolls over them as effortlessly as over sand."[9] Intermediary powers were seen as material and moral counterforces. More than simply remedies for social decomposition, they were said to constitute a *sociological* source of resistance, a dike to hold back the "ideas of uniformity" that led systematically to despotism.[10] Constant, following Burke on this point, repeatedly emphasized that liberty was the enemy of abstraction and the friend of particularity, always concrete. "What is bizarre," he insisted, "is that those who called themselves ardent friends of liberty always worked so zealously to destroy the natural principle of patriotism and to replace it with a factitious passion for an abstract entity, a general idea shorn of every quality capable of striking the imagination and speaking to memories! How bizarre that in order to build a building, they began by reducing to dust all the materials they would need."[11] Here, the author of *Adolphe* is not very far from sharing the views we previously saw expressed by Royer-Collard.

Several other prominent public intellectuals took up this theme in the 1820s. Among them were Jean-Marie Duvergier de Hauranne in *De l'ordre légal en France et des abus d'autorité* (1826) and Pierre Claude François Daunou in his *Essai sur les garanties individuelles* (1818). In the 1831 debate on municipal organization, Daunou directly attacked Guizot. At that time he urged the French to "seek a counterweight to power," and for this he regarded the potential power of municipal councils as essential.[12] For both writers, free associations and institutionalized intermediary bodies set limits to the action of other powers, thus endowing liberty with a well-defined structure. A youthful Rémusat shared their enthusiasm in this period. "The spirit of association marches hand in hand with the spirit of liberty," he proclaimed well before Tocqueville. "England and America are living examples. It is therefore advantageous and politic to extend the empire of the spirit of association."[13]

This view of the connection between liberty and particularity was not shared by all liberals, a majority of whom identified, as we shall see, with the culture of generality. It was not without influence in the field of law, however. In some quarters, opposition to the totalizing vision of the revolutionary period developed steadily, leading ultimately to a more pragmatic and modest approach to the law. The cult of codification gave way to growing interest in the works of the German historical school and its leader, Friedrich Carl von Savigny. To take the full measure of this very significant intellectual shift, we would need to undertake a full-scale review of the history of legal philosophy in the Restoration. Eugène Lerminier, the author of a thesis on Savigny, played a decisive role in this area. A series of articles that he published in *Le Globe* between 1825 and 1830 introduced the cultivated reading public to the works of the German historical school. Treating Savigny as a disciple of Montesquieu, Lerminier portrayed the latter as a philosopher tired of theories and abstractions and concerned instead with rules. For Lerminier, "a love of what is national and a feeling for what is historic" pointed the way toward a more solid conception of liberty.[14]

The interest that Lerminier and others took in the work of Pellegrino Rossi stemmed from a similar interest in the philosophical treatment of politics. Rossi, who played a key role in formulating the constitutional doctrine of Louis-Philippe's regime, developed in the 1820s a critique of utopian codification that left its mark on French liberalism. The cultivated public also encountered Savigny's work through Rossi. His articles of the early 1820s and especially his *Traité de droit pénal* (1829) lent intellectual authority to an approach that allowed ascribing due weight to history and facts while adhering politically to a frank acceptance of 1789. By expounding the idea that "the law is a language," Rossi brought grist to the mill of those who saw particularity as the true ally of liberty.[15] Hence in this period the historical school of law reinforced those who saw intermediary bodies as ramparts against tyranny.

Liberty-Association

The idea of association in the early nineteenth century was polysemic and therefore difficult to grasp. As we have seen, it was linked in the very early years of the Restoration to cultural resistance to the idea of an atomized society. In this regard it was common to speak of a *spirit* of association whose role was to serve as an antidote to social dissolution. "Association," in this connection, referred to a principle that was inextricably moral and sociological and opposed to the principle of individualism. By the 1820s, however, the term also had a more precise meaning, referring to an alternative *mode of organization* of economy and society. Charles Fourier of course blazed the way with his *Traité de l'association domestique et agricole* (1822). In the 1830s and 1840s, the language of association was linked to a wide variety of proposed countersocieties: limited experiments here and now with a society of the future (modeled on Fourier's celebrated *phalansteries*); more modest and pragmatic attempts to set up producers' cooperatives; and utopian speculation about radically different forms of social organization (such as neo-Babouvist communities of property). It would be useful but tedious to construct a typology of the many faces that "association" wore in these years as a form of resistance or radical alternative to what was not yet called capitalism. The works of Charles Fourier, Victor Considérant, Théodore Dezamy, Philippe Buchez, Auguste Ott, Etienne Cabet, Pierre Leroux, and Flora Tristan are among the most striking examples of a vast literature that left its stamp on the period.

The term "association" also had a third referent in this period: it denoted a *freedom,* which was demanded with ever-increasing insistence. Association was seen as a means of action and defense, an instrument for implementing and extending the more basic freedoms of the individual. The problem was that the exercise of what was seen as an essential right was severely limited by Article 291 of the Penal Code of 1810, which required prior government approval for any meeting of more than twenty individuals (this being the limit arbitrarily established by law as the dividing line between an inoffensive domestic or social gathering and a public assembly with a possible political dimension). A point left vague by revolutionary legislation was thus given sharp relief.[16] Article 291, which in theory applied to all types of association, including literary and learned societies, had been debated only cursorily under the Empire, when it was only one of a range of draconian restrictions, others of which were seen as more fundamental threats to liberty. The Restoration maintained the law but enforced it only loosely, and in practice it affected only the more prominent citizens in their social and political lives. The liberals criticized it but did not make the issue a priority. Except for Duvergier de Hauranne, they devoted little attention to the problem.[17] After 1830 things changed abruptly. With the dashed hopes of the July Revolution and the emergence of a "workers' question" came a new social and political climate in which the issue of collective action was central. The fears of the new regime combined with the demands of the opposition to make the right of association one of the central issues of the period.

The issue was pressed initially by workers, who insisted on the right to organize in groups as a necessary condition of their emancipation. Thus what might be called a "militant" justification of association arose in conjunction with the emergence (or revival) of a corporatist ethos. One of the first workers' newspapers, *L'Artisan,* offers a good example of this new political (as opposed to simply societal or sociological) dimension of worker groups. The paper's journalists regarded associations as organs of resistance and means of action.[18] As the first publication to refer to the "working class" in its title and to make the organization and mobilization of that class one of its goals, *L'Artisan* offered its readers a careful analysis of the effects of abolishing the crime of coalition in England in 1824.[19] For these pioneers of worker action, the principle of association was virtually identical with the right of coalition. Another important publication of the period, *L'Echo de la fabrique,* repeated this demand in column after column championing the collective actions that proliferated in the early 1830s. "The deplorable isolation and long slumber of the working class must give way to a new social fact, association. This will have to be accepted soon, and the thousands of coalitions that have sprung from it and extended their branches far and wide are just the beginning."[20] In this context, the association was clearly defined as "the surest means to emancipation" of the world of labor.[21]

A type of action and organization that decades later would be associated with trade unions thus emerged in the early years of the July Monarchy. Many workers' associations were founded at this time, and most called themselves "corporations" or "societies," with relatively few adopting the name *chambres syndicales*. Countless brochures authored by obscure militants straight from the shop floor—a complete novelty—became the hallmark of the movement. For these humble spokesmen, association was the remedy for the ills of the proletariat. It saved them from isolation and dispersion, gave them visibility, and allowed them to resist their masters. The idea was orchestrated in numerous appeals, manifestos, and organizational bylaws drafted by these early militants. Everywhere there was talk of organizing bureaus, committees, and assistance funds in support of emergency collective action.[22] These groups called loudly for repeal of Article 291 and of the Le Chapelier law banning coalitions.

In the aftermath of July 1830, republican commentators defended the right of association from a similar instrumental point of view. In *Le National,* Armand Carrel and his friends supported the workers' call for associations to resist the oppressive organization of industry.[23] Lamennais, a recent convert to the democratic faith, also placed freedom of association at the heart of his agenda, explaining that "wherever all classes and corporations have been dissolved, so that only individuals remain, each man is left defenseless if the law isolates one individual from another and refuses to allow them to join together for common action."[24] The tone was the same in more radical circles, which formed organizations like the Société des Amis du Peuple and, later, the Société des Droits de l'Homme et du Citoyen. Albert Laponneraye, the author of the celebrated *Lettre aux prolétaires* that was at the heart of this agitation, ran a campaign that included the publication in 1831 of a *Petition à la Chambre des députés pour demander la radiation de l'article 291 du Code pénal.* The prosecution under this law of various republican societies naturally lent impetus to calls for a right of association.

This view of intermediary bodies as the essential underpinning of one form of liberty was further reinforced when the government, destabilized by growing political and social unrest, attempted to tighten legal restrictions on associations in the spring of 1834. The great debate that preceded the adoption of the law of 10 April 1834 saw a vigorous reaffirmation of the idea that freedom of association was a fundamental liberty.[25] People active in workers' associations and republican societies were naturally the first to protest the proposed new restrictions. Publications such as *Le National*, *Le Précurseur*, the *Revue républicaine*, *La Glaneuse*, *L'Echo de la fabrique*, and *La Tribune* unsurprisingly denounced a bill widely seen as "infamous." Liberty, they all repeated in chorus, was meaningless without a right to organize and act collectively. For them, "free man" meant "social man," who defined his place in society in terms of the associations that gave him influence. But not all the attacks on the allegedly liberty-destroying new law came from highly committed militant circles. In the Chamber of Deputies, more moderate voices joined legitimists and the dynastic left in protest. "Not only does the right of association exist," said Odilon Barrot, "but no society is possible without it." He went on: "Taken in isolation, individually, man can do nothing . . . No useful result can follow without association. The right of association in itself is therefore far more than just a right, far more even than a faculty. It is a *necessity*, the first of all social necessities."[26] For Barrot, then, it was clear that political liberty could not be based on individualism and that it needed the support of intermediary bodies. Lamartine and Pierre Antoine Berryer shared this view. The latter, who would become the most eloquent of the attorneys who argued on behalf of workers prosecuted for forming coalitions under the July Monarchy and Second Empire, also called the right to associate a "basic right" and a "generating right within the social order."[27] For these men, association was not simply a "sociological" means of resisting social dissolution but also a cornerstone of liberty. Hence the right of association was for them more than a mere *modality* or *variety* of liberty (akin to freedom of the press, for example); it was a *social condition*.

Functionality and Liberty

The Revolution demonstrated its suspicion of popular societies, which were accused of disrupting the legal operation of public institutions whenever they exceeded the limits of their role, narrowly defined as the elimination of counterrevolutionary intrigues. As we have seen, moreover, the electoral process left them no space in which to operate, since in the absence of declared candidacies there was no official need to organize or guide citizens in their choices. The two-stage voting system made this system possible by instituting a different procedure for reducing the number of people involved. The few hundred second-stage voters responsible for electing the deputies from each *département* were often chosen in a rather confused manner, but one could assume that the final choice was based on personal knowledge of those individuals who emerged victorious from the ballot box. All this would change with the introduction of direct suffrage under the Restoration. Despite the restrictions of the *censitaire* regime, which imposed property qualifications on suffrage, the number of "real" voters (those who effectively chose the representatives) increased considerably under this system.[28] The problem of organizing candidacies thus took new forms. Once it was no longer materially feasible to prohibit organized candidacies, the question of *electoral committees* arose. Although political *parties* were not yet envisioned (the word retaining much of the negative, factional connotation it had in the eighteenth century), the practical implementation of the electoral process was the order of the day.

It nevertheless took some time before the first electoral committees were established. In the early years of the Restoration, elections were still in effect confined to the social circles of the prominent. Elections were nothing like those with which we are familiar today. Voters assembled in meetings that could last hours or even days. They elected officers, listened to patriotic speeches by the chair of the session, and did not adjourn until all business was concluded, which, if no candidate commanded an immediate majority, could take a considerable period of time. We might call this procedure *assembly voting* (with electors forming a "college"), and one observer described it as a "high-society function" rather than a truly political event.[29] Nevertheless, the liberal-ultra divide ran through most of these assemblies. There was no rigorous organization of these factions, however, though it was not uncommon to see published brochures for both sides addressed to the several hundred electors in each *département*. We do find unofficial committees forming to influence the elections of 1819, and later we will encounter some of the criticism that this aroused, but in any case this development did not go very far.[30] Everything changed with the election of 1828. Long years of ultra power had led the liberal camp to organize against what had become a stiflingly reactionary regime. In 1827 the younger generation of the movement—men like Guizot, François Mignet, Rémusat, Charles Marie Tanneguy Duchâtel, and Ludovic Vitet, together with various more radical elements—took the initiative to form a society called Help Yourself and Heaven Will Help You, which was conceived as an action committee to coordinate the election campaign.[31] A manifesto was drafted, a subscription drive was launched, and 100,000 copies of a *Manual for the Juror-Voter* were published, a truly extraordinary figure for the time. Local committees were formed in nearly all *départements,* the initial objective being to persuade voters to register on the voting lists (which coincided with the jury lists). Nearly all of these committees published brochures of their own, adapted from those drafted in Paris.[32] A central committee was simultaneously established by leaders of the movement. This committee was the first glimmering of a modern political party in France.[33]

Did these committees fall within the scope of Article 291, which required authorization for all meetings involving more than twenty people? A case was brought on this basis in 1819 against the Société des Amis de la Presse, which had been created in 1817 to collect funds to pay the fines meted out to writers for violations of the press laws. This group was accused of acting during elections as a head committee in correspondence with affiliated local societies (and the indictment also mentioned an associated "central committee").[34] Sanctions were imposed. The founders of Help Yourself and Heaven Will Help You took steps to avoid repeating the same outcome. Their manifesto acknowledged the existence of an association but stressed that there were "no secret associations or shadowy plots" and no violation of Article 291 because the associations in question were temporary and met only irregularly.[35] It also insisted that as a matter of practical necessity, voters had to be able to communicate if the right to vote was to have any real meaning. After some hesitation, apparently, the government decided not to crack down on the group.

In the spring of 1828, when the Chamber of Peers was presented with a petition from fifty-nine voters in Niort complaining that the prefect had refused to grant their committee legal recognition, it refused to rule that the group was illegal.[36] Benjamin Constant spoke in favor of "the right, indeed the duty, of citizens to meet to discuss their choices when they are called upon to elect a deputy . . . The alleged head committees are legal assemblies."[37] The ministry backed this position. In an important circular sent out to prefects, Jean-Baptiste de Martignac wrote:

In several *départements* assemblies have formed under the denomination of bureaus, electoral consultative committees, or analogous terms with the announced purpose of facilitating the registration of entitled individ-

uals as voters or jurors . . . These groups fall outside our laws. No express
provision of our law is applicable to them. None prohibits their formation. None regulates the conditions under which they exist. So long as
they do not disrupt public order by illegal acts or written texts deserving
of the attention of the courts, you need not take any steps against them.[38]

This decision left matters in legal limbo, but the recognition of electoral
committees was in any case clearly separated from the general question of
the right of association. This "exception" to the rigorous reign of generality
was sanctioned by the July regime. Even after the crackdown on associations was reinforced in 1834, the government instructed the minister of
justice to clarify its position to the Chamber: "Electoral meetings are not
within the purview of the present law. We are making a law against associations, not against accidental and temporary assemblies for the purpose of
exercising a constitutional right."[39] It thus acknowledged that an electoral
committee could not be considered an ordinary intermediary body, that it
was merely a sort of technical interface, a simple material extension of the
recognized right of suffrage.

Electoral committees thus encountered no obstacles in establishing themselves under the July Monarchy, whereas other political associations were
harshly persecuted, while at the same time, as we shall see in due course, a
monistic vision of the social to rival that of the revolutionary period took
firm hold. So, for instance, in 1837, a Democratic Central Committee led
by Etienne Arago, Louis Blanc, and Dupont de l'Eure came into being. In
the summer of 1845, with a dissolution of the Chamber impending, two
committees were established on the left. When the dissolution was announced in 1846, a powerful Central Committee of the Opposition was organized with branches in all *départements*.[40] The governmental right also
established networks of its own,[41] while Charles Forbes de Montalembert
put together an important Electoral Committee for the Defense of Religious Liberty. Electoral committees thus became a regular feature of the
electoral process. The advent of universal suffrage in 1848 consecrated
their role in two ways.[42] Legally and politically their role was confirmed by
recognition of the right of association. At several points the provisional
government explicitly called upon citizens to form committees to discuss
candidacies and participate in the electoral process.[43] But the formation of
committees was also seen as a technical necessity given the vast numbers of
people voting under universal suffrage; the procedure of voting by lists

only reinforced this necessity. A newspaper in the Beaujolais explained this in terms worth reproducing verbatim:

> How would [the voters] understand one another if there were no organization to help them evaluate the qualifications of the competitors and allow them to express their attitude toward each candidate before the election? How could candidates hope to win if their candidacies were left to chance? How can this mass of more than 100,000 voters proceed in an orderly manner, aim for a definite goal, or see where it is being led unless someone imparts a direction to it and points out the path it ought to follow and the goal it ought to seek? Electoral committees are indispensable for achieving a common understanding.[44]

It was thus for technical reasons that electoral committees came to be seen as integral to the right to vote, of which they were merely an extension.

— 8 —

Resistance and Reconfiguration

Ineffective Criticism

The vision of generality passed on by the men of 1789 was essentially political. Their intention was to affirm the unity of society, to posit the nation as an indecomposable whole. This original significance of generality continued to be decisive in the nineteenth century, and the prospect of "states within the state" was still seen as a terrible menace. We shall encounter some recurring manifestations of this later on. By itself, however, this persistent cult of unity would probably not have been enough to withstand the pressure to admit that revitalized intermediary bodies might play a positive role in social life. In the preceding chapters I therefore stressed the terms in which an imperative of governability, a sociological constraint, and an insistence on liberty chipped away at the initial suspicion of agencies situated between the state and individuals. The issue of decentralization, which has come up in several contexts, is exemplary in this respect. Fervent pleas in favor of decentralization were heard throughout the early years of the Restoration, and reform proposals from a variety of angles could soon have filled an ample library. Yet for a long time the French model of centralization remained unaffected by all this. There is much to be learned here. In the 1820s, opinions seemed to converge on the idea of decentralization as a symbol of the reforms needed to give real influence to the new spirit of association, which it was hoped would bring the shattered society together while guaranteeing basic freedoms. The issue of municipal and departmental reform therefore remained on the agenda throughout this period. After the fall of Charles X, the newly installed July regime made action in this area one of its most urgent priorities. Yet none of this ferment and urgency yielded tangible results. How can we explain why a need for reform that seemed so obvious failed to become a reality? Why did repeated denunciation of the destructive consequences of a society shaped by utopian generality not give rise to the correctives called for by reformers? An analysis of this capacity to resist pressure is essential. Indeed, the key to understanding the French model lies in this negative dialectic between the political culture and critiques of that culture.

Why, moreover, did the French not draw the consequences from their obsessively analyzed aversion to an all-powerful, omnipresent state? In virtually no other country in the nineteenth century do we find such an abundance of criticism of bureaucracy, and of the allegedly exorbitant power of functionaries accused of being divorced from reality. From the turn of the century on, denunciation of bureaucracy became almost a literary genre unto itself. From the panoramas of Ymbert to the satires of Georges Courteline, the verve of the pamphlet writers never let up. It would be no exaggeration to say that nineteenth-century France wrote the book on criticism of the centralized state. "Decentralization! Decentralization! That is the cry that resounds everywhere nowadays, expressing one of the most imperious needs of the day," according to one mid-century commentator.[1] Decentralization had its manifestos, its committees, its journals and newspapers. It had its cult books and the most eloquent of advocates. The list of its champions, from Constant to Tocqueville, from Proudhon to Lucien Anatole Prévost-Paradol, from Ernest Renan to Taine, spans virtually the entire gamut of French political thought. It was a powerful movement whose charges were backed by glaring facts, yet nothing came of it. Why? To answer this question is to penetrate to the heart of the French enigma.

This chapter will look at various factors that can help us to understand how Jacobinism reorganized and reestablished itself in the first half of the nineteenth century. The influence of the political culture of utopian generality was not merely a continuation of the forces that led to its inception. Although there is no denying its durability, the French model was able to overcome the resistance it faced throughout its history by reconfiguring itself in the face of challenge. It adapted in four ways: by reformulating the centralizing impulse in administrative terms, by broadening the definition of generality, by "liberalizing" Jacobinism, and by invoking democracy as grounds for criticizing intermediary bodies. At a more basic level, moreover, circumstances helped to ensure the permanence of the French model, and it is those circumstances that I examine first.

Order and Opportunism

Circumstances and their attendant conflicts played an important role in the rejection of intermediary bodies. This fact becomes clear when we look at decentralization. It would of course be possible in this case as elsewhere to point to various forms of inertia and hidden bottlenecks that prevented ideas from becoming realities. The analytical tools forged by the sociology of organizations can help clarify many things by demonstrating how special interests "internal" to the state apparatus operated. This analysis does not go far enough, however, given the many potent factors promoting decentralization. One fact is too stark to overlook: those who were the most ardent decentralizers while in opposition invariably seemed less motivated once they held the reins of power. This phenomenon was particularly flagrant when Villèle became president of the council in 1822 and suddenly forgot that he had been an outspoken apostle of local liberties. It was also apparent when the Martignac ministry abandoned reforms it had proposed in 1829,[2] and again in 1848. It may come as something of a surprise, for instance, to learn that Tocqueville remained silent on the subject in 1848 and felt that it was inappropriate even to raise the issue before the committee entrusted with drafting a new constitution, although this was only ten years after he had theoretically expounded and vigorously denounced centralization as "the French disease"!

In France the banner of decentralization was of course often brandished by political minorities. In 1816 and again in 1819, for example, Guizot made fun of legitimists who hoped to find in the *communes* the power from which they were excluded in the government.[3] By contrast, it is no surprise to find François-Dominique de Montlosier somewhat later mocking liberals who, "having been unable to establish the Republic from above, are now trying to establish it from below."[4] Examples are also abundant for other periods. It might indeed be worthwhile to take a fresh look at the whole history of abortive decentralization proposals with an eye to measuring the importance of opportunism as an explanatory variable. It was far from negligible.

Throughout the nineteenth century, fear of disorder also played a decisive role in fostering suspicion of intermediary bodies. The specter of "popular societies" and workers' coalitions loomed whenever associations were mentioned. This was clear as early as 1810, when Article 291 of the Penal Code was introduced. The rapporteur in the Corps Législatif saw only "deplorable memories" in the word "association."[5] The conditions under which the complementary law on associations of 1834 was passed reveal this attitude even more strikingly. (Recall that this was an important text because it provided for considerably harsher penalties than did Article 291.)[6] To be sure, it was debated in troubled times. In Paris and Lyons, riots and demonstrations by workers had been going on almost without letup since 1831. First the Société des Amis du Peuple and later the Société des Droits de l'Homme et du Citoyen had learned to coordinate the action of resurgent republican groups, and worker coalitions fed by discontent born of economic depression were proliferating. These early years of the July Monarchy thus bore the mark of chronic political and social unrest. The regime, obsessed by the need to restore order, therefore made stamping out associations a central element of its policy. Barthe, the justice minister who presented the proposal, saw associations as instruments "aimed at destroying institutions and laws" and forming "a sort of insurrectional government" representing a minority of society that had allegedly "declared war on the mores and laws of the vast majority."[7]

No other parliamentary debate in this period revealed as clearly or bluntly the reigning bourgeois ideology. In a context dominated by elemental social fears and without the linguistic subterfuge that limited suffrage had allowed, the rejection of associations was rooted in an obsession with disorder. Legal, philosophical, and sociological arguments carried little weight in this context. Dupin Aîné, for instance, maintained that the right of association did not fall under the head of individual freedom, since every association was by its very nature a corporation.[8] Emile de Kératry meanwhile explained that association was a way of bringing individuals together characteristic of "societies in their infancy," a primitive form of the social contract.[9] Yet among the men of July it was far more common to speak in terms considerably blunter than this, and without such elaborate oratorical subterfuge or logical subtleties. Speakers were more likely to evoke "the stifling atmosphere of 1793" and to denounce the popular societies for "corrupting the Revolution of 1789."[10] Guizot, then minister of public instruction, set the tone for the ruling majority. He was blunt: "Security for respectable members of society: that, gentlemen, is the rule that guides our policy, and that is why we believe that associations represent so great a danger."[11] Hence there was no need to tread carefully: "We do not intend to wait until associations have committed crimes; we intend to prevent crimes by banning associations," Guizot continued with equal candor. Nor were the frightened gentlemen in the legislature interested in subtle distinctions among types of groups. All were to be banned as a way of ensuring the restoration of order. To be sure, lip service was paid to the idea that "true associations" existed. Some speakers mentioned literary societies, for instance. But no one wanted to restrict the law in any way: "The most dangerous associations might all too easily have evaded the requirements of the law. All associations therefore had to be subjected to a common rule," in the view of the rapporteur in the Chamber of Peers.[12] Earlier thoughts about the role of intermediary bodies were thus summarily dismissed. The trouble was that the fundamental question became confused with the circumstantial argument in the minds of contemporaries, who therefore lost sight of the former.[13]

The obsession with order in this period was also significant in another way: beyond the fear of association, it amounted to a stigmatization of the idea of a minority and an opposition, which were themselves perceived as threats.[14] Indeed, the hope was that the majority could rule without opposition or protest of any kind, a view that allowed for no middle ground between routinized government and insurrection. The celebration of the bourgeois order can thus be seen as an extension of the Jacobin worldview. It was a paradoxical extension, however, in that it was expressed in a totally "pacified" form while partaking of Jacobinism's exclusionary radicalism. The persistence of the political culture of generality in France was not unrelated to the existence of this moderate absolutism. To be sure, men like Berryer, Lamartine, Odilon Barrot, and Portalis spoke out against the proposal in the Chamber of Deputies. Memories of demonstrations against the law in April remained fresh in everyone's mind. Yet the fact that the 1834 law was not repealed until 1901 proves that behind the circumstantial reasons for its passage more powerful forces were at work.

This is not the place to rehearse the history of the various circumstantial laws that restricted the right of association in France. The legislation of 1849 on clubs was particularly significant, however. Less than a year after the enthusiastic outpouring of the spring of 1848, which witnessed both a celebration of association and a flourishing of political societies, severe restrictions were imposed on the existence of clubs and their activities.[15] In this case the law of 19 June 1849 was initially presented as a stopgap measure. Now the threat to public order that was to be avoided was "the dangers of socialism."[16] The Second Republic had to renew the law twice, first in 1850 and again in 1851, to keep it on the books. In nineteenth-century

France it was sometimes hard to distinguish between "exceptional circumstances" that tended to become permanent and the old *doctrinaire* reluctance to accept the existence of associations.

Administrative Reformulation

As we have seen, the culture of generality initially combined two main influences: a unitary conception of the nation forged by the Revolution, coupled with an older political rationalism. Although the rationalizing character of French centralization was reinforced over the course of the nineteenth century, the monist vision of the social was open to challenge. One might characterize this reformulation of the culture of generality as "administrative," and the ability of the Jacobin model to withstand criticism was greatly enhanced by it. The administrative system established by the celebrated consular law of 28 Pluviôse, Year VIII, was justified primarily on the grounds that it would make government action more efficient. The goal was no longer the same as in the fall of 1789: to design an administrative organization that would contribute to the establishment of a united egalitarian society. "From the First Consul to the mayor of a village in the Pyrenees, everything is connected; all the links of the chain are in place," one of the organs of the new regime commented. "The government will be able to move rapidly because it has a direct line to every locality in the country. *Obedience* is everywhere and *opposition* nowhere. The government has all the instruments it needs, and nothing stands in its way."[17] In a similar vein, the minister of the interior, Jean-Antoine Chaptal, rejoiced that "orders and laws can be transmitted with the speed of the electric fluid," thus making it possible to administer an empire of forty million people.

Thirty years later, Adolphe Thiers invoked the same grounds in his successful effort to thwart attempts to increase local powers, which many of his contemporaries favored. In a memorable speech in 1833, he portrayed himself as the defender of "old opinions," meaning opinions of the revolutionary era. He evoked the specter of anarchy to denounce the danger that would result from "37,000 little states within the larger state" and attacked the "reactionaries" who wanted to emancipate localities.[18] For him, decentralization would open the door to laxity of every sort, create new feudal strongholds, and plunge France right back into the Old Regime. Thiers was a "liberal" who boasted of his admiration for the Convention and Napoleon. He had no words strong enough to celebrate the benefits and beauties of centralization, which as he saw it made France the envy of all the world. "Can one imagine anything more admirable," he asked, "than a government that, thanks to the telegraph, can be sure of commanding within instants the obedience of the most remote corners of the kingdom? . . . The influence of the center on the extremities and of the extremities on the center is felt constantly. Thirty-two million of you live together as if assembled in the public square, thanks to your press, which has worked wonders. Owing to the press, people think but a single thought from Dunkirk to Perpignan. Thanks to the press, the same order is carried out with astonishing promptness throughout France. It is this perfect unity that has given you the means to achieve matchless power."[19] Hence municipal liberties were harmful in the first instance because they interfered with the action of the administration.

Similar criticism was directed at those who proposed restoring corporatist forms of organization in order to make economy and society easier to govern. In this connection, Vital-Roux's 1805 *Rapport sur les jurandes et les maîtrises* for the Paris Chamber of Commerce was typical. This thick document offered a methodical defense of the practical superiority of "liberal statism" over government through intermediary bodies. Vital-Roux's first concern was to restore the debate to what he considered its proper context: "The abuses of unrestricted liberty have led people to forget those of exclusive corporations."[20] His critique of proposals to restore corporations was developed around three essential points: first, corporatist forms of organization were intimately associated with privilege; second, the market offered a superior system of economic regulation; and finally, where restrictive rules were necessary, it was better that they be formulated and administered in terms of public laws.

"The history of corporations is nothing but a long series of rigorously enforced privileges."[21] In making this point, Vital-Roux was merely following in the footsteps of the men of 1789. His lengthy attacks on "the partiality and injustice" inherent in the corporatist spirit were intended more to demonstrate his attachment to the new France and tax his adversaries with backwardness than to put forward original arguments. His plea on behalf of the market was equally conventional, but his arguments were more solid than those of eighteenth-century economists, who had been largely content to denounce the perverse effects of the corporatist system and the dysfunctions to which it gave rise (such as slowing innovation and distorting competition in such a way as to keep prices artificially high). By contrast, Vital-Roux tried to show that regulation by the market yielded *better information*. The interests and tastes of consumers were "more perspicacious than all the regulations" of the corporations because consumers constantly evaluated their needs and weighed one against another. Corporate syndics were thus useless as intermediaries, because they were more costly and less accurate than market signals in transmitting information about the state of consumer needs. "The consumer is the sovereign judge," he emphasized. "His is the only competent tribunal, from which there is no appeal . . . For one cannot change the will of the consumer. *One cannot be cleverer than he is, by virtue of his experience.*"[22]

If consumer taste was thus "the most useful rule for all manufacturers to follow,"[23] Vital-Roux nevertheless recognized the need for certain rules of public order (such as public health regulations governing the sale of meat), although he tended to place greater emphasis on consumer vigilance than on administrative surveillance.[24] In such cases, however, public laws were more effective than professional authorities. Only such public laws could guarantee both efficiency and impartiality, in his view.[25] In other words, the most effective regulation would result from a combination of the market with public laws and a rational administration. Such a two-pronged approach was the only way to prevent disorder and dysfunctionality. Corporations suffered from two related defects: they were neither "particular" enough where particularity was needed (for the decentralized management of a large volume of information) nor "general" enough when it came to enforcing rules. As far as Vital-Roux was concerned, it was the very idea of intermediary bodies that was faulty. As he saw it, no intermediary was possible between regulation by law and regulation by the market, between administrative intervention and the role of the consumer, between the individual and the nation.[26] There was only one economy of information and action, and this provided the basis on which he rejected intermediary bodies. On the one hand, the market itself offered a sufficient interface, while on the other hand, only administrative action could effectively reach every part of the society. "If the number of intermediaries between the people and the government is increased," he wrote, "the work of the public administration is impeded, while the chain binding subjects to the state is unnecessarily made heavier. The administration has no need of master tradesmen to bring its benefits to the people whom it administers."[27]

In contrast to a Vincent de Gournay or a Turgot, in other words, Vital-Roux was not content to rest his case on natural liberty. He wanted both more market and more legislation (when legislation was needed). For him, the goal was to concentrate in one place all rules governing manufacturing (rights and duties of workers, patents for inventions, and so on). All effort should therefore be directed to the establishment of a true *industrial code* covering all aspects of manufacturing.[28] Such a "monument of legislation" would constitute a counterpart to the Civil Code in its own realm and make it possible to establish an efficient government of generality far superior to that which would result from the usual overlapping of corporatist regulations. Vital-Roux thus showed himself to be a proponent of the rationalistic view of the state and the law whose origins and successive forms we have examined. In one of the first major treatises on French administrative law, Louis-Antoine Macarel summed up the idea as follows: "An enlightened government must look at industry from a general point of view. It must regard itself as a kind of providence, which observes the whole range of events from a very lofty height, abstracting entirely from individuals and the interests of localities."[29]

Vital-Roux's report was exemplary. Instead of simply examining the 1805 petition by winesellers to reestablish a corporatist system of organization, it laid out a complete and coherent doctrine. It developed a true "theory of generality" for public action in the economic sphere. It was to the early nineteenth century what the Le Chapelier law had been to the Revolution: a symbol of the French model put forward by a thinker. That is why the report should be regarded as a major document. It was repeatedly cited, indeed pillaged, by everyone who took part in the debate on this issue during the Restoration. Jean-Baptiste Say, Benjamin Constant, Prosper Duvergier de Hauranne, Chaptal, Dupin, Ganil, and of course all the functionaries and merchants tapped to defend the commercial order or the prerogatives of the state would recite their Vital-Roux. The only novel contributions to the debate would come from jurists, who proposed a new theory of economic regulation intended to make it easier to adapt legal rules to the complexities of the real economy.[30]

Significantly, the administrative relegitimation of the Jacobin model was accompanied by vigorous criticism of theories claiming to take the place of the only recognized general science of society, namely, political science, or the art of government. Thus we find the "liberal" officials of the July Monarchy strenuously opposing political economy's claim to define the general interest. In one of the pioneering works of the discipline, *De la liberté du travail,* Charles Dunoyer posed the problem as follows: "Of the two sciences, that of politics and that of political economy, which is more naturally and more appropriately suited to treat society?"[31] His answer was unequivocal: "This role should indisputably be awarded to political economy. To abandon the study of society to politics is to reduce it to far too limited an object . . . Only political economy is concerned essentially with society, with its nature, object, and purpose . . . Hence only political economy can speak properly of society in a general way."[32] This view was vigorously opposed by men such as Guizot and Thiers. For them, only the state could claim to administer generality in a rational way, and thus political science was the only form of knowledge that could claim to shed light on the operation of society as a whole. The administrative cult of political centralization thus gave rise to a sort of "epistemological Jacobinism," which proposed a general science of society standing above all other modes of knowledge. This would serve as the intellectual basis for resisting the formation of new intermediary bodies.

Generality's New Guises

Of course the administrative reformulation of the Jacobin spirit is not enough to explain the observed resistance to the revival of intermediary bodies. Other factors played a part. One of the most important of these was the fact that this was not the only response to the advent of a society of individuals. To overcome the "sociability deficit" in postrevolutionary society, three broad options presented themselves: the constitution of a new aristocracy, new conceptions of order and organization, and renewal of the social bond by way of a new religion. In each case, the proposed remedy to social disintegration ran *counter* to the traditional understanding of intermediary bodies.

It was chiefly among the *doctrinaire* liberals that the effort to overcome the fear of numbers and find a new way to make society governable again took the form of redefining aristocracy. They sought a new principle of social control and stability in the relationship between elites and masses. Prosper de Barante summed up their point of view well in a book that was widely read and commented on, *Des communes et de l'aristocratie.*[33] "For the past thirty years," he wrote in 1820, "the constitution of society has never been less aristocratic, individuals have never been more isolated from one another, and the public spirit has never been more attenuated."[34] The solution? In order to "rebuild the nation," society would have to be reorganized around real elites. There could be no stable society, indeed no society at all, the *doctrinaires* insisted, without a true aristocracy at its center: such was the gist of their message. All their efforts went into defining and shaping that aristocracy. They never tired of reminding people of the etymological sense of aristocracy: government of the best. Only such a concept of aristocracy, together with the concept of self-interest as its polar opposite, could breathe life into the social bond.[35] "Superiority perceived and accepted is the original and legitimate bond of human societies," wrote Guizot. "It is at once fact and right [*le fait et le droit*]. *It is the true and only social contract.*" Furthermore, "power belongs to superiority. Among equals it would never exist."[36] The distinction between governors and governed rested on the superiority of the former over the latter: for Guizot, that was the basis of any ordered society. In this respect his sociology and his political philosophy were inextricably intertwined.

In the minds of the *doctrinaires,* this "new" mobile aristocracy deployed within egalitarian society stood in stark contrast to the exclusive, privileged aristocracies of the Old Regime. Modern society, by virtue of its functional and organizational superiority, was able to stand on its head the old representation of the relation of individuals to situations. "Society," Guizot wrote, "consists of just two elements, individuals and situations. Situations are facts; real individuals possess rights. The flaw of previous legislation was that it considered individuals only in terms of situations and thus sacrificed rights to facts. The principle of modern legislation will be to recognize rights where they really exist, which is to say in individuals, and to return facts, which is to say social situations, to the natural course of things."[37] Under these conditions, the new aristocracy would not be able to stand still and close its ranks. It would also be a positive and flexible principle of order. The new aristocracy was thus the appropriate solution for the problem of postrevolutionary society. It would perform the *functions* of the old local administrations and associations in the new egalitarian world of mobile individuals. In the new aristocracy, the recognition of particularity and the practice of generality would support each other.

A second remedy for social disintegration was proposed in the 1820s, in the form of a project to establish a new organic unity and impose a novel form of leadership. The works of Saint-Simon and Auguste Comte were particularly influential in this regard. For Saint-Simon, the goal was to restore order not by consolidating the social structure itself but by imagining new ways of managing it. In his eyes, the major problem was the impotence of modern politics. "My ambition is to give politics a positive character": such was his program as he stated it in his early works. His solution was to promote a new "science of social organization."[38] What Saint-Simon had in mind was a reorganization of society *from above*. Thus the new politics should be viewed as yet another attempt to rationalize social management and administration. The government of men was transformed into the administration of things.

Comte sought to systematize this effort after the death of his teacher in 1825. He criticized Saint-Simon for having drifted toward a philosophy more sentimental and religious in its outlook than truly scientific. Comte's ambition was also to bolster and give structure to society by developing a *positive politics*. Like Saint-Simon, he borrowed from the *doctrinaires* the idea of a new ruling class destined to play a structuring role. He accordingly called for "a class . . . constantly and exclusively occupied with providing general rules of conduct for the other classes of society."[39] But his primary objective was to elaborate a social science (social physics) that would reveal the organizing structures at work behind the appearance of aimlessness, as well as to develop a theory of order that would enable post-revolutionary society to establish itself on a durable footing. The work of both Saint-Simon and Comte left an indelible mark on their contemporaries. Indeed, they made it possible to update and reformulate the rationalist approach to politics and thus to offer a novel *managerial* solution to the ills of atomized society. The idea of reinstating or reinventing intermediary bodies was thus discredited from this angle as well.

Rather than reorganize civil society and grant it increased autonomy, many people expected that the necessary associative tonic would come from a revival of religious feeling. Among the apostles of such an approach, Lamennais naturally stands out. He was one of the first to emphasize the intrinsic social function of Christianity. "Religion is not only necessary to society," he wrote in one of his earliest texts; "it *is* society, and a unified nation can never be created from a group of men who share no common beliefs, which are the basis of common rights."[40] For him, the absence of religion was to blame for the disintegration of society; as he put it, "civil society does not exist because it is above all religious society."[41] This was one of the major themes of his *Essai sur l'indifférence en matière de religion*. One of the key ideas of this immensely influential book was that no society can rest solely on a human foundation, for spiritual society must exist prior to civil society. Without religion, Lamennais believed, there could be no society, only unrelated individuals whom no social contract or association could organize. To renounce the spiritual power was thus tantamount to annihilating society.

The remarkable thing is that Lamennais's vision was not confined to circles bent on a traditionalist revival. It was widely shared. We have seen, moreover, that religious sentiment came to occupy an increasingly important place in Saint-Simon's thinking. Even in his earliest writing he did not shrink from stating that religion was "the only kind of political institution that aims at the organization of humanity."[42] Ultimately Saint-Simon came to think of religious society as organic, as is evident from his last book, *Nouveau Christianisme* (1825). His disciples followed this logic to its natural conclusion, creating a veritable "Saint-Simonian religion" under the aegis of Prosper Enfantin in the 1830s. Auguste Comte also followed this path. There wasn't a single utopian or socialist in this period who did not see the formation of a transfigured religion as the solution to the woes of the age. Pierre Leroux, for example, called for a "new religion of humanity," and this formula was soon picked up by many other writers, as well as drawing comment at the Sorbonne and the Collège de France. For the author of *Réfutation de l'éclectisme,* the true philosophy would inevitably become a religion.[43] That was how the associative ideal, of which Leroux was one of the most inspired prophets, would become a reality. Also worth mentioning is Etienne Cabet, who proposed a Jacobin interpretation of the Gospel in *Le Vrai Christianisme selon Jésus-Christ* (1846). In order to do justice to the relation between the religious sentiment and the effort to promote social regeneration, we would need to explore the history of ideas in this period in all its ramifications.

Historians like Michelet and Quinet also turned to the idea of a new religion of the human race in search of a way to a more harmonious world. To be sure, their religion was rather vague, little more than a diffuse spiritualism serving as a sort of prop to the democratic ideal, but they expected much from it in the way of giving substance to modern society. It was supposed to put people in tune with one another, reduce their isolation, and "strip the individual for the sake of enriching the species," in Quinet's remarkable formulation.[44] In short, religion was to provide a real remedy for social disintegration. For Michelet it was France and all mankind that embodied the new reunifying god. "I call upon you, my noble country, to assist me," he proclaimed. "You must take the place of the God who has

slipped from our grasp and fill in us the incommensurable abyss left by ex-
tinct Christianity. You must be for us the equivalent of infinity. We all feel
our individuality dying. May the sentiment of social generality, of human
universality, of the world, be born anew."[45] What Michelet hoped to see was
a true transfiguration of generality. The failure of revolutionary unity was
thus redeemed by the adoption of a new guise.

Ways of Jacobin Liberalism

The reluctance to regard intermediary bodies as instruments of freedom,
means of action, ways of defending individual and group autonomy and
organizing institutions of government was also rooted in French liberalism
itself. The impulse to discredit and reject associations did not come only
from "outside," from the Jacobinism that supposedly embodied the dark
side of French political culture. Jacobinism did not simply persist; it un-
derwent a *liberal recomposition*. This phenomenon was made unmistak-
ably clear for the first time in the arguments that the *doctrinaires* raised
against ultra decentralization proposals during the Restoration. The essence of their case is contained in a well-known article that Guizot published in 1818.[46]

In that text Guizot traced the history of liberty as a struggle for emancipation. "Under an absolute government, in which all power is concentrated in the hands of the supreme royal authority, which is answerable to
no one, citizens enjoy no protections against the exercise of this central authority and therefore need to seek them elsewhere. They kneel in capitula-
tion before the sovereign and establish their defenses where they can. Thus
the courts became political bodies, and provinces and municipalities constantly sought privileges, independence, and anything else that might enable them to minimize the damage and enhance their security in the face
of the unchallenged actions of the supreme authority." In other words,
Guizot limited the utility of the various types of intermediary bodies to the
predemocratic age. He thus accepted the aristocratic theory of liberty but
only to historicize it and circumscribe its validity. The advent of representative government led in effect to an "emancipation within the emancipation" transcending its initial forms. "Now, the principle and form of our
government are no longer the same," Guizot went on.

> Its principle is the greater good of all with respect for the rights of each.
> Its essential form is public debate, which ensures that its principle is not

forgotten but guides its action. Therein lie all the citizen's guarantees. Voting on taxes, elections, freedom of the press, an independent judiciary, the right of petition—these constitute a complete system of defense of his civil rights. How much less perfect would these safeguards be if one were to look to a local institution to provide them?[47]

"In ages of political freedom, centralization seems to offer nothing but advantages," Rémusat summed up for his part;[48] while Thiers, still more incisive, insisted that "liberty requires unity" and accused the ultras of being the sort of people "who prefer liberties to liberty."[49] The *doctrinaires* held steady, as we see clearly in 1831 and 1833, when they were obliged to institute reforms of departmental and municipal administrations in the wake of the July uprising. Prosper de Barante, the rapporteur on the departmental proposal, offered a very sharp appraisal of the benefits likely to result from granting increased powers to decentralized institutions:

> Local administration, as our mores, laws, and social constitution have made it, does not encompass our primary rights, those that we hold dearest and most sacred. The word *commune,* which in the Middle Ages had such an impressive ring and was once almost synonymous with the nation, today has a limited and modest significance. Civil liberty, the protection of individuals and property, the administration of justice, the apportionment and manner of taxation—all of these things are governed by the constitution of the state and not that of the *commune.* For forty years, no liberty has been granted to us or taken from us by changes in the local administration.[50]

For all these men, it was generality in the form of (representative) political power and its closely associated legal forms rather than particularity that offered protection against oppression. Oppression, in their view, arose exclusively from the threat of particularity as arbitrariness.[51] "If the central mechanism of the Charter is sufficient to maintain public liberties and general rights," Guizot observed, "any impediment to that mechanism is a cause of disorder."[52] To protect was thus to centralize.[53] The liberals of the 1820s continued to insist on this point. An article published in *Le Globe* in 1829 put it strikingly:

> Historically, the existence and even independence of cities preceded the advent of all political liberty. It was indeed characteristic of the Middle Ages that practically everything was particular and local, and liberty be-

gan with the extremities. The philosophical civilization of the Moderns has proceeded in the opposite order. It generalized everything first and then gradually descended the ladder of generalization, particularizing as it went. Since the beginning of the revolution, politics and legislation have followed no other path. Liberty radiates from the center to the extremities.[54]

The author of the article thus sketched out a whole philosophy of liberty against the background of the history of centralization over the centuries. In this as in other areas, Guizot established the interpretive framework, most notably in his celebrated 1828 course on the history of European civilization. Two major achievements characterized that civilization, in his view: the formation of nation-states (reflecting centralization and embodying a principle of unity) and emancipation of the human spirit (reflecting a move toward greater liberty and embodying a principle of equality). Guizot divided this history into three broad periods. The first ran from the beginning to the twelfth century and was characterized by fragmentation: separation of social estates (feudal nobility, clergy, communes), geographical division, and, in law, complex overlapping jurisdictions. The middle period, from the thirteenth to the sixteenth centuries, saw the emergence of nation-states. Political power was secularized and began to integrate the diverse local powers inherited from the feudal period. Finally, the modern period involved a simplification of the social associated with the process of centralization. In place of the spirit of specialty and localism, two important new tropes emerged under the impetus of the monarchy: the people and the government. In parallel with this sociopolitical movement, man's spiritual evolution, driven by developments within Christianity, culminated in the Reformation of the sixteenth century, which marked a decisive advance for scientific inquiry and freedom of thought. Thus for Guizot, modernity began in the sixteenth century, when the Reformation converged with the centralized nation-state. But this convergence also initiated a crisis, in that the principle of free inquiry was to a degree in contradiction with the principle of centralization of power, "the former being the defeat of absolute power in the spiritual realm, the latter its victory in the temporal realm." The resolution of this contradiction, Guizot argued, came in the form of representative government, which synthesized centralization with liberty. This analysis broke sharply with customary interpretations of French history. Few of Guizot's contemporaries (with the notable exception of Edgar Quinet) would follow him in his assessment of the historical role of Protestantism, but this fact simply meant that his demonstration of the progressive role of centralization was appreciated all the more.

Guizot's philosophy attracted a good deal of support, to the consternation of the *sociological* champions of stronger intermediary bodies as a way of diminishing the effects of social atomization. Guizot's concept of liberties was also related to a very specific vision of democracy, which I have called *polarized*: the central institutions were said to "express" sovereignty in its entirety, the voice of the people being represented entirely by the results of elections.[55] One influential deputy summed it up perfectly in 1821: "When power is absolute at the summit of society, democracy is useful in inferior institutions; when democracy tempers power at its source, inferior institutions should be that much less popular."[56] Duvergier de Hauranne even used the term "democratic anarchy" to characterize a regime in which democratic principles and procedures fed into the society.[57] Thus the ardor for centralization concealed a certain fear of universal suffrage and popular intervention. There was dread at the thought of not being able to control pressures from below that had been successfully contained by property qualifications on voting and representative government.

This apology for centralization—"liberal" even before it was republican—might seem to be a somewhat watered-down version of the old "Jacobinism." Indeed, it falls within our definition of the political culture of generality, with its unitary conception of the nation, polarization of public and private, preeminence of the law, and so on. But it was above all a *pacified adaptation* of that culture, divorced from revolutionary imagery and formulas; and this adaptation allowed it to establish itself permanently at the center of gravity of French political culture. "Jacobin liberalism" derived its strength from the fact that it linked a philosophy of power with a philosophy of liberty, refusing to consider the latter in isolation. It was by way of liberalism that Jacobinism acclimatized itself in France. That is why it easily supplanted "traditional" liberalism, which had always enjoyed the support of some of the country's most brilliant and profound writers, from Benjamin Constant to Prévost-Paradol, Daunou to Edouard Laboulaye, and Tocqueville to Paul Leroy-Beaulieu. But its failure to constitute a culture of government allowed men like Guizot and Thiers to place themselves at the center of action. Thiers did not even mention the issue of local collectivities or associations in his celebrated Address of 11 January 1864, in which he discussed the five necessary liberties.[58]

Charles Dupont-White exemplified the culture of liberal Jacobinism in the 1860s. A liberal who opposed the Empire but was a firm proponent of order, he was also a conservative highly suspicious of universal suffrage yet devoted to the principles of 1789, like Prévost-Paradol and many others. Reason also made him a republican, who believed that questions about the nature of the regime were a thing of the past. His work is a remarkable example of the "pacified adaptation" of Jacobinism. In a series of important volumes—including *L'Individu et l'état* (1859), *La Centralisation* (1860), *La Liberté politique considérée dans ses rapports avec l'administration locale* (1864), to name only the most significant—he offered a theory of the new philosophy. He broadened the base of the "traditional" centralizing vision so as to incorporate it in a comparative history of liberties.[59]

Dupont-White's originality lay first in his having proposed the idea that what was distinctive about France was that its Parisian "intellectual centralization" served in a sense as an antidote to its political centralization. Centralization in France was great, to be sure, but also "intelligent" because perpetually subject to independent judgment. While it might appear that the people were subject to a remote, repressive administration answerable to no one, the reality was different: the machinery of state, Dupont-White argued, was balanced by a proportionate "power of public opinion." Centralization, he wrote,

> incorporates a corrective that remains to be discovered. That corrective is a capital. The word conceals a number of things. A capital is not one of the enumerated and classified constitutional powers. Writers on public affairs have yet to define the role of this organ in the physiology of nations. Yet a capital is just as much a power as the constituted powers. It is an organ, or, rather, it is to the body politic what the "vital form" is to the human body, the vital form that physiologists cannot locate and yet recognize as playing a role more important than all the visible organs and functions. Its function is to create ideas outside the churches and academies, to create a fashion and a society outside the court, and to create an opinion outside the government.[60]

Thus the capital, for Dupont-White, was in a sense that element of representative government which was associated with centralization. It established a connection between power and independence, centralization and liberty. France, he continued, "achieves the full measure of its thought only by way of its capital and achieves the full measure of its strength only by way of the government. The history of France is a riddle, the solution to which is unity."[61] Vigorous thought combined with strong government: this was in a sense the realization of the ideal of political rationalism forged in the eighteenth century.

Dupont-White also added new arguments to the arsenal of those skeptical of decentralization, arguments based on a comparison of France and England. Rejecting the view shared by most of his contemporaries, he did not believe that English liberties stemmed from the existence of strong local powers. He saw them rather as the product of a vigilant aristocracy coupled with a powerful sentiment of individuality (which he attributed essentially to the "English race"). Nothing of the sort existed in France, where there had never been a true aristocracy owing to the leveling role of the monarchy and where the "French race" was of quite a different character. Unlike the Anglo-Saxons, who were empirical individualists, the French were sociable and rational. "A sociable race," he argued,

> is a race that needs to be governed and is therefore open and vulnerable to a host of official interventions and mediations, which are not superfluous in the contentious environment it prefers. If, in addition, it has the philosophical spirit, this, too, leads to and culminates in a certain luxuriousness of government. It leads to this because thought rather than will is its dominant attribute, so that the state may well be required to make up for a certain national inertia by its action. It culminates in this, as well, because it will determine the extent and vigilance of government on the basis of theoretical reason.[62]

France was thus a country that needed a powerful government in virtue of both the nature of the sociability and the "philosophical spirit" that prevailed there. Hence there was no point in seeking to regenerate French society by invoking the spirit of individuality alone. Emancipation in France must take account of "the preference for public interests and public powers."[63] Identity was not a liberty but a potential. Political liberty in France was therefore the fruit not of individual independence but rather of government's ability to act in harmony with the deepest needs of society. The idea was that government could protect and educate the society because it knew the people's needs.

In this respect Dupont-White articulated the common thinking of republicans. It is disturbing to note that little differentiated his thinking from the implicit philosophy of the Empire ("Liberty begins with government," in the words of one of the Empire's leading theorists, the great jurist Raymond-Théodore Troplong).[64] He pointed to "the illusion of the liberal party," the fundamental error of thinking that liberty consists in the abasement of power. For Dupont-White, by contrast, the only true guarantees lay in the "firm organization of power." In his eyes, liberty was in effect *a protective framework* that allowed for combining authority with stability and democracy. Here, the assumption was that individuals should be satisfied with guarantees of their *purely individual* rights, which need not be bound to any collective institutions. Utopian generality was thus linked to a passive understanding of democracy as consent and legitimation rather than social creation.

The French model (and its philosophy of liberty) was thus founded, ultimately, on a certain understanding of power and a certain vision of civil society. That understanding of power involved the certainty that liberty was defined by the strength of its guarantees, with the question of individual autonomy totally subordinated to that of independence of the collectivity (and with the associated confusion of interior with exterior related to a broad historical representation of the self). Furthermore, the vision of civil society contained the implicit idea that the individual was not capable of being his own master. What ultimately accounted for the resistance to decentralization was a *culture of capabilities (culture capacitaire)*. Among nineteenth-century political writers, Leroy-Beaulieu understood this most clearly. "True decentralization," he wrote, "involves more than just shifting decisions on local matters from a larger or higher district to a smaller or more proximate one, or even from a functionary to an elective council. It has more to do with expanding the sphere of action of the individual and family and reducing to a bare minimum the number of prior authorizations and formalities required, which in France is so great as to stifle the spirit of initiative."[65] At bottom, this is why the rhetoric of decentralization had so little influence. There was a lack of confidence in civil society and its capabilities. Montalembert, in a melancholy mood, once observed that it was not the centralized state as such but the figure of the state as pedagogue that cast its shadow over the society: "As soon as any party, without exception, achieves control of the government, it treats France not as a victim or a conquest but quite deliberately as a pupil. It sets itself up as the country's teacher . . . It makes this great country its ward and awards itself the right to teach it what it ought to want, know, and do."[66] His was an accurate assessment.

Democratic Rhetoric

Resistance to the formation of intermediary bodies was also based on a certain conception of democracy and social representation. We see this clearly when the issue of restoring corporations comes up during the Restoration. Opponents raised not only economic objections but also political ones, questioning the *representativeness* of those who favored reinstating or reinventing corporations. At bottom, the charge was that the various petitioners constituted a minority, whereas the legal institutions represented the majority. Thus officials and spokesmen for the Paris Chamber of Commerce accused Levacher-Duplessis of not revealing the names of the 2,000 people he claimed had signed his petition, and they further objected that the very nature of their institution made them more representative. When the case was submitted to the Board of Manufactures, that body also emphasized the difference in representativeness between a legal institution and a group of petitioners: "You [petitioners] have avoided submitting your petition to the only institutions currently recognized by the Government, which were specially created to act as organs and interpreters of the wishes and needs of two very precious branches of public wealth. The Chamber of Commerce of Paris is not, as it is wrongly alleged to be, an insignificant commercial council designated by the prefecture. It is legally instituted, chosen by its peers."[67] The Board of Trade, ruling on the same case, rejected the petitioners' claim to be acting as delegates of the merchants and artisans of the city of Paris, pointing out that they could claim no mandate, not having been elected, and that in any case they represented only a very small percentage of the city's licensed tradesmen.[68] On another occasion, the same council drew a contrast between a group of "self-interested and unknown petitioners" and "more suitable and independent authorities"[69] and in consequence sternly rejected the petitioners' claim to be regarded as in any sense representative.[70]

This polemic was a significant event. It was the first time that a genuine battle had been waged between civil society and the official corporations about which should be considered representative. The question was at the heart of the debate about the role of intermediary bodies, and it highlights the fact that resistance to them had been strengthened by the advent of democracy. That is why *democratic illiberalism* is such a crucial feature of the French political culture. The sociological rejection of intermediary bodies and the vision of a democracy corseted in legal formalisms stem from the same sources. Those sources were multiple and intertwined: first, the claim to reduce the uncertainty of democracy by introducing an idea of representation-incarnation in theory and practice; second, the assertion that any definition of the public that exceeded the bounds of legal institutions was illegitimate; and finally, the rejection of all political intermediary bodies that could be charged with interfering with the authentic expression of the general will. Illiberal democracy thus radicalized the monism of the Revolution and linked it to a utopian resolution of the problem of representation. In other words, the suspicion of intermediary bodies in France amounted to a judgment on the meaning of democracy. Ultimately the question was far-reaching: Was it possible to conceive of any form of social representation between the two extremes of broadly generalized representation (the market or public opinion) and narrowly focused representation (suffrage)?

Criticism of campaign committees during the elections of 1849 and under the Second Empire can be seen in a similar light. The committees were denounced as "antidemocratic" on the grounds that they were the result of private initiatives, hence "particularistic" and therefore susceptible to distorting the formation of the general will. This "democratic" argument was invoked by the imperial regime in its crackdown on efforts by prominent republicans to organize resistance at the polls in 1863 and 1864.[71] Bonapartist spokesmen spoke of "occult government" and denounced the committees for "substituting the views of a few ringleaders for the imperial common sense of the masses" and for forming an "external administration" that posed illegitimately as a "rival and hostile" competitor to "the august and lawful administration."[72] For the same reason the Bonapartists were vehemently opposed to voting by a list or ticket of candidates, which they deemed incompatible with universal suffrage freely exercised. Thus they countered the legal argument (that the right to organize was essential if the right to vote was to be meaningful) with what they took to be a superior political argument regarding the nature of democracy. There was nothing new in their reasoning. Earlier, under the Restoration, the right had attacked so-called leadership committees, or groups of prominent citizens who met to lay the groundwork for elections, as an *imperium in imperio*.[73] In an 1828 debate in the Chamber of Peers, speakers had also attacked "a sort of power organized by individuals without authorization."[74] Under the Second Empire, however, this criticism took on a more systematic and radical form that led to an illiberal theory of democracy.

Campaign committees were unacceptable, it was argued, unless they were themselves chosen democratically. In 1870, some went so far as to propose legalizing the committees as institutionalized components of the electoral machinery.[75] Behind this rejection of intermediaries, what was at stake was the belief that democracy could organize itself without outside assistance. Reinforcing this vision was a certain conception of the relation between institutions, which were seen as "general," and civil society, whose constituents were inevitably branded "particular" (or "special interests," as it would be more natural to say in English).

The illiberal democratic conception of politics cast its shadow on the state, where it served to justify certain kinds of state monopoly. Just as the general interest was defined *in opposition* to all particular interests, civil society's claims to take charge of certain collective functions were opposed by the argument that all services exhibiting a public character ought to be the exclusive province of the state. The French theory of democracy thus encouraged a radical approach to the administration of scarcity, leaving no middle ground between public monopoly and the market. The history of telecommunications in the nineteenth century offers a striking example of this propensity to treat monopoly as a democratic political form. In presenting the law of 2 May 1837, reserving the use of the telegraph to agents of the government, the minister of the interior offered this extraordinary argument: "We do not like monopolies as such, and we would be happy to extend to everyone the benefits that the telegraph brings to the government. But the guarantees that we have been offered are misleading . . . The only way to prevent a monopoly is to assign it to the government."[76] This was another way of formulating French monism. The French model cannot be understood without taking account of the essential link between Jacobinism as an administrative form and a polarized conception of democracy.

Systematic Ambiguity

As we have seen, the political culture of generality survived the criticism leveled at it by adapting and reformulating itself. In addition, it hid behind a number of ambiguities that allowed it to dissimulate the manner in which it governed. It is striking to discover, for example, the extent to which it adopted the very terms in which it was contested, in some cases obscuring for contemporaries the true divisions and the significance of effective reforms. The evolution of the language in which the issues of centralization and association were discussed offers a good example of this phenomenon. In addition, the ambiguities of anti-Protestantism maintained a cultural confusion that ultimately served the interests of the Jacobin vision. Let us consider each of these examples in turn.

Proponents of decentralization invariably described the need for reform as imperative yet couched their proposals in the vaguest of terms. Recurrent doubts about what centralization meant are a case in point. "Centralization is a word that is constantly repeated of late but whose meaning no one seeks to clarify," Tocqueville characteristically observed at the beginning of his career.[77] To dispel the confusion, the author of *Democracy in America* proposed a distinction between *administrative centralization* and *political* or *governmental centralization*. The goal of administrative centralization was to concentrate the management of various (particular) local institutions, whereas governmental centralization sought to take charge of the *common interests* of the various parts of the nation in a unified and organized way. There was nothing original about this distinction, which was a centerpiece of legitimist rhetoric. It was explored, for example, by Ferdinand Béchard and his friends.[78] In fact, it had been suggested even earlier, in the late 1820s. *Le Globe* distinguished between "political domination" and "administrative domination," emphasizing that the former was limited and contained (by publicity, debate, the press, elections, and so on), while the latter encountered neither checks nor balances.[79] Under the July Monarchy the distinction became something of a commonplace. Liberals employed it as well as legitimists, as we have seen. It was also used descriptively by Alexandre François Auguste Vivien in his famous *Etudes administratives* (1845). Most remarkable of all, it was ultimately adopted and even instrumentalized by republican writers. Thus in the early 1830s François-Vincent Raspail was one of the first to argue in favor of combining centralization for general interests with decentralization for local interests.[80] Marie-François de Cormenin introduced the same idea in 1840 and later invoked it in his celebrated pamphlet *De la centralisation* (1842).[81] Louis Blanc also appropriated it: "Necessary as political centralization is, administrative centralization is stifling." The distinction recurs at a number of places in his writing.[82]

There is something disturbing about such a consensus. The contrast between a good and a bad centralization in support of a policy combining political (or governmental) centralization with administrative decentralization ultimately did more to obscure the issue than to illuminate it. Two points are taken for granted: that political action is by nature and definition centralized, since the essence of government is to act with unified means,[83] while administrative management is functionally hindered by bureaucratic paralysis. The difficulty, however, was to distinguish what was political from what was simply administrative. Even Thiers, a ferocious centralizer in the ordinary sense of the word (meaning strict limitation of the autonomy of local authorities), declared himself in favor of "decentralization of affairs."[84] While everyone readily agreed that it was a good idea to decentralize the administration of particular or local interests but to maintain unified control of general interests, the difficulty lay in how to draw the dividing line between the two categories. As we have seen in detail, what defined the political culture of generality was a certain way of relating public and private. Without detailed knowledge of that relationship, the "formula" was thus purely tautological. Its ambiguity was demonstrated in striking fashion in 1848. Take, for instance, the committee charged with writing a constitution. "To do away with centralization or even to weaken its fundamental principles is out of the question," said Tocqueville, "*but* centralization was used as a way of hiding abuse"; while Vivien insisted that "centralization must be modified . . . *but* if the republican system does not preserve and even increase centralization, we will be heading toward federation."[85] In both cases, a general assertion was limited with a partial restriction, a rhetorical device for hiding the ambiguity involved in proposing contradictory approaches in the same statement.[86] The distinction that people began to make in this period between "concentration" and "centralization" was also misleadingly instrumental.[87] Although the problem was to distinguish between two methods and two spheres of action, these antinomian pairs sowed confusion by suggesting that their mere assertion somehow offered a solution to the problem.

The "formula" thus served to confuse the issue and in effect to legitimize the French model while pretending implicitly to correct it. Evidence for this paradox can be seen in the fact that one of the first important laws of the Second Empire unabashedly claimed "administrative decentralization" as its goal when in fact it increased the direct power of the prefects.[88] The abuse of language in this instance was patent, but what allowed the Bonapartist regime to get away with it was the earlier equivocation by liberals and republicans. The distinction between the political and the administrative was maintained throughout the nineteenth century. Jules Simon, Jules Ferry, and Léon Gambetta all had recourse to it on numerous occasions. It is worth noting that Pierre Larousse chose a large number of citations to introduce the entry "centralization" in his dictionary. It was also invoked repeatedly by those who passed as official philosophers of the Republic: Alfred Fouillée, Charles Renouvier, and Emile Auguste Chartier Alain. Its posterity would be very long indeed.

The idea of association was similarly ambiguous. As we have discussed at length, when the "spirit of association" was invoked in the early 1820s, the objective was to find a remedy for the anomie of the new society of individuals. At that time the term "association" referred to efforts to reconstitute intermediary bodies as a way of giving palpable substance to the social. It was used in that sense with nostalgic connotations by legitimists but also with progressive connotations in the form of communitarian alternatives to the reign of individualism. Soon, however, these early understandings, which were linked to an appreciation of civil society, were to some extent supplanted by efforts to reformulate the revolutionary perspective of a "unified whole" in the language of association. Quite a number of authors rejected "partial" associations and intermediary bodies in favor of establishing a *greater association*. It is in these terms that one should seek to understand the link that exists in France between the republican perspective and a certain conception of socialism. Indeed, the socialist idea originated as a radical alternative to individualism. Although Buchez and Louis Blanc defined association in the same way, they took different approaches to it in practice: a group of limited solidarity for the former, a Rousseauist form of integral collectivism for the latter.[89] Pierre Leroux condemned what he called "absolute socialism" on the grounds that it distorted the associative ideal, with its notion that society constituted a single vast body.[90] The great debate of the 1830s and 1840s on workers' associations should be understood in this light. The idea of the association as intermediary body came to be opposed to the idea of the association as a greater whole. In the latter case, "unity" was the key word.[91] Louis Blanc discussed the various aspects in his work, portraying socialism as the culmination and transfiguration of a vision of unit that had previously existed only in what he took to be the distorted forms of monarchy and Catholicism. Thus he revived the old political culture of generality as part of the language of socialism.[92] "Association means progress only if it is universal," Blanc summed up in his *Organisation du travail*.[93]

This revival of the political culture of generality in the language of socialism created a link between the French republican tradition and the socialist ideal that became a distinctive feature of French political culture. Everywhere else, socialism was simply and directly opposed to bourgeois liberalism and republicanism. Raspail expressed this division very clearly in the early 1830s. "Whenever we speak of the omnipotence of association," he wrote, "we refer not to the kind of association that plays politics [*qui joue à la cité*] as children play soldier. We intend to build an association on a far broader foundation, that of the entire nation [*la grande cité*], which monarchy shattered into little pieces and which we intend to make our business."[94] In the 1840s Auguste Billiard, who would be one of the first to respond to Tocqueville and Guizot with his own theory of the democratic republic, proposed a similar contrast between limited (particular) and overarching (general) associations. He spoke with the accents of 1789 but with an admixture of the social, extolling the Republic against intermediary bodies.

> Certain pious congregations will no doubt make admirable efforts to alleviate our miseries, and teaching *corps* will surely contribute mightily to the spread of learning among the various classes of the people . . . But if the nation is itself the pious congregation and the teaching corporation, as well as the magistracy that metes out justice and the army charged with defending our national institutions, and if in these various functions the cooperation of all the members of which the state is composed is constantly and simultaneously required, won't an association of this kind be ten times, nay, a hundred times more charitable, more enlightened, more just, and more powerful than all the corporations authorized or organized by the government?[95]

The various republican dictionaries of the period resolutely spread this philosophy, as can be seen by a glance at the most popular and representative of the lot, the *Dictionnaire politique*, published by Pagnerre in 1842. There we are told that "if the great Association of all were organized for a common purpose, any particular association that operated independently of that goal would be either silly or dangerous. Everything that destroys unity where unity exists must be prohibited."[96] The only grudging concession, as had been the case a half-century earlier, was to admit the circumstantial utility of "partial" associations.[97] Similarly, in the early 1830s the *Revue républicaine* revealed its skepticism about workers' associations, which it viewed as a "provisional means of slowing the progress of the malady" but not as a genuine alternative.[98] The language of association was thus ambiguous, since it could refer to the state as well as to civil society.

The spirit of 1848 exemplified this ambiguity in a striking way. The revolutionaries in effect celebrated the two contradictory aspects of association. If 1848 marked "the rebirth of peoples" across Europe, it also marked a rebirth of associations in France. With universal suffrage now established, the right of association symbolized the break with the immediate past. Political clubs, producers' cooperatives, and workers' societies of all sorts proliferated in the space of a few months, as if a whole compressed universe had suddenly exploded into being. A decree of 25 February 1848 implicitly recognized the right of workers to associate, and the law of 28 July 1848 legalized freedom of association and assembly as a matter of principle. These new rights were consecrated in the Constitution, whose Article 8 proclaimed that "citizens have the right to associate, to assemble peacefully and without arms, to petition, and to express their thoughts by way of the press or other means."[99] It is incorrect, however, to conclude that revolutionary doubts about intermediary bodies had been dispelled. The recognition of various rights (to assemble, form cooperatives and clubs, and so on) was not intended as approval of a corporatist form of social organization. It was just as common in 1848 for the word "association" to refer to a new way of thinking of society as a totality: a fraternal and hopefully more egalitarian totality, but still a totality. As one political writer of the period put it, summing up a widespread feeling, "the organization of society can be seen as a single vast association."[100] In this respect the fraternal spirit of the spring of 1848 did not indicate a rupture with the political culture of generality. It kept faith with the spirit of Jacobinism, in a more sentimental, less militant version. The utopian form of association that was celebrated in 1848 thus served to express the old aspiration of 1789: the aspiration that unity and consensus might be achieved through a political transfiguration of the social bond.

The anti-Protestantism that developed in France after 1820 also contributed to the proliferation of ambiguities on which a reconfigured Jacobinism thrived.[101] This was a new type of anti-Protestantism, no longer that of men like Louis de Bonald and Joseph de Maistre, who had characterized reformed Christianity as "religious sans-culottism" and seen it as the source of harmful democratic doctrines indistinguishable from the views of Robespierre.[102] Now, however, Protestantism was blamed above all for the individualism of the modern world and hence indirectly for the disorder that was the issue of the day. Lamennais unsurprisingly lashed out at "the protestants of the social order,"[103] whom he held responsible for rampant social dissolution as well as "muddling" the science of public law.[104] The charge was echoed in diverse circles. Saint-Simonians were particularly vehement. For instance, Prosper Enfantin denounced "Protestants who preach only diversity and division, individualism, and, to put it bluntly, selfishness."[105] Leroux was also violently hostile to Protestantism. Buchez accused the disciples of Luther and Calvin of having contributed to the "divinization of the self" and the "deification of the individual," in contrast to Catholicism, which "is not only a religion but also a national feeling; it is in all things love of and faith in unity."[106] It is noteworthy that when the first signs of skepticism about American democracy appeared, it was its Protestant character that was attacked. Criticizing Tocqueville, a writer close to Buchez drew a parallel between individualism in religion and morality, supposedly a reflection of the Protestant spirit, and individualism in politics, supposedly the road to federalism.[107] Here the sociological critique of individualism that was implicit in anti-Protestantism was transformed into political praise for centralization, though the link between the two was not made explicit.

Writers sometimes expressed contradictory views of society without being aware of it. Under the banner of anti-Protestantism, one could slip imperceptibly from Pierre Leroux to Louis Blanc. When Blanc, in the well-known introduction to his *Histoire de la Révolution française* (1847), attacked Luther for introducing a "misunderstanding" that led to confusing the advent of individualism with that of liberty, he had no wish to establish a communitarian society of the sort that would have appealed to the author of *De l'humanité*.[108] Indeed, the Catholicism that he praised in the course of his argument could even be identified with the Jacobin state. Again, we see how the political culture of generality drew its strength from its ability to reformulate itself in terms that might seem at first sight to be associated with its antagonists.

— Part III —

Jacobinism Amended

— 9 —

The Great Turning Point

Caught between forces and counterforces, the French model under the July Monarchy settled into a reconfigured Jacobinism. Later, however, the situation began to evolve again under the double impetus of social and intellectual forces. The social factors included the fear of socialism and the specter of the welfare state, which led in the period 1848–1870 to a fresh look at the critique of revolutionary individualism. There was also a growing sense that professional associations might be useful in establishing a better-organized and better-regulated society. A change in the intellectual climate also led to a different understanding of the role of intermediary bodies. Under the combined effect of revolutionary historiography and the new discipline of sociology, one version of Jacobinism lost credibility.

The Fear of Socialism and the Specter of the Welfare State

In the previous chapter I noted that repression of associations before 1848 was often justified by the new ruling class's obsession with subversion. To round out the picture, however, I should add that some workers' associations were also regarded as highly useful instruments for maintaining social order. This was especially true of mutual aid societies (or *sociétés de secours mutuels,* also known as *caisses de secours* and *sociétés de prévoyance*). Already under the Empire these groups were exempt from the strictures of Article 291 of the Penal Code. Although the authorities, for obvious anticorporatist reasons, insisted that the mutual aid societies be made up of individuals from various walks of life, they soon modified their stance to allow the revival of old confraternal ties among workers in a single trade.[1] The Ministry of the Interior even encouraged the creation of associations

149

of this type as "guarantors of order" laudable for their "moral influence."[2] To be sure, the phenomenon was limited in scope: in the early years of the Restoration there were only about 160 mutual aid societies encompassing 11,143 subscribers. Nevertheless, the attitude that was taken toward these groups is worth noting if we want to appreciate the full complexity of the issue of associations. Throughout the Restoration and the July Monarchy, social leaders included workmen's societies of this type in their depictions of a well-ordered society. The well-known Société Philanthropique, whose membership included parts of the old aristocracy as well as the new elites, even made material subsidies available to such groups.[3] On the left, the Société de la Morale Chrétienne also offered its assistance. One member of this group, Guizot, who was normally quick to voice alarm at the peril of numbers, praised the role of such associations in "combatting the malaise" of modern life and "not endangering the general order."[4] In 1834, when alarm about working-class unrest was at its height, Frédéric-Gaëtan de La Rochefoucauld–Liancourt thought it useful to publish a pamphlet listing workers' mutual aid societies, in which he urged readers not to judge such groups "in general" because, quite apart from those political organizations deemed menacing, useful associations like these also existed.[5] He invited his colleagues to look upon the latter as a means of "shoring up order" more effective than the repressive measures that had mainly monopolized their attention previously.

Under the July Monarchy, a similar conservative view in favor of restoring modernized workers' corporations emerged as the second wave of a movement that had already begun under the Empire and Restoration. The case for these was made repeatedly by a small but active group of writers and philanthropists who were looking for a remedy for the problem of pauperism, which had suddenly cropped up as a pressing issue. At first they saw this type of association as a new form of community capable of restoring "re-embedded" solidarity. Eugène Buret, Joseph Fodéré, Joseph-Marie de Gerando, Sismondi, and Alban Villeneuve-Bargemont discussed the issues in works that attracted attention in the 1830s and 1840s. All five saw pauperism as a consequence of social dissolution, and several went so far as to remark that serfdom had avoided this malady by obliging masters to take responsibility for the welfare of their dependents. But the interest in corporatist associations went beyond social considerations of this sort. There was a certain nostalgia for the corporatist system stemming from anxiety over the threat of worker unrest and the need for oversight and moral instruction. A symptom of this state of mind was the "plan for a disciplinary reorganization of the industrial classes in France" that Félix de La Farelle published in 1842.

Before 1848, however, such openness to workmen's associations remained limited, a reflection of fear that workers would band together to make demands or to plot insurrections. After the February uprising, everything changed, in the first place because the new government had to satisfy long-standing demands. Yet the term "association" connoted hope as well revenge. It was almost symbolic of the new course that the people desired. There was also a political dimension to the issue of associations and intermediary bodies. As both conservatives and liberals were quick to recognize, a society of individuals leads almost automatically to demands for an ever-growing state. Repression of the working class in the 1840s had hidden this problem from view. In 1848 it became glaringly apparent. In the absence of associations and intermediary bodies, demands from every quarter poured in to the state, which represented the only alternative to a dissipation of energies and the only conceivable embodiment of the general interest. The experiment with national workshops in the spring of 1848 demonstrated both the implacable logic and the inevitable consequences of this change—consequences that were quickly deemed catastrophic. Clamor around the "right to work" soon crystallized the issue in concrete form.

The great debate on this question reveals that a shift in perception was under way. Arguments on both sides were laid out clearly in the course of conflict in the National Assembly over the new constitution. The conflict also revealed a number of underlying concerns and fantasies. The question was whether the constitution should limit itself to a general statement of society's "duty" to assist or provide work for the unemployed or should go further and declare a "right" to work. Tocqueville accurately reflected the emergent thinking on this subject on the right.[6] Like many of his peers, he resigned himself, at least temporarily, to seeing the state play a greater role, yet he worried that an inexorable logic would lead to a continual expansion of that role. "The state," he alleged, "will seek to give work to all workers who want it, and little by little this will turn it into an industrial power . . . It will be led surreptitiously into becoming the principal and, before long, the only industrial entrepreneur . . . After thus gathering all private capital into its own hands, the state will ultimately become the sole owner of everything. And that is communism."[7] In 1848 that was the central problem of democracy for Tocqueville: how to escape what he called the "fatal" necessity that would slowly transform the liberal democratic state into a socialist one, that is, "the vast and sole organizer of labor" as well as "the director of society" and "substitute for individual assistance [*la prévoyance individuelle*]." That question had never arisen before. Suddenly it had become unavoidable. No longer was the issue simply the Jacobin centralization resulting from the Revolution's establishment of a society of individuals. The advent of universal suffrage and its attendant social demands on the state radicalized and complicated the issue: now it was possible to see socialism as the consequence of individualism. The republicans carefully avoided dealing with the crux of the question. Alexandre Auguste Ledru-Rollin, responding to Tocqueville, skirted the difficulty in his plea on behalf of the right to work. "I do not want to turn the state into a producer or manufacturer," he reassured the deputies. "I want to turn it into an intelligent protector."[8] An "intelligent" state: the word could hardly disguise the vagueness of his approach, which for the first time turned a glaring spotlight on the ambiguities of the republicanism of the day.

The right drew a fundamental lesson from this episode: if socialism was to be stopped, new thinking about the issue of association and intermediary bodies was needed. Antoine-Elisée Cherbuliez, a highly conservative economist of the time, summarized the view that he and many of his friends shared: "The influence of communist ideas can be neutralized only with analogous ideas of association and patronage . . . The worker believes or senses that he is disassociated. He sees himself as standing outside society in the strict sense . . . Communist associations can be neutralized only if capital and property penetrate them."[9] Still, the specter of communism or socialism was not the only thing that moderated the rigor of the French model at this time. The figure of the welfare state (*l'état-providence*) emerged during the Second Empire as a threat that needed to be dealt with. The term *état-providence* was coined in 1860 to denote what, in the absence of any real socialist threat, many people regarded as a new moral and social peril.[10]

In a work devoted to associations for poor relief, Emile Laurent, after attacking the state "for setting itself up as a kind of Providence," called upon his contemporaries to "restore the idea of association in French society."[11] Hence even before associations were proposed as a way of preventing the working class from drifting toward communism and socialism, associations were portrayed as an alternative to a tutelary state playing the role of society's protector. Many others joined with Laurent in calling for a system of insurance or a network of workers' associations in the hope that a revitalized society would prevent the advent of a welfare state, which was accurately seen as the natural consequence of an atomized society in which the government alone remained as general protector. For instance, Emile Ollivier noted that

> it is not true that there exist only, on the one hand, individual bits of dust unconnected to one another and, on the other hand, the collective power of the nation. Between the two, as the transition from one to the other and as the means of preventing the individual from being crushed by the state, exists the group, formed by elective affinity and voluntary agreement. It is the province of the group to perform works of labor, assistance, expression, and progress that lie beyond the power of the individual and would become impossible or oppressive if they could only be carried out by the power of the public authorities.[12]

The old moral and social critique of dissolved society was now reinforced by hostility to the welfare state in granting greater legitimacy to associations than in the past. This was the first factor in favor of a relaxation of the rigid French model.

The Trade Union as Source of Order

Another factor leading to relaxation of the French model was a banal need for order. Obsession with order in the 1830s had led to repression of workers' societies, which were perceived as a threat. Thirty years later, the same obsession yielded a different result. This is one way of interpreting the process that resulted in legal recognition of trade unions. Social history made changes in the law necessary. We can see this as early as the mid-1860s, when the first decisive break with the past came in the form of abolition of the old crime of coalition. The law of 29 May 1864 that laid the groundwork for new laws on occupational or professional associations already reflected a new political calculus. The Empire, seeking to quell opposition from workers, tried to drive a wedge between them and the republican opposition. Napoleon III adopted this line soon after his seizure of power, when he came down in favor of increasing the number of mutual aid societies and offered assistance to the first workers' retirement funds. In the same spirit, he indirectly encouraged the sending of delegations of workers to the International Exhibition in London in 1862, which prepared the way for worker candidacies in the elections of 1863 (to the consternation of republican notables).[13] The regime was also obliged to take note of the fact that the courts punished workers' coalitions more frequently and more harshly than employers' coalitions, a fact that gave rise to considerable resentment.[14] Napoleon's supporters therefore called upon industrialists to recognize the collective character of working-class life, described as a "fatal necessity" to which employers must submit.[15]

This 1864 law marked a turning point. The transformation was by no means complete, however. The new law on coalitions clashed with other measures. Article 291 of the Penal Code and the law of 1834 requiring prior authorization for associations of more than twenty persons remained on the books, for example. So did Article 416 of the Penal Code, which in very general terms prohibited interference with the freedom of labor. Workers were still prosecuted for forming associations or even for going on strike whenever collective action was deemed to involve "coercion" of workers.[16] Workers' organizations were in fact merely tolerated. This tolerance was not fully institutionalized until 1884, twenty years later. Even then, practical considerations and contemporary events played a crucial role in moderating the basic republican credo in order to expand the right to associate.

Progress was slow: eight years elapsed between the filing of the first bill to legalize trade unions in 1876 and the final vote. The length of the discussion is in itself a good indicator of the skepticism and resistance that greeted the unions' effort to gain recognition. Concerns about the social consequences of recognition weighed more heavily and more directly than any other consideration in the minds of both supporters and opponents. In fact, a new social issue had arisen in the period. Although the memory of revolutionary episodes had begun to fade by the late 1870s (the return of the last banished Communards having been authorized), the social climate had worsened. Strikes multiplied: there were more work stoppages in 1879 than in the five previous years put together. The movement gained strength in the early 1880s.[17] The *Statistique annuelle de la France* began tabulating the number of days lost to strikes in the late 1880s, an indication of the salience of the issue.[18] This was the "golden age" of the strike in France. Spontaneous walkouts were legion, and workers began coordinating work stoppages in different parts of the country. The proliferation of walkouts and of revolutionary propaganda worried both the bourgeoisie, still haunted by the specter of the Commune, and republicans of various stripes, who feared that the still-young regime might be dangerously weakened as a result. At the same time, social conflict grew more acute as many unions, still just barely tolerated, began to amass war chests for the express purpose of supporting strike actions.

This was the context in which the institutionalization of trade unionism was contemplated. The hope was that such a move would moderate the workers' movement and result in a more coherent set of demands. At the height of the strike movement, for instance, one prefect wrote to Paris: "When union bodies are firmly established, we will see no more of the noisy strikes that have occurred recently in Roubaix, Armentières, and Reims. Workers will know that they can achieve their ends more reliably and less dangerously" by other means.[19] In Paris the prefect of police made a similar plea. This argument played a key role in parliamentary debate. François Henri René Allain-Targé, the rapporteur on the bill in the Chamber of Deputies, opened with this point: "Experience has shown that wherever trade unions exist, strikes are rare or end very quickly."[20] Henri Tolain, the rapporteur in the Senate, hammered on the same point: "It is our profound conviction that the trade unions will soon prove to be the most powerful factors in fostering public security, industrial progress, and social order."[21] Addressing the assembly of an organization of important Paris businessmen, Gambetta also pleaded for recognition of the trade unions:

> You will not be truly on the road to progress and social peace until you have persuaded other associations and organizations enjoying the same independence and personal autonomy to work closely with you in such a way as to encourage free debate and open deliberation, which are almost always the prelude to an accord . . . It is cause for congratulations that the workers have now also organized as autonomous and completely free union groups. It is to be hoped that in addition they will approach and seek contact with you.[22]

The hope was that responsible, organized trade unions would replace the old strike resistance funds, whose explicit purpose was to finance lengthy conflicts. The example of England, where trade unions had been legal since 1824, was frequently invoked from the late 1860s on.

Despite a few dissident voices, the majority of deputies took a favorable view of the English experience.[23] The comte de Paris set the tone with the book *Les Associations ouvrières en Angleterre,* published in 1869.[24] As he explained at length, recognizing the unions had deprived the most violent workers of the influence they had derived from exercising a hidden and irresponsible power. At the other extreme of the political spectrum, Anthime Corbon, the author of the cult book *Le Secret du peuple de Paris* (1863), also devoted an enthusiastic study to the English trade unions.[25] Speakers of many shades of opinion rose in the Chamber and Senate to extol the positive effects of unions, whose power was said to give them the ability to resolve labor conflicts peacefully. The rarity of strikes in England was contrasted with their anarchic proliferation in France. Edouard Lockroy, Martin Nadaud, and many others developed this theme at length. "Friendly Societies" were also universally praised.

Thus trade unions, which militant workers saw as means of "defense" and "conquest," were viewed by others as a source of order. One worker deputy, Georges Brialou, summed up the general sentiment that led to passage of the law of 1884:

> What leads to strikes is the lack of serious organization, which leaves [worker] corporations at the mercy of a few impulsive leaders, who send their followers out on strike over a trifle. Whereas with unions, usually made up of the most serious and intelligent men in the corporations, you can be certain that every available means of reconciliation will be exploited to the full, and then you will no longer have the kinds of strike that erupt overnight in many cases over misunderstandings or minor slights that could have been resolved without conflict.[26]

Was this vision simplistic and idealized? Probably. Nevertheless, it captured what was seen as a fundamental problem: how to make society more organic and less volatile, and how to structure it so as to make it easier to comprehend. Even if unions were still seen by some as a lesser evil, a concession to events, they were no longer regarded solely as instruments of struggle and conflict. They were also perceived as necessary for the regulation of society. Legalization, it was hoped, would dispel the specter of revolutionary passions and usher in an era of stability. France in the nineteenth century was indeed obsessed with fear of the multitude, the pervasive threat being that of social decomposition associated with the rise of the individual. People imagined society as an amorphous mass, a pure human magma, a juxtaposition of identical units. They saw an uncontrollable revolutionary mob, a potential for riot that could not be quelled, a vague, unpredictable mass, a faceless, shapeless force that could not be represented because it was the organic at its most basic level. The limited suffrage that remained in force from 1814 to 1848 had been established to contain this fear of numbers. In the 1880s, in an age of universal suffrage, trade unionism was seen as a way to exorcise the same demon, to compensate for the deficit of representation that was a structural feature of modern society.

It was in this spirit that leading businessmen appeared before parliamentary committees to testify in support of the trade unions bill. A delegation from the Union Nationale du Commerce et de l'Industrie, a distant ancestor of the group that represents French industry today, put it this way: "There is no discussion with a mob or even with a hundred people, no negotiation, no compromise; yet economic life is merely a series of agreements and transactions. A new ingredient is therefore necessary, and that new ingredient is the organization of labor, or, to put it another way, the organization of production. It is free and open professional association formed on the basis of the affinities, needs, and interests of the moment."[27] The ministerial circular implementing the law, which Pierre Marie René Waldeck-Rousseau sent out to his prefects on 25 August 1884, stressed the usefulness of the trade unions from the standpoint of governing society: "The association of individuals in accordance with their professional affinities is not so much a weapon of combat as an instrument of material, moral, and intellectual progress."[28]

It was hoped that legalizing the unions would make them more "responsible" (and some even dreamed of making them conservative).[29] This hope reflected a perception of social violence as a result of occult influences. "If you deny any form of legal existence [to professional associations], they will take refuge in the shadows, and it will be impossible for you to reach them," argued Barthe, who for a time served as rapporteur on the bill in the Senate.[30] Operating in the light of day, the unions would become more reasonable. Openness would also eliminate the "misunderstandings" between workers and employers that arose because of lack of contact between them and fed on fantasies born of isolation and marginalization. Indeed, it was hoped that recognition of the unions would integrate workers into society more effectively than universal suffrage alone. Now that the ballot box had supplanted the rioter's rifle, there was hope that organized negotiation would put an end to wildcat strikes. "On the day when union associations are able to operate in the open," remarked a respected social observer in the ranks of the moderates, "they will shed their occult and illegal status to become the real and effective representatives of each professional corporation. Their spirit and role will change. They will be seen as authorized defenders of the interests of the working population. Tolerated illegality will give way to a regular legal mandate, adding new life and vigor to the forces of society."[31] Granting a certain autonomy to the social sphere was supposed to cool political passions or even induce workers to abandon the realm of politics. The Republic thus pursued a goal similar to that of Napoleon III: to organize labor in such a way as to diminish the danger of revolution. If workers stayed out of politics, they would be tranquil and happy: that naive hope led republicans to make trade unions an exception to their general view of the world. In order to keep politics from turning into "the unhappy multitude versus the legislature," they agreed to allow workers to organize in their own sphere. A more "organic" social sphere would avoid the danger of "inorganic universal suffrage."[32]

Blame Le Chapelier

Thus the need for order played a key role in the legalization of the unions. Yet such a decision could not have been taken on that basis alone, because intellectual resistance to the legitimation of organized special interests was so powerful in France. From a legal point of view, recognition of the unions meant abolition of the decree of 14 June 1791, which in many respects symbolized the very soul of revolutionary political culture. Hence there was a contradiction that needed to be resolved. The cost of doing so was nothing less than a rewriting of the history of the famous decree. It was necessary to "invent" an imaginary Le Chapelier Law so as to exonerate its critics of the charge of overturning the principles of 1789.

It is important to remember that historians long regarded the Le Chapelier Law as one of the less important acts of the Constituent Assembly. It was seldom referred to before 1860. Neither Thiers nor Louis Blanc mentioned it. Michelet did briefly allude to an earlier proposal of April 1791 to ban collective petitions and grievances from popular societies, but he had nothing to say about the text of 14 June. All that changed with the Second Empire. It was Berryer, in one of his most famous cases, who set the tone in the early 1860s, while defending typographers charged with the crime of "coalition." He attacked the law of 1791 "abolishing collective forces" and poured scorn on what he characterized as "the utopia of the time." He reproached the government for seeking "to abuse the law of

1791. But do you know where that absolute principle will take you? . . . It will take you straight to the theory of the right to work."[33] The warning would be heeded. Emile Ollivier repeated the charge when he defended the proposal to abolish the crime of coalition in 1864. The Le Chapelier decree was suddenly rescued from oblivion, only to be subjected to withering scrutiny and attacked as "the fundamental error of the French Revolution."[34] A leading member of the republican opposition went even further: "The law we are discussing is one of the most important that we can approve. With a stroke of the pen it erases one of the greatest errors of the Revolution."[35] Thus a new way of talking about the Revolution emerged in this period. To be sure, this was not the first time that the individualism of 1789 had been attacked. We have already examined in detail the history of this recurring criticism through the first half of the nineteenth century. Now, however, the connotations of the critique ceased to be exclusively negative. The attack on the Le Chapelier Law made it possible to incorporate a certain suspicion of the Revolution within republican political culture itself. This move proved to be particularly effective and adaptable because criticism of the law came in many shades and varieties.

The minimalist version of the critique of the decree of 14 June 1791 merely stated that it had outlived its usefulness. Lockroy, in the bill that he filed in 1876 jointly with much of the republican left, from Louis Blanc to Alfred Naquet and from Désiré Barodet to Clemenceau, emphasized this point from the beginning: "We do not associate ourselves with the criticisms that have been directed at this law of 1791."[36] In fact, this saving reservation merely encapsulated the view that the law "had been a good and useful measure in its time." Lockroy was quick to balance this opinion with the observation that "since 1791 a revolution has taken place in the world of production."[37] With industrial conditions profoundly changed, fidelity to the spirit of the Revolution might make it necessary to violate the letter. Recognition of individual freedom had been valuable in its day, but progress now required workers to band together to press their common interests. Thus it was possible to present the repudiation of a key feature of revolutionary law as an expression of continuing progress. For instance, Tolain spoke soberly of "bringing the law into harmony with the new customs and mores that have taken hold among workers."[38] Hence it was perfectly possible that Le Chapelier's work had been absolutely "necessary" in its time but had since become undeniably dangerous.

This rhetoric of maladaptation and obsolescence was typical of one type of justification for the repudiation of the Le Chapelier Law. The revolutionary text was absolved of any blame. Hence it comes as no surprise to find the most intransigent republicans reasoning in these terms. Other champions of repeal were somewhat more critical, attributing the original passage of the law to a neglect of its full implications owing to the circumstances in which it was conceived. Gambetta, for example, did not hesitate to brand it a "fatal law." While deploring the fact that the men of the Revolution had shied away from making "a concession to collective freedom," he blamed their error entirely on the urgent climate of the times. "They were in a fight for their lives," he argued, "and did not make distinctions. They had no time to analyze, categorize, and classify or to determine which associations would be harmful and which useful."[39] In a similar vein, Allain-Targé spoke of a "mistake."[40] A law maladapted to the times and a mistake: the same arguments had already been invoked repeatedly by those who had defended associations in previous legal proceedings. What many saw as "the Constituent Assembly's greatest blunder" was still understood as a tactical error, a result of unfortunate overzealousness in waging a just war on the corporatist legacy of the Old Regime. In fact, the term "overzealousness" recurred frequently in explanations of why the Le Chapelier Law had solidified into an obstacle to further progress. "The French Revolution's great and invaluable triumph over the guild system was all too complete. The goal was exceeded. Let us return to it." In such terms was the situation summed up by one authoritative analyst of state-society relations.[41]

Other participants in the great debate on trade unions were not so cautious. Traditionalist Catholics, led by Albert de Mun, offered an authentically reactionary critique of the 1791 law, calling for a return to corporations in the form of unions composed of both workers and employers. As they saw it, such professional associations would "save France from the Revolution" and had nothing to do with adapting the principles of 1789 to contemporary realities. From a radically opposed perspective, the extreme left viewed the Le Chapelier Law as a symbol of the politics of the bourgeoisie, a celebration of the individual citizen at the expense of the proletariat. Paul Brousse saw the law as nothing more than a weapon for keeping wages down and preventing workers from improving their condition.[42] In the same spirit, Jean Jaurès denounced what he called a "terrible law" responsible for straitjacketing the working class.[43] What socialists denounced was thus not just the Le Chapelier Law but the behavior of the exploiting classes, which led Marx to write a celebrated attack on this "wretched" legislation.[44]

What we have here, then, is a broad spectrum of views of the Revolution, from Albert de Mun to the socialists, from conservative republicans to radicals. All rejected the Le Chapelier Law, though for different and even contradictory reasons. This state of affairs proved to be the basis of one of those "equivocal convergences" that so often cause the wheel of history to turn. We see this clearly in the celebration of the Revolution's centennial in 1889. There was certainly an unbridgeable cultural gap between the diatribes of the bishop of Angers, Monseigneur Freppel, against what he continued to call "revolutionary satanism," and the moderate republican synthesis embodied in the commemoration. On certain points, however, crucial resonances linked writers of radically different political persuasions. No longer was criticism of the Revolution reactionary by its very nature. Now even moderates were puzzled by or hesitant about what had been done, and the left condemned it.

Sociology versus Jacobinism

Thus, for political and social reasons, the terms in which the question of intermediary bodies and associations was approached were modified in the second half of the nineteenth century. Changing views of the Revolution also led to criticism of the strict anticorporatism of the Le Chapelier Law. But another factor, this one of an intellectual order, also played an important though less clear-cut role: the emergence of the discipline of sociology in the 1870s led to a new understanding of society. We cannot rehearse that history in detail here. It is highly complex, and to study it properly we would need to examine the work of many earlier writers, starting with Auguste Comte, who invented the word "sociology" if not the thing itself. We would also need to look at the rich tradition of social surveys, from the early work of Louis René Villermé and his associates in the *Annales d'hygiène publique et de médecine légale* in the late 1820s to the major monographs inspired by Frédéric Le Play fifty years later. Ignoring all this, we begin our examination at a later date, 1877, when Alfred Espinas published *Des sociétés animales*. "His book marks the first chapter of sociology," Emile Durkheim noted shortly afterward, and we therefore take the date of its publication as our point of departure.[45]

Espinas belonged to the generation of 1870, which had been shocked by the French defeat in the Franco-Prussian War—a failure that was seen as moral and social as much as military. Members of this generation therefore set to work restoring the intellectual and political foundations of the French model. The situation was not unlike that of the generation of 1815, which came of age after the experiences of the Revolution and the long night of empire. In 1870 as in 1815, young men felt the same need to revive a tired nation and repair institutions that had for too long been battered by opposing principles.[46] In the wake of the Empire, however, there had been a tendency to meet the urgency of the situation by building grand systems, of which the oeuvres of Comte and Saint-Simon are merely the best-known examples. The response later in the century was different. Scholars set out to study reality and to rebuild politics on the basis of in-depth knowledge of the facts. This shift accounts for the interest in scientific psychology (first with Hippolyte Taine and later with Alexis Ribot) and sociology. Espinas exemplifies the new approach. "He was the first to study social facts as a science rather than as a complement to some grand philosophical system," Durkheim noted.[47] The nature of the critique of individualism changed. The attack no longer focused on a moral attitude. Writers emphasized the fact that the actual structure of society did not correspond in any way to the atomistic assumptions praised by some and attacked by a good many more. Jacobinism, with its statist-individualist worldview, thus came in for a new kind of criticism: since it did not correspond to the facts, it could be seen as an *ideology.*

Espinas began as a follower of Herbert Spencer, a writer whose immense intellectual influence in Europe in the last four decades of the nineteenth century is rather hard to imagine today. In *The Principles of Sociology* he compared society to a living organism: sociology was for him a continuation and further development of biology. Espinas's work was rooted in a similar organicism, to which he added the idea of collective consciousness (which Spencer rejected). His organic theory, as set forth in *Des sociétés animales,* led him to see society as a whole, a complex collective being, and not as a mere juxtaposition of sovereign individuals united by a formal political compact. It also led him to reject monist representations of the individual, now also described as a complex being. We cannot delve further here into this powerful and fundamental work. For us, the important thing is to point out the political consequences of Espinas's analysis. Rousseau was the principal target. "For the author of *The Social Contract,*" Espinas wrote, "there is no conceivable middle ground between direct sovereignty by individuals, which is pure anarchy, and collective sovereignty of the political body they constitute, which leads *in fine* to totalitarianism." This political and philosophical vision was based on an assumption that the social body could be seen as comprising individuals on the one hand and the state on the other, which for the sociologist was not an accurate reflection of reality. As Espinas saw it, scientific observation led to a different idea of the relation of the whole to its parts. Treating society as an organism encouraged a different way of understanding social function, as a complex of differentiated, interacting organized entities working together with one another. Between individuals and society as a whole there existed a large number of organs, associations, and intermediary bodies.

The immediate political consequence of this analysis was to reject the Jacobin view of sovereignty, which was tied to an obsessive fear of "states within the state," as the insistent formula has it. If society is an organism, it is nothing other than a dynamic, functional arrangement of other organisms.[48] In a system of this type, social power is inevitably diffuse. As Espinas wrote, "the doctrine of the social organism, which holds that everything is done by degrees [*par gradations*] and admits only the relative, is the only theory that reserves for citizens a part of the action they have delegated. This doctrine is also a doctrine of government. Organization is inconceivable without concentration, and concentration without delegation."[49] He thus rejected earlier republican conceptions of politics and institutions derived from natural law philosophies. To be sure, he allowed that the principles of 1789 were worthy of admiration in a historical and moral sense. They had played a crucial critical role and facilitated an effective attack on the Old Regime, but they were not based on an understanding of the facts sufficient to found a new order. "*Immortal principles*," he concluded, "cannot provide us with any solution to the most pressing problems of social organization."[50] With this he mentioned several of the day's more controversial issues: decentralization, the relation between the individual and the state, the right of secession, the organization of property. He then called on progressives among his contemporaries to reject the simplistic views of Le Chapelier. It is worth noting that Espinas also wrote a book on the Revolution, *La Philosophie sociale du XVIIIe siècle et la Révolution* (1898), in which he stressed the logic that led from the individualism of 1789 to the radical socialism of someone like Babeuf. For him, Babeuf was merely "the natural culmination and ultimate expression of Jacobinism."[51] In his view, the best way to move beyond the French model, with its perverse coupling of individualism with statism and related "denial of the right of association,"[52] was to study how society really functioned. "Sociology," he argued, "finds that association, or grouping, is the general law of all organic and inorganic existence."[53]

Espinas's work did not reach a wide audience in France. Spencer attracted far more readers. But Espinas was eagerly read and passionately discussed by scholars and left his mark on an entire generation. Among his readers was the philosopher Alfred Fouillée. Fouillée, along with Charles Renouvier, was one of the leading pedagogues of the "absolute Republic." His defense of a thesis on free will and determinism attracted Gambetta among other enthusiastic and admiring spectators. Twenty years later, he was the primary inspiration of Léon Bourgeois, the father of solidarism, whose tenure as prime minister marked the first application of a new social philosophy of the state. In 1880 Fouillée published his most influential book, *La Science sociale contemporaine*. In this work he took his inspiration from Espinas as well as Spencer and offered a synthesis of their approach with that of social-contract theorists from Rousseau to Kant. The key concept with which he hoped to join the two traditions was that of a "contractual organism."[54] His point was more normative than Espinas's. Fouillée wanted to synthesize the organic with the voluntary and thus individualism with socialism. He therefore emphasized the usefulness of associations and argued that the representation of society as a simple confrontation of individuals and the state was outmoded. Higher-order societies had moved beyond this to an "ideal synthesis of centralization and decentralization, a synthesis that is at once the ultimate form of the organism and of society."[55] Accordingly, he, too, viewed intermediary bodies and associations in a different light from those who subscribed to the revolutionary political culture of generality.

> The state of the future will be an association of associations, a free centralization stemming from decentralization itself, in which the interest and liberty of all will be in harmony with the interest and liberty of each individual. The contractual organism, in its perfection, is the reconciliation of two seemingly contradictory things: individuality and collectivity, decentralization and centralization, liberty of the parts and cohesion of the whole.[56]

Fouillée developed these propositions in numerous works, especially *La Propriété sociale et la démocratie* (1884), *Le Socialisme et la sociologie réformiste* (1909), and *La Démocratie politique et sociale* (1910). His sociology went a long way toward persuading people that the Republic could step away from the statist-individualist principles of 1789 without betraying itself. "When the Revolution in France (rightly) destroyed privileges and monopolies, it allowed itself to go so far as to destroy the principle of association as well. This was its great blunder."[57] He also criticized the Le Chapelier Law for "leaving workers as isolated as motes of dust" and rejected a system in which "the state allowed scarcely any major association to exist in France other than itself."[58] In order to overcome the errors of "individualist democracy" he sought to make sociology the basis for a reorganization of republican politics that would allow France to move beyond the liberal-versus-socialist antinomy characteristic of the late nineteenth century.

Durkheim's contribution should be understood in a similar light. His scientific and methodological contributions to sociology need not detain us here. We are interested in what he did to separate republicanism from Jacobinism. His first steps were guided by careful study of the work of Espinas, Fouillée, and Spencer, as well as Albert Schaeffle, the author of *Bau und Leben des sozialen Körpers,* which influenced a new generation of social scientists, even as another great German scholar, Otto von Gierke, left his stamp on jurists. Nothing illustrates Durkheim's position better than a review he wrote in 1890 of a book by Thomas Ferneuil, a writer specializing in educational issues, titled *Les Principes de 1789 et la science sociale.* Published to mark the Revolution's centennial, Ferneuil's book had a special place among the various encomia and critiques spurred by the occasion. The author was a committed republican, but he called upon his readers to take a fresh look at 1789. At a time when republicans were still engaged in debate with the last remnants of legitimism, Ferneuil focused on a different problem. For him, the heart of the matter was to distinguish between the principles of 1789 as "social faith and patriotic religion" and the same principles as analytical concepts. As analytical concepts, the principles of 1789 had been demolished by science, he argued. No society had ever been constituted by way of a formal contract among isolated individuals. As a reader of Espinas and Fouillée, he argued that analysis of the facts compelled us rather to view societies as organisms. "Hence there is a profound and flagrant contradiction between the ideas of the Revolution and the findings of modern sociology," he concluded.[59] Nevertheless, the severity of this judgment did nothing to diminish his republican ardor.

"Science may well have demolished the principles of 1789," he wrote, "but it is still our duty today to approach the legacy of the Revolution in a spirit of piety, to take from it those inestimable treasures of patriotic faith, devotion to the public good, and national solidarity that our fathers left for the edification of their offspring."[60]

Durkheim fully agreed with this approach. "The French Revolution, once an object of faith, is increasingly becoming an object of science," he began.[61] What about the principles of 1789? These could be viewed as either a historical event or a political fact. Following Ferneuil, Durkheim noted that "they were once a religion, which had its martyrs and apostles, which profoundly moved the masses, and which, when all is said and done, inspired great things."[62] As a scientific theory of society, however, those same principles had largely been invalidated, because man in reality bore no resemblance to the abstract entity envisioned by the revolutionaries. This conviction formed the basis of Durkheim's political vision. He was thus able to reconcile his critique of 1789 with his republican faith. His strictures on individualism were of a scientific order and no longer merely moral or political. Rousseau could thus be set aside dispassionately, for the simple reason that his concept of the social contract "bore no relation to the facts."[63] If sociology showed that the social system comprised not only individuals in confrontation with the larger society but a whole network of "secondary" groupings, it would be necessary to examine the legal and political implications. Although the liberation of the individual in France had been historically associated with the advent of a leveling state, it was now crucial, Durkheim argued, to accept that the conditions of modern society suggested that further emancipation depended on the creation of a coordinated hierarchy of new "centers of regulation."[64]

Finally, to take the measure of the intellectual transformation that marked the end of the nineteenth century, we must turn to the work of Léon Duguit. Duguit was a legal scholar by training, but as a young professor in the early 1890s he focused primarily on sociology.[65] At that time he was closely associated with Emile Worms and the group of scholars connected with the *Revue internationale de sociologie*. His work on the constitution of "objective" law originated in this period. Like Fouillée and Durkheim, Duguit regarded associations as a fact, the importance of which had to be appreciated. These writers were not interested simply in expressing their nostalgia or voicing their criticisms in the manner of Le Play and Taine. For them, associations were first and foremost a *social fact*, and their importance was increasing despite all the legal and political obstacles. "It is impossible," Duguit argued, "not to notice the fact that over the past twenty years particularly, there has been an immense reaction against the individualist doctrines of the Revolution in the form of a vast associationist movement, exemplified above all by the prodigious growth of unions of workers, farmers, and industrialists in France and abroad. No politician or legislator can remain indifferent to this development."[66] In dealing with the question of associations, Duguit thus initially adopted the position of observer. He, too, hoped to establish a new politics on the basis of "scientific sociology," taking what he believed to be an objective finding as his starting point: namely, the fact that society was a living being, an organized whole governed by laws of aggregation and cooperation.[67]

Revolutionary monism thus found itself under scrutiny as a result of a powerful intellectual movement that arose in the last quarter of the nineteenth century, a movement that can be conveniently summed up under the name "sociology." Many other writers could be invoked to demonstrate the full scope of this movement.[68] Of course this was not the only thing that shook the original French model. But there is no denying that, combined with the other factors we have examined, it brought the situation to a crossroads. The need for order and the emergence of new social fears encouraged people to look at associations in a new light, but it was the fact that the very core of the Jacobin system was now subject to intellectual challenge that made it vulnerable. Sociology helped to change the contours of the conceivable in late nineteenth-century France. Fouillée spoke of "fundamental new ideas," and Durkheim spoke of new representations of the social as playing an active role and serving as a real driving force. Change was undeniable, even if it was still only in its early stages. In the next few chapters we shall try to measure its extent.

— 10 —

The Trade Union Exception

A century after the Le Chapelier Law, the law of 21 March 1884 granting legal recognition to trade unions opened a breach in the French system. It not only repealed the celebrated law of 14 June 1791 but also marked a break in terms of political culture. It came late in the day, to be sure, especially when compared with the experience of other countries: union action had been legal in England since 1824, for example. But still, the break was undeniable. Nevertheless, the history of the trade union movement cannot be reduced to the passage of a single law. One indicator of the complexity of the situation is that it took a significant amount of time after 1884 for associations in general to be granted legal recognition: this did not happen until 1901. In many respects, the law governing associations lagged behind the law governing unions (for example, in regard to such technical matters as "civil person" status and institutionalization). We shall return to this later, since it tells us a great deal about the ambiguities of the French case. First, however, we need to appreciate the significance of the legislation on professional associations and assess its broader implications by looking beyond the circumstantial factors whose importance we noted in the previous chapter.

A Special Law?

Although Lockroy was the first to file a bill to legalize trade unions in 1876, his proposal followed a series of earlier initiatives in regard to freedom of association. The whole issue had been broached as early as 1871, as we shall see in detail in the next chapter. Nothing came of it at that time, however, owing to a combination of conservative suspicions and philosophical doubts. Seen in this light, the 1876 initiative reveals a calculated lowering of sights on the part of reformers. "Today," as one contemporary observer put it, "one no longer hears calls for broadening the law [of association in general]. The only demand is for workers' unions to be granted the freedom to associate and the right to assemble."[1] Yet even this incrementalist policy was a long way from garnering universal support. In fact, it drew criticism from various quarters on the grounds that it would grant a privilege to a particular category of citizens. In the late 1870s and early 1880s, bills to authorize the right of association generally were repeatedly tabled, while the bill to legalize the unions was delayed frequently. The paradoxical thing about the history of intermediary bodies in France is that procedural particularity (partial reform) was rejected as firmly as social or political particularity (the association of particular interests). Doctrinal aversion to a certain kind of reformism was thus rooted in the very essence of Jacobin culture.

The battle was especially fierce in the Senate. Pierre Jouin, a moderate, summed up the sentiment of many senators: "Until now, I have lived in the conviction that all the French were supposed to be equal before the law and that the law was supposed to be the same for all citizens. I do not understand the theory that there are individuals and categories for whom organizing freedom is the easiest thing in the world."[2] A special law for unions? The honorable republican did not shrink from calling this a "privilege accorded to some," thus revealing how potent the old argument remained. In the same vein, his colleague Joseph Brunet deplored the proposed bill as a "law of exception."[3] In the Chamber of Deputies a number of members made similar statements. Félix Cantagrel, a Fourierist disciple, agreed with his Radical colleagues that the association issue could not be broken down into "unions" and "others" and voiced serious doubts about the union bill.[4] Similar sentiments emanated from the benches of the center left, where one liberal republican, Alexis Ribot, thought it useful to rehash the whole history of the struggle against corporations before expressing his "regret that we now seem ready to pass a law benefiting certain class interests" and evoking the "real danger" of showing such favor to a particular group.[5] These hesitations and doubts would be overcome by powerful political pressures that favored passage. "The question," as Lockroy put it, "is what the Republic is going to do for the workers who have done so much for the Republic."[6]

The bill's sponsors felt that defending the bill against these fundamental objections called for a broad and substantive approach. As if afraid of unleashing old demons that they would be unable to control, however, they chose a rather oblique strategy. Tolain's argument is noteworthy in this light. He did not reject the charge by the bill's adversaries that it was a "law of exception" but rather justified it as a paradoxical way of restoring normality to what was itself an exceptional situation: "All classes of citizens except manual laborers have found ways of organizing that are tantamount to granting themselves certain privileges . . . Only manual workers have never enjoyed the right to assemble and associate. They still live under this exceptional and draconian legislation, which it will be the honor and dignity of republican assemblies to eliminate at last."[7] Lockroy spoke in similar terms in the Chamber: "It is because we recognize that workers are in an exceptional and special situation that we need exceptional and special laws to fix it."[8] Thus proponents of the trade union bill acknowledged that it was a law of exception but shrank from considering the theoretical implications.

It became increasingly common to distinguish unions from associations in general without any clear understanding of what this meant. One sign of this trend is the semantic shift that took place between 1848 and 1870. In 1848, any grouping of workers, whether in the form of a producers' cooperative or a protest delegation, was automatically classified as an association. It was only toward the end of the Second Empire that the term *syndicat,* or trade union, began to be applied to organized labor. This process of semantic differentiation deserves close attention. There is no mystery about the origin of the word: it was the French translation of the British term "trade union" (and the history of the British trade unions became more widely known in France after a delegation of French workers was sent to the London International Exhibition in 1862); the French word chosen for this purpose was an archaic term borrowed from the corporatist and administrative vocabulary.[9] Before the word *syndicat* came into general use, another old formulation, *chambre syndicale,* was widely employed, at first by employers, who applied the term to their earliest professional organizations.[10] In 1863, Tolain, who was then a leading figure in the Proudhon-inspired workers' movement and would become one of the principal drafters of the "Manifesto of Sixty," called for the formation of *chambres syndicales ouvrières.*[11] One finds in his writing hints of social separatism, since he believed that organizations of workers belonged to a class unto themselves. At about this time the trade union movement came into its own as something distinct from the earlier associative movement. The word *syndicat* gained favor in the context of this differentiation, and it was in 1866 that an association of shoemakers became the first to call itself by this name.[12] Now at last there was a specific word for a specific social reality, and this addition to the lexicon helped to lay the groundwork for a specific law.

The Disputed Terrain of the Trade Union

The legalization of unions was fraught with contradiction. At first, as we have seen, it was proposed that unions be treated as a *particular type* of association, but this approach raised the old hobgoblin of "privilege" and therefore aroused opposition. At the same time, however, people feared that the unions harbored ambitions to broaden their *field of action* to such a degree of generality that they might be tempted to enter the realm of politics. This worry, which afflicted most parties in the 1870s and 1880s, was of course partly tactical. For those who saw the unions as instruments for effecting a functional division between the social and the political so as to confine labor conflicts to the social sphere, where there would be less danger of their exploding into revolutionary threats, it was obviously desirable that the unions should be institutionalized in such a way as to preserve that fundamental distinction.[13] Such a move entailed limiting their field of action strictly to the economic realm, that is, to representing the "particular interests" of a specific group of workers.

The various drafts of the trade union bill reflect this concern, which many saw as fundamental. Lockroy's 1876 draft was content to ascribe to the unions the purpose of "defending the common industrial interests of their members." In the Cazot-Tirard proposal of 1880, this clause was tightened and made more precise: "Unions have as their exclusive purpose the study and defense of those professional, economic, industrial, and commercial interests common to all their members." The goal was not only to broaden the definition of a union to include economic activities in general and not just the industrial sector, but also to extend the permissible field of action by allowing unions not just to present worker demands but also to engage in occupational training or to organize themselves as mutual investment or mutual aid societies. The crucial word, however, was "exclusive," which conveyed the clear intention to limit union action strictly to the economic and social sphere. This issue was central in debates in the two assemblies between 1881 and 1884. Concern was heightened by a proposal, briefly entertained, to include a reference to the "general interests" of the occupational groups concerned.[14] It was rejected. There were two reasons for this: first, to make it clear that a union represented only a particular segment of society and thus to prevent any "encroachment on generality"; second, to squelch any temptation on the part of the unions to trespass on the political realm. As the rapporteur in the Chamber of Deputies stressed in 1882, it was important to make sure that the words "general interest" could not "serve as a pretext for discussions unrelated to occupational issues."[15]

Debate on the composition of the unions took up where questions as to their nature left off. Article 2 of the law of 1884 stipulated that professional organizations must consist of individuals "exercising the same profession, similar trades, or related professions cooperating in the production of specific goods." The final phrase was added as the debate proceeded to take account of evolving forms of industrial organization, which tended to erode the traditional category of "trade" (métier). The guiding idea, however, was that the union structure should be based on the narrowest possible definition of shared interests. "If the unions are to render the services that many people expect of them, they . . . should be made up of individuals engaged in the same industry so as to maintain the purely professional character of the institution," according to Paul Lafitte's summary in the Revue politique et littéraire.[16] In smaller towns, however, the number of workers in each occupational category might be too small to support independent unions, so amendments were proposed to authorize organizations of workers from different trades; these were firmly rejected, however. Residual elements of the old corporatist culture among workers (based on a distinct identity for each trade) reinforced conservative fears of a vast class-based organization deemed to be inconsistent with republican principles.[17]

The issue of unions of unions was approached with a similar mind-set. Although Lockroy said nothing about the subject in 1876, Allain-Targé had proposed in his spring 1881 report to the Chamber of Deputies that the law authorize unions of syndicats professionnels. Both employers and trade unions had asked for this provision. Employer groups had already engaged in several attempts to create larger organizations. On the workers' side, a first "Union des Chambres Syndicales Ouvrières de France" brought together moderate trade unions under the leadership of J. Barberet (Waldeck-

Rousseau would enlist its support in the final stages of parliamentary debate on the proposed law). All militant workers aspired to some form of super-union, as was evident during the Congress of Lyons (1878) and of Marseilles (1879). Unions of unions offered undeniable practical advantages. Labor negotiations and conflict resolutions often involved a range of trades associated with a particular industry or a range of organizations associated with a particular locality. The Chamber of Deputies acknowledged the reasonableness of such an approach, but the Senate took the opposite view, and it was on this new battlefield that opponents of the law preferred to wage their campaign to ban unions of unions.

Most senators found it possible to regard unions organized for a strictly limited and disciplined purpose as elements of order, but super-unions were an altogether different matter. The fear was that trade union federations might become revolutionary instruments. Some went so far as to speak of the advent of a "central power" or "veritable government" and evoked the "terrifying concept of a universal union" as a potential threat to society. As René Bérenger asked, "Is it possible to believe that a million men united under common leadership might not pose a danger to the state?"[18] Old fears of the multitude thus converged with critiques of corporatism on this issue. The clearest indication of this effect came when Emile Lenoël, the wizened old senator from the Manche, mounted the podium to speak as a self-described "old republican." He implored his colleagues not to legalize trade union federations, whose power, he argued, would ultimately strike at the very foundation of the representative republic. If huge masses of people were to band together in a professional organization, the result would be "to create a veritable counterweight to the action of national sovereignty freely exercised in electoral meetings."[19] Small trade unions strictly limited to the defense of clearly defined special interests could be tolerated, but for Emile Lenoël the change of scale implied a change of nature, the result of which was likely to be a partisan association intent on substituting its particular interests for the generality of the public sphere. "The federations," he insisted,

> will be precisely the opposite of Parliament, because all shades of opinion are represented in the assemblies elected by the nation. In the federations, however, only the exclusive interest of the members will be represented, and exclusive interest is always blind . . . If you have three million feder-

ated workers, you have a very large faction, but it is still only a fraction of the nation, and my personal gospel holds that sovereignty is one and indivisible and that no faction can arrogate it unto itself.[20]

With powerful unions possessing many branches, the Republic would thus be in danger: this was Lenoël's position, and it was supported by a good many of his colleagues.

At first these prejudices commanded a majority in the Senate, and it took Waldeck-Rousseau quite some time to overcome them. Facing a chamber whose members did not hesitate to wrap themselves in the old banner of the crusaders against privilege, the minister of the interior did not attack his adversaries head on. Significantly, he limited himself to laying out the practical political advantages to be gained by legalizing the unions.[21] He began by expressing his faith in the moderating virtues of large numbers in the face of aroused minorities, thus applying another article of the republican credo that had been developed earlier in support of universal suffrage itself.[22] Hence, for example, Waldeck-Rousseau invoked the "conservative instincts of the masses" to reject the dark forebodings of those who saw nothing in the organized masses of workers but an "army of disorder." In other words, he based his case on the republican image of a virtuous French people. At the same time he stood the argument against particularity on its head by emphasizing that the development of super-unions would reduce the corporatist peril by encouraging broader social sympathies. This notion of a "generalization" of the interests of the working class remained fragile, however, because it did not answer the question of how a class interest related to the national interest. It did have an immediate rhetorical effect, however, in countering the arguments of those who saw the proposed law as leaving society vulnerable to the corrosive anarchical power of particular interests.

The Process of Institutionalization

Legal recognition of the trade unions led to a rapid increase in their number, from 68 in 1884 to 1,006 in 1890, 3,287 in 1900, and 5,354 in 1908. In 1884 only a handful of workers had been unionized in small, isolated groups, but by the turn of the century nearly 600,000 belonged to unions, and by 1914 the number had risen to more than a million. National federations developed with similar rapidity. Although the percentage of workers

belonging to unions was much smaller in France than in Germany or England, the situation differed sharply from what it had been before passage of
the law of 1884. This fact did not prevent many militant workers from feeling hostility toward a law that they believed had subjected the working
class to government oversight by requiring unions to file for official authorization.[23] A decade of practical experience gradually dispelled the doubts,
however. The reigning republicans were glad to see the strike threat diminish even if the number of strikes did not. As Waldeck-Rousseau was able to
say in 1900, "the new phenomenon, the precious and heartening fact, is
that unions do more than go out on strike. They impose rules and discipline strikers. [Shouts of 'Very good! Very good!' from the left, extreme left,
and center.] That is the social progress to which the legislation of 1884 has
given rise."[24]

The granting of the long-awaited freedom to organize was not the end
of the story, however. The unions very quickly became the institutional
representatives of the workers. As early as 1891, certain union representatives sat *ex officio* on the new Board of Labor, which was charged with
informing the government about "the true needs of the working population."[25] In the exposition of the bill filed by Emile Eugène Gustave
Mesureur and Alexandre Millerand, we read that "since the workers' unions are the only legal organization to which we can appeal, we ask them to
determine the representation of workers."[26] This role was reaffirmed when
the council was reorganized in 1899 and further reinforced by the establishment of regional councils in 1900.[27] A short while earlier, Millerand
had reorganized the Inspectorate of Labor, urging inspectors to work with
the unions to gather information about working conditions and uncover
abuses by employers. The editor of *La Petite République* congratulated him
on this initiative: "It transforms workers' organizations from pariahs into
organs of the state. In a way it makes them a part of the executive branch
by subjecting the officials responsible for executing laws in which the proletariat has an interest under the unions' control."[28] Jaurès, even more enthusiastic, spoke of "a first step for the working class toward taking possession of the capitalist organization" and even went so far as to call it "the
beginning of a social revolution."[29] In themselves these comments are an
indication of the change that was under way. The fact that a traditional liberal like Leroy-Beaulieu vigorously criticized this measure only confirms
its importance: "This amounts to a revival and official recognition of the
Old Regime corporation that Turgot fought against and the Revolution

eliminated, and if it doesn't yet restore all its abusive rights, it nevertheless marks a first step in that direction," he thundered. "It is the most colossal change that has been made in France since 1789."[30] Things had truly changed: the old suspicion of intermediary bodies had been dispelled.

The instrumental perspective, in which the unions were seen as a means of maintaining social order, continued to play a crucial role in the process of institutionalization. We see this influence in various proposals to extend the civil capacities of the unions. Many conservatives supported these because they believed that allowing the institutionalized unions to acquire property would have a moderating, pacifying effect by turning "corporatist activities toward peaceful works rather than dangerous activities of propaganda and militancy."[31] People intent on managing their property ceased to think about social reform, these grave gentlemen insisted. Thus unions were permitted to do what other associations were not at this point. In 1920 a bold new law capped this line of thinking. Unions not only could appear in court but also could own property virtually without restriction; establish and administer contingency funds, training institutes, and low-cost housing; subsidize producers' and consumers' cooperatives; and sign contracts or agreements with commercial companies.[32] The trade unions had become institutions.

Attitudes toward the right to work (and hence the closed union shop) also evolved. In the 1890s the Cour de Cassation still held that unions could speak and act only on behalf of their members. In 1893 the court issued a celebrated decision in which it saw what it called "syndical tyranny" in a union's refusal to allow a nonmember to agree to a wage below the rate negotiated by the union. The judges vehemently refused to accept the argument that the union could express its own general interest as distinct from the sum of its individual members' interests. Judicial opinion on this point slowly evolved, however, to the point where a "general interest of the profession" was recognized. A 1913 decision of the entire court settled the matter by affirming that the union was a legal person distinct from its individual members and that its inherent responsibilities included defending the interests of the profession.[33] A few years earlier, the Labor Code of 1910 officially recognized the existence of a legal realm distinct from both public law and private law. Although some people warned at the time of the perils of "class-based legislation," the code marked a turning point.[34]

As additional occupational groups organized, the union form of organization became more and more institutionalized. The first unions had been

composed of either employers or industrial workers, but now farm workers and sales personnel also formed unions. All wage earners were concerned by legislation affecting the unions. Reporting on a bill before the
Senate, Tolain noted that the law "will be used by a large number of people
to whom no thought was given initially: for instance, office workers, accountants, clerks, and all sorts of white-collar personnel. In short, everyone engaged in an occupation is concerned."[35] To be sure, unionization of
these categories of workers proceeded much more slowly and less broadly
than unionization of industrial workers, but the door was now open. In
1892, various professionals (most notably in medicine) were authorized to
form unions. The movement proceeded until unions were accepted as a generic mode of representing and defending collective interests in all spheres
of social activity. In 1910, for instance, tenants formed a union in Paris. As
social conflicts over housing increased in the period between the two
world wars, a Confédération National du Logement was organized, and
by 1920 it boasted of having signed up 100,000 members. In 1928, a consumers' union known as the Confédération Générale pour la Défense des
Consommateurs claimed as many as four million members. The social
landscape no longer resembled that envisaged by the Le Chapelier Law.

New Forms of Collective Regulation

Institutionalization of the unions meant more than just integrating them
into the regulatory machinery and involving them in various councils of
government. It also reflected new realities and practices in the workplace.
To sum up a complex set of changes, one might say that recognition of the
unions marked the beginning of a more organized phase of economic and
social regulation. The "individualist" contractualism envisaged by the Civil
Code of 1804 gave way to new procedures and to a novel form of "collective" law. One should be careful, of course, not to make this contrast too
absolute, because collective negotiating *practices* did exist in the first half of
the nineteenth century, as exemplified, for instance, by the wage schedules established in the textile, printing, and construction trades.[36] Yet such
agreements remained isolated and were associated more with the survival
of old procedures than with the emergence of a new legal framework.
There were no standards governing such schedules where they existed,
and agreements of this kind enjoyed no legal status. This state of affairs
changed at the end of the nineteenth century, for reasons that were above

all economic, associated with the rise of large-scale industry. As Charles Floquet explained to the Chamber during the debate on the law of 1884, "until now the commodity known as labor was sold retail, parcel by parcel, by isolated individuals; now, by way of associations, we must set up whole-sale, collective trade in this commodity, which we call human labor."[37] As one contemporary observer noted, when dealing with a large-scale indus-try that "de-individualized" the factors of production, one had to forge a suitable tool, a type of collective agreement capable of serving as the "in-dispensable legal machinery" required by the new industry.[38] Older forms of regulation, such as the *conseils de prud'hommes,* whose role was much more important than used to be recognized, were indeed eroded in the 1860s, not only by narrow decisions rendered by the Cour de Cassation but also by the effects of industrial change itself.[39]

The nature of what might be called "the collective" (to use the language of the nineteenth century) also changed in this period. For a long time it had manifested itself only in strikes, when common action in a sense fused workers into a unit. "The striker is not an individual. There is no such thing as 'a striker,' only 'strikers,'" Maxime Leroy pointed out. "In a time of strike, only the collectivity exists."[40] By the end of the century, this was no longer the sole mode in which the collective existed; it no longer appeared only in exceptional circumstances.[41] It was now the regular and permanent form of workers as a group. What would soon be called the "working masses" was quite simply a by-product of the rise of big industry.

It was in this context that the need for new forms of labor regulation be-came apparent. Initially the concern was with managing conflicts. This was the purpose of the law of 27 December 1892 on conciliation and arbitra-tion, which proposed detailed procedures for employers and workers to follow in attempting to resolve labor disputes.[42] But the most important change was in the nature of the labor contract itself. As early as 1902, a bill was filed in the Chamber of Deputies concerning "collective contracts per-taining to working conditions."[43] The term *convention collective* was coined shortly thereafter to designate the new legal form that many hoped would lead to efficient regulation of labor relations in the modern firm. The new collective agreement marked a break with the definitions and implicit constraints associated with the traditional contractual model of the Civil Code. The *convention collective* in effect assumed the existence of a group and was binding on each of its members independent of their individual consent. It set forth general rules to be respected by subsequent, more specific labor contracts. "When looked at solely in the light of a strict interpretation of existing laws, the collective contract seems to us something close to a legal monstrosity," one panicky law professor observed at the time.[44] The economist Charles Gide did not hesitate to observe that the new type of contract was "perhaps the latest and most significant development in the history of wage labor."[45]

The conception and application of this new hybrid legal form would enlist the energies of law professors as well as reformers of various stripes, all working in close consultation with republicans in government keen to resolve the "social question." These people came together in places like the young Société des Etudes Législatives and the Association Nationale Française pour la Protection Légale des Travailleurs. The work done by the Committee for the Codification of Labor Laws created by Millerand in 1901 offers a convenient window into this milieu. A number of names pop up in several of these contexts. One such was Raoul Jay, a professor in the Faculty of Law in Paris. Millerand assigned him to draft the first part of what would become the Labor Code of 1910, dealing with "conventions pertaining to labor." He was also the secretary general of the Association pour la Protection Légale des Travailleurs, closely associated with the Musée Social circles; and, along with Barthélemy Raynaud, Raymond Saleilles, and Souchon, he was also a member of the subcommittee of the Société d'Etudes Législatives, which drafted the first proposed bill on collective conventions in 1904.[46] Thus he played a central role in the reform effort. "We are dealing here with matters on the boundary between public law and private law," he wrote.

> Does not the union in some respects figure in the collective labor contract as the delegate and precursor of the legislator? What is certain is that we would be giving an incomplete and therefore inaccurate idea of the collective labor contract, and fail to make clear what future it might portend, if we did not point out the undeniable implication of a contract of this type, namely, that it tends to create a *professional legislation* more or less directly binding on an entire line of work.[47]

The idea guiding the reformers' efforts was to bring the conditions of a certain social order into line with a new juridical order. Some spoke of the contract as a law "establishing permanent and lasting relations between two social groups," a convention "governing the relations between two social classes."[48]

The idea of a collective agreement was widely accepted by the early twentieth century, but support for it drew on various doctrines that could conflict in practice. Broadly speaking, attitudes clustered around two poles. One group took a contractualist approach, viewing the collective agreement simply as a mechanism for coordinating the individual with the collective, and some went so far as to suggest that collective agreements should be ratified by every affected individual. A second group took what might be called a regulatory approach: the collective agreement established a set of regulations that differed from state regulations only in the fact that they stemmed from private bargaining within an industry rather than from some government agency. The issue gave rise to a large volume of legal writing over a number of years.[49] Various elaborations of the traditional notions of "mandate" and "stipulation for others" were mooted: "anonymous contract," "rule-act," "legal mandate," "law-convention," and the like. None of these concepts won unanimous approval, and it seems that the collective convention was seen as something of a hybrid by nature, resembling a contract in the manner of its inception and a regulation in the manner of its application.

Because of its ambiguous nature, the collective convention was slow to catch on. It was recognized as a social necessity before being seen as a new legal category. Even this de facto recognition was slow in coming. The bills filed by Mesureur in 1906 and René Viviani in 1910 never passed, and it was not until 1919 that the law finally recognized collective conventions.[50] It took the war to move things along by requiring new forms of engagement with the unions. Before that there existed an unmistakable gap between the generous visionary spirit of the handful of jurists and social republicans who hailed the collective agreement as "the social formula of the century"[51] and the inextricably intertwined political and philosophical doubts of successive parliamentary majorities. In any case, the law of 1919 was quite limited in scope. Although it stipulated that the collective agreement took precedence over individual contracts and that the union could take legal action on behalf of individuals suffering harm in case of a breach, it also limited the benefits of the agreement to members of the union. Thus the idea, widely accepted after 1900, that the collective agreement was meaningless unless it created a general obligation was ignored. The final break with the traditional law of contracts did not come until the law of 24 June 1936 was approved. At that point the collective agreement truly became the law of the workplace, binding on all and benefiting all.

Capping this advance was what was known as the extension procedure, which established a mechanism for extending a collective agreement to all firms in a given branch of industry, including firms not belonging to the employer group that had signed the agreement.

The Workers' Corporation

The reluctance to allow intermediary bodies (in this case both an association and a governing institution) was thus finally overcome in the case of the trade unions. The reason why this was possible is sociological in nature: it was possible to see the union as giving *form* to workers as a group. Establishing the unions, Millerand noted, "is tantamount to replacing an inorganic mob of workers with an organism capable of reflecting, willing, and acting."[52] The assumption was that the union represented the workers collectively. This assumption was not universally accepted at the turn of the twentieth century, when the proportion of workers belonging to unions, though it had increased rapidly in just a few years, remained low. Millerand thus drew criticism for his decision to allow only unions to represent workers on the regional labor councils established by the decree of 17 September 1900. He was vehemently attacked for this in both the Chamber and the Senate. Most republicans rejected a system in which "the unions are to be imposed as intermediaries on the nonunion majority."[53] Millerand's answers reflect his embarrassment. He spoke of the danger of "mobilizing universal suffrage too often" as well as of undermining the authority of the unions.[54] Two months later, he therefore joined with Waldeck-Rousseau in proposing a system of *elected* delegates within firms for the purpose of attempting to reach amicable settlements of disputes over working conditions. The same bill also required any strike decision to be put to a vote, with the decision of the majority to be binding on all workers.[55] The bill was harshly attacked by smaller firms, which warned of workers' being compelled to strike against their wishes and alleged that the proposed law would "leave employers at the mercy of workers."[56] Officials and militants of the Confédération Générale du Travail (CGT) were also adamantly opposed to what they contemptuously characterized as "democratism."

Instead of atomized individual voters, mere numeric constituents of an abstract collective will, the founding fathers of syndicalism wanted what they believed to be a more realistic form of cohesion rooted in the economic organization of the trade. "Democratism" was therefore seen as radically antagonistic to syndicalism both practically and culturally. The two concepts were opposed in every way: democracy consecrated the reign of opinion, whereas syndicalism was based on an identity of interests; democracy was a regime of discourse, whereas syndicalism was organized around the problem of production; democracy asserted a purely formal equality, whereas syndicalism instituted real equality among its members; democracy encouraged resignation, as individuals delegated responsibility to others, whereas syndicalism could not exist without the involvement of its members and was therefore a source of energy and identity. They also (as Millerand had predicted) rejected the idea of a secret individual ballot: "The secret ballot," they said, "destroys the unity of the masses; the voter feels isolated, alone with his ballot. The intention is thus to destroy the will of the masses and to discourage voters."[57] The philosophy of these militants was that of an active minority. The "ringleaders" who aroused the suspicions of wise republican reformers were seen as the soul of the labor movement, and they were hostile to any proposal that might lead to "parliamentarizing" the workers' organization.

Capitalist fears and militant aversions thus combined with the doubts and perplexities of the republican majority to scuttle the Millerand proposal. Apart from the socialist Jaurès, virtually no one overtly supported the idea, and Jaurès went so far as to suggest that the unions be empowered to make laws based on the direct mandate of the wage earners.[58] Indeed, the institutionalization of the unions raised the whole question of their representativeness. Since it seemed impossible to deny that they did represent something, there was a need to find a practical expression of this fact. How? By reducing the distance between law and fact and combining the two faces of the unions—on the one hand, representatives of an entire trade, on the other hand, delegates of their membership: in other words, by closing the gap between the individualist logic of membership and the "public" institutional logic of a regulatory function. Any number of proposals to that end emerged in the early 1900s. For instance, the jurist Georges Scelle suggested that union membership be made compulsory and even that a single union be designated as the official representative of workers.[59] This step would eliminate the difficulty posed by the gap between the associative nature of unions and the role it was hoped they would play: that of governing authorities in their industries. The representing organization would then coincide perfectly with the representative organ, and there would no longer be any reason for jurists to feel uneasy about the a priori assumption of representativeness. The theoretical problem of syndicalism would be resolved by the practical elimination of the dual nature that had created it. In October 1908 a deputy named Louis-Lucien Klotz filed a bill that would have created a National Federation of Labor composed of the presidents or secretaries of union groups, and this federation would have had quasi-official status.[60] It was to have been chosen by a system of regional elections in order to ensure that the union officials selected would be seen as representatives of all workers. The CGT vehemently denounced this proposal. "This is a childish and pitiful attempt to parliamentarize the unions," in the view of Alphonse Merrheim, the secretary of the CGT metalworkers' federation. "They want to treat the organized working class the way they treat the mass of voters."[61] On the other side of the fence, employers were terrified by the prospect of a "compulsory union." Hence these proposals went nowhere. Opposition from both sides converged to prevent any clear resolution of the question of the unions' representativeness. The growth of the unions took advantage of this ambiguity.

Representativeness would either be implicitly assumed or else in some vague way be taken as an ultimate goal. Views that might at first sight seem incompatible were thus able to coexist and even be combined, at the price of a certain ambiguity. Revolutionary syndicalists took a maximalist approach, defending a purely essentialist view of the unions,[62] whereas social republicans preferred a more prosaic arithmetic view of the unions; but in practice these distinct views ceased to clash once the proposals for "voting tests" were abandoned. Commenting on the law of 1884, Hubert Lagardelle, reflecting the first point of view, wrote that "for the first time the legislature has begun to recognize the concept of a 'collective worker' as opposed to the isolated worker. *The corporation of workers has been recognized as having a personal existence* . . . The complex but unified personality of the working class is already beginning to emerge."[63] For Lagardelle and his friends, the working class was indeed a corporation, a *corps*, a body, "a solid unit," of which the union was in a sense merely the form. Hence the question of membership was secondary, because "the union through its action in fact transcends the narrow circle of its members."[64] In defending the system of union nominations to the Board of Labor, Emile Mesureur tried to relativize the issue by treating it as a temporary condition: as he saw it, the unions would evolve to the point where nearly all workers would belong to them.[65] In that case, the distinction between election and nomination would in effect be abolished, and the essentialist and democratic qualities of the unions would coincide perfectly. Millerand ultimately adopted this pragmatic point of view himself; he even invoked Fouillée in support of the idea that the union was nothing other than the organized working class.[66]

The jurists who elaborated the notion of a collective agreement also sought ultimate support in the idea that actual labor collectives did in fact exist. Indeed, Raoul Jay went so far as to predict that "the twentieth century will witness the rebirth of corporations."[67] Raynaud, for his part, remarked on "the de facto sovereignty of the workmen's association" and noted that it was practically the governing authority for a given population of workers. From this he concluded that the domination of the unions—which he did not hesitate to call "syndical tyranny" in order to show that he was not averting his gaze from the realities of the situation—had a real basis and amply justified the view that the majority should take precedence over the minority on labor-related issues. In his view there was a "general interest of labor" that deserved priority over the particular interest, for in this respect the social was structured in the same way as the political.[68] Paving the way for works by people like Duguit and Georges Gurvitch, Saleilles went even further, arguing that the emerging social law was "the revenge of the idea of the social solidarity of the homogeneous group on the dispersion of isolated units in the individualist system."[69] He developed this theme, the right of integration, at length in his pioneering major work, De la personnalité juridique (1910). "What individualists found only in what constitutes the essence of the human personality, what theologians sought only in God, sociologists find realized in history," he argued. "And without having to ask where society comes from or who its author was, when they want to know what the laws are and how to define and enforce them, they think it sufficient to discover a fact susceptible of scientific observation and ineluctably necessary in the sense that law is necessary in its relations with the social organism."[70]

Saleilles, like his colleagues at the Société des Etudes Législatives, was influenced by the German legal literature of his day. He closely followed the drafting of the new Civil Code and was an attentive reader of Gierke. In one of his early works he gave a detailed analysis of the problems Germany had faced in defining legal persons in public law (a category that included associations, unions, and corporations), and among judicial reformers he was therefore foremost in moving in the direction of social law.[71] The role played by this small group cannot be understood solely in terms of doctrinal rigor, however. What is striking, in fact, is how imprecise the foundations of their approach to the social still were. They did not embrace either the essentialism of the revolutionary syndicalists or the corporatist nostalgia of Catholic traditionalists. It is easy to see, for example, what set them apart from people like Maxime Leroy and Georges Sorel, who thought that unions might become the sole legislators in each profession they organized. They also did not share the vision of Albert de Mun and his friends, who idealized "natural groups."[72] Nor did they share the rigorous sociological vision of "occupational groups" developed by Durkheim. In a sense the influence of these jurists stemmed from their distances from the various juridical, political, and sociological models that dominated the theory of the day. As social Catholics, the language they spoke and the references they used were such that the republican camp did not need to feel alienated from its inherited political culture. They could also be heard by socialists influenced by their German counterparts or by Jaurès. In their hands, the syndical exception ceased to seem radical. It could be presented as a modest instrumental adjustment. The question of intermediary bodies was pared down to a practical question of social organization.

— 11 —

Liberty and Institutions

One Word, Many Things

The political and intellectual changes whose broad outline we have described gradually diminished suspicion of the associative principle. The passage of the law of 1901 symbolized an undeniable shift in opinion. Yet we should be wary of focusing exclusively on this legal milestone. The rigors of the law throughout the nineteenth century were one thing; actual practice was another. When we look at how things were actually done, the picture that emerges is rather different from that derived solely from the law and stated principles. Beneath the Jacobin rhetoric, a civil society had in fact been constructed, and this society had a solidity of its own. Standing Tocqueville on his head, one might say that underneath the imaginary republic a real France was built little by little.[1] Political societies, charitable associations, student groups, and literary societies had already emerged during the Restoration; improvement came across the board in 1848; and the end of the Second Empire proved to be yet another high point of associative activity.[2] The French model has always exhibited a sort of split personality, operating more pragmatically than its stated principles would lead one to assume.

A number of factors help us to understand this gap. One is simply that the government demonstrated a degree of tolerance. To be sure, Article 291 of the Penal Code required all associations of more than twenty people to apply for official authorization. In practice, however, this law was not rigidly enforced. Nothing demonstrates this relaxed attitude better than the instructions that Thiers sent to his prefects regarding application of the repressive law of 1834. The prefects were explicitly told to concentrate on political groups and not to apply the strict general provisions of the law to industrial, literary, charitable, or mutual aid societies. With respect to the latter, the instructions of the minister of the interior were unambiguous: "You will apply to my administration for authorization if they ask for it; you will ignore their existence if they conduct themselves in a manner worthy of being ignored . . . If a society of this type displays insolence in refusing to apply for authorization or openly defies the law, then and only then will you be obliged to intervene."[3] The instructions also called upon the prefects to keep hands off even those circles "formed by men of the opposition" as long as they caused no trouble. In other words, the July Monarchy was close to preferring an absence of authorization, because a policy of tolerance allowed it some room for maneuver if necessary. It is symptomatic, moreover, that very few violations of Article 291 were prosecuted in the nineteenth century. Only one case was brought under the Restoration, in 1819 against the Société des Amis de la Presse. Under the July Monarchy, and especially in its early years, quite a number of republican societies were prosecuted but mostly on other grounds (for threats to the security of the state, conspiracy, incitement to violate the law, and challenging the king's authority). The penalties for these other crimes were of course much greater. The only important cases stemming from a violation of Article 291 were the "trial of thirteen" in 1864, which concerned campaign committees, and the prosecution of a group of leagues in 1899.[4]

By contrast, successive governments were always interested in controlling associations and kept a watchful eye on various circles and societies and especially bars and taverns, mostly in the provinces.[5] It was in the bars and taverns that the alleged troublemakers from the poorer segments of society gathered. Whereas there were at most a few hundred or perhaps a few thousand circles and societies in France in the middle of the nineteenth century, there were some 300,000 cafés, bars, and taverns. One of the first steps taken after the coup of 2 December 1851 was to tighten controls on these establishments by requiring them to apply for authorization to remain open. Nearly 20,000 taverns were closed for violating this law under the Second Empire.[6] This impressive statistic shows how vigilant and active the authorities were in this area.

What can we say in general about civil-society associations in the nineteenth century? Broad overviews of the subject are lacking, and too few specific studies have been produced. From the available works we can nevertheless offer a preliminary characterization of associations in this period. There were three main types: social associations, cooperative associations, and associations aimed at shaping the collectivity.

Initially, most associations were social. Circles, clubs, and men's groups of all sorts were common in France in the first half of the nineteenth century. Maurice Agulhon was the first to call attention to this phenomenon and to demonstrate its importance.[7] A few other works flesh out our understanding of this aspect of associational life. What emerges is a picture of various groups creating a level of sociability distinct from that defined by either family or citizenship. These associations fostered direct contact among neighbors. Often they created, within the new society of equality, a masculine space distinct from the feminine space of the home. The social bond itself was their province. These circles, clubs, and societies were microcosms of a sort, "little societies" within the larger society, like the "little nations" within the larger nation but on a different scale. Here, a different kind of civic life was constructed, a life no longer structured by either the legal organization of the professions or by imposed collective identities. These groups offered protection while at the same time allowing members to discover new forms of collective organization within a society of individuals. Agulhon offers the useful suggestion that the development of these kinds of association can be seen as part of a "natural history of sociability," which is one aspect of the history of civilization.[8]

Besides the purely social associations, various recreational associations were formed for the purpose of playing music or games such as *boules*. The musical societies that began to develop in the second half of the nineteenth century and flourished under the Second Empire were typical. France was blanketed with wind ensembles, choral societies, and brass bands, often subsidized by municipal governments.[9] The gymnastics societies and shooting clubs that sprang up after 1870 in response to the Prussian challenge reflected a similar need to socialize.[10] A statistical analysis of sporting club charters from the second half of the nineteenth century shows that the primary objective was most often to form ties of friendship and solidarity, followed by the need to encourage patriotism and prepare for the national defense, with training for competition ranking last.[11] Sporting and musical groups also linked distant places together as members discovered France by participating in festivals, competitions, and celebrations in other towns and regions. As one band leader put it, "these friendly competitions have allowed the humblest of us to become familiar with the geography of France. Traveling to competitions has fused the various parts of the nation . . . Bretons, Gascons, Burgundians, and Normans have become French thanks to the village band. The ancient soul of France lives on and perpetuates itself in these raucous, cordial festivals."[12] Thus social groups were transformed into schools of generality. Jules Ferry went so far as to say, "the gymnast is the Republic made flesh."

Cooperative associations were different. By pooling individual resources they made it easier for people to act. Workers' associations and mutual aid societies fall into this category. Although such associations existed in the 1820s and 1830s, as we have seen, 1848 marked an important turning point. The increase in the number of producers' and consumers' cooperatives was relatively modest, but mutual aid societies proliferated rapidly after the law of 15 July 1850 and above all the decree of 25 March 1852 granting them legal and financial status. At the beginning of the Second Empire there were already 2,438 such societies boasting some 271,000 members; ten years later the numbers had increased to 4,721 and 676,000, respectively. Producers' and consumers' cooperatives were not animated by the same spirit as the mutual aid societies, but their numbers also increased as economic change and the need for social protection made socialization more attractive. The spirit of 1848 received a boost when legislation passed under the Second Empire allowed new associations to spring up everywhere.

The third type of association included groups such as political parties and trade unions, whose purpose was to mold the collectivity. Parties and unions operated in different ways. The party (or campaign committee or political club) primarily played a functional role: it was a *moment* in the reflexive process of producing the political community, a kind of interface. By contrast, the trade union was designed for action and for the defense of workers' interests; it helped to create and give voice to a particular community within the economic order: workers. Both party and union thus helped to bridge the gap between the individual and the collective, the party as an organ of political expression, the union as an instrument for the formation of the working class. Hence the histories of both are best understood in relation to the history of democracy and capitalism.

The three major types of association had different histories, and the authorities treated them differently. Furthermore, each type of association related to the social generality in a different way. By 1901, however, one fact stood out: the number of associations of all types had grown quite large. A nationwide survey undertaken in 1899 in connection with the Convention on Freedom of Association showed clearly that numerous associations of all kinds had been organized with or without the permission of the law.[13] A survey conducted by the Office du Travail in 1900 counted 45,148 associations. By that date France had already come a long way from the model described by Tocqueville a few decades earlier. The main categories and numbers recorded in this survey are instructive:

Professional associations of all kinds (not just trade unions): 7,246
Mutual aid societies: 11,232
Cooperative associations: 1,918
Scholastic associations: 2,468
Charitable associations: 990
Associations for study, patronage, education, learned societies, etc.:
    2,203
Associations for sports and games: 7,480
Musical associations: 6,453
Circles: 3,677
Miscellaneous (military, patriotic, and undefined): 1,481

Using our typology, we find that social associations account for some 48 percent of the total, cooperative associations for 30 percent, and collectivity-shaping associations for 22 percent. (Bear in mind that the figures do not include political organizations, and no account is taken of the number of members of groups of different types, a key variable.) The geographic distribution of these associations is unknown, but we can get some idea of it by looking at "circles," which since 1871 had been subject to a tax proportional to dues collected from members.[14] Statistics derived from this tax indicate that circles were numerous in three areas: southeastern France along the Mediterranean coast (Bouches-du-Rhône, Var, Vaucluse, Gard, Alpes-Maritimes), southwestern France (Gironde, Gers, Lot-et-Garonne), and western France (Maine-et-Loire being the department with by far the most circles, nearly 20 percent of the total for all of France).[15] Owing to the virtual absence of departmental monographs, it is impossible to compare the local histories of the various types of association across regions.[16] Despite all the caveats, however, it is clear that associations were a vital force in late nineteenth-century France. This vitality stands in striking contrast to the slowness of the law to adapt itself to the facts. For some contemporaries, this legislative sluggishness was a minor problem: "If the new law has yet to pass Parliament, it has been made outside; it has entered into mores," observed Jean Macé, the founder of the Ligue Française de l'Enseignement in the late 1880s.[17] Still, the delay needs to be explained, particularly since it is important to understand that ultimate passage of the bill did more than just bring the law into line with reality. It also removed obstacles that still remained in place, as we can see from the fact that large numbers of new associations were created after 1901.

The Thirty-Year Delay

On 8 March 1871, Tolain, the indefatigable champion of the workers' movement, who was still a long way from becoming the sober senator we found him to be in 1884, filed a bill with the new National Assembly for the purpose of repealing Articles 291 and 292 of the Penal Code as well as the law of 10 April 1834. There is nothing surprising about this move, given the fall of the Empire. While in opposition to Napoleon III, legitimists, liberals, republicans, and militant workers of all stripes had repeatedly included freedom of association among their primary demands. Gambetta's famous Belleville Platform (15 May 1869) called for "full and complete" freedom of association, setting the tone for any number of campaign manifestos in this period. For nearly twenty years, the prosecution of workers and campaign committee organizers for the crime of "coalition," not to mention the famous trial of the Association Internationale des Travailleurs in 1868, had stirred the wrath of all the regime's adversaries to the point where repeal of the old "liberticide" laws was considered an absolute imperative. Berryer, Jules Favre, Simon, and Thiers all spoke as one on this issue. When Ledru-Rollin and others drafted the first platform of the Alliance Républicaine in December 1870, they naturally called for "the right to meet and associate as guarantees against the errors of the majority and safeguard of the rights of the minority." The Union Républicaine did the same a year later. From good intentions to reality a long road remained to travel, however.

On 14 December 1871, a law professor named Charles Bertauld, a leader of the center left and close associate of Thiers, submitted a report on Tolain's proposal. Bertauld raised no objection to the substance of the bill. For him, the freedom of association and the right to assemble (the two were not clearly distinguished, as we shall soon see in greater detail) were mere corollaries of the freedom of speech and action. The honorable republican remained circumspect, however: although the right of association was "a powerful instrument of civilization and progress, it could [also] be a powerful source of disruption and disorganization . . . Too many dangers are associated with the exercise of such liberty not to call for close surveillance."[18] This was not much different from what lawmakers were saying in 1834. In the great parliamentary debate that followed in the wake of this report and led ultimately to the law of 1901, this philosophical affirmation of a necessary freedom had to contend in one way or another with anxious fears of social disorder. To be sure, this was the heyday of the Ordre Moral, and the majority once again lashed out, for example, at the Association Internationale des Travailleurs with the law of 14 March 1872, which took aim at all groups calling for "cessation of work or abolition of the rights of property, family, country, religion, or freedom of worship." Bertauld himself had expressly warned against allowing associations whose purpose was to organize and subsidize strikes or to pursue revolutionary political goals. If we leave aside the recommendation to monitor associations and punish violators of the law rather than ban them outright (which, from a legal point of view, did indeed mark a decisive step forward), then the debates on the association issue that took place in both the newspapers and parliament have a depressingly familiar ring. Again we hear the same hopes and fears that had been expressed since the turn of the nineteenth century: on the one hand, anxieties about the atomization of society and the dissolution of the social bond; on the other, old concerns about the dangers of "states within the state."[19]

Bertauld's proposal came to naught. The wheels had been set in motion, however, and thirty years later the law of 1901 arrived. Thirty-three bills would go down to defeat, however, before that result was achieved, at last proving wrong the politician who referred to "the proposed law of association as a bill that is always being submitted for consideration only to be withdrawn without ever being debated."[20] Most observers have been content to treat this delay as a mere transitional period of no particular significance. For instance, Paul Nourrisson, the first great historian of the right of association, tried to trace the history of the "scraps of freedom wrested from the state one by one" in these years.[21] Among them were the law of 1875 concerning higher education, the law of 1884 on professional unions, the law of 1890 on syndicates of communes, and the law of 1898 on mutual aid societies. Thus it was possible to take the view that the right of association emerged gradually, in the form of "piecemeal" legislation[22] leading up to the "Copernican revolution" of 1901.[23] Historians have also called attention to the authorities' growing tolerance of associations created without prior authorization (as we ourselves noted earlier).

Republican historiography has always emphasized the law of 1901 as one of a series of triumphs for liberty that began in 1879, when the resignation of Edme Patrice Maurice de Mac-Mahon brought the Opportunists definitively to power. On this view, the right of association was merely the crowning achievement of a series of measures beginning with the laws of 1881 on freedom of assembly and of the press. The deputies who voted in the spring of 1901 in favor of the long-awaited law would ultimately characterize it as the logical culmination of a century-long battle against conservative forces. In the Senate report that marked the final stage of the parliamentary process before the law was adopted, Ernest Vallé set forth a bizarre history of the events leading to this outcome. Forgetting the Le Chapelier Law and the recurrent denunciation of intermediary bodies by Jacobins of one stripe or another, Vallé asserted that "the republican party has steadfastly insisted on the need for freedom of association, which derives from natural law, and when in power it took pains to enshrine that freedom in our laws."[24] Offering the ambiguous decree of 21 October 1790[25] and the legislation of the spring of 1848 as proofs of republican dedication to the associative cause, he traced a magical history in which the only resistance to recognizing the right to associate came from the forces of reaction, from Thermidor to the Second Empire by way of the Restoration and the July Monarchy. "Why all these abortive attempts?" he asked, as others had done before him. "Because certain people were unwilling to grant freedom."[26] On this view, the law of 1901 was a logical culmination and not a rupture. The law fitted naturally within the trajectory of French history; there was no turning point. In the same spirit, Maurice Agulhon remarked that "1880 was certainly a more important date than 1901," with the implication that the real turning point came when republicans at last outmaneuvered all their rivals for power; the freedom of association was but the culmination of a series of liberal laws.[27]

But why did it take another twenty years, from 1880 to 1901, to achieve this result? Most historians share the view of many contemporaries that this "delay within the delay" was due to issues raised by religious congregations. To conclude our survey, we therefore turn to this matter.

Blame the Congregations

"The main difficulty with the law comes from the congregations," Jules Simon observed with some bitterness when he revived Senate debate on the right of association in 1883, to no avail.[28] Georges Trouillot, the ultimate rapporteur in the Chamber of Deputies prior to final adoption, made the same point in explaining why the process had bogged down: "The triumph of the cause of freedom of association has been delayed in the Chambers by the perpetual conflict between those who demand the privilege or unlimited advantages of this freedom for the congregations and those who see in its extension to the congregations the greatest danger to civil society. All the bills filed over the past thirty years bear traces of these concerns. Only eleven of them insisted on absolute conceptual equality between lay associations and religious congregations. All the others allowed for special precautions in dealing with the latter . . . These precautions themselves demonstrate the difficulty of the problem and *explain the delay in finding a solution*."[29] For more than a century, historians have accepted this interpretation of the thirty-year delay as self-evident. Maurice Agulhon, the undisputed authority in this area, has embraced it.[30] In my view, however, there are reasons to question whether it is correct.

There is no denying the fact that hostility to the religious congregations dominated all parliamentary debates prior to passage of the law. It is no exaggeration to say that anticlerical sentiment "permeated the general discussion."[31] After 1870, republicans did in fact increasingly transform anticlericalism into a philosophical program and campaign slogan. Gambetta's celebrated war cry in the Chamber of Deputies in 1877—"le cléricalisme, voilà l'ennemi"—of course became an essential element of their political credo after May 16. We need not delve further into the reasons for this political choice, which have been thoroughly studied. It is enough to recall Alfred Noël François Madier de Montjau's expression of the dominant republican sentiment in 1880: "Promise that you'll soon bring us the bodies of our defeated enemies, the hated congregations!"[32] Hatred of the congregations was much more powerful at the time than the will to establish a right of association. Hostilities with Catholics only increased after the government repeatedly rejected requests to allow the authorized congregations to create new schools and, after the decrees of 29 March 1880, did away with the tacit exception granted to unauthorized institutions. When the Assumptionists, led by the newspaper *La Croix*, abruptly mobilized for the 1898 elections and engaged in vehement anti-Dreyfusard activities, hostility rose to a fever pitch. "Conspiratorial monks" were denounced everywhere. It was also in this period that Waldeck-Rousseau, the president of the Conseil, raised the specter of the congregations' "billion" and dramatized the opposition between "two groups of young people separated not so much by their social condition as by their educa-tion."[33]

All these events are a matter of record, and the subterranean as well as overt history of these conflicts has been studied so often that there is no point in even trying to summarize it here.[34] The repercussions of this hos-tility on the debates and on the content of the law have also been abun-dantly documented.[35] The distinction between "associations" and "congre-gations" in the law of 1901 stems from this controversy. When Vallé bluntly told the Senate that the law granted associations a freedom that it had de-liberately denied to congregations, he was merely expressing the dominant sentiment of the republican camp. That is why Title III of the law imposed particularly severe restraints on the charitable and teaching activities of the congregations while requiring them to seek authorization from the gov-ernment simply to exist. But why did it take twenty years to hit upon this "solution" to the republican dilemma (the contradiction between the "ob-vious necessity" of associations and the fear that they would be used as a weapon by the enemies of the Republic)? In my view, the simple, direct in-terpretation is untenable.

At the dawn of the 1880s, freedom of association was loudly proclaimed to be a *public liberty*. Yet latent problems remained, problems having to do with the kinds of *institutions* to which such a freedom might be expected to give rise. The process that led to the distinction between associations and congregations was intimately intertwined with questions about the nature of association. In effect, the congregation as *social form* (and not just religious institution) epitomized everything that worried republicans about associations in general. The distinction incorporated in the 1901 law can thus be understood as a means of distinguishing the good aspects of association from the bad. The congregations were seen as the embodiment of all the most negative aspects of intermediary bodies. The republicans of the 1880s did not invent this way of looking at things, but they radicalized and politicized it.

Thus the opposition between associations and congregations at the end of the nineteenth century changed the terms in which the specter of cor-poratism was raised. The congregations became the butt of all the criticism directed at intermediary bodies. A moderate and relative form of that criti-cism was incorporated into a "Jacobin representation" of state and society. Or, to put it another way, the criticism distinguished between a modern view of the association as a factor for civilization and progress and an archaic variant. That is why the congregations were not seen merely as a religious form of association. They were not associations for a particular purpose but a particular type of association. A congregation "is far more than an association," the Cour de Cassation observed under the Second Empire.[36] Various features of the congregations—their communitarian dimension, their internal discipline, their perpetual character—made them the very epitome of corporatism for many observers. No one expressed this view better than the socialist Eugène Fournière, who took part in the 1901 debate in the Chamber. "Corporations and congregations, all more or less closed, hieratic, authoritarian, and monopolistic, are survivals of the old coercive form of association rather than products of deliberation and contract," he emphasized. "They exhibit few or none of the distinctive features of modern associations, which are based on freedom of choice . . . Freedom of choice means the freedom to exit as well as to enter. It should not be forfeited when an individual joins an association, and no legally valid contract can compel an individual to remain a member."[37] In attacking the congregations, republicans thus conveniently separated the old from the new and combined the resolution of a historical question with the pursuit of a political controversy linked to anticlericalism.

The congregation was also seen as the consummate embodiment of the threat implicit in association, the threat of a "state within the state." A typical expression of this sentiment came from Jules Roche, a close associate of Clemenceau:

> The Church is a state—a vast society directed by an organized public authority, a political body with laws of its own, a strictly hierarchical and extraordinarily devoted cadre of functionaries, a budget drawn from a thousand sources, subsidiary corporations that amass savings constantly and never spend, and an all-powerful sovereign who commands obedience across borders—and this formidable power is irreducibly opposed to the basic principles of modern society . . . France is no less entitled to defend itself against this power than to defend itself against any other empire in open war against it.[38]

The French view of laïcité needs to be understood in this context. Only in a derivative sense did it stem from anticlerical sentiment. It was based primarily on a concept of moral sovereignty. In this sense, the congregations symbolized the institution that stood as the radical competitor of public authority in its various guises. In particular, they claimed to be able to replace the state as society's teacher, as the agency capable of shaping the naturally disorganized collectivity. In an immensely successful book that came out in 1860, *Les Moines d'Occident*, Montalembert celebrated the religious orders in just this spirit, as associations that had advanced the cause of civilization long before any organized public powers existed. The congregations could thus stand against the state as an adverse moral and educational authority, a spiritual power to rival the power of Leviathan. This distinctive totalizing vision of the role of the state vis-à-vis society played a central role in the debates leading up to passage of the law of 1901.

So even though the anticlerical dimension of this late nineteenth-century controversy is apparent, its origins were of a different order. Evidence for this can be seen in the fact that government liberals who favored a strong state strongly opposed the congregations throughout the century. The reasons for their opposition to the Jesuits under the Restoration are well known. Beyond the Gallican wrath of Montlosier, one thinks of Jean-Marie Duvergier de Hauranne, who, in one of the leading liberal works of the time, *De l'ordre légal en France et des abus d'autorité* (1826), delivered to his fellow citizens a warning against the danger that the religious orders posed to the state.[39] In 1845, moreover, Thiers had this to say about the Jesuits: "The state cannot suffer there to be a state within the state, or tolerate the existence of congregations over which there would be no oversight and no power of authorization or dissolution."[40] Dupin, Lamartine, and Odilon Barrot spoke in similar terms, and Berryer was quite isolated when he defended the religious orders by suggesting that in the eyes of the law they were nothing more than private voluntary associations.[41] Even the most conservative elements within the government made a point of defending the state's right to grant itself a monopoly on secondary education. The moderate Guizot did not take a very different position in this regard from the fiery Emile Combes.

In these circumstances it comes as no surprise that Waldeck-Rousseau and his allies presented their doubts and hesitations as the culmination of a long tradition. What is more, they portrayed the history not only as the continuation of the revolutionary measures discussed earlier but also as an extension of the liberal legacy. They were quick to cite Thiers and Etienne Pasquier and to emphasize precedents in the discussions of 1826 and 1845. More broadly, they claimed to be carrying on the tradition of the French monarchy and presented themselves as upholding the letter of the celebrated edict of Saint-Germain-en-Laye of 1666, which solemnly reaffirmed the state's right to oversee the organization and activities of corporations, colleges, monasteries, and religious and secular communities. Trouillot, the rapporteur, summed up with this familiar argument: "Thus—leaving aside the Revolution, which eliminated all orders—from the Old Regime and the Empire to the Restoration, July Monarchy, and Second Empire on down to the present time, we find a perfect unity of doctrine concerning the religious congregations."[42] He continued to hammer home his point:

> The thesis that the congregations are to be treated under a special regime is neither Jacobin nor republican. In view of the social and economic perils that excessive growth of such associations represents, all our regimes, whether of old France or of the Revolution, have repeatedly warned against them. In every one of these periods mistakes may have been made concerning the effectiveness of the precautions taken, but there has never been any mistake about the need to protect both persons and property against this awesomely expansive power.[43]

Paradoxically, he saw this assertion of continuity as a justification for rejecting the earlier ban on associations. In order to make the right of association possible, it was thus necessary to revive and deepen the ancient distrust of the congregations. In a sense, it was essential to diminish the importance of the right before it could be granted, to reduce its implications by allowing a cathartic and protective exclusion.

In this respect, the question of the congregations was far broader than a question of the relations between church and state. What was really at stake in the impassioned debates about the right of association was the very definition of the state in its relation to society. The result was a singular conception of civil society in France. It was framed not in terms of its difference from the state but rather in terms of its distance from the world of religion. In an often-cited speech, Waldeck-Rousseau forcefully asserted "the supremacy of civil society," but he contrasted civil society only with "the preeminence of religious power."[44] This marked a return to the old definition of civil society, the definition given by seventeenth-century authors such as Locke in seeking to assert the independence of the political power. This "civil-political" society has nothing to do with the "civil society" of writers from Hume to Hegel who conceived of the autonomy of the social. The difficulty of conceptualizing intermediary bodies in France is intimately connected with this archaic view of civil society.

Utopian Association

The reference to congregations as a social form was thus charged with all the negative connotations that were to be exorcised. For republicans, the congregations symbolized the most radical and most unacceptable aspect of corporatist society: the total, irreversible absorption of individuals in a single whole and in a form of collective property not subject to control of any kind but rendered autonomous by virtue of a detested mortmain. This demonized vision was contrasted point by point with the rosy picture of the type of association that they intended to empower.

So on the one hand we have the vow whereby freedom and will were alienated, while on the other we have the contract whereby individuals who remained absolutely sovereign were united. Obviously this dichotomy was simplistic in the assumptions it made about religious vows.[45] But it played a fundamental role in the republican imagination, dispelling suspicions of archaism that had been linked to the idea of associations since the Revolution. "How can anyone fail to see the difference between a contract and a vow?" Jules Simon asked. "Between an association that brings a new collective force into the body politic and a congregation that annihilates individual forces?"[46] Viewed in this way, associations could be fitted easily into the framework of a purely individualistic society, whereas congregations exemplified the most basic characteristics of corporatist society. Waldeck-Rousseau went so far as to say, in striking phrases, that the essence of associations, as he understood them, was to stimulate "the enlargement of the human personality" and bring about an "increase of individual power."[47] This was tantamount to saying that associations were not intermediary bodies in any way, shape, or form. In no sense were they the "partial associations" that some people believed ought to be created within the "larger association" so as to clarify its organization and facilitate its expression. "An association is a contract, nothing more and nothing less," was the way Waldeck-Rousseau summed up his case in a formula that is still celebrated.[48] For him, then, an association was simply a contract whereby two or more individuals agreed to pool their resources, knowledge, and energy for some specified purpose. It was an instrument of individualism, not a form of communitarianism. It was unambiguously modern. It belonged completely to the private sphere and did not interfere in the public. Hence "associations do not appear to me to be concessions of the political order," Waldeck-Rousseau observed. "They appear to me as the natural, primordial, and free exercise of human energy."[49] If an association was a contract like any other, it could be dealt with adequately in terms of the categories of the Civil Code. "What we are doing with respect to associations is merely what has been done for sales, rentals, exchange, and all other contracts," he logically concluded.[50]

The freedom of association envisaged by these definitions was therefore relevant only to modern individualistic society. It had nothing to do with the ancient rights it was alleged to be reviving. In that vein, the earliest republican commentators on the law of 1901 stressed that "freedom of association was unknown" in antiquity as well as under the Old Regime, when the various communities and corporations were public institutions.[51] In their eyes, this circumstance also explained why the issue of association had arisen in such a peculiar form in France, where the "organic temptation" was deeply ingrained, as opposed to a country like the United States, where the powerful and durable presence of the individualistic spirit made it possible to tolerate the existence of congregations without anxiety. Unlike in the 1830s, when the individualistic spirit of Protestantism was denounced as a force for social dissolution, now it was Catholicism's discipline and esprit de corps that were attacked as a danger to a society of individuals.[52]

In this restrictive framework, associations could not own property in their own name, nor were they endowed with a civil personality. Waldeck-Rousseau took a radical position, arguing that whatever an association possessed should remain divisible and transferable to individual members in case of dissolution. Members were thus regarded as veritable partners with shares in the association, just as in a commercial partnership. In other words, if an association was primarily an association of intelligences or interests, it was secondarily a partnership that implicitly agreed to hold in common whatever property it acquired in furtherance of its purposes.[53] Waldeck-Rousseau would modify this position in the final debate by accepting first of all that certain (limited) types of property needed by the association for its express purposes could be construed as undivided property and, second, that an association could be treated as a moral person and endowed with civil capacity under the law without the issuance of a certificate of public utility by the state. These concessions were purely pragmatic, however, and had no implications for his philosophy of association.

The ultimate version of the bill differed somewhat from earlier drafts, and in particular from Waldeck-Rousseau's initial proposal. There is no need to trace the various stages of revision here.[54] It is enough to recall that the law ultimately distinguished three types of associations: undeclared, declared, and recognized as being of public utility. Only declared associations enjoyed full legal capacity. Waldeck-Rousseau's initial distinction between simple contractual associations and recognized organizations was thus extended and modified. The right to own property and receive donations and bequests varied according to the type of association involved. Thus the law evolved to reflect certain pragmatic necessities, yet it did so without betraying the spirit in which the originators of the legislation had conceived of the associative process.

Liberty and Institutions

There is no denying the fact that the law of 1 July 1901 symbolized a repudiation of the century-old refusal to countenance associations. It reflected a certain erosion of the rigid, doctrinaire Jacobin understanding of the relation between the individual and the state, between the particular interest and the general interest, which had broadly prevailed throughout the nineteenth century. This rupture must be placed in its proper context, however. In previous chapters we saw how various imperatives associated with the dynamics of society itself led authorities *in practice* to weaken formal restrictions on associations to the point where any number did in fact exist. Yet these accommodations remained a matter of *tolerance,* which meant that the tolerated associations could be restrained or banned in certain instances, as circumstances required. It was essentially this regime of exceptions that the new law did away with. Tolerance was replaced by legalization (except in the case of religious congregations). Was that all that happened? Some historians think the change was more significant, arguing that the law of 1901 represented a kind of "compromise" between the individualistic legacy of the Revolution and a recognition that intermediary bodies could be useful.[55] This perspective may be pertinent in social and political terms, but it makes no sense in legal terms.

As we shall see in due course, some jurists proposed a new (for France, at any rate) legal doctrine in regard to associations as early as the turn of the twentieth century, but the ensuing controversy among legal scholars had little impact on the interpretation of positive law. Most specialists followed the legislators of 1901 and continued to treat associations as contractual arrangements unambiguously belonging to the private sphere. For them, associations were like commercial partnerships, purely instrumental arrangements that allow individuals to structure their activities and expand their scope.[56] They do not operate in the public sphere and have no access to generality. To be sure, the law provides for different legal regimes for different types of association (declared, undeclared, or recognized as being of public utility).[57] Nevertheless, the dominant and characteristic feature of all associations is that they are excluded from the production of the general interest. Thus the legal recognition of associations at the turn of the twentieth century was combined in a rather curious way with a certain blindness to the economic and sociological transformations of the modern world. The terms in which the mortmain issue was dealt with illustrate this in a striking way.

That eighteenth-century economists and philosophers were highly critical of mortmain, the legal term for real property held inalienably, is well known. A century later, nothing had changed. Although the word (*main-morte* in French) fell out of use for a time,[58] it made a dramatic comeback after 1880, when the right of association began to be debated seriously.[59] "Ah, that dreaded word! Among our contemporaries, be they ordinary citizens or lawmakers, what incredible terror it arouses!"[60] Naturally it conjured up denunciations of the notorious "billion" imputed to the congregations (which itself summoned up collective memories of another mythical "billion," that imputed to émigrés during the Restoration), while at the same time hinting at obscure powers that posed a threat to the state as well as its citizens. But how solid was this myth? Wasn't it just an "enormous soap bubble to which someone has ascribed a mysterious and almost macabre name"?[61] The reality was more complicated. The idea of mortmain served to widen the gap between associations and congregations and thus helped people to think of the association as a form of freedom rather than a type of institution. This divergence justified a very narrow approach to the associative phenomenon and had a great deal to do with the limitations placed on the "moral personality" of associations.[62] Above all, the fact that the specter of mortmain was associated almost exclusively with property owned by religious congregations reflected a lack of understanding of the economic and social evolution of the late nineteenth century. By then, the whole question of mortmain was different from what it had been a century earlier. Very little of the property held in mortmain belonged to religious congregations.[63] More than that, the nature of property in mortmain had changed. No longer was it held in the form of sterile, immobile capital and thus removed from the circuits of exchange and unavailable as an economic resource. Increasingly it took the form of *social capital,* either as insurance held in reserve against some risk or as wherewithal for the exercise of some collective function.

An important fact about the economy in the late nineteenth century is what some writers referred to as "workers' mortmain."[64] The trade union law of 1884 and, to an even greater extent, the supplementary acts that followed made this possible by authorizing the unions to acquire property. Some on the right objected to this. "Has fear of religious mortmain caused you to lose sight of the vast amount of lay mortmain and its growing influence in this country?" one conservative deputy asked his colleagues. "Has it caused you to lose sight of the vast latifundia in which the smoldering wrath of the proletariat is every day gaining in intensity? What is it that you say? That the only illicit associations are religious? What are you doing, what are you thinking, about the unions, the trusts, the omniums, the corporations, the coalitions, and the bogus contracts you heard about the other day?"[65] In a related vein, it was not uncommon to hear corporations in the modern sense, incorporated businesses—*sociétés anonymes* in French—attacked for being "anonymous" to the small merchants and craftsmen who owned and were responsible for their own businesses. Republicans had difficulty grasping the scope of this social evolution and were therefore incapable of integrating it into their concept of association. While one can hardly fault them for ignoring Jules Guesde's analyses of the need for collectivization of the economy, it is striking to find that they paid just as little attention to the work of liberal economists such as Léon Say and Paul Leroy-Beaulieu. Writing in the 1880s, Say noted what he considered to be an irreversible trend toward the constitution of a powerful "lay and social mortmain."[66] Leroy-Beaulieu, for his part, insisted on the positive and necessary aspect of this new form of mortmain, which reflected the emergence of new collective functions.[67]

Paradoxically, traditionalist Catholics were more lucid than republicans on this point. For instance, Albert de Mun observed that "corporations and collective enterprises are growing bigger every day. This is the great economic evolution of society."[68] At times, his aversion to the individualistic society spawned by the Revolution led him to prefer the audacity of the socialists to the caution of the republicans. In his eyes, the "workers' mortmain" helped to fill the gap that had opened up between the state and individuals. His approach to association was set within the broader context of reconstituting and promoting intermediate bodies in a society that had outlawed them. Waldeck-Rousseau and his allies did not reason in the same terms. For them, recognizing the right of association had nothing to do with the history of similar organizations but was merely a phase in the expansion of civic freedoms. In some circles, the prospect of an emerging workers' mortmain was associated with the revival of a long-repressed corporatist ethos; it was hoped that associations would become the driving force in the struggle against "unbridled individualism." In Catholic circles that prided themselves on being "social" as well as "traditionalist," the goal was clearly to offer an alternative to socialism and communism where there existed a "growing tendency to increase the social residue."[69]

Some socialists also viewed the growth of associations as a necessary step in building the type of society they hoped to encourage. Viviani, for example, observed that "the truth is that associations are destined to play a social role, that they are created to replace the state in certain of its offices and functions, the very diversity of which poses a challenge to the state's initiative. To complete my thought, I should add that associations are thinner and lighter than the state and can therefore slip into narrower niches than the more ponderous and powerful government can reach."[70] The specter of mortmain did not frighten him. In a sense, collectivism was merely a generalization and socialization of the concept of property held in mortmain. Viviani took this idea a step further. Although he was ferociously anticlerical, his anticlericalism was different from that of the republicans. While he detested the congregations, he paradoxically recognized that they performed social functions that would have to be taken over by others. He was therefore convinced that they could not simply be banned. His astonishing argument deserves to be stated in full. "Like it or not," he argued,

> the congregations are a political and economic fact. Although the law of the law books can sometimes destroy a political fact, it cannot destroy an economic fact. What, then, is to be done? We must go into the congregations and take up their task. For the charity that is bestowed on known individuals, we must substitute the solidarity that embraces all men anonymously. We must constitute a system of social insurance and channel all that is powerful and disinterested in lay society into this focus of energy and enlightenment. We must take over teaching and make people under-

stand . . . that there is no reason to hesitate in choosing between the de facto monopoly created by the Church and the monopoly of civil society whose benefits flow to the state.[71]

Understood in this way, socialism could be defined as the nationalization (and not the elimination) of the congregations! For Viviani, this conception, quite removed from the classical republican idea of strict separation between private and public spheres, implied the need for a third pole, the "social." This form of socialism reconstituted the old "sociological" and functional idea of intermediary bodies with the new political idea of an actively egalitarian society.

This vision of socialism as recycling the old in the new played a central role in shaping the imagination of several generations that aspired to do battle against the rival social paradigms of individualism and hierarchy. From the 1830s until the end of the century, this was a constant element in one of the two main traditions of French socialism. (The other, growing out of the republican distinction between public and private spheres, aimed for maximum expansion of the public sphere.) The position that Viviani took in the debates on the law of association was not that of his allies in the Chamber. Fundamental questions about the nature of socialism and the best way to achieve it interested them less than more immediate political concerns. Deeply involved in the anticlerical struggle, they were among the vanguard of those who wished to banish the religious orders. The most extreme speech on this issue was delivered by one of this group, Alexandre Zevaès.[72] Yet their chief concern was to make sure that their militant activities enjoyed the protection of the law. With memories of the prosecution of the Workers' International still fresh in mind, they were wary of any provision that might interfere with the organization of socialist workers nationally and internationally. Like trade unionists in the 1880s, they objected to any declaration procedure that might facilitate repression of socialist groups by the government.[73]

Thus both republicans and socialists approached the issue of association primarily in terms of public liberties, the very liberties that Gambetta called "the crown of democracy."[74] No one in either camp attached any special importance to this particular liberty,[75] and it was only in conservative Catholic circles that it was referred to around the turn of the century as "the great liberty."[76] The dominant view remained that of Jules Ferry, who said in 1881 that the Republic needed "a good law of associations, one that will finally regulate the exercise of a necessary liberty without injury to the rights of the state, the first, the highest, and most necessary of associations."[77] What was consecrated in 1901 was indeed a liberty and not a social institution with a role to play in determining the public good. This fact explains the remark that one opposition senator addressed to Waldeck-Rousseau on the eve of the bill's passage: "In the political realm the chamber has given you everything; in the legal realm, nothing."[78] For the majority in 1901, associations remained a legal imponderable. The law they approved recognized only the *act of association* while ignoring the institution that resulted from that act.

The Impossibility of Generalization

The refusal to characterize associations as substantial institutions extending beyond the act of inception accounts for the failure of the law of 1901 to serve as a legal framework broad enough to encompass the many ways in which individuals form groups and act cooperatively. A comparison of the law of 1901 with the law of 1884 on trade unions gives a stark view of the difficulty. Recall that the 1884 law marked the culmination of a process that began with Lockroy's bill of 1876, which was presented as an attempt to address one aspect of the problem of associations at a time when a more comprehensive solution seemed out of reach. Why, then, was it not possible to subsume the "partial" law of 1884 within the "general" law when it was finally adopted in 1901? In fact, as Article 21 of the law of 1901 clearly stipulates, "Nothing in the present law is to be construed as prejudicial to the special laws concerning professional unions." Clearly the problem was that the law of 1884 was in some respects more favorable to the unions than the law of 1901. For instance, unions enjoyed the material advantage of being allowed to occupy space in the *bourses du travail*, or labor exchanges. They were entitled to receive gifts and bequests without special authorization, whereas the law of associations was restrictive in this area. Labor leaders also enjoyed better protections, since the law of 1901 specifically imposed heavy penalties on leaders who illegally attempted to reconstitute a dissolved organization.[79] As a result of this last feature, employers pushed to combine the two laws in the hope that the provisions of the law of 1901 would free them to take more effective action against the young Confédération Générale du Travail.[80]

The difference between the law of 1901 and that of 1884 goes beyond these specifics, however. The heart of the matter is that under the 1884 law the unions were recognized as a social institution. This institutional character increased with time thanks to various legislative measures that gradually recognized the unions' status as quasi-public organizations, whereas the framework laid out in 1901 for associations scarcely evolved at all.

— 12 —

Polarized Democracy

1884 and 1901: The Scandalous Gap

The law of 1901, though severely limited by its cautious, hesitant approach to the whole issue of associations, nevertheless marked a break with the past. We have examined the reasons behind the law's limitations, which have told us a great deal. But perhaps the most surprising aspect of this whole story is what happened, or, rather, what did not happen, subsequently: the law survived the twentieth century virtually intact but for minor revisions.[1] It was as if the revolution of 1901 was immediately stopped in its tracks, its limits established once and for all. This outcome soon led many people to feel that the reform had been incomplete, especially among those who had been most active in bringing it about. In the early 1920s, for instance, Duguit spoke of a liberty that had "fallen by the wayside."[2] The "little personality" that declared associations were granted afforded them only a limited legal capacity, which the legislature refused to expand. The ability of associations to acquire property was severely constrained by Article 6 of the law of 1901, which the courts interpreted in the narrowest possible manner. Saleilles was thus perfectly justified in speaking of the "very impoverished and constricted form of association given us by the law of 1901,"[3] the fundamental error of which had been "to allow liberty only on condition of poverty."[4]

How is this disturbing and persistent lack of progress to be interpreted? The answer to this question takes us back to the heart of the French enigma. We start with an observation: the original rigors of the law of 1901 were strictly maintained even after the reasons that had been cited to justify both the restrictions in the law and its belated passage had practically evaporated. The specter of the congregations, which had hovered over the

208

debate, gradually faded. To be sure, anticlerical sentiment peaked in the early years of the twentieth century, and the laws of 1902 and 1904 cracked down hard on the congregations.[5] Shortly thereafter, however, passions died down somewhat, and the "Union Sacrée" made necessary by the outbreak of the Great War virtually ended all frontal assaults on religion. A ministerial circular of 2 August 1914 suspended application of the various anticongregation measures *sine die,* and subsequent legislation confirmed and expanded this initial relaxation of the rules.[6] Thus the much-feared congregations saw Article 3 of the law, which covered them, evolve with time, while ordinary associations remained subject to provisions that did not change. Meanwhile, the danger of mortmain turned out to be nonexistent, yet nothing was done to increase the ability of associations to acquire property, as restrictions on gifts and bequests remained in place and the source of revenue was limited to dues.

While associations remained subject to the same strict rules, the law regarding trade unions evolved considerably after 1884. As noted earlier, the unions were eventually granted the privilege of representing the collective interests of a whole profession and not just of their own members. Article 2 of the law, which ascribed to the unions responsibility for "the defense of economic, industrial, commercial, and agricultural interests," was thus quickly interpreted in the broadest possible way. To be sure, this evolution did not go uncontested. The courts dealt with the various categories of the collective interest in different ways. In regard to trademarks and trade names, for example, it was not long before unions of producers were viewed as repositories of the general interests. The earliest decisions in this area dealt with wine appellations. In 1889, for instance, a judgment was handed down in favor of a syndicate of Champagne wine producers, who had filed suit against a competitor in Saumur who had attempted to label his product "champagne." The decision noted that the Champagne syndicate "represented a general interest absolutely distinct from the individual interest that a wine dealer from the Champagne region might have to complain about the counterfeit of his trademark."[7] A law of 5 August 1908 concerning fraudulent practices confirmed this decision by granting the syndicates involved "the rights accorded to the civil party throughout the territory of France and its colonies."[8] The evolution of the law governing trade unions came more slowly. Thus at the turn of the twentieth century, the Cour de Cassation was still holding that trade union action had to be based on individual rights. But this was merely a delaying action. The crucial turn came in 1913, when the full court affirmed that a union was a legal person that could not be reduced to its individual members and that it had a broad legal mission to defend the interests of a profession.

Since that date, the collective right to act in the interests of a profession has been part of the definition of a union, and there was thus a radical distinction between a union and an association, since the latter was still strictly an organization of individual members. At the beginning of the twentieth century, French jurists engaged in a great debate on the nature of "moral persons," and there can be no doubt that this debate helped to change legal thinking about unions. Proponents of the theory of the moral person as a "legal fiction" or "doctrinal fiction" lost out to those who favored treating unions as a "real moral person."[9] The works of Léon Michoud and Raymond Saleilles enjoyed considerable influence in this realm.[10] But this concept was not applied to associations. The courts systematically refused to allow associations to act as civil parties on behalf of a general social interest.[11] One of the few exceptions was granted to temperance leagues, which a law of 9 November 1915 recognized as being of public utility. Only much later, toward the end of the twentieth century, was this restriction relaxed somewhat in the areas of environmental law and child abuse. By contrast, the Labor Code from the beginning stipulated that unions "may, in all jurisdictions, exercise all the rights reserved to a civil party in regard to acts resulting in direct or indirect harm to the collective interest of the profession they represent." Clearly, this unequal capacity for legal action was an essential difference between an association and a union.[12]

As for the ability to acquire property and what kinds of property were authorized, unions and associations were initially subject to similar limitations, and fears that either would acquire property in mortmain were openly expressed. But new legislation soon created an enormous gap between the two. As we have seen, the law on associations remained static, whereas the law concerning unions evolved rapidly. The law of 12 March 1920 expanded the unions' civil capacity considerably. In addition to members' dues, unions were authorized to receive bequests and gifts without limit or authorization, including bequests and gifts of foreign origin. They could engage in various kinds of commercial activity as long as no profits were distributed. They could operate mutual aid societies, build low-cost housing, and establish and administer various charitable trusts of interest to the profession in the areas of training, insurance, and industrial and agricultural experimentation. Maxime Leroy summed up the changes thus: "In 1884, they wanted the unions poor. In 1920, they want them rich. In 1884, they were afraid of union mortmain; in 1920, they want it."[13]

What is more, the government helped and supported the development of the unions, whereas associations were left to fend for themselves. In 1886, for instance, the first *bourse du travail* (labor exchange) was opened in Paris. Reporting on this initiative to the municipal council, Mesureur noted that

> the existence of union headquarters will always be tenuous, since most workers will find their cost prohibitive. It is therefore important that unions be provided with space and offices where members can go without fear of making sacrifices of time and money that would otherwise be beyond their means. The free and permanent availability of meeting halls will allow workers to discuss the various issues pertaining to their industry and influencing their wages in a more mature and informed manner. To guide and instruct them they shall have all necessary means of information and correspondence, statistical data, and a library.[14]

Thereafter labor exchanges sprang up like mushrooms. Yet no city envisioned creating a "house of associations." Here, too, there was a double standard.

In the 1920s Léon Duguit deplored this "duality of legislation," which created such a wide gap between the law of unions and the law of associations. He was not the only one alarmed by the situation. In 1927 a Congress on the Freedom of Association was held in Paris, and its deliberations tell us a great deal about the kinds of questions that were being raised.[15] Most of the speakers discussed the ways in which the laws had diverged. The restrictive regime might have been justified in 1901, when the country still had little experience with the freedom of association, but many argued that it no longer served any purpose. "The steady growth of associations has given us the spectacle of what some have called the revolt of the facts against the law," one speaker noted, expressing a widely shared sentiment.[16] Indeed, it was already clear that many associations had been forced to procure needed resources illegally, for example by taking up public collections or holding raffles. This state of affairs gave rise to a crucial question, one that was repeated with monotonous regularity: Why were unions treated so favorably when charitable, scientific, and cultural associations were still viewed with suspicion and governed by rules that in effect prevented them from organizing and growing? What made this difference all the more incomprehensible was the fact that many unions professed avowedly revolutionary goals, whereas the activities of most associations posed no threat to anyone. "Today," one jurist complained, "a person can bequeath a million francs to a union whose sole purpose is to organize strikes and create trouble in industry. Such a bequest is perfectly legal and not subject to any administrative oversight. But if a person wants to make a bequest to a charitable association, an educational association, or a cultural association, that bequest will be declared null and void."[17] Conservatives of this sort stressed the political advantages that might result from improving the legal status of associations, whose influence could then counter that of the unions in French society. "It is reasonable," the sage Berthélemy summed up, "and by no means dangerous, to eliminate the last vestiges of suspicion remaining from the legislation of the revolutionary era, since these attitudes no longer make sense in the current state of our mores."[18] A variety of arguments and warnings were advanced in the hope of winning a relaxation of the 1901 rules, but without success.

The gap between unions and associations also widened because the Conseil d'Etat adopted a very strict policy after passage of the law of 1901 when it came to granting recognition of public utility, on the grounds that the law allowed enough scope for most charitable associations to operate as "declared" rather than "recognized" organizations. The high council thus clearly indicated that the underlying issue in this whole debate was the need to distinguish sharply between the category of general interest and the realm of social activity. The peculiar rules governing foundations under French law are another striking illustration of the fierce obsession in France with limiting responsibility for the general interest exclusively to the state. Surprisingly, the rules governing foundations have never been legally codified in France. They have been established through administrative practice, ratified by decisions of the Conseil d'Etat.[19] Every foundation is thus a special case, to be looked at in the light of its own peculiar circumstances. A series of *statuts types,* or typical models, can be modified to fit each new situation and serve only as general guidelines. Each foundation therefore requires approval from on high. Each is a special case, a sovereign creation of the state. Thus it is really the government that institutes foundations. Without government approval, a foundation enjoys only a virtual existence, as a mere intention, without legal form. In many countries, foundations have served as an instrument for improving the welfare of the public through individual initiative, but in France they remain suspect, and very few receive authorization.[20] A number of jurists belonging to the Société d'Etudes Législatives mobilized at the beginning of the century to propose reforms in this area. Saleilles headed a committee that produced numerous reports and suggestions.[21] None of this effort did any good. Although the advice of the society played an important role in formalizing the notion of a collective contract, its proposals in regard to the law of foundations got nowhere. Virtually the same men who successfully moved the law of unions forward failed to make any progress toward reforming the law of associations.

Republican Janus

Dynamic openness with respect to unions versus suspicious rigidity with respect to associations: such was the situation in republican France at the beginning of the twentieth century. It is important to try to understand what this difference tells us about the nature of the French political model. To begin with, one thing stands out: the disparity points not to two contrasting visions of politics or society but rather to an *internal* tension of the republican model. This tension is symbolized by a name: Waldeck-Rousseau. The man who led the Défense Républicaine in 1899 was directly linked to both the law of 1884 and the law of 1901 (though he played a smaller role in drafting the former than the latter). "The son of a republican of 1848, no ambition lay closer to his heart than to avenge the Republic of 1848 by bringing the definitive Republic into being." So reads the inscription on the monument dedicated to him in the Tuileries Gardens in Paris, which also bears the dates of the two great laws. The "definitive Republic" is thus clearly identified with the duality of associations and unions. Like Waldeck-Rousseau, it was willing to allow the unions to become a quasi-public institution, yet it feared that if the prerogatives of associations were broadened, they might build themselves up into a power to rival that of the state.

Waldeck-Rousseau was a staunch advocate of the general interest in politics but a pluralist on social issues. Thus he wrote a warm preface to a book by his collaborator Joseph Paul-Boncour, *Le Fédéralisme économique, étude sur le syndicat obligatoire*, even as he was fighting in the Assembly to limit the freedom of association. The contrast is all the more striking because Paul-Boncour did not merely plead the case of trade unionism and point out, as many others had done before him, how the unions could contribute to more effective social regulation. He treated the unions as the agents of a veritable social revolution and predicted that their growth would lead to a complete reorganization of the relations of production. Waldeck-Rousseau, normally quick to express alarm at any threat to the general interest, found nothing to criticize in Paul-Boncour's notion that the relations between individuals and professional groups "tend to become relations of sovereignty."[22] The notion of "syndical sovereignty" at the heart of Paul-Boncour's book apparently gave him no pause. Clemenceau also approved of the book, and when he became president of the Council in 1906, he even urged Viviani, the first minister of labor, to take Paul-Boncour as his chief of staff. What we see, then, is wary republicans taking an almost Proudhonian approach to the social question. This separation of the social and political, which scholars have not emphasized strongly enough, is essential for understanding the French republican model. Strict monism in the political sphere coexisted easily with a certain pluralism in the social sphere from the late nineteenth century on.

Waldeck-Rousseau was not the only embodiment of this dualism. Léon Bourgeois is an equally exemplary figure. Bourgeois, a friend and admirer—one might almost say a disciple—of Alfred Fouillée, completely shared Fouillée's anti-individualist ethos. The author of *Solidarité* considered himself a social thinker, and the words "association" and "organism" recur constantly in his writing. He, too, sought to reject the abstractions of the social contract. For example, he wrote that "by destroying the abstract and a priori notion of the isolated individual, knowledge of the laws of natural solidarity also destroys the equally abstract and a priori notion of the state."[23] Bourgeois's philosophy and sociology had little in common with the Jacobin worldview. He had no objection, for instance, to Fouillée's comment that "the law of 1884 is the most important law of our time," marking the beginning of a new social era, "the germ of a general organization of labor."[24] Yet while the great radical was socially reformist and even economically revisionist (advocating a sort of synthesis of liberalism and socialism), he nevertheless remained a republican fundamentalist in regard to the constitution. He refused to follow his friend Fouillée when the latter imposed his organic vision of the social on the country's political institutions with his call for a Senate that would represent collective interests and social functions to be established alongside a Chamber that would express individual wills by way of the ballot box. When Fouillée asserted that the absence of such an institution meant that "we are not, as we believe, living in a true republic," Bourgeois obviously did not approve.[25]

The jurists, philosophers, and sociologists who were the intellectual sponsors of the "great turn" we have described need to be reread in this perspective. Their social influence was considerable, while their political weight turned out to be almost nonexistent. The reception of Duguit's work provides a good example. Duguit, who initially thought of himself as a jurist-cum-sociologist, gave voice to the perception of an entire generation that a new social age had arrived. "Syndicalism," he wrote, "is the constitution within society of powerful, coherent groups with a well-defined legal structure and composed of men already united by a community of social employment and professional interest."[26] This definition was widely accepted. He was still understood, though conservatives may have been somewhat more skeptical, when he predicted that syndicalism "is not just a transformation of the working class" and that it would gradually extend to all classes of society in "a development that will give definite legal structure to the various social classes."[27] By contrast, Duguit encountered vigorous opposition when he called for making syndicalism an element of the reconstruction of political society itself by establishing, as Bourgeois had also suggested, a system for the representation of interests. One of the first to criticize him for this proposal was Thomas Ferneuil, the author of an important book, *Les Principes de 1789 et la sociologie*, whom we encountered earlier. Ferneuil, who described himself as an admirer of Durkheim, had been unsparing in his critiques of revolutionary abstraction, and in this respect he felt himself to be in sync with the dean of Bordeaux. He also agreed that the avenues opened up by the laws of 1884 and 1901 should be pursued. But he strongly opposed both Duguit's proposal for a Chamber consisting of elected representatives of the unions and his idea of corporatist and administrative federalism. Summing up his differences with Duguit, he located them "on political ground," as if it were possible and natural to distinguish the political from the social.[28]

We find the same distinction in Joseph Caillaux's comments on Duguit's work. Caillaux was a left-wing republican with advanced ideas on economic and social issues (he was the father of the progressive income tax, for example). He was alert to changes affecting the conditions of labor and open to new ideas. For instance, he supported the CGT's proposal to create an economic council. He also supported a proposal to set up "broad economic councils alongside parliamentary assemblies" and hoped that they would be charged with the complex task of managing what he did not shrink from calling "the economic state."[29] By contrast, he was hostile to Duguit's idea that the professions should be represented in the legislature, on the grounds that such an arrangement was incompatible with the republican understanding of governing in the general interest. "A Chamber consisting of representatives of the trades would become a free-for-all," he protested. "Each representative would want a larger share of the pie, and in order to get enough for themselves, they would all form coalitions against the general interest."[30] He angrily rejected the suggestion of Duguit and many others that politics be subsumed in a sort of decentralized government of the economic and social, which he believed would lead to a "fragmented state, decomposed into a thousand pieces," giving rise to the threat of "corporatism unbound" and of a France "bristling with a myriad of small citadels."[31] Thus Caillaux, too, accepted a radical distinction between the social and the political. Although he could agree with Duguit's sociological vision, in constitutional matters he resolutely rallied to the more traditional banner of another leading jurist, Adhémar Esmein, the proud guardian of the revolutionary political and legal philosophy of sovereignty.[32]

From Illiberal Democracy to Polarized Democracy

The separation of the social from the political was at the heart of the reformed republican model that established itself in the period 1880–1914. This model characteristically linked political loyalty to the heritage of revolutionary political culture while taking account of a whole range of factors that militated in favor of granting certain intermediary bodies a place in social and economic regulation. Although this model did not establish itself securely until the end of the nineteenth century, it had begun to emerge as early as the Second Empire. At that stage it was to some extent the result of a political calculation. Napoleon III had been willing to allow greater autonomy to civil society in order to legitimate a political centralization that was all the more rigorous for having been conceived in terms of a fundamentally illiberal democracy. As the emperor noted in the late 1850s, "If we can combine our political unity, which is a source of power, with the strength that derives from the spontaneous cooperation of free individuals and associations, our country will achieve the great things envisioned for it by the illustrious citizens of 1789."[33]

The political model stemming from this approach would be carefully formulated and rationally implemented in the mid-1860s. It began with a letter from the emperor to Eugène Rouher, who at that time was the minister presiding over the Conseil d'Etat:

> Our system of centralization, for all its advantages, suffers from the serious drawback of leading to an excess of regulation. As you know, we have already tried to remedy this, yet much remains to be done. In the past, constant administrative oversight of a host of matters may have been justified, but today it is only a hindrance . . . The more I think about this situation, the more I am convinced of the urgent need for reform.[34]

The Conseil d'Etat was thus called upon to develop proposals for new legislation and administrative action in a variety of areas. Edmond About, a prolific novelist and the author of numerous essays who was also a much-heeded private advisor to Napoleon III, had this to say about the new orientation: "The government that we have is enlightened enough to understand that we must decentralize, that is, that we must limit the domain of the state to political matters and leave all the rest to citizens freely associated in accordance with their affinities, needs, and resources."[35] He thus revealed how one ought to understand the term "liberal empire," which soon came into currency to describe the turn the regime took in the 1860s: it meant liberalism in the social and economic spheres but not at all in the political realm. The press was still muzzled, the opposition's campaign committees were still prosecuted in the courts, and parliamentarism was merely a façade. When About recommended that "association in all its forms be preached" to the French, he had no intention of suggesting any sort of "democratization" of the regime and thought only of greater autonomy for civil society.[36] To that end, a variety of reforms intended to reshape the French political model were undertaken. In this situation, "association" and "hyper-Jacobinism" formed an unexpected and unprecedented tandem.

The law of 1864 abolishing the crime of "coalition" has been taken by historians as the symbol of this shift in the imperial regime, as we saw earlier. Emile Ollivier, who reported on the bill to the Corps Législatif, insisted that the group spirit, the associative spirit, "would in the future yield untold benefits in the form of prosperity, wealth, labor, order, and tranquility."[37] In the minds of contemporaries, however, this first step toward recognition of the trade unions was not isolated from a series of other measures.[38] For instance, a law of 21 June 1865 on *associations syndicales* played a key role in the organization of rural France by establishing a flexible and efficient legal framework for landowners seeking to undertake collective projects for the common good (draining of marshes, channeling streams, cleaning up menaces to health, and so on). "In place of helpless isolation we wish to establish fruitful association," read the preamble to this law, which expressed the underlying philosophy of the reform effort in the following terms: "To promote French agriculture, industry, and commerce by associating interests and sources of capital and through the spontaneous action of citizens."[39] This was a long way from the vision of a tutelary state conceived as the sole agent of the common interest.

The reform of the law governing commercial corporations in 1863 and again in 1867 enables us to take the measure of these changes. At the beginning of the nineteenth century, under the Empire, the formation of corporations had been strictly regulated by the Commercial Code. Napoleon had insisted on "the inappropriateness of abandoning corporations to private individuals."[40] Hence no corporation could be formed without authorization from the state. In fact, commercial corporations were subject to regulations similar to those governing simple associations. They were viewed with a suspicion that was as much political as it was economic or legal. There was fear of monopolies that might constitute a power capable of threatening the public authorities. More broadly, it was impossible to imagine that an important area of social activity might escape from state control.[41] The bourgeois governments of the July Monarchy were as intransigent on this point as Napoleon and refused to heed the arguments of the liberal economists of the period.[42] At the time, state authorization was both a regalian right, supported by a broad swath of public opinion that feared the advent of new dominant powers, and an instrument in the hands of certain firms for manipulating competition.[43] By the 1860s economic arguments had begun to change minds,[44] but it was Napoleon III's determination to recast the French model that played the key role.

The first step was taken in 1863 with the formation of *sociétés à responsabilité limitée* (limited-responsibility partnerships). The rapporteur for the Corps Législatif introduced the bill as the embodiment of one aspect of a new philosophy of government. "The Emperor," he said, "has sought to stimulate citizens to free themselves gradually from state tutelage. He has identified civil liberty as the best and most solid foundation upon which to establish our political liberty."[45] The same point would be made again in 1867, just before the vote on the crucial law that made the formation of corporations in France totally free.[46] Spokesmen for the regime again sang the same old tune, celebrating the "vivifying principle of association" and remarking on "the imperious need" to encourage its development.[47] Indeed, the "centralizing spirit" of the First Empire was now openly criticized and dismissed as old-fashioned. In part, the new attitude reflected fears of the advent of an uncontrollable welfare state, which we analyzed earlier. "Wherever the state intervenes," it was said, "the individual abdicates; he considers himself relieved of the need to make any effort, he sinks into veritable lethargy, and he expects everything of the state, which he blames for all his disappointments."[48] Yet it was not just prudence of this sort that made people open to associations. Developments in two areas also contributed to the change in attitude. First, there was a general feeling that universal suffrage and expanded educational opportunity inevitably meant that the state would play a smaller role in overseeing the economy and society. Even more important, however, was a new understanding of the way in which the general interest was expressed. Generality was now seen as being defined within a novel economy of power, linked to the development of society in all its forms (in terms of rights, education, and level of activity). In order to be effective, political government now had to be more concentrated, more focused on essential tasks. A certain liberalism, or social pluralism, was therefore seen as essential for reinforcing government and even for ensuring its survival. This perspective did not, however, lead to a redefinition of the political. No new philosophy of the general interest emerged. On the contrary, it was an attempt to rescue the political culture of generality within a process of *polarization.*

Pursuing this line of thought, the Second Empire launched numerous reforms intended to allow civil society greater latitude to regulate itself while maintaining a highly centralized state. Within this framework, social liberalism and political illiberalism meshed neatly. This convergence affected many areas in addition to those discussed here. For instance, the flourishing of mutual aid societies and producers' cooperatives warrant more extensive discussion than space allows. The Third Republic inherited this model without modifying its overall structure. The only change—a noteworthy one to be sure—involved the expansion of public liberties. For instance, fetters on the organization of campaign committees and political parties were removed. Yet this expansion did not lead to any substantial modification of the underlying conception of democracy. What happened was simply a shift from a *radically illiberal democracy* to a *polarized democracy*. Both should be seen in contrast to what might be called *complex democracy*, that is, a plural political formation in which the society can make its voice heard and participate in decision-making in a succession of venues ranging from proximate to remote, from extremely informal to highly institutionalized.

From this point on, the question of decentralization becomes a good test case, as well as a symptom, of this difference and of the problem that it reflects. Let us therefore consider it for a moment.

The *Commune* between Civil Society and Political Society

The terms in which local government reform was described in the late nineteenth century show clearly that the obstacles to true decentralization stemmed more from a certain conception of politics and democracy than from mere bureaucratic inertia. The oft-celebrated municipal organization law of 1884 undeniably marked a turning point in this regard. It temporarily brought to a close a long period of questioning and doubt concerning the regulation and administration of local government *(communes)* and established a new framework that persists to this day. The law was essentially a codification of a long series of previous measures of more limited scope. It established a coherent institutional structure and gave local government legal autonomy and financial "personality." It steered a middle course between contradictory goals and achieved a compromise acceptable to all republicans as well as to adherents of other political persuasions. This compromise involved the attribution of powers, the definition of the respective roles of mayor and municipal council, and the relation between local authorities and various forms of state oversight.[49] Nevertheless, the new law did not represent an intellectual breakthrough, and in no way did it transcend earlier ambiguities in regard to the idea of decentralization. The vision of local government that emerged from it rested entirely on the vision of polarized democracy that was described in the previous section. Hence it is quite revealing to reread the debates and commentaries of the time with this perspective in mind.

Before the new law was passed, local government was seen as almost entirely an administrative instrument. It was common for republican candidates in this period to tell voters that "what you have to choose are not deputies, or legislators, but municipal councilors, or administrators."[50]

This attitude explains why the debate on the municipal law drew little public attention, as if it were a technical question of interest only to specialists.[51] Louis Emile Gustave de Marcère, who reported on the subject to the Chamber of Deputies, insisted on this point: "Municipal corporations cannot and must not concern themselves with politics."[52] At the time this was taken to be self-evident. It was the culmination of a long history. Since 1831, when a reform had reinstituted elections to municipal councils, it was common to distinguish between "political elections" and "administrative elections," with the former designation applying only to the election of deputies, the latter to municipalities. In the first half of the nineteenth century and under the Second Empire, the leaders of the principal parties therefore showed little interest in municipal votes, which they saw as nothing more than "beauty contests."[53] Remember that mayors were still *appointed* by the prefects or the government. Under the July Monarchy, the leaders of the Republican Party showed no interest in these elections except perhaps in Paris and a few other big cities.[54] In 1884, too, just as in the 1830s, local governments were not regarded as "political bodies." This circumstance is an important key to understanding the nature of the French model. Marcère's treatment of the subject is thus quite enlightening.

"Local government [*la commune*] is not a creation of the law," the rapporteur wrote. "It is born of the nature of things."[55] In other words, local government was a natural body, not an artificial (political) body. To put it another way, local government corresponded to a *level of organization* of collective life (in essence comparable to the family, for example) and not to a mode of social generality. Local government was merely one form of civil society among others and not a form of political society. This point is crucial. Let us therefore attend closely to Marcère's argument: "It [*la commune*] has collective interests of property, security, health, and police that it may manage as it sees fit," he noted.

> It has moral interests, to which it must attend. It needs resources and has the ability to create them. In a word, it enjoys full administration of its affairs. But however freely it may act within its own sphere, it is subject, like any other moral or individual person, to the general laws of the state, and it cannot violate them without making France again vulnerable to falling into a veritable state of anarchy. In this sense, local governments are subjects, and, as such, they are subject to oversight by the public authorities.[56]

In other words, the local government was just one moral person among others. Marcère took this approach one step further. He asserted that a local government was a moral person of a particular kind, which must be "treated as minor." In his view, it could be regarded only as the beneficiary (and not the owner) of the collective goods in its charge. From this he deduced that "it is not in consequence of the tyranny of the state that, from the standpoint of disposing of its wealth, it is subject to certain rules. It is because of its very nature, which has made it necessary to deprive it of some of its powers in the interest of future generations."[57] In effect, duration was to time what generality was to a determinate field. State oversight of local government was thus in no sense bureaucratic but solely a consequence of "democratic" order, a circumstance that made it necessary to ensure the supremacy of generality over particularity. Marcère continued: "The justification of governmental oversight rests on the following grounds: respect due to general laws, protection of collective interests against individual interests, and the guarantees made to future generations against the incompetence and wastefulness of contemporaries."[58] In this framework, so-called decentralization had only instrumental meaning: it belonged strictly to the realm of *management* and had nothing to do with the operation of governmental authorities.

If we are to understand this conception properly—and we must if we want to understand why it has been almost impossible to reform the French model—we must clear up one ambiguity concerning the electoral principle in the municipal realm. In the republican vision of the 1880s, as in the liberal vision of the 1830s, municipal elections were essentially functional devices: their purpose was to establish confidence, to qualify and legitimate the authority of an administrator. They had nothing to do with extending representative government. This was precisely what Marcère and Antonin Dubost, the spokesman for the committee that reviewed the draft of the bill, objected about to the deputies of the extreme left who proposed alternative frameworks based on the principle of local autonomy.[59] Dubost, for example, was critical of the risks involved in "plans that would shatter national sovereignty."[60] His attack on one of those plans could not have been more unambiguous: "M. Lacroix's proposal is based on the exercise of representative power, and its purpose is to constitute a municipal government that is entirely independent, not subject to any control, or at any rate not subject to any control other than that of the voters, to whom all elected representatives are of course subject."[61] In other words, local governments were not to be subject to majority rule.[62] For the critics, then, the first wrong idea was to look upon local governments as political bodies solely because they were elected. This perspective also explains the recurrent resistance in France to reducing the number of local government units, which is exceptionally high. The fact that there are 40,000 such units means that they must remain administrative agencies and may not set themselves up as political powers.[63]

The right of municipal councils to choose the mayor was not granted until 1882, although Paris remained an exception, on the grounds that its position as capital meant that its local government would inevitably be political in character.[64] Even more important, it was not until 1882 that France abandoned the system under which a town's biggest taxpayers participated in the deliberations of the municipal council when these involved floating a loan or imposing a new tax. This procedure had been adopted in 1818 and was consistent with the idea of the citizen as property owner (though less compatible with the *censitaire* suffrage, which was based on a notion of equality within difference, since payment of the *cens* (poll tax) defined a certain minimal capacity beyond which distinctions no longer counted).[65] It was strongly reaffirmed in 1837 and never challenged thereafter.[66] This procedure, known as "adjunction of the leading taxpayers," seriously limited the effects of universal suffrage, since the number of taxpayers summoned to participate in council deliberations was equal to the number of regularly elected council members. This arrangement was tantamount to treating local government as a "syndicate of interests" rather than as a political community. On the eve of its abolition, this procedure was still in common use: 99.5 percent of all towns invoked it regularly.[67] That this was the case nearly half a century after the adoption of universal suffrage would be incomprehensible were it not for the fact that contemporaries viewed local government as "nonpolitical." Bear in mind, too, that the law of 1884 itself still contained unusual restrictions on the eligibility of municipal councilors. For instance, Article 32 stipulated that no person could be elected to the council who was "a domestic servant in the exclusive employ of another person" or "who was exempt from contributing to municipal expenses or supported by public assistance offices."[68] This point was not even debated, as if the residue of the idea of citizen as property owner did not seem out of place when applied to municipal matters.

Article 72 of the 1884 law strictly prohibited municipal councils "from publishing proclamations and addresses or expressing political wishes or, except in cases envisioned by the law, entering into communication with other municipal councils."[69] The formulation is troubling: it repeats almost word for word the revolutionary decrees of 1791 and 1795 on political societies, which were intended to indicate that such societies could not be organs of sovereignty but only "partial" associations. This resemblance shows clearly that local governments were regarded in a similar light in 1884, as particular associations, of which there were many.

Subsequent decisions by the Conseil d'Etat only confirmed this republican vision of the municipal realm. In a series of decrees issued in the last decade of the nineteenth century and the first decade of the twentieth, the Council defended the idea of a community of taxpayers, as distinct from a community of residents.[70] The eminent jurist Maurice Hauriou produced a masterly and deeply original analysis of these decisions that sheds new light on the French political culture of generality. It is worth pausing to take a closer look at it. The Council's various interventions all came in response to taxpayers' objections to what they regarded as illegal decisions by municipal assemblies (approving allegedly excessive expenditures said to reach beyond the prerogatives of local government). In one of his notes, Hauriou carefully probed the distinction between the "political reality" of the town (people residing in the same place) and the "economic reality" (administration of expenditures) in order to justify the Council's intervention.[71] In the first case, he pointed out, only common interests were concerned; hence there were no grounds for challenging the actions of municipal governments as "exercising excessive power," because "the representative mechanism is intended to ensure proper administration of these interests."[72] If "the elected authorities manage things badly, the voters can vote them out of office. Elective mandates are of short duration, and at the next election culpable officials can be summoned to give an account of their actions and rejected at the polls if found wanting."[73] Universal suffrage thus sufficed to judge matters of common interest. But, Hauriou continued, there was another, more economic dimension to local government, and in this case it was possible that a taxpayer's *personal* interest might be harmed by a mad decision. This distinction between the *voter* (representing generality) and the *taxpayer* (representing particularity) was basic to the Conseil d'Etat's interventions in matters of municipal administration. (Obviously such a distinction would make no sense at the national level, where the taxpayer and citizen are inevitably one, there being only one mechanism, political in nature, causing them to act.) Hauriou approved of this distinction without reservation and went so far as to express his regret that elections had obscured the "civil" nature of local government. His thoughts on the subject are recorded in terms whose bluntness merits our attention: "The operation of universal suffrage has led to a gradual shift in the political center of gravity, so that the biggest taxpayers no longer hold power. Here we are examining this new situation not from the standpoint of general politics but from a strictly financial standpoint. This is not without drawbacks for the interests of taxpayers as well as of the collectivity."[74] The view that taxpayers were not sufficiently protected against mistakes by elected local officials shows clearly that local government was seen as a hybrid organ, somewhere between civil society and political society.

What was invoked in this case was not the regulatory power of a government of judges as opposed to democratic government but rather a kind of economic oversight. Hauriou, for example, spoke of a "judge responsible for ensuring proper administration."[75] In effect, he offered an *economic critique* of universal suffrage on the grounds that "democratic assemblies are spendthrift because they have to satisfy their electoral clientele."[76] Even though the law of 1884 had just been passed, he was glad that the Conseil d'Etat operated as an "organ of centralization" by separating administrative oversight from any consideration of electoral politics.

To be sure, the refusal to regard local government as a true political body was not based entirely on fundamental republican doctrine. Republicans joined with conservatives in fearing the rise of "municipal socialism," which some thought had begun to move toward a silent revolution from below.[77] Observers had been impressed by the election of Guesdist socialists in Roubaix in 1892 and then, in 1896, in Dijon, Lille, Marseilles, and Toulon. Taine, who had always been so quick to denounce the ogre of centralization, suddenly discovered its virtues: "If nothing else, authoritarian centralization is good in at least one respect, namely, that it can still save us from democratic autonomy."[78] Nevertheless, the crucial fact remained that local government stood at the point of contact between two different worlds and was divided by the contradiction between its *form* (which seemed political as a result of its elective basis) and its *nature* (which was economic).[79]

In this connection, it behooves us to pay particularly close attention to the terms in which municipal referenda were condemned.[80] Once again it was the Conseil d'Etat that ruled them out in 1905 on the grounds that they involved an inherent confusion between taxpayers and residents.[81]

Neither intermediary body nor political body, local government is thus an excellent indicator of the tensions that existed in the French model. This also helps us to see why the idea of decentralization met with such difficulty in France: it could be interpreted on the one hand as political decentralization, which was deemed to be impossible by definition, or, on the other hand, as administrative decentralization, which was believed to be incapable of being economically effective without the oversight of a superior power. Decentralization has thus continued to seem doubly impossible.

The Impossibility of Decentralization

Decentralization: the word retained a quiet power of attraction in the late nineteenth century. Even the imperial regime found it useful at times to wrap itself in its folds, as much to decorate its policy of deconcentration with an adjective deemed to be flattering as to celebrate the modest increase in the prerogatives granted to municipal and general councils in 1866 and 1867. The opposition rallied beneath the same banner after the publication of its "Nancy Program" in 1865, which called for election of mayors, elimination of the office of prefect, and abolition of the Conseil d'Etat so as to loosen the vise of centralized control. Thirst for revenge among local notables in this period meshed neatly with the liberal and republican ambition to attack "smothering centralization."[82] A newspaper appropriately named *La Décentralisation* was even founded in Lyons in 1868. As Flaubert noted in *L'Education sentimentale* (1869), "Some wanted the Empire, others the Orléans, still others the comte de Chambord, but all agreed on the urgency of decentralization." The enthusiasm attained its zenith in 1870. With much fanfare the Empire, a few months before its fall, established a "committee on decentralization" as evidence of its reformist intentions.[83] Once the regime was gone, its adversaries took up the baton. Raynouard sponsored a "Ligue de la Décentralisation," and a *Revue de la décentralisation* commenced publication.

The movement briefly picked up speed in 1871 but then suddenly ran out of steam. As under the Restoration and July Monarchy, circumstances again played an important role. Now in firm control, liberals and conservatives showed less enthusiasm for reform than before, or at any rate no longer saw any need to act quickly. Furthermore, the idea of decentralization took on certain communalist overtones, which the right found worrisome. The memory of the Parisian insurrection, which had been carried on in the name of federalist principles, stood as a warning. In 1871, therefore, Thiers, as he had done in 1834, emphatically insisted that the party of order was inevitably the party of centralization. The shock of defeat at the hands of the Prussians also played a part by discrediting the idea of a weak state in the eyes of a humiliated country. On the left, republicans also turned their backs on the position they had taken while in opposition. Gambetta's evolution gives striking evidence of this shift. Under the Second Empire the author of the Belleville Program had been in the forefront of critics of the prefects and Conseil d'Etat. After 1877 these views were quickly forgotten, and he became one of the main proponents of "national centrality" or "French centrality" as the necessary and indispensable basis for organizing a country that was happy to identify with the state.[84] To be sure, he was also quick to contrast political centralization with administrative decentralization, but the only function of these words was incantatory, for as he bluntly put it one day from the podium in the Chamber of Deputies, "I am not a decentralizer."[85]

Thus from the early 1870s to the mid-1890s, the theme of decentralization disappeared almost entirely from public debate. The skirmishers on behalf of Ordre Moral and, later, the founding fathers of the Third Republic had more urgent tasks before them. The issue did reemerge at the end of the century, however, as if some mysterious thirty-year cycle governed the political agenda. First in the 1820s and 1830s and then in the period 1865–1870, decentralization had seemed an obvious response to the problems of the moment: the fear of social disintegration in the first case and the need to organize resistance to an oppressive central government in the second. The issue resurfaced along with doubts about the foundations of the new regime and a sense of new threats looming on the horizon. The Boulangist crisis had an important effect, revealing the shakiness of the ground on which the democratic republic stood. There were also fears that the provinces would wither economically at a time when the population of the capital was increasing rapidly. After the elections of 1893, the spectacular progress of the socialists triggered deep anxieties that the central government might succumb to a frenzy of taxation and regulation. Local notables across France felt their power threatened.[86] All this was enough to create a situation favorable to a new round of decentralizing enthusiasm.

The France of Paul Deschanel was in sync with that of Maurice Barrès in celebrating the virtues of the countryside and denouncing the power of bureaucrats barricaded in their citadels.[87]

Everything came together in 1895. An extraparliamentary commission "charged with looking into the means of achieving decentralization and simplifying the administrative services" of the state was appointed.[88] Its members included ministers, deputies, elected officials of major cities, and well-known writers on public affairs. The work of the commission involved a study of governmental reorganization and redistribution of power between local and national authorities. The emphasis on "administrative simplification" is significant. Indeed, it was as much the bureaucracy as centralization itself that caused anxiety.[89] Within the space of a few months a spate of books and pamphlets flowed from the presses. The *Revue politique et parlementaire,* the *Echo du Parlement,* and *La Nouvelle Revue* published countless analyses of the problem and proposals for reform.[90] The last of these journals even featured a regular "chronicle of decentralization" (by Marcère) and a column on "The Provinces." In March 1895 the Ligue Républicaine de la Décentralisation was organized, but it was soon renamed the Ligue Nationale in order to cast as wide a net as possible. It was headed by Marcère, the former minister of the interior, whom we encountered earlier, and drew support from both the left and the right. Léon Bourgeois was its vice-president, but the membership also included young monarchists linked to Barrès and Maurras.

Vigorous debate continued for several years, engaging both the general public and the political class through the turn of the century. Then it died down. New publications became scarce, the commission's work bogged down, and the Ligue Nationale was dissolved in 1899. A small band of activists regrouped around the Fédération Régionaliste Française, which was organized in 1900. But it was fairly limited and soon saw itself pared down to members nostalgic for the "organic life" of prerevolutionary France and sympathetic to the politics of Charles Maurras.[91] Once again, enthusiasm for decentralization fizzled. What accounts for this? To be sure, circumstances again played a part. Waldeck-Rousseau's formation of a "republican defense cabinet" in 1899 helped to reorder political priorities, for instance. "The truth," as Paul-Boncour sadly noted, "is that decentralization has been relegated to the scrap heap along with other discarded pipe dreams, issues that are useful while in opposition but embarrassing when in power, and akin to such other juvenilia of radicalism as the election of judges and elimination of the office of president of the Republic."[92] Equally important was the outrage expressed by the Action Française, which condemned the Republic as a regime by its very nature unable to decentralize, an accusation that became a sort of self-fulfilling prophecy.[93] But what we need is an explanation for the recurrence of failure.

The first thing to note is that the meaning of "decentralization" is quite elastic. "'Decentralize' is a rather vague word . . . It is like a cry from a thousand oppressed bosoms, but it is a word whose meaning is undefined," as Marcère himself conceded in 1895.[94] For nearly a century, the word "decentralization" had been taken for granted, with tacit silence as to its precise meaning. The *Dictionnaire des idées reçues* had every reason to include "decentralization" along with "self-government" (a word that was particularly fashionable in the 1870s). It is certainly true that deploring the ravages of centralization has been one of the great commonplaces of French political discourse and that recurrent calls for decentralization have been a constant of French political culture. To note the phenomenon is not to explain it, however, or to account for the regular return of the word, even if it is of the essence of politics to offer comforting illusions.

The rhetoric of decentralization in French political discourse is in the first place a mark of the difficulty of representing reality. It substitutes imprecation for analysis and thus allows for convergences and coalitions that would otherwise be improbable or impossible. It is as if an imaginary France—a bureaucratic monster reigning over society from on high—had to be invented before an agenda for change could be formulated—with "change" here of course also situated in the realm of the imaginary. In other words, whenever decentralization was invoked, it was trapped in a vicious circle of unrealistic assumptions. From time to time the circle was broken by some political or military emergency, which justified a return to some form of "realism." But even this realism was interpreted as an immediate imperative that required no explicit discussion of its underlying assumptions. Thus, little by little, the political culture of generality ceased to recognize itself for what it was and gave way to an immediate and self-referential form of political discourse. Ideology is born when discourse surreptitiously frees itself from facts, setting up a fantasy that serves as an obligatory substitute for reality. The idea of decentralization, which in its dominant formulations bore only a remote resemblance to the way things were, thus ended up as the expression of two kinds of failure, intellectual and political, perversely weaving together the unthinkable and the impossible.

This analysis explains why the history of decentralization repeatedly followed an identical pattern. Indeed, the twentieth century began with one of the most distorted formulations of the decentralizing dilemma ever given. It emanated from Radical Party circles. In various platforms and manifestos of the early 1900s, the young party frequently resorted to bombastic denunciations.[95] It spoke of excessive centralization, "absolutely contrary to the republican regime." It demanded that the post of subprefect be eliminated. One of its leaders, Georges Clemenceau, proclaimed: "Not only am I firmly in favor of decentralization, but so far am I from deserving the charge of Jacobinism that my ideal of government is federalism."[96] Everyone proclaimed in unison that "we must do away with Napoleonic centralization, which has fallen into the hands of a government of faceless pencil-pushers."[97] The same Clemenceau, though quick to insist loudly on the need for communal autonomy, softly added "within limits compatible with the unity of France." Thus the same dilemma inevitably returned, yet no one seemed bothered by this, because everyone was perfectly capable of separating the two components. The republicans of this period sounded like Tocqueville but continued to think like Robespierre.

The Radicals of the early twentieth century also emphasized a different approach to decentralization, which might be called managerial or economic. In this perspective, the principal charge against centralization was that it contributed to waste. In 1902 Radicals denounced a "veritable army of civil servants, whose numbers could easily be reduced by half."[98] The idea that the French bureaucracy needed to be slimmed down (défonctionnarisée) became a commonplace of the period. Ultimately, therefore, to decentralize was "to economize." The expression "decentralization of business," which came into widespread use at this time, reflects a shift in thinking consistent with the idea of "nonpolitical" local government. Much later, the utopian ideal of reducing the cost of bureaucracy became the core of the argument that led to the reform of 1982. Yet even then the fundamental structural ambiguities of the republican discourse on decentralization remained untouched.

— 13 —

The Network State

The original French model also evolved for another reason: associations and intermediary bodies, once the embodiments of particularism, were themselves integrated into the general scheme of things. This integration took three forms. First, associations and intermediary bodies were co-opted as political agents of the monist republican vision. Second, they became functional auxiliaries of the state. And third, the state reorganized itself along corporatist lines by constituting so-called *grands corps*.

Agents of Democratic Generality

"Revolution must not remain external and superficial. It must penetrate and permeate."[1] These words, from a lecture that Michelet gave in 1848, nicely capture the republican concern with bringing hearts and minds into harmony with new institutions. Mirabeau, in his *Travail sur l'éducation publique,* had earlier formulated a similar wish, calling upon his fellow citizens to fill "the *immense gap* that has suddenly opened up between the way things are now [as a result of the adoption of the Constitution of 1791] and what we were accustomed to."[2] To harmonize mores with institutions: the imperative was felt all the more acutely in the second half of the nineteenth century, because universal (male) suffrage had with one stroke put the fate of the nation in the hands of the man in the street. It was with this new state of affairs in mind that Jean Macé founded the Ligue de l'Enseignement in 1866. The purpose of the association, which soon had chapters all across France, was to contribute to the education of the average citizen, who, in Macé's eyes, was still "an uncouth master."[3] In 1870, on the eve of the Franco-Prussian War, the Ligue boasted some 18,000 members. At the time, all republicans looked upon universal education as a necessary condition of universal suffrage. "Democracy and education need each other and are intimately intertwined," as Eugène Spuller, an ally of Gambetta, put it.[4] Formally, this objective was achieved in 1882, when a law was passed making education compulsory. The ardent republicans who had campaigned for the new law naturally believed that it was up to the state to take charge of the educational system. By itself, however, the law could not ensure complete success, for the goals of the project were at once pedagogical (to educate the people) and political ("to transform," as Spuller put it, "generations of former French monarchists into French republicans"). Republicans, Spuller added, could not wait for time to do the work of "professor of the Republic."[5] Something would have to instigate and accelerate public action: this was the role assigned to organizations such as the Ligue de l'Enseignement and the Association Philotechnique. Such associations served as allies and auxiliaries of the state. Macé did not hesitate to say that "we are with the government";[6] he even went so far as to observe that an association of the type he headed was a way of "universalizing the governmental function."[7] What we have here, in other words, is quite the opposite of a state functioning within the state as an adverse and competing power.

An auxiliary association thus engages in public action, but it does so on its own schedule; and it also reduces the resulting tensions. Jules Ferry, speaking as minister of national education to independent groups in favor of secular public education, was clear about the complementary role of these auxiliary groups: "The republican university needs collaborators like you, pioneers like you, independent societies that explore unknown areas *before the university does and on its behalf,* that develop new methods and carry out experiments that the state has neither the time nor the right to conduct until they have been consecrated by experience. The teaching *corps* of the Republic needs this auxiliary army."[8] For Ferry, clearly, an association was also a partner of the state. He insisted on this relationship on numerous occasions, as, for example, when he spoke of the Association Philotechnique as an "indispensable auxiliary to ministers of national education."[9] What Ferry had in mind, however, was not a mere complementary relationship in which the private association simply backed the action of the state. As the incarnation of social generality, the state as he saw it had no functional need of "private" support. The auxiliary association was justified only if it could be shown that the state somehow lacked the power or the means to get the job done. The association intervened in a time frame appropriate to its purpose, which was to experiment. Thus, he explained, the Association Philotechnique was in fact "a small avant-garde university."[10] If the state was defined by the generality of its procedures and actions, innovation obliged it to step outside its own system, since by definition innovation implies a break with the past and the temporary establishment of a new order. The association is better able to manage this *moment of particularity* and is therefore charged with this responsibility. It thus remains tied to the state and in a subordinate position. Once the innovation is incorporated into the administrative machinery and becomes the norm, the association steps aside.

Taking as an example the education of girls, in which the Association Philotechnique played an important role, Ferry stressed the need for the association to withdraw once the reform was complete. "Once freedom's torch is passed to the state," he said, "once the people's school is established and secondary education for young women overcomes all the resistance and hostility and is accepted by the academy where it was nurtured by vigilant hands and allowed to thrive, the associative spirit must seek out another task, find a new agenda, and resume its place in the avant-garde."[11] He therefore called on the association's members to turn to other projects, such as professional education, which was then in its infancy. In other words, there was a "division of labor" between the state and the associations,[12] or, to put it yet another way, a dialectic of particularity and generality relating distinct temporalities (the shorter time frame of associative innovation and the longer time frame of state permanence). Macé offered a clear formulation of the rules governing this division of responsibilities: "The league must march ahead of the government to lay the groundwork for the reforms we desire . . . But when the law is passed, we must follow behind the state in order to make sure that the law is enforced."[13] In other words, the association in this case served as a kind of intermediary body, though it did not declare itself to be one and retained the form of a private organization. Many other "good works" of secular organizations were similar in nature. These must be taken into account if we are to understand the nature of the republican state that took hold at the end of the nineteenth century, for the practical construction of this new type of state depended on such associations.

This conception of the association's role posed no threat to the original republican model. It merely described the specific conditions under which associations could play a role without undermining the monist vision of politics. Bear in mind that this did not betoken a new approach to democracy or a redefinition of the political. The old political culture of generality continued to dominate thinking. It is symptomatic, moreover, that Macé, though quick to celebrate the role of associations as auxiliaries, remained strongly opposed to campaign committees, because he took a very traditional view of democratic immediacy, in which such committees were "a way of evading universal suffrage."[14]

If associations served as auxiliaries of the state, they were also psychological and sociological instruments in the service of generality. "An association," Léon Bourgeois observed, "is an apprenticeship in social life . . . It is a way of creating in a small area, a limited space, a restricted domain, a reduced image, visible to a few, of what the greater human society ought to be."[15] To borrow a famous expression of the time, the association was seen as a sort of *petite patrie*, a phase in the achievement and representation of national unity. It was a way of learning about unity and translating it into action.[16] Association was a necessary instrument of totality in a world of individuals in which totality was no longer immediately available. Contrasting modern society with the Old Regime, in which the unity of national will was an almost natural consequence of the interpenetration of church and state, Bourgeois saw associations as an indispensable tool for reconstructing a palpable totality that could no longer be taken for granted. "In a state like ours," he observed, "will is in the hands of the delegates of the sovereign masses, and the idea of it is scattered or dispersed throughout that immense mass. Who will give it cohesion and unity?"[17] Here, association was understood as a means and moment of totality, and thus had something in common with Lanthenas's conception of the pedagogical role of popular societies in the revolutionary period.[18] This perspective was quite remote from any vision of social and political autonomy in a world that had supposedly rejected Jacobin culture. Here, association was merely an agent of generality.

Props of the State

If associations served as agents of political and public action in the establishment of republican France, other intermediary bodies saw their roles legitimated even earlier as direct auxiliary agencies of the state. Indeed, this was how the anticorporatist rigor of the revolution was first moderated.

We can follow the thread of this "exception" to the initial postrevolutionary rule from the restoration of the chambers of commerce in 1802 to today's practice of allowing associations to perform certain functions of the
state. The revival of consular institutions blazed a symbolic trail just ten
years after they were banned as incompatible with the new France. The ban
on these intermediary bodies was lifted because of the technical assistance
they could provide, and at the same time their operations were made subordinate to the state apparatus. The chambers of commerce are symbolic
in this regard. A brief investigation of their history will enable us to grasp
the extent and significance of yet another bending of the founding principles of the culture of generality.

The banning of the chambers of commerce was a logical consequence of
the principles of 1789, since the deputies to the Constituent Assembly had
held that "administrative bodies established in major cities should suffice
for all purposes, covering those engaged in commerce along with all other
classes of citizens." In June 1791, Le Chapelier was persuaded to bend just
enough to make one (and only one) exception to his strict denunciation of
corporations of every kind: "Some say that an exception should be made
for chambers of commerce in the cities. Of course you can well imagine that none of us intends to prevent merchants from coming together to
discuss business."[19] Chambers of commerce were thus explicitly excluded
from the decree of 14 June 1791. What drove this decision is not very clear,
since the deputy from Brittany felt no need to justify himself on this
point. But the obvious role of chambers of commerce in promoting economic development surely persuaded him that they should not be lumped
together with those corporatist institutions whose very nature allegedly
made them impediments to innovation and progress. This probably explains why his comment was accepted without debate. On 27 September 1791, however, the Assembly reconsidered this decision and reversed
course after hearing a report read by Pierre-Louis Goudard on behalf of
the Committee on Agriculture and Commerce. "The existence of chambers of commerce," Goudard explained, "offends against the principles of
the Constitution, which proscribes corporations. These particular administrations must therefore be abolished so that they may be incorporated
into the general administration."[20] The chambers of commerce, he observed, had proved useful in the past, as had the inspectors of manufacturing instituted by Colbert. But times had changed. Now the market, coupled
with the bureaucratic machinery of a representative government, sufficed

to ensure adequate regulation of the economy.[21] Thus even as Goudard was arguing in favor of eliminating the inspectors of manufacturing and chambers of commerce, he was also singing the praises not only of the market, which in itself sufficed to limit "combinations of labor," but also of a beefed-up bureaucracy to monitor and assist commerce. On 26 October 1791 a "central bureau for the administration of commerce" was established in the Ministry of the Interior. In other words, the decree of 27 September 1791 had reaffirmed the supremacy of revolutionary principles in public law.

Eliminating the chambers of commerce was not accomplished without difficulty, however. In April 1792, for example, Jean-Marie Roland de la Platière, the minister of the interior, sternly reprimanded the directorate of the department of the Somme for allowing a "committee of commerce" to organize for the purpose of discreetly reclaiming certain of the professional prerogatives of the old chambers. "All interests must be concentrated in administrative bodies," Roland wrote. "They alone are charged with representing the public. No sort of aggregate entity can be allowed to control any portion of the general administration that is entrusted to them, and only in them can nonindividual demands be allowed to take shape."[22] This insistent reaffirmation of revolutionary doctrine showed that many of the old problems remained. For example, because the system of tax collection linked to the chambers of commerce had not been reformed, it became necessary to name liquidators chosen from among the merchants who had been members of the chambers (laws of 6 September 1792).[23] It soon became apparent, however, that the central office of the commerce administration was not well suited to do the jobs assigned to it. Under the Consulate, Jean-Claude Beugnot, the prefect of Rouen, carried on a very instructive correspondence on this subject with the minister of the interior, Jean-Antoine Chaptal. Looking at the issue purely in terms of practical administration, he offered numerous examples to show that many of the functions of the old chambers were not being properly filled by the new administration. "In a department like this one," he wrote on 24 Thermidor, Year IX, "it is impossible for one man to understand, embrace, grasp, and combine the countless reports involved in this administration."[24]

The minister of the interior found these arguments persuasive. As a first step, he asked his prefects to establish councils of agriculture, arts, and commerce.[25] A more important step was taken on 3 Nivôse, Year XI (24

December 1802), when he presented to the consuls a proposal to reinstate the old chambers of commerce.[26] His brief emphasized the role that the chambers could play in informing the government of ways to promote the nation's prosperity. He also mentioned that they could serve as councils. His proposal drew an immediate response in the form of a directive issued the same day. It mentioned only the functions he had discussed, as well as the mission of auxiliary to the administration.[27] Thus the restored chambers were not simply copies of the Old Regime institutions bearing the same name. Chaptal expressly stated that they must not in any way be "invested with a portion of the [responsibilities of the] administration." Significantly, the directive was careful to indicate that the chambers must "correspond directly with the minister of the interior" (Article 5), meaning that they were not permitted to correspond with one another. Bear in mind that in the language of the time, "to correspond" meant to rise above one's particular sphere of activity and to assume functions of coordination, that is, of generality.[28] A few years later, the new minister of the interior, Jean-Baptiste Champagny, rebuked the Paris Chamber of Commerce for printing a brochure and seeking to communicate with peer groups elsewhere. Champagny issued a warning to all chambers of commerce:

> His Majesty the Emperor wishes me to inform you that no written document or memorandum is to be printed in the name of either the chamber or a committee operating under its auspices without my express authorization. The work of the chambers of commerce belongs to the administration. This work achieves its purpose when it has been submitted to the administration for further consideration. It is up to this higher authority to evaluate the costs and benefits of publication.[29]

Clearly, chambers of commerce conceived in these terms posed no threat to the legal principles of the Revolution. They were in effect reduced from being part of a system of professional self-regulation to serving as a new type of cog in the bureaucratic machine. In Chaptal's estimation, "these establishments are nothing but auxiliaries of the administration" and therefore ought to be "limited to merely consultative functions."[30] The goal was to enhance the efficiency of the state by improving its sources of information, so as to secure its power. Hence it is wrong to describe the chambers of commerce as "intermediary bodies" in the full sense of the term. The chambers as "restored" by Chaptal were in no sense autonomous public institutions; they were merely part of the administrative machinery. Note that this represented a novel "Jacobin" conception of the relation of corporation to state: the corporation in this case was not an economic or social community but a *competence,* a type of knowledge. Its form was totally submerged by its function (whereas in traditional corporatism, the two were inseparable).

Does this example suggest that we are witnessing the emergence of a model? At the very least it must be conceded that other institutions were conceived in a similar spirit. Take, for example, the consultative chambers of manufacturing, factories, and arts and crafts that were established a short while later, in 1803. Regnault de Saint-Jean-d'Angély, a member of the Conseil d'Etat, prepared a report on the issue for the Corps Législatif in which he expressed many of the same concerns that Chaptal had touched on in connection with the chambers of commerce. "Who is a shrewd enough judge of conditions and a clever enough student of political economy to decide unambiguously what ought to be done in our present situation, which offers such an abundance of means, such a wealth of resources, and such a variety of new commercial combinations?" he asked.

> We must look to councils of wholesale and retail merchants themselves to ponder their situation and provide the means to decide what measures might be beneficial to commerce. That is why the government proposes that you authorize the formation of consultative chambers of manufacturing, factories, and arts and crafts. These chambers, well informed about local interests and made up of men of experience, will stimulate the thinking of the government. They will tell us what the needs of commerce are.[31]

Once again, the role of the institution was limited to functions of information and advice. The intermediary body was recognized as a superior source of information, and nothing more. This outcome is quite similar in spirit to Chaptal's suggestion that the imperial prefects rely on networks of local notables to collect statistical information that the administration might not always be in a position to collect on its own.[32] To be sure, these councils were elected, but the representativeness stemming from the election carried no democratic significance for the government that instituted it. The basis for election was rather moral and technical, in that it impressed upon the members the seriousness of their task and guaranteed the quality of the information they were to supply.[33]

These chambers posed no obstacle to state supremacy. In fact, they served it and increased the government's ability to sink its roots deep into society. Indeed, it was the same minister of the interior, Chaptal, who was both the principal author of the stringent law of 28 Pluviôse, Year VIII, which defined the framework of administrative centralization, and the active promoter of these new institutions. What we see here, in other words, is complementarity, not contradiction. The tasks assigned to the new institutions grew steadily over time. At first the government entrusted them with overseeing public works pertaining to commerce (such as port maintenance), but later their mission of advice and information was expanded to questions of taxes and tariffs. They were consulted as needed on questions of railway rate-setting and on matters of economic policy in general.[34] The responsibilities of the chambers increased as their number grew, culminating in their elevation to the status of *établissements publics* in 1851.[35]

In a very different realm and a somewhat less institutionalized manner, the government in the late nineteenth century began to turn its attention more and more to social and health issues, and in this too it felt a need to call on auxiliaries and intermediaries. Here, the Pasteurian revolution played a crucial role, reinforcing the shift in the perception of the relationship between individuals and the community that sociology had begun. In his treatise on "the politics of social welfare," Léon Bourgeois, who belonged to the second wave of founding fathers of the Republic, nicely summed up this sense of a revolution in thinking:

> Thanks to Pasteur, a new idea of humanity has emerged and taken root in people's minds. He encouraged us to develop a more accurate picture of the relations that exist among human beings. He proved beyond a shadow of a doubt that all living things, all creatures, are profoundly interdependent. What he taught about microbes proved how much each of us depends on the intelligence and morality of others. He made us understand how each of our individual organisms contains within it a vast army of infinitesimal creatures that in a sense attack all the other organisms in the world, and in consequence he taught each of us what we owe to everyone else . . . With this wonderful demonstration, which is the high point of his work, he achieved not only a scientific revolution but also a moral revolution.[36]

A new generation of social republicans seized on these ideas in an effort to transcend earlier antinomies of individual and collective. A new conception of society as a system of interaction and interdependence replaced earlier approaches in which the social bond was conceived exclusively in terms of composition and aggregation. The role of the state in instituting the social was thus completely redefined. It also became more complex as its scope rapidly broadened. Hence the state could no longer pretend to be able to accomplish the immense task facing it on its own.

The new "social hygienist" state turned to a whole network of allied associations, which helped to prepare, carry out, and extend its actions. Disciples of Pasteur joined with militants of the new Republic to assemble a vast range of auxiliary institutions. At the national level, for example, there was the Comité National de Défense contre la Tuberculose (founded by Léon Bourgeois), the Société Française de Prophylaxie Sanitaire et Morale, the Alliance d'Hygiène Sociale (1905, also presided over by Léon Bourgeois), the Association Française de Climatothérapie et d'Hygiène Urbaine (1905), the Alliance Nationale pour l'Accroissement de la Population Française (founded in 1902 by Bertillon and Emile Cheysson, an industrialist who also promoted social housing and parks for workers). But a host of local associations also assisted in orchestrating this effort to develop a new type of public action. A whole array of journals, conventions, and expositions marked this effort, which was both intellectual and political. Far from fearing associations as potential focal points of opposition, the state now called on a dense network of them to assist in its undertakings.

Once again the goal was not a more autonomous society but a more effective collective power. The militants of social hygiene did not disparage the state but praised it as confirmed centralizers.[37] Often it was the same men who did battle on both fronts: the name of Léon Bourgeois should suffice to indicate the degree to which the two roles were combined. The author of *Solidarité* hit upon the most striking phrases to describe the role of new intermediary bodies in this new vision of the state: "Between the individual and the state," he lamented, "there is at present no intermediary whose existence is obligatory . . . This bond should exist in the form of voluntarily created associations. The associations are created by the mind and by the heart. They are nothing other than the *intrinsic framework of the state.*"[38] Bourgeois went so far as to say that the goal was to broaden the traditional understanding of the state.[39] Thus the new intermediary bodies that the French Beveridge was calling for were supposed to attach themselves to a state with broader prerogatives and a more complex structure than ever before.

There was yet a third way in which associations, conceived as powers allied to the state, gained a place for themselves within the republican order, namely, as auxiliaries in the areas of police and justice. Over the course of the nineteenth century, the feeling had grown that the agents of the state could not be everywhere and that effective sanctions against violations of the law required the cooperation of citizens. Such cooperation was easily conceived when it came to testifying in court or assisting law enforcement in emergencies. Every citizen was required to assist people in danger and authorized to use force if urgent circumstances demanded it.[40] Yet there were any number of relatively common minor offenses in regard to which the individual was not in a good position to intervene, while the state was too distant. In such cases action by associations could be particularly effective. The imaginative Edmond About, whom we encountered earlier in the entourage of Napoleon III, was one of the first to stress this novel way of legitimating associations. Taking the example of poaching and cruelty to animals, he expressed the view that prosecution of such offenses by associations of hunters and animal lovers would be the only effective way of stopping them, since public officials could not be everywhere at once.[41] The issue was widely debated at the end of the nineteenth century as many people became alarmed by rising crime rates and falling arrest rates. The response of the authorities to, for example, truancy, child abuse, alcoholism, vice, pornography, and fraud of various kinds was deemed insufficient, and it was also judged to be ineffective because too remote from the places where these offenses were committed.[42] Many saw the reporting function of associations well integrated into the social fabric as indispensable.[43] Jurists pondered the issue, and even the Académie des Sciences Morales et Politiques took up the subject.[44] Alfred Fouillée put in a word as well.[45] Some people believed that public authority had declined so rapidly that the time had come to explore the possibility of a reform intended to allow associations to prosecute offenses as crimes and not merely as civil suits for damages, as was already the case in certain areas such as fraud involving wines.[46] These people held that associations could efficiently replace the public prosecutor. Such proposals never came close to fruition, but the fact that they were entertained at all shows that people were looking at associations in a new light at the dawn of the twentieth century.

Thus old prejudice against associations gradually gave way to a more pragmatic and utilitarian approach. Subsidies, which became increasingly common after 1920, allowed the state to favor those associations it deemed most useful.[47] Whenever it became necessary for the state to become involved in some new area where, for political or technical reasons, it either could not or did not wish to take things directly in hand, it regularly turned to associations for help. This was frequently the case in areas pertaining to economic regulation, social protection, and recreational development. Thus the concept of the auxiliary association expanded over the years to the point where it became possible to think of certain associations as pure instruments of the administration. What gradually emerged was thus something that might be called a network state, whose reach extended far beyond the strict limits of the administration. This development by no means indicated an eclipse of the state by an increasingly autonomous civil society. It was rather a reinforcement and dissemination of state functions, which were now exercised through a wide variety of subsidiary agencies.

Paths of the Corporatist State

The French model changed markedly when it enlisted quasi-intermediary bodies to serve as state auxiliaries and to shore up democratic generality. These efforts involved what one might call "external" use of associations by the state. But it also departed from its original principles in another way, by restoring actual corporate entities within the state itself. Hatred of these corporate bodies *(corps)* had formed the nucleus of revolutionary political culture, as we have see in countless examples. Rigorous enforcement of this principle had soon abated, however. One sign of this is a certain continuity of vocabulary. Indeed, it is striking to note that while the Revolution banished *corps* as such, it continued to make determined use of the underlying metaphor. It was not the political idea of the *corps* that was rejected but the fact that there could be many autonomous bodies. The new society that the men of 1789 hoped to create consisted of one *grand corps,* unified and regenerated. Note that the Constitution of 1791 preferred to call the legislature the Corps Législatif rather than the Assemblée Nationale, because the former more strongly connoted the desired idea of unity.[48] It was common during the revolutionary period to speak of *corps administratifs* and *corps constitués* to describe the administration.[49] The Consulate and, later, the Empire ratified these usages.[50] But it was always the idea of unity that was paramount—an idea as remote as possible from any suggestion of separate organizations. In theory, then, these *corps* had nothing in common with *corps intermédiaires,* or intermediary bodies.

Under the Empire, however, this situation changed with the introduction of a *corps enseignant,* or teaching *corps.* Apparently it was Napoleon who coined this term in 1806, while planning for the establishment of a university.[51] With this innovation the emperor hoped to establish a purely public system of education extending from the primary grades through advanced studies. The system he imagined was to be distinct from the regular system of administration. If administrative centralization was based on what might be called a "mechanical" principle, the educational system was to be run by a more "organic" administration. Why this difference? Because of the different purposes of the two systems: although regular administrative procedures were suitable for governing things, they were not appropriate for forming individuals. What the educational venture needed was a common spirit, something beyond the literal curriculum and its associated procedures. Napoleon saw the teaching *corps* as the lifeblood of the system, the necessary link between state and society. "This great body will have its feet planted among the school benches and its head in the Senate," he noted in summing up his intentions.[52] This would be an intermediary body, but one associated with the state and fully integrated into its operations. Thus the Empire laid the groundwork for a sort of "state corporatism," which neutralized whatever threat this intermediary body might contain, leaving only the positive aspects.

To explain the meaning of this innovation, Napoleon used the most eloquent of images: what was needed, he explained, was to incorporate into the state instruments equivalent to what the religious orders had once been, as these orders embodied the very essence of the corporate form. In his own words: "I want a corporation not of Jesuits whose sovereign is in Rome but rather of Jesuits who have no ambition other than to be useful and no interest other than the public interest."[53] The goal was thus to *secularize* and *nationalize* the corporatist idea, not to reject it. On this interpretation, the corporation did not rival the state but fortified it. First, it strengthened the state by establishing a durable basis for government ("I want a corporation, because a corporation does not die," as Napoleon put it).[54] Second, it strengthened the state by making it more efficient in an area where ordinary administrative instruments were of no use, namely, teaching. The Empire thus marked a break with the revolutionary period. To be sure, there had been no shortage of ambitious plans for organizing a national system of education during the Revolution. From Talleyrand to Condorcet and Mirabeau to Lepelletier, numerous proposals had been made, but without effect, because their implementation was still conceived within a traditional administrative framework, with a hierarchical chain of command transmitting orders from summit to base. The institution of a teaching *corps* was supposed to change all this in a manner set forth in the decree of 17 March 1808 on the organization of the university.

In the early years of the Restoration, a young political theorist by the name of Guizot developed a theory of how these redefined intermediary bodies could play a role in establishing a strong state and effective government. Though a "liberal," Guizot in this respect followed in the footsteps of the authoritarian emperor, starting with the idea that modern government had a dual nature: on the one hand it was a traditional administrative power, while on the other hand it was what he called "interior" government (and would soon redescribe as "government of minds").[55] Guizot explained the consequences of this distinction as early as 1816 in his *Essai sur l'histoire et sur l'état actuel de l'instruction publique en France*, in which he tried to show that the term "administration" was inappropriate when applied to public education, because education required a particular type of action best carried out by creating a *"grand corps"* associated with the state.[56] Guizot's idea, like Napoleon's, was to establish a sort of congregation entirely devoted to the public good but having a life of its own, thus ensuring its vitality and longevity. In this perspective, *esprit de corps* was no longer opposed to generality but actually served it: it became a "principle of union and energy, which has only advantages when it brings individuals together and binds them to one another without separating them from the state."[57] For both Guizot and Napoleon, the teaching *corps* was to the modern state what the Jesuits had aspired to be for the earlier state.[58]

The "government of minds" rested entirely on implementing this scheme: autonomous regulative and organizing poles were to be established within civil society but structured by and wedded to the state. The degree of autonomy would vary from case to case, with learned societies and academies being more autonomous, teaching *corps* less so. Guizot thought of power in terms of flows rather than stocks. Hence his notion of *corps*, as he used it in connection with the teaching *corps*, did not precisely overlap the traditional notion of corporation. Indeed, it was intended to transcend the historical contradictions in that traditional idea. The corporations of the Old Regime actually fostered an autonomous sociability. This outcome was positive, in the sense that they organized the social, but at the same time they stood as an obstacle to social unity. The march of civilization simplified the social by leaving nothing standing between individuals and the state, but this consequence increased the risk of disintegration. Hence Guizot felt the need to promote *social effects* equivalent to those achieved by the old corporations but without reproducing the form of those corporations. In short, his intention was to help *modern corps* to establish themselves.

Far from constituting an obstacle to social unity, these modern *corps* helped to bring it about. They offered a means of supplementing the "mechanical" operation of administrative centralization with a more profound kind of centralization, at once intellectual and spiritual, thus completing the revolutionary project. "Under these conditions," Guizot emphasized, "the state obviously needs a lay *grand corps,* an important association profoundly wedded to society and intimately familiar with it, living with it, but also wedded to the state, from which it derives its power and direction, to exert on young people the moral influence they need to develop a sense of order and discipline."[59] The new teaching *corps* had nothing in common with the teaching corporations of the past, "existing on their own, alien to the state, competing with it, and monopolizing the realm of public education."[60] Victor Cousin, who would become the primary organizer of the teaching *corps* under the July Monarchy, also insisted repeatedly that public education required a special mode of administration, which could come only from a *corps* defined in Guizot's terms.[61] It is noteworthy that each of the successive regimes that governed France from 1820 on tried to weaken the new teaching *corps* in order to return to a more classical ministerial management of public education—a clear indication of the wide gap that separated legitimist apologies for the old corporatist world from this novel approach involving a *corps* wedded to the state.

The constitution of a teaching *corps* was not an isolated example. In many other areas, the Jacobin state allied itself to structures that reinforced its power: the case of the various *corps* of civil engineers is especially noteworthy.[62] These institutions were soon celebrated as the most powerful expressions of the French state. By the time of the July Monarchy they already stood for a "responsibility that does not die." The expression is that of Lamartine, who joined many of his contemporaries in honoring "these beautiful special administrations, these *corps* that were born and have since grown and continue to grow with each improvement in public administration."[63] The Ecole Polytechnique was always respected because of this status, as well as because of the adeptness with which it reinterpreted elitism in a democratic key and reaped the glory of identification with the state.

Indeed, there was justification for pride in all the *grands corps*, as if their brilliance helped to reveal the true nature of the state.[64] This organization was supposed to flesh out and firm up an administrative structure that some feared might otherwise wither. Rules and procedures were thereby rooted in sociology in a way that justified their rigor. The *grands corps* were said to be "guardians" of the integrity of the great principles upon which the state was founded. They guaranteed "permanence of thinking . . . in the interest of French unity."[65] To view the state in this way was not without problems, however, since each *corps* could be seen now as a protection, now as a threat (again, the specter of corporatism). In the early 1870s, for example, Jean-Gustave Courcelle-Seneuil charged the *grandes écoles* (the most prestigious institutions of higher learning in France) with having produced a "new mandarinate" and attacked the harmful effects of *esprit de corps*, which, he alleged, led inevitably to social paralysis, with society straitjacketed by a rigid, inflexible organization of the professions. But his was the point of view of a liberal economist, to whom people paid no more heed than they had to Frédéric Bastiat a few years earlier, when he attacked the baccalaureate, the symbol of academic ranking, for promoting a homogenization of knowledge and therefore encouraging socialism.[66]

In any case, government officials in the late nineteenth century became concerned with the tenuous boundary between the modern *esprit de corps* and the old corporatism. The issue was implicit in the main questions surrounding the status and unionization of civil servants in the early twentieth century. Indeed, the issue of unionization brought the tension between *corps* and corporatism into sharp relief.[67] Nevertheless, the figure of the "corporatist state" remained at the heart of the French model.

— 14 —

Differences and Repetitions

From 1880 to the First World War, the French political model took on far more supple contours than it had had earlier. Between "network state" and "polarized democracy" a compromise was struck, balancing civil society's demands for autonomy against the administrative imperatives of modern bureaucracy and the demands of revolutionary political culture. In terms of political organization, "balanced democracy" *(la démocratie d'équilibre)* emerged in the same period as the dominant form, the translation of "revised Jacobinism" into the language of state-society relations.[1] The French system did not become frozen in place, however, and it would be misleading to think that it had overcome the tensions and contradictions that had defined the contours of its earlier history. In the 1920s and 1930s, for example, many called for a reconsideration of the place of intermediary bodies in the system. This new cycle of utopian proposals and nostalgic reactions quickly came to an end, however. The revised Jacobinism that had dominated thinking at the beginning of the twentieth century survived more or less intact to the end. Although it continued to evolve in response to successive transformations of the economy and society, its structural framework remained unchanged. Hence in this final chapter we can move fairly quickly through the twentieth century—more quickly than might seem warranted at first sight.

The New Cycle of Utopias and Nostalgias

After the law of 1901 was passed, culminating years of effort, many proponents of associations continued to plead the case for allowing them to play a more active and more institutionalized role. For instance, leading social

247

Catholic writers rehearsed conventional arguments that could have been made a century earlier. This literature, featuring such names as La Tour du Pin among the more traditionalist camp, Marc Sangnier among the progressives, and Abbé Lemire and the comte de Chambrun in the middle, is well known and has been widely commented on, so that there is no need to dwell on it here. But the theme also enjoyed a prominent place on the left, in circles where political thinking was informed by Proudhonian ideas bolstered by insights from the new discipline of sociology. Eugène Fournière typifies this school of thought. His brand of socialism stood in opposition, intellectual as well as political, to that of Jules Guesde. Fournière had been a trade union leader from the inception of the unions as well as an active champion of the cooperative movement. He joined the socialists at their 1879 Congress of Marseilles and later sat in the Chamber of Deputies alongside Jaurès. As a Freemason, member of the Ligue des Droits de l'Homme, and proponent of popular universities, he had all the characteristics of the progressive republican of his day. As director of *La Revue socialiste* and the author of numerous books, he was also the theorist of a liberal, reformist variety of socialism.[2] It is this aspect of his life that will interest us here.

In *L'Individu, l'association et l'état* (1907), Fournière developed the outlines of a political theory in which (political) democracy was combined with (economic) socialism and (social) association in such a way as to encourage the simultaneous development of all three. These ideas were developed further in the major work of Fournière's maturity, *La Sociocratie: Essai de politique positive.*[3] With this book he sought to address all the impasses of republican modernity at one stroke. What impeded the ultimate achievement of democracy, he believed, was the permanent tendency of democratic systems to degenerate into "Caesaro-democratic regimes"[4] or to succumb to domination by political parties.[5] He also believed that socialism operated under the permanent threat of degenerating into a bureaucratic system. In order to advance from formal democracy to real democracy and from an abstract collectivism to a concrete appropriation of the means of production, he proposed association as a sociological form capable of uniting a political category (directed toward effective self-government) and an economic category (the producers' group). This vision, which expanded on Proudhon's idea of federalism, was shared at the time by a considerable number of French socialists and stood as a rival to Guesde's vision of state socialism. Fournière strongly rejected both liberal individualism and regimented collectivism and proposed instead a third way, based on a synthesis of individual interests and social interests. A "regime of overlapping, interrelated associations" was supposed to make up for the "insufficiencies of the social contract" while at the same time preventing the formation of a "monstrous state economic power."[6] As such, the association no longer represented a dangerous "state within the state" but rather served as a direct instrument of both social sovereignty and individual self-improvement.[7]

Fournière was the last socialist theorist of his generation to propose a synthesis of this kind. The year of his death, 1914, marked the beginning of a period that would result in a complete redefinition of the meaning of socialism in the wake of the Russian revolution and the Great Depression. The issues treated in his work are still with us, but they would never again be combined in a unified view that was both theoretical and programmatic. In Fournière's day, however, the influence of his teacher Proudhon was still palpable. The author of the *Principe fédérateur* even became a reference for certain thinkers of the antiparliamentary and anticapitalist right.[8] A new critical edition of Proudhon's *Oeuvres complètes* began to appear in 1923.[9] But it was another nineteenth-century figure, Saint-Simon, whose ideas were even more in the air at the time. He, too, was rediscovered and reprinted in the early 1920s. Alfred Pereire published his *Lettres d'un habitant de Genève: Essai sur l'organisation sociale* and *De la réorganisation de la société européenne*. More important, Célestin Bouglé and Elie Halévy brought out a carefully annotated edition of the *Doctrine de Saint-Simon*.[10] In many respects Saint-Simon's thought seemed relevant to the circumstances of the day. The reason for this is easy to comprehend: for the author of *L'Industrie*, the idea of emancipation was inseparable from a "doctrine of organization."[11]

For many people, organization was the crucial variable in the early twentieth century.[12] The war had in effect discredited a state whose dysfunctional aspects (slow response, irrationality, waste of various kinds, and improper division of responsibilities) had seriously handicapped efforts to mobilize the nation. "Rationalization" (the word was all the rage in the 1920s) was seen as an absolute necessity. Henri Fayol and Charles Taylor once again gained influence, which now extended far beyond industrial circles. Ultimately, it was politics itself that was suspected as a source of inefficiency. As one respected member of the Conseil d'Etat wrote, "the exaggeration of what we call politics has eaten away at France like a cancer:

the proliferation of useless and unhealthy cells has choked off the life of the nation."[13] In this context the question of intermediary bodies was perceived in a new way. Now the problem was not so much to assist the actions of the government or to increase the autonomy of civil society as to *supplant* the devalued state with new and supposedly more effective economic and social powers. Along with the advent of a new technocratic current, what emerged in this period was a new approach to these kinds of intermediary bodies in which a certain degree of social pluralism was linked to the project of creating a "republic of producers."

In the 1920s, one man symbolized this coupling of Saint-Simonian themes with the legacy of Proudhon: Maxime Leroy. The great jurist, who had been supportive of syndicalism in the early years of the twentieth century, was steeped in Proudhonian culture, as is evident in his splendid work *La Coutume ouvrière* (1913). He also supplied notes and a preface for a new edition of the Besançon socialist's political testament, *De la capacité politique des classes ouvrières.*[14] Following the Great War, however, he, too, turned above all to the work of Saint-Simon, whom he saw as the originator of modern social philosophy.[15] "Let us state that the political era defined by Montesquieu is over." For Leroy, the key issue was now to replace the old government of men with a new form of administration of things.[16]

At this point the problem was no longer to modify the Jacobin tradition. It was to substitute management principles for the revolutionary political culture: the traditional art of government must now give way, many believed, to "social engineering" *(une technique sociologique).* Hence "intermediary bodies" were tapped to take the place of the state and the political system. This utopia of a "republic of producers" in which self-governing workshops would ultimately drain all substance from the sphere of politics points to the prevalence of economistic thinking in the 1920s. This came about as a result of numerous disillusionments. Leroy summed it up this way: "Our institutions and private actions should no longer be dominated by a philosophy of power but rather by a philosophy of labor, or, if you prefer a broader term, a philosophy of production . . . To serve is regalian; to produce is democratic."[17] Society in the twentieth century no longer resembled society at the end of the revolutionary period as described by Royer-Collard: dispersed individuals had been concentrated, grouped, and coalesced by way of economic categories; they came together through affinities of interest. Hence the problem was no longer what it had been in the nineteenth century, namely, to produce the sphere of "the social" between the state and the individual. It was rather to promote effective development of the social. "The constitutional innovation of our time," Leroy summed up, "is above all the public, visible organization of these bodies, which have until now remained hidden."[18] Thus "organization" served as a catchword connoting a new approach to the question of intermediary bodies, which were now seen as forces to be tapped to govern a world in which economics took the place of politics. In other words, the bodies in question were no longer "intermediary" so much as they were directly governing. This utopian idea of the 1920s was elaborated in a variety of guises by trade unionists and socialists.

In the 1930s another overarching idea gained prominence: *corporatism*. This ancient form of organization, long since relegated to oblivion, suddenly regained credibility, so much so that it was deemed a model for the future. Within a few years the word "corporatism" had found its way into the titles of countless essays and pamphlets.[19] Some countries openly embraced the idea. Salazar's Portugal defined itself in its 1933 constitution as "a unitary and corporatist republic," and Fascist Italy soon joined in celebrating the notion. It was enough to suggest to some that a "century of corporatism" had arrived to take the place of the "century of liberalism" just past.[20] Yet it was impossible to discern a clear political doctrine or school of thought behind the word, which was suddenly invested with so many virtues. Indeed, it was a long way from the nostalgic notions put forward by Georges Valois,[21] a veteran of Action Française, to the "neosocialist" views of Marcel Déat.[22] Clearly, however, the word now meant something quite different from what it had meant twenty years earlier. For Christian traditionalists as well as for academics like Durkheim, "corporation" was then a sociological category, a generic term for the intermediary associations that it was hoped would remedy the atomization of society.[23] By contrast, the corporatism of the 1930s was associated with reactions to the economic crash of 1929. Hence it must be understood as a response to the "crisis of liberalism" that many people saw at that time.[24] It was therefore seen primarily in relation to the problem of *regulation*.

There is, however, no escaping the fact that for many people the precise meaning of "corporatism" in the 1930s was rather vague. To begin with, this was because the word was still sometimes used in its primary sociological sense. For example, in the review *Esprit* in 1934 one could read that "the word 'corporation' has this advantage, that it crystallizes the idea of a socialization that is not statist and respects the interaction of the natural intermediary groups that stand between the individual and the state."[25] Meanwhile, the "nonconformists" of the group Jeune Europe criticized not only the vocabulary of the nineteenth century but also "the current conception of society that seeks to eliminate all intermediaries between the individual and the state and to turn the nation into a dust of individuals confronting an omnipotent and anonymous welfare state."[26] This view was indeed influential, but more often than not in this period references to corporatism were not so much "sociological" as "regulationist."[27] Evidence for this claim can be seen in the fact that it was during the 1930s that the term "intermediary bodies" truly became current in political and social discourse, as if to mark the difference I have indicated. Despite this fundamental distinction, confusion remained, however. Indeed, the reference to corporatism was offered as a response to a heterogeneous range of aspirations and reactions inspired by the Depression. For some, the most urgent need was to counter the dogma of class struggle by pointing to the possibility of peaceful collaboration among the classes. A determination to "smash the Marxist framework" can be seen in any number of advocates of the new corporatist doctrines. But it was around the search for new forms of economic and social regulation that things really came together.[28]

Although it is pointless to look for a coherent vision in this proliferating literature of the 1930s, because so many different points of view were represented, it is also true that much of it centered upon two questions: How were the professions organized internally? And what were their social functions, modes of intervention, and legal responsibilities? In each case, both liberalism and statism were criticized for leading to economic anarchy, and alternative solutions were proposed. Everyone was looking for a new form of "economic sovereignty" capable of dealing with the chaos and injustice of laissez-faire. At the core was a group of reformers with relatively coherent proposals in the realms of economics and public law,[29] and they were joined by many others concerned in one way or another with issues touching on the theme of corporatism. Indeed, it is striking to note that calls for economic planning, which began to be heard in precisely the same period, were based on a similar critique of liberalism. The planning theme thus concealed a familiar set of rejections.[30] This complex period deserves a more complex analysis than can be given here. The key is to understand what the new corporatist rhetoric meant in terms of *political culture* rather than "doctrine." Indeed, the concerns that were voiced in this context exhibit a certain unity. They point to something beyond Jacobinism, because the central issues of the day—class conflict and economic regulation—were associated with a new stage in the development of capitalism and society and therefore in a sense alien to the Jacobin mind-set.

The Turning Point: 1945

Sociocracy, the republic of producers, corporatism: each of these terms suggested a way of transcending, or an alternative to, what I have been calling "revised Jacobinism." For a time these ideas were at the center of public attention and widely debated, but after 1945 they were discredited or quite simply overtaken by events. Although the parliamentary republic continued to be criticized, it was now seen as an indispensable guarantor of liberty. The rise of one form or another of totalitarianism had made people more hesitant than before to embrace proposals that would have "done away" with politics. The revolutionary vision of something radically beyond the republican order survived, to be sure, but by 1934 all reformers saw defense of the Republic as a necessary prerequisite. While many changes were deemed necessary, proposals for reform were henceforth formulated within the overall framework of the Republic, as is clear from the projects entertained by various elements of the Resistance during the war.[31]

Meanwhile, the Vichy episode discredited corporatist ideas by associating them with a shameful moment in the nation's history.[32] Although the word "corporatism" was now banished from the vocabulary, certain innovations carried out in its name were nevertheless maintained. This was true, for instance, of a whole range of professional "orders" created in this period, including the Order of Physicians, the Order of Pharmacists, and the Order of Accountants.[33] Under this system, public service missions continued to be entrusted to private professional organizations. The example is interesting. Although this heritage was accepted, Vichy's attempt to establish a single overarching national union was categorically rejected.[34] Those reforms that made sense as continuations of the earlier revision of Jacobinism were easily integrated into the reconstituted Republic after the war, while those that stemmed from the radical alternative of corporatist labor organization were unequivocally rejected. In a related vein, the organizing committees that had been established in the major branches of industry were not completely rejected, and many of the objectives of those groups were incorporated into the economic plan developed under the leadership of Jean Monnet.[35]

Thus 1945 marked an important date: the stabilization of the French political model of revised Jacobinism, which had developed gradually in the period 1880–1914. After 1945 this model obviously did not remain frozen, but its essential features did not vary.

Deepening of the Model

Institutionalization of the trade unions progressed considerably in the second half of the twentieth century. The "governing" role of the unions had been recognized in the period 1920–1936, during which their civil capacities were broadened and their claim to represent the interests of labor in general through collective bargaining was recognized. Subsequently, their status as *organs* of wage labor was formally acknowledged, with major advances in 1945, 1968, and 1982. (The so-called Auroux Law of 28 October 1982 went so far as to recognize the right of the major unions to represent a firm's workers even if none of them were union members.) At the same time, a whole range of economic and social functions (including employment, professional training, and social security) was made subject to co-management, or in some cases even direct management, by professional organizations, which were thus implicitly equated with public institutions.[36] It was not just the increasing role of the unions that was noteworthy about this period, however. Even more significant, perhaps, was the narrowing of both the legal and the sociological gap between unions and associations. We have already noted one broadening of the union model, in the 1920s and 1930s, to include demands in the areas of consumption and housing. This trend only became more pronounced later on. It took two forms: on the one hand, the notion of "social body" was broadened, while on the other hand, associations acquired a new status through the establishment of certain mechanisms of public consent.

As we have seen, the acceptance of a certain "trade union exception" to the basic principles of French public law grew out of the recognition that there was a distinctively collective character to the organization of labor. In other words, workers really did constitute a "corporate body," and this fact justified the special role assigned to the unions. For a long time this "workers' corporation" was the only such body singled out by a society that believed it owed its emancipation to its indecomposable unity and to the consequent destruction of all intermediary organizations. In 1945 another "body" received similar recognition: the family. The state expressed its wish that a *corps familial* be established to represent the interests of families and to serve as an advisor and auxiliary to the public authorities.[37] A broad framework was established, with the objective of bringing the various relevant associations into contact with one another. The ordinance of 3 March 1945 established a Union Nationale des Associations Familiales, to which three tasks were assigned: to advise the government on family-related issues and make proposals in this area; to serve as the official representative of French families in dealings with the public authorities; and to manage services assigned to it by the state.[38] Insofar as thinking about associations is concerned, the spirit of 1884 rather than that of 1901 is discernible here. Yet at the same time the scope of the reform envisioned by the institution of a *corps familial* was far broader than that encompassed by the "trade union exception."

Although the unions were institutionalized and expanded in this same period, the most noteworthy developments came in the realm of relations between associations and the state. While the percentage of workers in unions peaked at the Liberation and declined sharply after 1975, the associative phenomenon gained momentum in France in the second half of the twentieth century, and its structure solidified. Freedom of association, an essential prerequisite, was increasingly recognized. The Constitution of 1946 explicitly mentioned this in its preamble, for example. In 1950, the Conseil d'Etat included freedom of association "among the basic public liberties" recognized by the Republic. Above all, the Conseil Constitutionnel solemnly reaffirmed freedom of association as an untouchable right in 1971 when Raymond Marcellin, then minister of the interior, proposed certain oversight procedures that would have led in some cases to requiring associations to obtain, in an oblique way, prior authorization from the government.[39]

During the second half of the twentieth century there was a veritable revolution in relations between the state and certain associations. As we saw in the previous chapter, certain associations became auxiliaries of the state in the early decades of the century. This trend became more pronounced after 1960. In part, it reflected a wish to "end congestion" in the bureaucracy and transfer certain functions, especially social and cultural functions for which the government bureaucracy had proved to be ill suited, to the local level.[40] Large parts of policy pertaining to children and special education were thus "subcontracted" to associations by a state obliged to cope with rapid changes in the health and social welfare sectors.

In exploring this development, however, we would do well to distinguish between associations subject to "administrative attraction"[41] and "directly administrative" associations. The former were associations that had functioned as experimental precursors or in support of administrative actions in the general interest and thus naturally tended to gravitate toward the administration. Such "auxiliary associations" (as we called them earlier) played a prominent role in the history of social innovation and expanded state action. The government entrusted them with tasks it did not know how to perform itself or for which it was not yet able to assume responsibility. In the 1930s, reformers in the top ranks of the civil service openly urged the government to take full advantage of this dialectic. In 1936, for example, François Bloch-Lainé advocated the creation of a "French Alliance for the Education of the People," an independent private agency whose pioneering work would gradually be placed under the supervision of the state as its various experimental programs were transformed into institutions.[42] Thus the old spirit of the Ligue de l'Enseignement lived on, but in a broader context and much more systematically coordinated with the political authorities. After 1960, these practices were consolidated as the state granted powers of consent to certain types of association.

The "directly administrative" associations were different.[43] Here, the relationship was not one of functional complementarity and usefulness but rather one of pure legal convenience. Associations in this category were directly created and financed by a ministry or public agency. These were especially common in the areas of education and research as well as in the social welfare domain. Such associations were not created by private initiative only to be instrumentalized later on by the bureaucracy; rather, they were "mere pseudopods of ordinary services."[44] This phenomenon became common enough that jurists coined the term "administrative associations" to describe it.[45] The Cour des Comptes also took a keen interest in these organizations, since the primary reason for their existence was to circumvent the rules for accounting for the use of public funds and for hiring and firing personnel.[46] Thus associations of this type were no longer social in form and had no link to what was vital in civil society.

The role of both auxiliary and administrative associations was consecrated by the fact that the state granted some of them privileges, in some cases going so far as to award them a monopoly on intervention in their area of responsibility.[47] Both of these types of "public" associations were rewarded with important subsidies, and for many these were the sole source of funding. Overall, public financing accounted for 58 percent of the resources of all associations in 1995.[48] Health, education, welfare, culture, and sports were the areas most heavily subsidized. State financial support goes a long way toward explaining why associations have become major employers in France, with some 1.2 million people on their payrolls at the end of the twentieth century.[49]

If the expansion of the associative world was related to the development and transformation of the interventionist state, as I have been suggesting, then we must pay particular attention to the emergence in the 1970s of a new and more political way of thinking about the role of associations. This went hand in hand with thinking about ways to change the nature of democracy. After May 1968, many people looked upon the parliamentary regime and government bureaucracy as having run out of steam, and celebration of the energetic virtues of civil society was accompanied by growing enthusiasm for associations. The issue was often discussed in terms of political culture. Proponents of what was called "the second left" looked to social movements as the representatives of a decentralized form of politics influenced by the ideal of self-management *(autogestion)*. This revival of the association issue was spurred by awareness of two related crises: a political crisis of representation and a cultural crisis centering upon a particular model of authority and action. In the wake of all these changes, the authorities themselves began to look at associations in a new light, apparently forgetting the old obsession with associations as impediments to generality and potential states within the state. Hence we would do well to take a closer look at this resurgence of interest in associations.

The government's new attitude toward the potential public role of associations was obviously influenced by the new spirit growing out of the events of 1968. The turning point in this respect came in 1975. In March of that year the Commission on National Development and Living Conditions issued a report intended to assist in the preparation of the Seventh Plan. This report noted the invaluable service that associations could provide through their ability to tune in to the precise needs of the population and suggest social innovations.[50] A few months later, a general report on the preliminary orientation of the Seventh Plan took up the theme again, emphasizing the importance of encouraging associations and "intensifying local social life."[51] Top civil servants (including François Bloch-Lainé) and activists joined forces to create an "Association for the Development of Progressive Associations," the purpose of which was to pressure the authorities not to forget about these good intentions. René Lenoir, the secretary of state for social action, spoke for the government, expressing enthusiasm for these initiatives in an op-ed piece published in *Le Monde*.[52] The tone he struck was new for a minister. Going beyond the rhetoric customary on such occasions, Lenoir did not shrink from contrasting Tocqueville's democracy with Rousseau's. "After the people have voted and gone home for five or six years," he wrote, "associations continue to function in permanent dialogue with the government . . . To the extent that these associations are in fact the people in the process of organizing themselves, they become democracy's teacher and messenger." He also expressed the hope that the coming years would witness the birth of a new age in state-association relations. Interest was expressed at even higher levels of government, since the president of the republic (in a letter dated 25 February 1975) urged his prime minister to look into "concrete ways of increasing the participation of the French in the improvement of their living conditions." As a result, Jacques Chirac appointed a commission chaired by Pierre Delmon, the president of the mining firm Houillères du Nord. The report of this commission, submitted in January 1976, marked an important date, in effect granting official recognition to the state's new attitude toward intermediary bodies.[53]

With an epigraph from the author of *Democracy in America* deploring the French administration's aversion to any movement claiming to deal with public affairs outside of government control, the Delmon report developed arguments of two kinds to justify a greater role for associations. First, it pointed to the government's own interest in being able to draw on sources of information closer to the ground. There was of course nothing new in thinking of associations as possible intermediaries between the bureaucracy and society. Taking a more original line, the report also considered associations from the point of view of democracy itself, extending René Lenoir's insights in a systematic way. To a bureaucracy accustomed to dealing directly only with elected officials, it suggested "bringing a third partner into the game in the form of associations."[54] The obstacles to such an approach were not neglected. Indeed, a list of them was duly provided: the legitimacy of the representative mandate was undeniable; there were risks involved in giving a voice to special or strictly corporate interests; many associations rested on a narrow social base; associations tended to represent only active minorities; and so on. But the report insisted that these scruples, though partially justified, should be overcome because of the evident need to fix what was not working in "traditional democracy" (most notably, the conflict between the long term of municipal office and the increased frequency of major decisions affecting the lives of citizens). In the network of associations the report saw "a reservoir of energy that one cannot fail to tap." It also called upon conservatives to overcome their nervousness about dealing with social movements seen as troublesome.[55] The Delmon Report and the work of the Seventh Plan set the tone for a new approach to the associative phenomenon. Others also spoke out in favor of encouraging associations "in order to defend the interests of citizens as users, consumers, and residents."[56]

Was the French model, even in its amended version, on the verge of a radical upheaval, or was all this activity merely a passing intellectual fad growing out of the climate of the moment and the activism of small groups with access to the media? It is easy to establish that this movement and its associated projects were essentially supported by elements of the second left,[57] allied with various groups of association activists and a loosely affiliated network of high civil servants (such as Lenoir and Bloch-Lainé, who were quite active). That much is undeniable, as is evident from the fact that similar series of articles were published in journals such as *Esprit*, *Faire*, *CFDT-aujourd'hui*, and *Echange et projet* (published by a club headed at the time by Jacques Delors). Interest in these developments was broader, however, extending initially to the new Socialist Party but also to liberal Giscardian circles. To be sure, the echoes and resonances that developed around the idea of association, or what people began to refer to as "the third sector," were not without ambiguity, since at times the voices of those who favored a radical reformulation of both the democratic project and the organization of the economy (in the direction of "self-management," to put it in a nutshell) seemed to mingle with other voices that were frankly conservative and interested mainly in reducing the role of the state. Still, one has to admit that when reform has come in France, it has often been the result of ambiguous convergences of this kind. Possibilities sometimes arise when one side's utopia coincides with the other side's calculation.[58]

As is often the case, the reforms actually put into practice fell short of the stated intentions of the reformers. There is no denying the fact that the philosophical foundations of French democracy remained unchanged. But things began to move in a new direction. To take the measure of the change, one needs to recognize that two different views of the role of associations coexisted at the time. The more sweeping of the two envisioned a complete transformation of democratic politics (by establishing a more direct form of democracy to supplement the elective democracy that already existed). *Politically,* the French model withstood the attack.[59] The other, more limited vision involved an extension of the trade union model (of functional representation). Bloch-Lainé's regrets concerning "the displacement of the activist by a coalition of the elected official and the technocrat" were never overcome in practice.[60] In this triangular relationship, the activist had always been accepted as a subordinate ally by one camp or the other, but his claim to intrinsic legitimacy revived old prejudices. The new celebration of civil society (a term that made a major comeback in the 1970s) and the criticism of "social-statism" shook the edifice but did not bring it down. An important shift in practice did take place, however: a series of reforms initiated by the various reports discussed above did lead to an increased role for associations.

On 25 February 1976, for example, the Council of Ministers decided that in the future all commissions charged with offering advice on matters of regional development, protection of certain sites, and urban planning would be required to include individuals qualified "by virtue of their membership in an association." The laws of 2 July 1976 on the protection of nature and 31 December 1976 on urban development reform solidified this inclusion of associations in the relevant decision-making processes. At the same time procedures were worked out for soliciting advice and consent from associations concerned with protecting the natural environment.[61] This recognition of a role for associations, initiated even earlier by the 1975 disabilities law, was in due course extended still further: in 1988, with the creation of the *revenu minimum d'insertion,* or minimum wage for entry-level workers, and the procedures associated with it; in 1990, with the Besson law on housing; in 1998, in connection with efforts to combat "social exclusion"; and in public health and risk prevention. Taken together, these changes added up to a change in the way in which the bureaucracy related to society, even if the procedures in question were often merely consultative and the functions auxiliary.

In describing the domains with which it was concerned, the Delmon Report used an expression that had gained a certain popularity: *syndicalisme du cadre de vie,* an untranslatable phrase linking trade unionism to the issues of living conditions and the social and cultural environment. The expression was emblematic of the changes taking place at the time. The associations involved were given an increased role, and their activities were compared to those of the trade unions in a sort of "general unionization of the social." Consumer groups and organizations concerned with the social and cultural environment did indeed begin to organize in ways reminiscent of labor unions, and on the basis of similar principles. Yet the old hatred of corporatism held its own against what political scientists at the time began to characterize as "neocorporatist regulation."[62] Apart from agriculture,[63] the French system was a long way from organizing social life and determining the general interest in the manner of Germany or the Scandinavian countries. Nevertheless, revision of the Jacobin model continued in this period.

The most significant feature of the evolution of the Jacobin model in the last quarter of the twentieth century was, as has been noted, a tendency to blur the distinction between trade unions and associations, thus encouraging generalization of what was originally (that is, in 1884) conceived as an exception. What bears emphasizing, however, is that this extension of the trade union model was not accompanied by a reform in the status of associations themselves. To be sure, the state increasingly paid homage to associations, as in 1983, when it created a Conseil National de la Vie Associative, and in 2000, when it established a Fonds National pour le Développement de la Vie Associative.[64] Yet despite proposed amendments to the law in 1976 and 1982,[65] nothing really changed in regard to the legal capacity and financial status of associations in general (unlike "officially approved" associations, which enjoyed a status similar to that of the trade unions). A minor reform of the rules governing tax deductions for gifts to certain associations was adopted in 1987, but that was the end of it. So while associative activity mushroomed, the law hardly budged. The 1901 edifice stood firm, proving in retrospect that the religious issue had merely been a façade hiding more fundamental reservations.

Still, the immobility of the law should not be allowed to mask the crucial development, namely, a vast expansion of associative activity. A few figures will help us to measure the extent of the change: 5,000 new associations were created annually in the 1950s; 10,000 in the 1960s; 25,000 in the 1970s; 40,000 in the 1980s; 60,000 in 1990; and 68,000 in 2001. Growth was exponential, and it has not slackened since. When the centennial anniversary of the law of 1901 was celebrated, it was estimated that roughly twenty million French men and women (or 40 percent of the population above the age of fourteen) belonged to one or more associations,[66] of which there were some 700,000 across the country (or twenty times more than a century earlier). So while the law went nowhere, practice was revolutionized. Striking evidence of this could be seen at the Assises Nationales de la Vie Associative, which took place in Paris in February 1999 at the behest of the prime minister.[67] The centennial celebration was capped by the adoption of a charter between the state and associations formally recognizing the contribution of associations to the search for the general interest.[68] At the local level, relations between communities and associations also evolved, and both sides agreed to "mutual recognition."[69] All this goes to show that a century after 1901, associations had become commonplace.

These findings suggest that we need to reconsider the widely held view that France is an exception when it comes to associations. Comparative international studies carried out in the 1990s show that while membership in trade unions and religious organizations is less common in France, the gap that once existed between France and other major industrialized countries with respect to association membership has been greatly narrowed.[70]

The much-revised Jacobinism of the early twenty-first century thus points to a France that has shed some of its former characteristics. Further evidence of this change can be seen in the history of decentralization, although philosophical doubts and institutional impediments were noticeably more pronounced in this regard. Following halting efforts at reform in 1946, it was not until the 1980s that the modest reforms of 1871 and 1884 were truly revisited. This is not the place to trace the history of all this, which has been told often. Here I want merely to point out that relations between the state and local communities had long been governed by what Pierre Grémion has called "tamed Jacobinism."[71] In practice, the political-administrative system had long since abandoned the ideal type of Year VIII, as various sociologists of organization showed in the 1960s and 1970s. Jean-Pierre Worms gave a brilliant analysis of the way in which there gradually developed a sort of complicity between the prefect and "his notables" that allowed the prefect to assert his authority in exchange for allowing the notables to act as intermediaries and arbiters between the state and the citizenry.[72] Pierre Grémion's work has also stressed that the state, seen from below, was a colossus with feet of clay and far from able to impose its will. Both of these writers have exposed the complex system of negotiation and compromise on which the French system was based, as the official legal authority of the bureaucracy was mitigated in practice by a whole range of accommodations and bargains. Behind the immutable rhetorical façade of the Jacobin state, a far more complex "rationalizing corporatist state" was actually at work.[73]

Thus the important reform of 1982 cannot be understood as a radical break except in relation to purely theoretical model. Its primary motive was administrative, a recognition of the fact that, as Pierre Richard, the *directeur général des collectivités locales,* put it at the time, "the state is doing too many things. It is omnipotent, and by virtue of its omnipotence, it has become impotent."[74] Like business firms and other large organizations, the state had to adapt its organization to new managerial constraints stemming from the need to regulate ever more complex systems and to process growing volumes of information. In proposing a preliminary new distribution of tasks and responsibilities, the main proponents of the 1982 decentralization reflected a shift in the structure of power and influence in twentieth-century France.[75] A course correction was at long last begun, even if it did not go far enough.

Democracy's Mental Block

Even granting this, however, can one really speak of "Tocqueville's revenge"?[76] After a century and a half, the melancholy judgments of the author of *Democracy in America* have undeniably lost some of their relevance. But caution is in order for one important reason: the growing gap between reality and representation. Despite the major changes described above, it is striking to find that the French still look upon their institutions with the same critical eye that has informed their thinking for the past two centuries. Although the unions have been institutionalized and associations have proliferated, old complaints about the gaping void that exists between individuals and the state continue to be recycled. Tediously ritual denunciations of the ravages of corporatism survive changes of government and transcend different shades of opinion.[77] The battle of ideas seems to have been waged largely in a theater of shadows. The French have barely managed to confront the real dynamics of their political and administrative model. It is as if they suffered from a permanent affliction, a need to exaggerate their woes by turning them into fantasies in order to justify their overcautiousness and hide their perplexities. Behind the recurrent denunciations of "the stalled society" and the Jacobin heritage—"the French disease," as it has been called—lies the difficulty of conceptualizing democracy and its history, which has indeed remained in the shadows.

The place of intermediary bodies was indeed reevaluated, as we have seen, yet the intellectual foundations of French democracy were not reconsidered in the wake of these changes. Although the original Jacobin *organization* was extensively modified, the *political culture* of generality has continued to dominate thinking, with all the consequences that persistence implies for the conception of sovereignty and the general interest. The claims of the political world to be the sole embodiment of social interest continue to be influential. Thus a certain illiberal tendency remains despite the undeniable advent of a more pluralistic society. In France, these two contradictory tendencies have established an unlikely equilibrium, and this has put discourse into an unusual position with respect to reality. Thus it has been possible for a certain republican fundamentalism to coexist with repeated attacks on the Jacobin model, the two together serving as a kind of exorcism, driving the realities of the situation out of the discussion. This mental block has had a number of deleterious effects, most notably a complication of the problem of conceptualizing change. This is the origin of what might be called France's penchant for a reformism that dares not speak its name: the state of the world and the balance of political power have led to changes in policies and institutions, yet it has been impossible to discuss openly what the implications of those changes are. Over time, therefore, the gap between facts and representations has only grown wider.

In 2001, the centennial of the law of 1901 on the right of association was celebrated in a spirit of unquestioned unanimity. Two years later, in 2003, there was no real debate when the "decentralized" character of the French Republic was officially inscribed in the constitution. Did this signify a decisive shift in the intellectual climate? No, because there was no genuine reflection on the issue: a consensus in favor of decentralization had simply replaced the blanket condemnation that had preceded it. The real history of what had taken place was thus obscured, yet its effects continued to make themselves felt. Now that openness to Europe and the world is imposing a new series of reforms and upheavals in the relationship between government and civil society, the time has come to look at this history with the kind of lucidity that may help us to uncover possible ways of confronting the future.

The New Age of Generality

This book has shown the gap that exists between the real France and its Tocquevillean caricature. It would be a serious mistake, however, to conclude that the influence of the Jacobin worldview has simply faded away. It remains a powerful presence in people's minds. There is still a long way to go before all the old prejudices against civil society organizations are eliminated in France. The law pertaining to associations needs to be developed further, and the status of foundations is due for a complete overhaul, to take just two examples. More generally, organizations representing particular social groups are still all too often attacked as corporatist, archaic, and not truly representative, thus calling the legitimacy of their actions into question in advance. All of this should be borne in mind. Nevertheless, the old approach to the issue is no longer tenable. We can no longer look at today's problems exclusively in terms of a long historic conflict between the state and civil society conceived as a zero-sum game. With the advent of everything that is summed up by the word "globalization," history has entered a new phase.

The issue now is no longer one of an absolute or relative "French exception" that must somehow be eliminated. Instead, what we see *everywhere* is a crisis of politics and a questioning of the real nature of democracy. The very definition of "generality" is an issue in all democratic countries. In this context questions have been raised about both the state and civil society as new puzzles have arisen about both the nature and the meaning of "the general interest."[78] In a day and age when "governance" is the fashionable word of the moment, magical thinking about the virtues of association and decentralization is no longer appropriate, nor are old institutional and procedural certitudes about the determination of the social good. Fresh thinking about the overall architecture of democracy is urgently needed. People everywhere are searching for new definitions of sovereignty and legitimacy, new procedures of representation, and new forms of public expression. At issue is the very nature of the political. To be sure, the question is too vast even to be posed properly in the brief space of a conclusion. Hence a more thorough examination will have to be deferred to another work.

Notes

Introduction

1. No strict legal or sociological definition of "intermediary bodies" is possible. The expression is generally used to refer to various social and political forms that occupy the space between the state and the individual, including associations, unions, parties, local governments, and a variety of self-regulating institutions of civil society. Like civil society itself (in which intermediary bodies operate as subjective instances within a defining framework), they can be understood only dynamically, within the context of social conflicts and demands that call them into existence and shape their development.

2. On this point, see Rosanvallon, "Fondements et problèmes de l'illibéralisme français," in Thierry de Montbrial, ed., *La France du nouveau siècle* (Paris: Presses Universitaires de France, 2002).

3. As used in the text, the term "Jacobinism" should be understood as synonymous with "political culture of generality."

1. Generality as Social Form

1. On this point see Rosanvallon, *Le Sacre du citoyen: Histoire du suffrage universel en France* (Paris: Gallimard, 1992).

2. Abbé Sieyès, *Projet d'un décret provisoire sur le clergé* (Paris, 12 February 1790), p. 5.

3. Quoted in Antoine de Baecque, *Le Corps de l'histoire: Métaphores et politique (1770–1800)* (Paris: Calmann-Lévy, 1993), p. 120. Quotations in this vein are abundant. For instance, Sieyès spoke of the nation as the sole "great body [*grand corps*] of citizens."

4. Toussaint Guiraudet, *Qu'est-ce que la nation? Et qu'est-ce que la France?* (1789), p. 9.

5. Ibid., p. 11.

268   Notes to Pages 14–16

6. Abbé Sieyès, *Qu'est-ce que le tiers état?*, ed. Roberto Zapperi (Geneva: Droz, 1970), p. 183.

7. André Chénier, "Notes," appended to his poem "Hermès," in *Oeuvres complètes* (Paris: Gallimard, 1958), p. 401.

8. Sieyès, *Qu'est-ce que le tiers état?*, p. 168. On this point see also his well-known comments on the various categories of interest that he claims can be found in men's hearts; ibid., pp. 206–210.

9. Ibid., p. 143.

10. *Dire de l'abbé Sieyès sur la question du veto royal* (Paris, 7 September 1789), p. 15.

11. Hence sovereignty in the Revolution cannot be conceptualized as a purely political matter. It combined a sociological vision with a political philosophy, thus breaking with earlier understandings of sovereignty (for instance, Jean Bodin and Johannes Althusius viewed the concept of sovereignty as capping and consolidating the harmony of a society of *corps*). In this connection, Jacques Guilhaumou accurately notes that "Sieyès in 1788–1791 preferred to use the notion of the 'whole' [*tout*], meaning coextensive with the nation, where political thinkers and jurists spoke of national sovereignty." See Guilhaumou, *Sieyès et l'Ordre de la langue: L'invention de la politique moderne* (Paris: Kimé, 2002), p. 87. See also Pasquale Pasquino, *Sieyès et l'invention de la constitution en France* (Paris: Odile Jacob, 1998).

12. "The assimilation of men," Sieyès wrote, "is the primary prerequisite for the great national union into a *single* people." See "Sur le projet de décret pour l'établissement de l'instruction nationale," *Journal d'instruction sociale*, no. 5 (6 July 1793), 146. This first encounter, which took place in "small associations," was followed by the decisive movement of "adunation," Sieyès's word for the way in which a coherent whole comes into being. (The term "adunation," introduced into French by Sieyès though recorded in English as early as 1551, denoted the process by which a group of individuals comes to "form a nation.")

13. Presentation by Le Chapelier on 14 June 1791 of a proposed decree abolishing corporations, in *Archives parlementaires,* published by Laurent and Mavidal, 1st ser. (cited hereafter as *A.P.*), vol. 27, p. 210. The preamble to the Constitution of 1791 expressly noted that "henceforth there are no guilds or corporations of professions, arts, or crafts." These prohibitions were reiterated in the Constitution of Year III.

14. The Allarde decree of 2 March 1791 had abolished *jurandes* and *maîtrises*.

15. The first source to consult on this question is now Steven L. Kaplan, *La Fin des corporations* (Paris: Fayard, 2001).

16. For an early treatment of this question, see Alphonse Aulard, *La Révolution française et les congrégations* (Paris, 1903). For what is now the comprehensive

reference on the subject, see Jean-Paul Durand, *La Liberté des congrégations religieuses en France,* 3 vols. (Paris: Editions du Cerf, 1999).

17. Pierre Athanase Torné, 28 April 1792, *A.P.*, vol. 42, pp. 488–489.

18. "Considered from the latter point of view, the clergy is exempt from the action of political law. The ecclesiastical hierarchy is not within its purview. The legislator has neither the desire nor the power to break its bonds or to alter its order. A corporation entirely spiritual in its hierarchy and functions matters little to the legislator. So long as its governance does not exceed the limits of the religious cult, it is of no importance in the civil state. So long as the exercise of a cult does not disturb the public order, it is beyond the law's prohibitions. How, in the spiritual order, and purely in relation to religious functions, could sacerdotal corporations be subject to the sanction of abolition? Their members are united only by mystical bonds, are subject to command only by virtue of the bonds of faith, and have nothing in common except hopes and fears of another life, metaphysical opinions, purely religious ceremonies, and religious functions completely unrelated to public functions"; ibid., p. 489.

19. Treilhard Report, submitted on 17 December 1789, *A.P.*, vol. 10, pp. 624–626.

20. See especially Le Chapelier's intervention on 12 February 1790, *A.P.*, vol. 11, p. 574.

21. See the speeches of Dupont de Nemours, Roederer, and Charles de Lameth on 13 February 1790, ibid., pp. 589–590. Lameth, for example, gave his solemn assurance that "the Catholic religion is in no danger."

22. Quoted in Paul Nourrisson, *Histoire de la liberté d'association en France depuis 1789* (Paris, 1920), vol. 1, p. 137.

23. "An ecclesiastic is an isolated person; a monk is always a *corps*," Condorcet noted in his 1788 "Essai sur la constitution et les fonctions des assemblées provinciales," which can be found in *Oeuvres de Condorcet*, ed. A. O'Connor and F. Arago (Paris, 1847), vol. 8, p. 142. On these grounds Condorcet denied monks the right to vote. On this point see Rosanvallon, *Le Sacre du citoyen*.

24. See the report on the male secular congregations presented by J.-B. Massieu in the summer of 1791, *A.P.*, vol. 32, Annexes, pp. 58–60. Of the secular congregations Massieu wrote: "All these associations are by their nature involved in functions of paramount social interest: educating the young, teaching religion, training ministers, caring for indigent patients. Yet in order to perform duties of such consequence and importance for the welfare of the public, is it necessary to belong to any corporation whatsoever? Are these functions not equally well discharged in governments that do not recognize establishments of this sort? . . . Let us establish national education instead . . . Let us organize a general establishment of public assistance to care for impoverished patients."

25. Le Chapelier, speech of 6 April 1792, *A.P.*, vol. 41, pp. 237–247.

26. Ibid., pp. 240–241.
27. It noted: "When the legislative body has completed the abolition of religious corporations, it should also banish forever all costumes formerly associated with them, which would inevitably remind people of them, perpetuate their image, or make people think that they still persist"; *A.P.*, vol. 48, p. 350.
28. On the many interesting debates on this issue from 1789 to the end of the nineteenth century, see "Les Insignes parlementaires," in Eugène Pierre, *Traité de droit politique électoral et parlementaire*, 2d ed. (Paris, 1902), pp. 1303–08; and Edmond Launay, *Costumes, insignes, cartes, médailles des députés, 1789–1898* (Paris: n.p., 1989).
29. For an earlier treatment of this subject, see Marie-Vic Ozouf-Marignier, *La Formation des départements: La représentation du territoire français à la fin du XVIIIe siècle* (Paris: Editions de l'EHESS, 1989).
30. Adrien Duquesnoy, 4 November 1789, *A.P.*, vol. 9, p. 671.00–000
31. Thus it is noteworthy that Sieyès, in writings from this period (such as the manuscript "Division du royaume," Archives Nationales, 284, *A.P.*, 3, dossier 2, sleeve 3), reproduced Hesseln's celebrated geometric map, which mechanically divided the country into eighty-one squares (Robert de Hesseln, *Nouvelle Topographie ou description détaillé de la France divisée par carrés uniformes* [Paris, 1780]).
32. Quoted in Mona Ozouf, *L'Ecole de la France* (Paris: Gallimard, 1984), p. 33.
33. Abbé Sieyès, *Observations sur le rapport du comité de constitution, concernant la nouvelle organisation de la France* (Versailles, 2 October 1789), p. 2.
34. Expressed at the time in the arithmetic notion of proportionality, a purely mechanical relationship between individuals and territory.
35. Duquesnoy, 4 November 1789, *A.P.*, vol. 9, p. 671.
36. See his well-known speeches to the Assembly on 3 and 10 November 1789.
37. Sieyès, *Dire sur le veto royal*, p. 10. He also wrote: "France is not a political charterhouse."
38. Jacques-Guillaume Thouret, *Rapport du comité de constitution*, 3 November 1789, *A.P.*, vol. 9, pp. 654–655.
39. Ibid. "Who will not feel," he continued, "that belonging to the great national union is worth a thousand times more than the state of partial corporation that will be disavowed by the Constitution?" (ibid., p. 656). "Let us not give up hope that a day will come when the national spirit will have been more firmly consolidated and all the French will have been united in a single family having but a single law and a single mode of government, so that they will abjure all the prejudices of the particularist corporatist and local spirit."
40. Jacques Revel, "La Région," in Pierre Nora, ed., *Les Lieux de mémoire*, vol. 1: *Les France* (Paris: Gallimard, 1992), p. 874.
41. To quote Jean Starobinski, *1789 ou les emblèmes de la raison* (Paris: Flammarion, 1979).

42. See Mona Ozouf, *La Fête révolutionnaire, 1789–1799* (Paris: Gallimard, 1967), p. 69. This is still the most penetrating work on the subject.

43. Louis Blanc, *Histoire de la Révolution française* (Paris, n.d.), vol. 1, p. 409 (on this point see chap. 15 of book IV: "Vision sublime de l'avenir").

44. Ozouf, *La Fête révolutionnaire*, p. 152.

45. Sarrette, Year II, quoted in ibid.

46. See ibid., p. 177.

47. Jules Michelet, Preface of 1847, *Histoire de la Révolution française* (Paris: Gallimard, 1952), vol. 1, p. 8.

48. Charles-Alexandre de Moy, *Des fêtes, ou quelques idées d'un citoyen français relativement aux fêtes publiques et à un culte national* (Paris, Year VII), p. 2.

49. *Le Rédacteur*, 23 Fructidor, Year IV, quoted in Albert Mathiez, *La Théophilanthropie et le culte décadaire (1796–1802)* (Paris, 1904), p. 30.

50. Moy, *Des fêtes*, p. 8. Robespierre, for his part, stressed that "the most magnificent of spectacles is that of a great people assembled." See "Sur les rapports des idées religieuses et morales avec les principes républicains et sur les fêtes nationales," speech of 18 Floréal, Year II (7 May 1794), in *Textes choisis* (Paris: Editions Sociales), vol. 3, p. 176.

51. *La Bouche de fer*, no. 11 (27 January 1791), 161.

52. Jean-Jacques Rousseau, *Lettre à d'Alembert sur les spectacles*, in *Oeuvres complètes* (Paris: Gallimard, 1995), vol. 5, p. 115. The article in *La Bouche de fer* paraphrased Rousseau.

53. Cf. what Rousseau said in 1755 in his *Discours sur l'économie politique* about the transformation of scattered individuals into united citizens: "If one habituates them soon enough to look at themselves individually only in terms of their relation to the body of the state and, as it were, to perceive their existence only as part of its existence, they will at last come to identify in some sense with this greater whole [*ce plus grand tout*]"; *Oeuvres complètes*, vol. 3, p. 259.

54. Rousseau, *Lettre à d'Alembert*, p. 90.

55. Ibid., p. 91.

56. "Premier discours prononcé par M. l'Abbé Fauchet," *La Bouche de fer*, no. 2 (October 1790), 19.

57. *La Bouche de fer*, no. 11 (October 1790), 178; emphasis added.

58. Ibid., p. 181.

59. Space does not permit discussion here of the Masonic influence on Fauchet, which led him to relate the virtue of locally expressed fraternity to the idea of humanity. "Let us extend this general love, in which the well-being of our brothers is identified with our own," he wrote, "and let us cause its infinite warmth to flow through the veins of all the human race"; ibid., p. 183.

60. See the analysis by Lynn Hunt, *Le Roman familial de la Révolution française* (Paris: Albin Michel, 1995).

61. Patrice Higonnet rightly stressed this point in *Goodness beyond Virtue: Jacobins during the French Revolution* (Cambridge, Mass.: Harvard University Press, 1998), p. 319.

62. Robespierre, speech of 18 Floréal, Year II (7 May 1794), on the Supreme Being, *A.P.*, vol. 90, p. 139. Earlier in the speech he said: "Bring together with the charm of friendship and the bonds of virtue people whom some have wished to divide"; ibid., p. 135.

63. Louis Antoine Saint-Just, speech of 26 Germinal, Year II (15 April 1794), on general order, *A.P.*, vol. 88, p. 615. "Revolutionary man is uncompromising with the wicked, but he is sensitive," he added (ibid.).

64. Idem, *Fragments d'institutions républicaines,* in *Oeuvres complètes de Saint-Just* (Paris: Editions Gérard Lebovici, 1984), p. 983.

65. Ibid., p. 984.

66. Bertrand Barère, *Rapport fait au nom du comité de salut public sur les moyens d'extirper la mendicité dans les campagnes, et sur les secours que doit accorder la République aux citoyens indigents,* 22 Floréal, Year II.

67. Idem, speech of 1 Floréal, Year II (20 April 1794), *A.P.*, vol. 89, p. 99.

68. See in particular Marcel David, *Fraternité et Révolution française, 1789–1799* (Paris: Aubier, 1987) and "De la philanthropie à la fraternité: À propos de deux thèses récentes," *Revue d'histoire du droit,* July–September 1994; Mona Ozouf, "La Révolution française et l'idée de fraternité," in *L'Homme régénérée: Essais sur la Révolution française* (Paris: Gallimard, 1989); Michel Borgetto, *La Notion de fraternité en droit public français* (Paris: LGDJ, 1993).

69. On this point see the important work of William Sewell: "The word *fraternité* had obvious revolutionary overtones, but it also belonged to the traditional corporatist vocabulary . . . It gave revolutionary respectability to the moral solidarity that found expression in trade guilds while adding more specific content to what was in other respects an abstract revolutionary term." See *Gens de métiers et Révolution: Le langage de l'Ancien Régime à 1848* (Paris: Aubier, 1983), pp. 279–280.

70. See *Motion de M. Thouret, sur les propriétés de la couronne, du clergé et de tous les corps et établissements de mainmorte,* 23 October 1789, *A.P.*, vol. 9, pp. 485–490.

71. Thouret, intervention of 30 October 1789, ibid., p. 611.

72. This was the central argument advanced by those who tried to justify the ownership of ecclesiastical properties.

73. We will see later that the issue of mortmain was central to the debates of the late nineteenth century that led to the law of 1901. Many republicans feared the prospect of associations in perpetuity.

74. Jean-François Essuile, *Traité politique et économique des communes, ou observations sur l'agriculture, sur l'origine, la destination et l'état actuel des biens*

communs, et sur les moyens d'en tirer les secours les plus puissants et les plus durables pour les communautés qui les possèdent et pour l'état (Paris, 1770). On this question see Nadine Vivier, *Propriété collective et identité communale: Les biens communaux en France, 1750–1914* (Paris: Publications de la Sorbonne, 1998).

75. See Edme Champion, *La France d'après les Cahiers de 1789* (Paris, 1897), pp. 152–154.

76. Responses to this survey and other material from this debate were collected in a stout volume by Georges Bourgin, *La Partage des biens communaux: Documents sur la préparation de la loi du 10 juin 1793* (Paris, 1908).

77. Ibid., p. 103.

78. The law of 14 August 1792 imposed compulsory division of communal land. The definitive text of 10 June 1793 made division optional.

79. Claude-Dominique Fabre, *Rapport sur le mode de partage des biens communaux, A.P.,* vol. 61, p. 429.

80. See for example the work of Geneviève Fraisse and Joan Scott.

81. Toussaint Guiraudet, *De la famille, considérée comme l'élément des sociétés* (Paris, 1797), pp. 8–9. On the question of the political status of the family, see Anne Verjus, *Le Cens de la famille: Les femmes et le vote, 1789–1848* (Paris: Belin, 2002).

82. P.-L. Roederer, *Quatrième Discours sur l'organisation sociale* (17 February 1793), in *Oeuvres du comte P.-L. Roederer* (Paris, 1869), vol. 8, p. 163. See also his *Réflexions sur l'ouvrage du citoyen Guiraudet,* ibid., vol. 5, pp. 98–100.

83. Charles-Guillaume Théremin, *De la condition des femmes dans les républiques (1789)* (Paris: Indigo et Côté Femmes, 1996), p. 58.

84. Ibid. Many nineteenth-century feminists adopted this logic in claiming the right to vote for *unmarried women* on the grounds that they constituted a family by themselves.

85. Unless one adopts a Rousseauian perspective, according to which power can be divided between direct government of institutions and "indirect government," with women exercising the latter. On this point see the stimulating reflections of Arthur M. Melzer, *Rousseau, la bonté naturelle de l'homme* (Paris: Belin, 1998), esp. pp. 400–411.

86. See the classic analysis of Hannah Arendt, *The Human Condition* (Chicago: University of Chicago Press, 1958), chap. 2.

2. Generality as Democratic Quality

1. Decree of 30 September 1791, *A.P.,* vol. 31, p. 624.

2. Isaac-René-Guy Le Chapelier, *Rapport sur les sociétés populaires,* 29 September 1791, ibid., p. 617.

3. Debate of 25 Vendémiaire, Year III (16 October 1794), *A.P.*, vol. 99, pp. 203–216.

4. See, for example, Jean-François Reubell's speech, ibid., p. 208.

5. Ibid., p. 210, for this and subsequent quotations from Bourdon. Reubell meanwhile railed against "people who want to put themselves above the law, people who communicate among themselves as citizens but want to be more than other citizens, indeed, want to communicate as a corporation"; ibid., p. 208.

6. During the same debate, Jacques Thuriot made a similar point: "Sovereignty resides in the universality of the nation. Society's guarantee does not rest, as some have said, upon the popular societies"; ibid., p. 214.

7. Le Chapelier, speech of 29 September 1791, ibid., p. 617.

8. Robespierre, speech of 29 September 1791, ibid., p. 620.

9. Law of 25 July 1793. See the text of the law and its presentation by Jean-Etienne Bar in *A.P.*, vol. 68, p. 487, and vol. 69, p. 479.

10. The Committee of Public Safety remarked that "the popular societies should be the arsenals of public opinion, but the Convention alone shapes that opinion as it should be shaped and sets the objective to be achieved." Quoted in Lucien Jaume, "Les Jacobins et l'opinion publique," in Serge Berstein and Odile Rudelle, eds., *Le Modèle républicain* (Paris: Presses Universitaires de France, 1992), p. 65.

11. Robespierre, speech at the Jacobin Club, 6 Nivôse, Year II (26 December 1793), in Alphonse Aulard, *La Société des Jacobins: Recueil de documents* (Paris, 1895), vol. 5, pp. 578–581. See also Albert Soboul, "Robespierre et les sociétés populaires," *Annales historiques de la Révolution française*, April–June 1958.

12. For an analysis of this conflict, see Albert Soboul, *Les Sans-Culottes parisiens en l'an II* (Paris, 1962), part 3, chap. 5: "Institutions populaires et sociétés sectionnaires."

13. See the monographs collected in "Existe-t-il un fédéralisme jacobin?," in *Actes du 111e Congrès des sociétés savantes* (Histoire moderne et contemporaine I, 2) (Paris: Editions du CTHS, 1986); the dossier "Les Congrès de sociétés populaires et la question du pouvoir exécutif révolutionnaire," *Annales historiques de la Révolution française*, September–October 1986; Jean Boutier, Philippe Boutry, and Serge Bonin, *Les Sociétés politiques*, vol. 6 of *Atlas de la Révolution française* (Paris: Editions de l'EHESS, 1992).

14. Marc-Antoine Jullien and Georges Auguste Couthon, 15 May 1794 (26 Floréal, Year II), at the Jacobin Club, in Aulard, *La Société des Jacobins*, vol. 6, pp. 126–129.

15. See the bill proposed by Boissel on 14 June 1793, *A.P.*, vol. 66, pp. 613–635.

16. On this point see Rosanvallon, *Le Peuple introuvable* (Paris: Gallimard, 1998).

17. See my foreword to Marcel Détienne, ed., *Qui veut prendre la parole?* (Paris: Editions du Seuil, 2003).

18. *Seconde Motion de M. l'abbé Fauchet, sur les droits des représentants et du peuple, fait à l'Assemblée générale des représentants de la Commune de Paris*, 25 November 1789, pp. 2–11.

19. Ibid., p. 8.00–000

20. Ibid., p. 9. Fauchet makes his point even more brutally clear: "Negroes would be enlightened enough to consent to a law that granted them all the rights of man and the citizen; it is impossible for Frenchmen to reject it" (p. 15).

21. These phrases are taken from his "Thirteenth Discourse" (on Rousseau), *Annales de la confédération universelle des amis de la vérité*, first supplement to *La Bouche de fer* (1791), 35–36.

22. See "Organisation des assemblées souveraines d'un peuple libre," *La Bouche de fer*, no. 76 (28 June 1791), 1–4.

23. *La Bouche de fer*, no. 11 (October 1790), 183.

24. See François-Xavier Lanthenas, *Des sociétés populaires, considérées comme une branche essentielle de l'instruction publique* (Paris, Year IV [April 1796]). His position was set forth earlier in "De l'instruction publique par les sociétés populaires," *La Chronique du mois ou les cahiers patriotiques*, 2 (April 1792).

25. Idem, *Bases fondamentales de l'instruction publique et de toute constitution libre ou moyens de lier l'opinion publique, la morale, l'éducation, l'enseignement, l'instruction, les fêtes, la propagation des Lumières, et le progrès de toutes les connaissances au gouvernement national-républicain* (Paris, 20 March 1793), p. 16.

26. Lanthenas, *Des sociétés populaires*, p. 16.

27. Idem, *Motifs de faire du dix-huit août un jubilé fraternel* (Paris, 1793), p. 26.

28. Idem, *Des sociétés populaires*, p. 16.

29. Idem, *Motifs*, p. 19.

30. See Bertrand Buffon, *Espace et délibération parlementaires: Une comparaison de l'Assemblée nationale avec la Chambre des communes*, thesis, DEA in Political Studies (Paris: EHESS, 1998). The standard work on this subject is still Armand Brette, *Histoire des édifices où siégèrent les assemblées parlementaires de la Révolution française* (Paris, 1902), vol. 1 (no other volume was published).

31. Quoted by Jean-Philippe Heurtin, "Architectures morales de l'Assemblée nationale," in Détienne, *Qui veut prendre la parole?*, p. 60. See also Heurtin, *L'Espace public parlementaire: Essai sur les raisons du législateur* (Paris: Presses Universitaires de France, 1999).

32. On this point see the data presented in Patrice Gueniffey, *Le Nombre et la raison: La Révolution française et les électeurs* (Paris: Editions de l'EHESS, 1993).

33. Quoted in Serge Aberdam et al., *Voter, élire pendant la Révolution française,*

1789–1799: Guide pour la recherche (Paris: Editions du CTHS, 1999), p. 459. This is the book to consult for the text of all laws pertaining to the organization of elections.

34. Quoted in *La Bouche de fer*, no. 7 (October 1790), 98.
35. Pons (of Verdun), *Rapport fait au nom d'une commission spéciale, sur la suppression des listes de candidat*, Year VI, quoted in Gueniffey, *Le Nombre et la raison*, p. 512.
36. Quoted in Aberdam et al., *Voter, élire*, p. 512.
37. *Loi contenant instruction sur la tenue des assemblées primaires et communales du 18 ventôse an VI (8 mars 1798)*, chap. 2: "De la fête qui doit précéder des assemblées primaires et communales."
38. Law concerning the elections of 25 Fructidor, Year III (11 September 1795).
39. Directive concerning the primary, communal, and electoral assemblies of 5 Ventôse, Year V (21 February 1797). Title IV of the law said this about candidacies: "This straightforward manner of offering to accept the trust of the voters is the most worthy of a republican and is preferable in all respects to the secret intrigues and obscure maneuvers of conspiratorial ambition." On the application of this law, see Bernard Gainot, "Les Troubles électoraux de l'an VII: Dissolution du souverain ou vitalité de la démocratie représentative," *Annales historiques de la Révolution française*, July–September 1994.
40. Law of 24 Pluviôse, Year VI (12 February 1798).
41. Quatremère de Quincy, *La Véritable Liste des candidates, précédée d'observations sur la nature de l'institution des candidats et son application au gouvernement représentatif*, 2d ed. (Paris, Year V [1797]), p. 17. "For now," the author continued, "the true list of candidates should not be a compilation of names exposed to criticism but a rational compilation of the principles on which that criticism should be based. The true list of candidates should not be a collection of individual portraits but a set of features appropriate to serve as a model or type that every candidate should resemble. It should not be a material list on which the parties will inscribe names of people who may be terrified of being with the others; it should rather be a series of notions and rules that has no need of a list or of candidates" (pp. 18–19).
42. On this point see the interesting documents collected by Bernard Gainot, *1799, un nouveau jacobinisme?* (Paris: Editions du CTHS, 2001), esp. pp. 122–125. See also idem, "Les Troubles électoraux de l'an VII." The various electoral codes of the period should also be consulted.
43. See esp. J.-P. Brissot, *Réflexions sur l'état de la société des électeurs patriotes, sur ses travaux, sur les formes propres à faire de bonnes élections* (Paris, 25 December 1790).
44. Le Chapelier, speech of 29 September 1791, *A.P.*, vol. 31, p. 617.

45. P.-L. Roederer, *Des sociétés populaires* (Brumaire, Year III), in *Oeuvres du comte P.-L. Roederer* (Paris, 1869), vol. 7, pp. 17–22.

46. See Articles 360–363. Art. 360: "No corporation or association contrary to public order may be formed." Art. 361: "No assembly of citizens may call itself a popular society." Art. 362: "No private society concerned with political issues shall correspond or affiliate with any other, nor shall it hold public meetings in which members and other attendees are distinguished from one another, nor impose conditions for admission and eligibility, nor arrogate to itself rights of exclusion, nor allow its members to wear any external sign of their association." Art. 363: "Citizens may exercise their political rights only within Primary or Communal Assemblies." See also the implementing law of 6 Fructidor, Year III (22 August 1795).

47. In the pamphlet cited above, it is significant that Roederer quoted from Rousseau's *Lettre à d'Alembert sur les spectacles* to illustrate the kind of circles and societies he regarded as "respectable and innocent institutions." Bear in mind, however, that literary academies and societies were themselves banned for a time; see the abbé Henri Grégoire's *Rapport* and the edict approved on 8 August 1793, *A.P.*, vol. 70, pp. 519–524.

48. See for example the speeches of Raisson and Jean-Augustin Crassous at the Jacobin Club, 25 Vendémiaire, Year III (reprinted in *Moniteur*, 30 Vendémiaire, Year III [21 October 1794], vol. 22, pp. 269–270).

49. Law of 19 Fructidor, Year V (5 September 1797). See especially Article 35.

50. See Brissot's *Discours sur l'utilité des sociétés patriotiques et populaires*, delivered on 28 September 1791 to the Jacobin Club, p. 23.

51. Report of 8 Germinal, Year IV (28 March 1796), *Moniteur*, vol. 28, p. 95.

52. This distinction continued to be made throughout the nineteenth century as grounds for opposing freedom of the press to freedom of book publication, the former having an avowed public dimension (see the Restoration debates on this issue).

53. On this point, see the very interesting remarks of Emmanuel Pastoret, *Discours sur les associations ou réunions s'occupant d'objets politiques* (Council of Five Hundred), 4 Thermidor, Year V (22 July 1797). Pastoret contrasted the "rapid reverberation" of eloquence at a meeting with the "delayed effect" of a printed work. He expounded on this distinction at some length in a discussion of the theory and practice of representative government.

54. See Christine Peyrard, "Les Débats de l'an VII sur l'association politique," in *Les Droits de l'homme et la conquête des libertés: Actes du colloque de Grenoble-Vizille, 1986* (Grenoble: Presses Universitaires de Grenoble, 1988); and Isser Woloch, *Jacobin Legacy: The Democratic Movement under the Directory* (Princeton: Princeton University Press, 1970).

55. See P.-L. Roederer, *Des sociétés particulières: Telles que clubs, réunions, etc.*, August 1799, in *Oeuvres du comte P.-L. Roederer*, vol. 7, pp. 88–95.

56. See the arguments of Jacques-Paul Duplantier, *Rapport au nom de la commission de la classification et de la révision des lois administratives, suivi du projet de code des droits politiques et des élections* (Paris, Thermidor, Year VII).

57. See the various speeches to the Council of Five Hundred on 11 and 12 Fructidor, Year VII, especially those of Nicolas Joseph Parent-Réal and Marie-Félix Faulcon.

3. Generality as Mode of Regulation

1. Urbain Domergue, quoted in Ferdinand Brunot, *Histoire de la langue française des origines à 1900*, vol. 9: *La Révolution et l'Empire*, part 2, p. 641. "We call a country ruled by a sovereign king [*roi*] a *royaume*. A country in which the law [*loi*] alone commands I would call a *loyaume*."

2. See Raymonde Monnier, *L'Espace public démocratique* (Paris: Kimé, 1994), pp. 95–96. See also Isabelle Bourdin, *Les Sociétés populaires à Paris pendant la Révolution* (Paris, 1937).

3. See Allessandro Galante-Garrone, "Gilbert Romme et les débuts de la société des amis de la loi," in *Gilbert Romme et son temps (Actes du colloque tenu à Riom et Clermont les 10–11 juin 1965)* (Paris: Presses Universitaires de France, 1966); and Elisabeth Roudinesco, *Théroigne de Méricourt: Une femme mélancolique sous la Révolution* (Paris: Editions du Seuil, 1989).

4. On this festival of 3 June 1792, see Marie-Louise Biver, *Fêtes révolutionnaires à Paris* (Paris: Presses Universitaires de France, 1979), pp. 49–52.

5. See the chapter "La Suprématie de la loi," in Jean Belin, *La Logique d'une idée force: L'idée d'utilité sociale et la Révolution française (1789–1792)* (Paris, 1939). See also Jean Ray, "La Révolution française et la pensée juridique: L'idée du règne de la loi," *Revue philosophique de la France et de l'étranger*, 128 (September–December 1939); Simone Goyard-Fabre, "Le Prestige de la loi à l'époque révolutionnaire," and Catherine Larrère, "Le Gouvernement de la loi est-il un thème républicain?" *Cahiers de philosophie politique et juridique de l'université de Caen*, no. 12 (1987).

6. Maximin Isnard, speech of 14 November 1791, *Moniteur*, vol. 10, p. 375.

7. Louis Antoine Saint-Just, speech of 24 April 1793, in *Oeuvres complètes de Saint-Just* (Paris: Editions Gérard Lebovici, 1984), p. 416.

8. Quoted in Belin, *La Logique d'une idée force*, p. 85.

9. These phrases come from two advocates-general, Du Belloy and Marion, quoted in Marie-France Renoux-Zagamé, "Royaume de la loi: Equité et rigueur du droit selon la doctrine des parlements de la monarchie," *Justices*, no. 9 (January–March 1998), 23.

10. The phrase is taken from Guillaume Du Vair, *garde des Sceaux* in the early seventeenth century, quoted in ibid., p. 24.
11. See the magnificent speech "L'Amour de son état," 1 Mercuriale, reprinted in *Discours de M. le Chancelier d'Aguesseau*, new ed. (Paris, 1822), vol. 1.
12. "De l'esprit et de la science," 7 Mercuriale, ibid., p. 268.
13. On this point, see Rosanvallon, "Physiocrats," in François Furet and Mona Ozouf, eds., *Dictionnaire critique de la Révolution française* (Paris: Flammarion, 1988); translated by Arthur Goldhammer as *Critical Dictionary of the French Revolution* (Cambridge, Mass.: Harvard University Press, 1989).
14. Guillaume François Le Trosne, *De l'ordre social* (Paris, 1777), p. 23.
15. *Maximes du Docteur Quesnay*, in Eugène Daire, *Physiocrates* (Paris, 1846), vol. 1, p. 390.
16. Pierre Le Mercier de la Rivière, *L'Ordre naturel et essentiel des sociétés politiques*, new ed. (Paris, 1910), pp. 82–85.
17. Ibid., p. 345.
18. See Akiteru Kubota, "Quesnay disciple de Malebranche," in *François Quesnay et la Physiocratie* (Paris: INED, 1958), vol. 1, pp. 169–196. See also Louis-Philippe May, "Descartes et les physiocrates," *Revue de synthèse*, July–December 1950.
19. Le Mercier, *L'Ordre naturel*, p. 346. Recall that Quesnay wrote the article on self-evidence in the *Encyclopédie*. He defined it as follows: "The term 'self-evidence' refers to a certainty so clear and manifest on its face that the mind cannot reject it."
20. Concerning this essential dimension of French public law, see Raymond Carré de Malberg, *La Loi, expression de la volonté générale* (1931) (Paris: Economica, 1984).
21. This definition was repeated in subsequent revolutionary constitutions. See, e.g., the Constitution of Year III: "The resolutions of the Council of Five Hundred, adopted by the Council of Ancients, are called law" (Article 92).
22. "Diverses réflexions sur les vies de Thésée, de Romulus et de Lycurgue," in *Discours de M. le chancelier d'Aguesseau*, vol. 2, p. 380.
23. Ibid.
24. "Loi," in *Encyclopédie* (Jaucourt).
25. Jean-Jacques Rousseau, "Des lois," in *Fragments politiques, Oeuvres complètes*, vol. 3 (Paris: Gallimard, 1995), p. 493. This text is a long diatribe against "the enormous multitude of laws" and the "terrifying multitudes of edicts and declarations."
26. See Jean-Guillaume Locré, *La Législation civile, commerciale et criminelle de la France, ou commentaire et complément des codes français* (Paris, 1829), vol. 16, p. 635.

27. Abbé de Saint-Pierre, *Mémoire pour diminuer le nombre des procès* (Paris, 1725), p. 36.

28. Ibid., pp. 30–31.

29. See Jacques Vanderlinden, *Le Concept de code en Europe occidentale du XIIIe au XIXe siècle* (Brussels, 1967); J.-H. Michel, "Quelques Observations sur la notion de code synthétique," in *Code et constitution: Liber amicorum J. Gilissen* (Antwerp, 1983); Jean Gaudemet, "Codes, collections et compilations," *Droits*, no. 24 (1996) (special issue on codification). Frederick II of Prussia proudly proclaimed that "everything will be anticipated" when he published his Civil Code in 1791.

30. A committee of jurisprudence was named as early as 5 July 1790. An edict stated that "the civil laws shall be revised and reformed by the legislators, and a general code of clear, simple laws compatible with the Constitution shall be established."

31. Cambacérès's report of 9 August 1793 is included in P. A. Fenet, *Recueil complet des travaux préparatoires du Code civil*, new ed. (Paris, 1836), vol. 1, p. 1.

32. See the preliminary report of the committee assigned to draft a plan (Germinal, Year IX), in Locré, *La Législation civile*, vol. 17, pp. 32 ff. See also the treatment of the same subject (in 1807) by Regnault de Saint-Jean-d'Angély, pp. 57 ff.

33. See Jacques Vanderlinden, "Code et codification dans la pensée de Jeremy Bentham," *Revue d'histoire du droit*, 32 (1964); Denis Baranger, "Bentham et la codification," *Droits*, no. 27 (1998); François Ost, "Codification et temporalité dans la pensée de J. Bentham," in *Actualité de la pensée juridique de Jeremy Bentham* (Brussels, 1987).

34. Bentham's proposal for a "Pannomion for the French Nation" can be found in the collection of his manuscripts at University College, London (see manuscript no. 100, cited in Elie Halévy, *La Formation du radicalisme philosophique*, vol. 1: *La Jeunesse de Bentham* [Paris, 1901], p. 367). See also his "Pannomial Fragments," in *The Work of Jeremy Bentham*, ed. John Bowring (Edinburgh, 1843), vol. 3, pp. 211–230; as well as his "Nomography or the Art of Inditing Laws," ibid., pp. 232 ff.

35. Jeremy Bentham, "On Codification: To the President of the United States of America," ibid., vol. 4, pp. 453–467.

36. Jean-Jacques Rousseau, *Du contrat social*, book 2, chap. 7, in *Oeuvres complètes* (Paris: Gallimard, 1995), vol. 3, p. 381; translated by Maurice Cranston as *The Social Contract* (New York: Penguin, 1968), p. 84 (translation modified).

37. Pierre Le Mercier de la Rivière, *De l'instruction publique ou considérations morales et politiques sur la nécessité, la nature et la source de cette instruction* (Paris and Stockholm, 1775), p. 13.

38. Merlin (de Douai), "Loi," in *Répertoire universel et raisonné de jurisprudence*, 5th ed. (Brussels, 1827), vol. 18, p. 385. In a Rousseauist vein, he also says that "in order for an act to constitute a law, it must not only be the case that the will from which it emanates be that of the greater number; the subject of the nation's exercise of statutory will must also be common to all; and if a nation exercises its power, or manifests its will, on specific objects, it does so not as sovereign but as government. In such a case it acts not as legislator but as magistrate, and rather than make a law, it merely gives an order or pronounces a judgment"; ibid., pp. 384–385.

39. "Liberty always follows the fate of law . . . The worst law is still worth more than the best master, for every master has preferences, and the law has none"; Jean-Jacques Rousseau, *Lettres écrites sur la montagne*, letter 8, in *Oeuvres complètes*, vol. 3, pp. 842–843.

40. Idem, *Manuscrit de Genève*, chap. 4: "De la nature des lois et du principe de justice sociale," ibid., p. 327.

41. Idem, *The Social Contract*, p. 82.

42. See the various articles on "La Fiction," *Droits*, no. 21 (1995). On this point see also Rosanvallon, "L'Age de l'abstraction," in *Le Peuple introuvable* (Paris: Gallimard, 1998).

43. Louis Antoine Saint-Just, *Discours sur la Constitution de la France* (National Convention, 24 April 1793), in *Oeuvres complètes*, p. 418. See also *Fragments d'institutions républicaines*.

44. Jean Carbonnier, "La Passion des lois au siècle des Lumières," in *Essais sur les lois*, 2d ed. (Paris: Répertoire du Notariat Defrénois, 1995), p. 240. "Thus," he continued, "there exists a passion to legislate, a passion for the law, which has nothing in common with the ordinary thirst for power or even with the more singular pleasure that one might experience in making one's will. It is a phenomenon of legal psychology—of individual and collective psychology inextricably intertwined."

45. Quoted in Carla Hesse, "La Logique culturelle de la loi révolutionnaire," *Annales: Histoire, sciences sociales*, July–August 2002, p. 918.

46. Cesare Beccaria, *Des délits et des peines*, French edition of *On Crimes and Punishments*, ed. Franco Venturi (Geneva: Droz, 1965), p. 13 (see the entire section on the interpretation of the law). On these points see Michel Porret, ed., *Beccaria et la culture juridique des Lumières* (Geneva: Droz, 1997).

47. Beccaria, *Des délits et des peines*, p. 12.

48. "None of these interpreters," he wrote. "Works of this kind should be burned in all civilized nations and prevented from coming into being in nations yet to be civilized." See Denis Diderot, "Observations sur l'instruction de Sa Majesté Impériale aux députés pour la confection des lois" (1769), in *Oeuvres complètes* (Paris: Club Français du Livre, n.d.), vol. 11, p. 252.

49. Voltaire, "Loi," in *Dictionnaire philosophique*.

50. See the old but still useful book by Adhémar Esmein, *Histoire de la procédure criminelle en France* (Paris, 1881). See also Ernest Lebègue's book on Thouret, the man who played a leading role in this judicial reform: *La Vie et l'oeuvre d'un constituant, Thouret (1746–1794)* (Paris, 1910).

51. For a comprehensive review see Jean-Louis Halperin, *Le Tribunal de cassation et les pouvoirs sous la Révolution (1790–1799)* (Paris: LGDJ, 1987). There were two phases to the debate, the first in May, the second in November 1790.

52. Speech of 8 May 1790, *A.P.,* vol. 15, p. 432.

53. Ibid.

54. The actual mechanism of appeal combined interpretation of the law with judicial review. In the presumably rare instances in which the meaning of the law was ambiguous, the legislature itself was to settle the matter. "The appellate court should be located within the legislative body," said Robespierre, to indicate that judicial review in the strict sense was to be regarded as a measure in the general interest and not as a case involving individual persons, hence a measure alien to the judicial order. See his speech of 25 May 1790, ibid., p. 671.

55. Intervention of 18 November 1790, *A.P.,* vol. 20, p. 516.

56. See the examples in Jean Belin, "La Notion de cassation," in *La Logique d'une idée force,* pp. 94–96. This concept was perpetuated in the Constitutions of Year III and Year VIII. We find it reaffirmed in the law of 16 September 1807 and in the Acte Additionnel to the constitutions of the Empire of 22 April 1815.

57. See Joseph Barthélemy, "De l'interprétation des lois par le législateur," *Revue du droit public,* July–September 1908.

58. Reprinted in Jean-Etienne-Marie Portalis, *Discours et rapports sur le Code civil* (Caen: Centre de Philosophie Politique et Juridique, 1989).

59. Ibid., pp. 7–8.

60. Jean-Guillaume Locré, "Conclusion du commentaire et du complément du Code civil," in *La Législation civile,* vol. 16, p. 631.

61. Ibid., p. 632.

62. "The judge who shall refuse to judge on the ground that the law is *silent, obscure,* or inadequate shall be liable to prosecution for *denial of justice."*

63. See, for example, the arguments of Joseph-Jacques Maillia-Garat before the Tribunate (10 December 1801), in P. A. Fenet, *Recueil complet des travaux préparatoires du Code civil,* vol. 6, pp. 143–169.

64. Benjamin Constant, *Commentaire sur l'ouvrage de Filangieri* (1822), in *Oeuvres de G. Filangieri,* new ed. (Paris, 1840), vol. 3, p. 210. See chap. 7: "De l'influence que Filangieri attribue à la législation."

65. Rousseau, *The Social Contract,* p. 101 (translation modified).

66. See Robert Derathé, "Les Rapports de l'exécutif et du législatif chez J.-J. Rous-

seau," *Annales de philosophie politique*, vol. 5: *Rousseau et la philosophie politique* (Paris: Presses Universitaires de France, 1965).

67. "Introduction à la Révolution," an introduction to *Révolutions de Paris*, 30 January 1790, p. 6.

68. Jean-Nicolas Billaud-Varenne, *Despotisme des ministres de France* (Amsterdam, 1789) and *Plus de ministres ou point de grâce* (Paris, 1790).

69. See "Le Discrédit de la fonction ministérielle," in Edith Bernardin, *Jean-Marie Roland et le Ministère de l'intérieur (1792–1793)* (Paris: Société des Etudes Robespierristes, 1964).

70. Bertrand Barère, speech of 27 August 1791, *A.P.*, vol. 29, p. 742. A similar statement can be found in Abbé de Mably, *Du gouvernement et des lois de la Pologne*, published posthumously in 1789.

71. See especially the terms suggested in the debates of September 1789 and August 1791.

72. These various formulas can be found in the fourth notebook of his *Délinéaments politiques*, reprinted in Christine Faure, ed., *Des manuscrits de Sieyès, 1773–1799* (Paris: Honoré Champion, 1999), pp. 396–401.

73. See his "Lettre d'un jeune mécanicien aux auteurs du Républicain" (16 July 1791), in *Oeuvres de Condorcet*, ed. A. O'Connor and F. Arago (Paris, 1847), vol. 12, pp. 139–241.

74. For an early overview, see Joseph Barthélemy, *Le Rôle du pouvoir exécutif dans les républiques modernes* (Paris, 1907); see also Michel Verpeaux, *La Naissance du pouvoir réglementaire, 1789–1799* (Paris: Presses Universitaires de France, 1991).

75. Barère, comment of 4 December 1793, *A.P.*, vol. 80, p. 649.

76. P.-L. Roederer, comment of 10 April 1791, *A.P.*, vol. 24, p. 691.

77. See the report by Lazare Carnot on the elimination of the executive council, 1 April 1794, *A.P.*, vol. 87, pp. 694–698.

78. Louis Antoine Saint-Just, *Rapport général sur l'état du gouvernement*, 10 October 1793, *A.P.*, vol. 76, pp. 313–316.

79. Billaud-Varenne, *Rapport sur un mode de gouvernement provisoire et révolutionnaire*, 18 November 1793, *A.P.*, vol. 79, p. 455.

80. In his report of Year VII, François de Nantes still spoke of "freeing the Legislative Body from its oppression by the Executive." Quoted in Bernard Gainot, *1799, Un nouveau jacobinisme?* (Paris: Editions du CTHS, 2001), p. 452.

81. Bertrand Barère, *De la pensée du gouvernment républicain* (Floréal, Year V), p. 11.

4. The Question of Origins

1. Edmund Burke, *Reflections on the Revolution in France* (Cambridge, Mass.: Harvard University Press, 1909), p. 331.

2. This crucial point was made by Charles de Rémusat in *L'Angleterre au dix-huitième siècle* (Paris, 1856), vol. 2, pp. 273–452.

3. See Abbé Barruel, *Mémoires pour servir à l'histoire du jacobinisme,* new ed. (Hamburg, 1803), 5 vols. See also J. E. D. Bernardi, *De l'influence de la philosophie sur les forfaits de la Révolution* (Paris, n.d. [1800]), which went through several editions.

4. See François Azouvi's illuminating analysis in *Descartes et la France: Histoire d'une passion nationale* (Paris: Fayard, 2002), pp. 145–161.

5. See Paul Bénichou, *Le Sacre de l'écrivain, 1750–1830: Essai sur l'avènement d'un pouvoir spirituel laïque dans la France moderne* (Paris: José Corti, 1973), pp. 116–123.

6. See Jean-François de La Harpe, *Philosophie du dix-huitième siècle* (Paris, 1821); and especially J. E. M. Portalis, *De l'usage et de l'abus de l'esprit philosophique durant le XVIIIe siècle,* 3d ed. (Paris, 1834), 2 vols.

7. See chaps. 33 and 34 of Portalis, *De l'usage.* The famous first chapter of book 3 of Tocqueville's *L'Ancien Régime et la Révolution* uses arguments disturbingly close to those of Portalis.

8. Portalis, *De l'usage,* vol. 2, pp. 357–375.

9. See Augustin Cochin, *Les Sociétés de pensée et la démocratie moderne* (1921) (Paris: Copernic, 1978), p. 18.

10. Ibid., p. 19.

11. Taine devotes pages to attacking the "abstract principles of speculative politics," "abstract men who belong to no century and no country, hatched from nothing by a wave of the metaphysical wand," a society composed of "abstract beings and individuals set side by side," and constitution-writers with the "rigidity of speculative surgeons" (see the part on the Old Regime).

12. See François-Dominique de Montlosier, *De la monarchie française depuis son établissement jusqu'à nos jours* (Paris, 1814).

13. François Furet, who was one of the first to "rehabilitate" Tocqueville in the 1970s, rightly emphasized this difference between the two analyses.

14. Alexis de Tocqueville, *L'Ancien Régime et la Révolution* (Paris: Gallimard, 1952), vol. 1, p. 135.

15. The Rouen magistrate Bigot de Sainte-Croix in 1775, quoted by Robert Descimon and Alain Guéry in Jacques Le Goff, ed., *L'Etat et les pouvoirs* (Paris: Editions du Seuil, 1989), p. 326.

16. Letter from d'Aguesseau to the *procureur général* Joly de Fleury (1743), quoted in Paul Nourrisson, *Histoire de la liberté d'association en France depuis 1789* (Paris, 1920), vol. 1, p. 82.

17. Tocqueville, *L'Ancien Régime et la Révolution,* vol. 1, p. 65.

18. See the very enlightening research of F.-X. Emmanuelli, *Un Mythe de l'absolutisme bourbonien: L'intendance du milieu du XVIIe siècle à la fin du*

XVIIIe siècle (France, Espagne, Amérique) (Aix-en-Provence: Faculté des Lettres, 1981).

19. G. W. F. Hegel, *The Philosophy of Right,* trans. T. M. Knox (Oxford: Clarendon Press, 1977), sec. 273, p. 176 (translation modified).

20. Idem, *Encyclopédie des sciences philosophiques en abrégé* (Paris: Gallimard, 1970), sec. 534, p. 452.

21. On this point, see the searching commentary of Lucien Jaume in *L'Individu effacé ou le paradoxe du libéralisme français* (Paris: Fayard, 1977), pp. 283–285.

22. G. W. F. Hegel, *The Philosophy of History,* trans. J. Sibree (New York: Dover, 1956), p. 454.

23. See Charles Taylor, *Hegel and Modern Society* (Cambridge: Cambridge University Press, 1979); and Jean-François Kervégan, "Tocqueville et Hegel, un dialogue silencieux sur la modernité politique," in *Influences et réceptions mutuelles du droit et de la philosophie en France et en Allemagne* (Frankfurt am Main: Vittorio Klostermann, 2001).

24. Hegel, *The Philosophy of Right,* sec. 261, p. 161.

25. Cf. Antony Black's chapter on Hegel in *Guilds and Civil Society in European Political Thought from the Twelfth Century to the Present* (Ithaca: Cornell University Press, 1984).

26. In the economic sphere, it was the triumph of the market that illustrated this important transformation of the substance and form of human relations, extending the effects of political secularization and assertion of the primacy of the individual. With the advent of the market economy, exchange was no longer linked to any collective function and no longer enclosed within any symbolic system. It became autonomous, establishing a realm of purely instrumental commensurability. In every domain, then, increased autonomy and heightened abstraction went hand in hand.

27. At the end of 1788 Thouret wrote: "It is not as friends, or as members of a secondary corporation, that you will act as voters. It is as Frenchmen, as citizens, as members of that great family, the nation"; *Avis des bons Normands* (n.p.: n.d. [1788]), p. 27. Sieyès, for his part, observed that "the citizen has the right to be represented only because of the qualities that are common to all citizens and not because of those that differentiate one from another." *Qu'est-ce que le tiers état?,* ed. Roberto Zapperi (Geneva: Droz, 1970), p. 88.

28. This is precisely the reason why Hegel believed that democracy would lead to an impasse. The homogenization of society to which the search for equality leads separates individuals from the groups to which they traditionally belong without providing tangible new sources of identity.

29. For example, Oxford and Cambridge Universities were corporations enjoying their own representatives in Parliament until 1948.

30. Claude Lefort has written brilliantly on this point. See his *L'Invention démocratique* (Paris: Fayard, 1981), pp. 171–173.

31. The expression "Gothic colossus" comes from Bureaux de Pusy (27 August 1789, *A.P.,* vol. 8, p. 492). "Invincible colossus" is from Cérutti; see Rosanvallon, *Le Peuple introuvable* (Paris: Gallimard, 1998), p. 35.

32. Cornelius Castoriadis has provided a very stimulating commentary on this text in *Sur le Politique de Platon* (Paris: Editions du Seuil, 1999), pp. 155–173.

33. Plato, *Statesman* 294b, in *The Collected Dialogues of Plato,* ed. and trans. Edith Hamilton and Huntington Cairns (New York: Pantheon, 1961), p. 1063.

34. Vincent Descombes, "L'Illusion nomocratique," *Droits* 31 (2000), suggestively links the analysis of this question to the philosophical critique of totalitarianism.

35. In law, the contrast would be between the Civil Code and common law.

5. The Imperative of Governability

1. See Steven L. Kaplan, *La Fin des corporations* (Paris: Fayard, 2001).

2. For details of these regulations, see the section "Règlements sur le commerce de la boulangerie," in *Traité de la police municipale du comte Napoléon de Champagny* (Paris, 1847), vol. 2, pp. 687–750.

3. See the statute published in *Collection officielle des ordonnances de police,* printed by order of M. le Préfet de Police (Paris, 1880), vol. 1 (1800–1848), pp. 5–7. This collection contains many similar statutes.

4. Louis-Charles Bizet, *Du commerce de la boucherie et de la charcuterie à Paris* (Paris, 1847); and Hubert Bourgin, *L'Industrie de la boucherie à Paris pendant la Révolution* (Paris, 1911).

5. See L. Lanzac de Laborie, *Paris sous Napoléon,* vol. 6: *Le Mondes des affaires et du travail* (Paris, 1910), pp. 248–281.

6. Statement reported by François Nicolas Mollien in his *Mémoires d'un ministre du Trésor public (1780–1815)* (Paris, 1898), vol. 1, p. 266.

7. See the comments in the daily reports of the Prefecture of Police in Alphonse Aulard, *Paris sous le Consulat: Recueil de documents pour l'histoire de l'esprit public à Paris* (Paris, 1904–1906). See especially the reports of August and November 1801 (vol. 2, pp. 457, 483, 615), as well as September and December 1802 (vol. 3, pp. 232, 504).

8. See for example the questionnaire sent by the prefect of police to the butchers of Paris asking for their opinions about the organization of the profession, reproduced in the master's thesis of Marie-Caroline Saglio, *Le Renouveau du débat sur les corporations de métiers: Représentation symbolique des résistances sociales (1799–1821)* (Paris: Editions de l'EHESS, 1993). A more general questionnaire was subsequently sent to all merchants regarding the advantages

and disadvantages of reinstating the corporations. See also Jean-Antoine Chaptal's letters to Nicolas-Thérèse-Bênoit Frochot, then deputy of the Seine.

9. Reported by Adolphe Thiers, *Histoire du Consulat et de l'Empire* (Paris, n.d.), vol. 3, pp. 483 ff.

10. Report of 12 Germinal, Year XI, reprinted in *Le Moniteur universel,* 13 Germinal, Year XI, pp. 869–871. I shall have more to say later about this bill, which was adopted and led to the creation of "chambres consultatives de manufacturers, fabriques, arts et métiers."

11. After the butchers of Paris filed several petitions, the Conseil d'Etat drafted an "opinion for the minister of the interior" (reproduced in Saglio, *Le Renouveau du débat*). See Claire Lemercier, *Un Si Discret Pouvoir: Aux origines de la Chambre de commerce de Paris, 1803–1853* (Paris: La Découverte, 2003), for the earliest opinions (1803–04) of the Paris Chamber of Commerce.

12. See the remarks on this point in Paul Nourrisson, "Les Tentatives de restauration des corporations sous Napoléon Ier," *La Réforme sociale,* 1 August 1915, p. 155.

13. This petition, dated 14 Fructidor, Year XII (1 September 1804), contains proposed statutes for reorganizing the profession. It can be found in the appendix to Soufflot de Merey, *Considérations sur l'utilité des corporations, l'hérédité des offices et le rétablissement des jurandes et des maîtrises* (Paris, 1805).

14. Vital-Roux, *Rapport sur les jurandes et les maîtrises et sur un projet de statuts et règlements pour M. M. les marchands de vin* (Paris, 1805). This 180-page report went through several editions. For further comment on it, see Chapter 8.

15. See Archives Nationales, F12-502 (26); and Saglio, *Le Renouveau du débat*). Costaz refers to Vital-Roux's report in a postscript.

16. Toussaint-Bernard Emeric-David, *Projet d'un mémoire qui pourrait être intitulé: Essai sur les maîtrises des arts et métiers et sur les faillites,* February 1806 (Archives Nationales, F7-4283).

17. The issue was broached again in 1810, for example, and then twice more, on 24 November and 8 December 1814, in the Board of Manufactures. See Bertrand Gille, *Le Conseil général des manufactures: Inventaire analytique des procès-verbaux, 1810–1829* (Paris: SEVPEN, 1961), pp. 42–43.

18. My analysis is based on examination of the documents collected in *Analyse des procès-verbaux des conseils régionaux de département* for the four sessions of 1818–1820 (documents published by the Ministry of the Interior).

19. There is no need for exhaustive investigation here, because one can consult the many documents reproduced in Georges Bourgin and Hubert Bourgin, *Le Régime de l'industrie en France de 1814 à 1830* (Paris, 1912), esp. vols. 2 and 3. The issue was still coming up frequently in 1828.

20. Etienne Martin Saint-Léon, *Histoire des corporations de métiers* (Paris, 1922), p. 628.

21. Etienne-Antoine Feuillant, rapporteur for the budget committee, 9 March 1816, *A.P.,* 2d ser., vol. 16, p. 457. In a similar vein, see the speech of the comte de Marcellus, delivered on 1 May 1819, in support of a request by stonecutters to reinstate the *maîtrise* in their profession.

22. Louis-Pierre Deseine, *Mémoire sur la nécessité du rétablissement des maîtrises et corporations, comme moyens d'encourager l'industrie et le commerce* (Paris, 1815), p. 18.

23. This point was clearly noticed by Francis Demier, "L'Impossible Retour au régime des corporations dans la France de la Restauration, 1814–1830," in *Naissance des libertés économiques: Le décret d'Allarde et la loi Le Chapelier* (Paris: Institut d'Histoire de l'Industrie, 1993). Demier writes: "This type of movement can also be permeated by a presyndicalist worker logic, which is common among status-defined workers accustomed to controlling the labor market, as well as by a defensive employer logic, which seeks to protect the threatened trade and cope with new wage pressures. The very notion of corporation is particularly fluid and unstable. In some cases it can serve as the framework for new forms of worker solidarity, in others as a new way of organizing employers on the local level, besides which the restructured or reinstated 'corporation' can also be seen as an institution for coping with technical advances in the field" (p. 121).

24. See Kaplan, *La Fin des corporations,* pp. 523–527.

25. G. P. Legret, *Sur les corporations* (Paris, 1818), pp. 18–23. The "six *corps*" referred to here are the six principal Paris corporations, which played a dominant political and economic role.

26. Intervention at the Conseil d'Etat, 22 November 1811, in Jean Bourdon, *Napoléon au Conseil d'Etat* (Paris, 1963), p. 173.

27. Prosper Enfantin, "De la concurrence dans les entreprises industrielles," *Le Producteur,* 3 (1826), 390–391.

28. Charles Béranger, *Religion saint-simonienne: La concurrence* (Paris, n.d. [1832]), p. 1.

29. Jean Charles Léonard Simonde de Sismondi, *Nouveaux Principes d'économie politique, ou de la richesse dans ses rapports avec la population,* 2d ed. (Paris, 1827), vol. 1, p. 435: "We must look to this experience for the limits that legislative authority should place on competition."

30. These expressions can be found in Bénard, *Mémoire sur le rétablissement des maîtrises et des corporations* (Arras, 1823).

31. See the examples in Michael David Sibalis, "Corporatism after the Corporations: The Debate on Restoring the Guilds under Napoleon I and the Restoration," *French Historical Studies,* 25 (Fall 1988), 722.

32. Legret, *Sur les corporations,* p. 27.

33. The expression is taken from Michel Frédéric Pillet-Will, one of the pil-

lars of the Paris Chamber of Commerce, quoted in Saglio, *Le Renouveau du débat*, p. 70.

34. See Kaplan, *La Fin des corporations*.

35. Quoted in ibid., p. 84. The image of a "vast sphere," which is used here to evoke a threat, was also used in a positive sense by Sieyès.

36. Intervention of Antoine-Louis Séguier, advocate-general, at the Parlement of Paris, 12 March 1776, in Jules Flammermont, ed., *Remontrances du Parlement de Paris au XVIIIe siècle* (Geneva: Megariotis Reprints, 1978), vol. 3, p. 346.

37. Emeric-David, *Projet d'un mémoire*, p. 39.

38. Antoine Levacher-Duplessis, *Réponse des délégués des marchands en détail et des maîtres artisans de la ville de Paris aux rapports et délibérations des conseils généraux du commerce et des manufactures établis auprès de Son Excellence le ministre de l'Intérieur* (Paris, 1821), p. 19.

39. *Requête au roi*, p. 39.

40. Ibid., p. 17.

41. Ibid., p. 39.

42. This theme, which we cannot develop here, played a central role in the portrayal of the nascent market society by writers like Adam Smith and Condillac. Condorcet also dealt with the issue in his *Quatrième Mémoire sur l'instruction relative aux professions*, in *Oeuvres de Condorcet*, ed. A. O'Connor and F. Arago (Paris, 1847), vol. 7, pp. 378 ff. Conversely, we find the opposite view at the center of all the militant writing about the need to reinstate the corporations.

43. Louis Costaz, *Projet d'une loi relative aux manufactures et aux gens de travail de toutes professions* (Paris, Fructidor, Year IX).

44. See especially William H. Sewell, *Work and Revolution in France: The Language of Labor from the Old Regime to 1848* (Cambridge: Cambridge University Press, 1980). See also the various works of Alain Cottereau.

45. These words were apparently coined by Fourier. See Berke Vardar, *Structure fondamentale du vocabulaire social et politique en France, de 1815 à 1830* (Istanbul, 1973), p. 224. The fifth edition of the *Dictionnaire de l'Académie française* (1814) gives a very broad definition of *corporation*: "Association authorized by the government and consisting of several persons who abide by a set of common regulations pertaining to their profession."

46. Soufflot de Merey, *Considérations sur le rétablissement des jurandes et maîtrises, précédées d'observations sur un rapport à la chambre de commerce du département de la Seine sur cette importante question, et sur un projet de statuts et de règlements de M. M. les marchands de vin* (Paris, Year XIII [1805]). It was published in response to Vital-Roux's anticorporatist screed of the same year, discussed later in the chapter.

47. Ibid., p. 54.

48. Louis-Pierre Deseine, *Mémoire sur la nécessité du rétablissement des maîtrises et corporations, comme moyens d'encourager l'industrie et le commerce* (Paris, 1815), p. 11. In the same spirit, see the remarks of a printer who played a highly active role in this debate: "When the community existed, the constant surveillance that all its members exercised over each of them, together with the desire to obtain municipal and other posts and the fear of being excluded from them, prevented dishonorable actions and bankruptcies. Merchants were judged as merchants and even more as citizens, and the result of this was a general probity, from which everyone benefited." See Stoupe, *Mémoire sur le rétablissement de la communauté des imprimeurs à Paris* (Paris, 1806), p. 2.

49. Soufflot de Merey, p. 89.

50. Claude-Anthelme Costaz, *Histoire de l'administration en France*, 3d ed. (Paris, 1843), vol. 1, p. 189.

51. Henrion de Pansey, *De l'autorité judiciaire en France* (1810), 3d ed. (Paris, 1827), vol. 2, p. 433. "The reasons for which the corporations were established have lost none of their force, and experience may demonstrate their wisdom," he concluded. The great Jean Domat had earlier insisted on the link between "oversight" and the ability to take account of "a host of small details," so that the state had good reason to delegate the task to men who practiced the same craft or profession. See *Droit public* (Paris, 1697), book 1, title 13, sec. 1: "De la police ou discipline des arts et métiers."

52. See Oliver E. Williamson, *The Economic Institutions of Capitalism* (Glencoe, Ill.: Free Press, 1998); and Oliver E. Williamson and Sidney G. Winter, *The Nature of the Firm: Origins, Evolution and Development* (New York: Oxford University Press, 1991); as well as Ronald H. Coase, *The Firm, the Market, and the Law* (Chicago: University of Chicago Press, 1990). Hilton Root, writing as a historian versed in economic analysis, points out that the evolution of corporate regulations in France showed how much transaction costs weighed on institutional choices. See *The Fountain of Privilege: Political Foundations of Markets* (Berkeley: University of California Press, 1994), pp. 110–113.

53. See Pierre Rosanvallon, *Le Moment Guizot* (Paris: Gallimard, 1985).

54. On the term *gouvernabilité*, see Ferdinand Brunot, *Histoire de la langue française des origines à 1900*, vol. 12, p. 382; and G. Matoré, *Le Vocabulaire et la société sous Louis-Philippe*, 2d ed. (Geneva: Slatkine, 1967), p. 38. Thus there is nothing very new about the question of "governance."

55. In *Oeuvres de Turgot et documents le concernant*, ed. Gustave Schelle (Paris, 1919), vol. 3, pp. 625–626.

56. Legret, *Sur les corporations*, p. 27.

57. Ibid., p. 26. Thus corporations were portrayed as an impediment to an inquisitorial state. With corporations, the government need not delve into

"family secrets" to be fiscally effective (thus allaying the great fear of eighteenth-century economists).

58. See, for example, Feuillant, rapporteur for the budget commission, 9 March 1816, *A.P.*, 2d ser., vol. 16, pp. 453–458.

59. *Réponse des délégués des marchands en détail et des maîtres artisans de la ville de Paris aux rapports et délibérations des conseils généraux du commerce et des manufactures,* p. 19.

60. Soufflot de Merey, *Considérations sur le rétablissement des jurandes et maîtrises,* p. 65.

61. Ibid., p. 92. "To oppose the spirit of system to experience," he went on, "is to oppose myth to history. It is to oppose definite, undeniable results to the brilliant sophisms of the innovative mind and the uncertain calculations of a dangerous theory" (p. 99).

62. Levacher-Duplessis, *Réponse des délégués des marchands,* p. 19.

63. Louis-Charles Bizet, *Du commerce de la boucherie et de la charcuterie à Paris* (Paris, 1847), p. 8.

64. Jean Charles Léonard Simonde de Sismondi, *De la richesse commerciale ou principes d'économie politique appliqués à la législation du commerce* (Geneva, 1803), p. 275. See chap. 5, pp. 274–298.

65. Idem, *Nouveaux Principes,* pp. 364, 498.

66. Idem, *Etudes sur l'économie politique* (Paris, 1838), vol. 2, p. 337.

6. The Sociological Trial

1. François Guizot, speech of 3 May 1819 to the Chamber of Deputies, *A.P.*, 2d ser., vol. 24, p. 166.

2. "It is not enough to constitute the government. It is also necessary to organize society," noted the jurist Henrion de Pansey, repeating a thought that was on everyone's mind. See *Du pouvoir municipal* (Paris, 1824), p. 8.

3. Quoted in Xavier Martin, "L'Individualisme libéral en France autour de 1800: Essai de spectroscopie," *Revue d'histoire des facultés de droit et de la science juridique,* no. 4 (1987). Concerning the question of social dissolution, see Rosanvallon, "La Peur du nombre," in *Le Moment Guizot* (Paris: Gallimard, 1985).

4. Félicité Robert de Lamennais, quoted in Paul Benichou, *Le Temps des prophètes: Doctrines de l'âge romantique* (Paris: Gallimard, 1977), p. 138.

5. Chateaubriand, *Essai sur la littérature anglaise,* p. 118; idem, *Mémoires d'outre-tombe* (conclusion) (Paris: Gallimard, 1951), vol. 2, p. 918.

6. Pierre Leroux, *Aux philosophes: De la situation actuelle de l'esprit humain* (1831), reproduced in David Owen Evans, *Le Socialisme romantique: Pierre Leroux et ses contemporains* (Paris, 1948), p. 213.

7. Speech of 29 December 1830 to the Chamber of Deputies, in François Guizot, *Histoire parlementaire de France* (Paris, 1863), vol. 1, p. 178.

8. Charles de Rémusat, "Des moeurs du temps," *Le Globe,* 5 (26 August 1826), 29.

9. See Rosanvallon, "Déchiffrer la France," in *Le Peuple introuvable* (Paris: Gallimard, 1998).

10. Joseph de Villèle, speech of 6 February 1817, *A.P.,* 2d ser., vol. 18, p. 588.

11. Leroux, *Aux philosophes.*

12. Conversation between Joseph de Maistre and Charles de Lavau, 1820, in *Oeuvres complètes de Joseph de Maistre* (Lyons, 1886), vol. 14, p. 286.

13. See François de Corcelle, *Documents pour servir à l'histoire des conspirations et des sectes* (Paris, 1831), pp. 19–20. This "Society of Individualists" appeared on the scene in 1823.

14. See Jean-Jacques Goblot, *La Jeune France libérale: Le Globe et son groupe littéraire, 1824–1830* (Paris: Plon, 1995), pp. 172 ff. For preliminary work on the history of the word, see Konraad Swart, "Individualism in the Mid-Nineteenth-Century (1826–1860)," *Journal of the History of Ideas,* January–March 1962.

15. See Laurent, "De la foi de l'examen," *Le Producteur,* 2 (1826), 538, on "the spirit of hostility [that is] inseparable from the reign of individualism." He also used the word in "De l'inégalité," ibid., 3 (1826), 492–494; as did Prosper Enfantin in "Conversion morale d'un rentier: Deuxième lettre," ibid., 4 (1826), 241.

16. Philarète Chasles, *Etudes sur les hommes et les moeurs au XIXe siècle* (Paris, 1849), p. 253.

17. Balzac, *César Birotteau,* in *L'Oeuvre de Balzac* (Paris: Le Club Français du Livre, 1966), vol. 2, p. 354.

18. See Georges Matoré, *Le Vocabulaire et la société sous Louis-Philippe,* 2d ed. (Geneva: Slatkine, 1967); and Francis Wey, *Remarques sur la langue française au XIXe siècle,* vol. 1 (Paris, 1865).

19. Ferdinand Béchard, *Essai sur la centralisation administrative* (Paris, 1836), vol. 1, p. 53.

20. Félix de La Farelle, *Plan d'une réorganisation disciplinaire des classes industrielles de la France* (1842), reproduced in *Du progrès social au profit des classes populaires non indigentes,* 2d ed. (Paris, 1847), p. 466.

21. See his celebrated chapter "On Individualism in Democratic Countries." A properly philosophical history of the concept of individualism would need to make room for Théodore Jouffroy's *Cours de droit naturel* (1834). On this point, see Lucien Jaume, *L'Individu effacé ou le paradoxe du libéralisme français* (Paris: Fayard, 1977).

22. Benjamin Constant, preface to *Mélanges de littérature et de politique* (Paris, 1829), p. vi.

23. François Guizot, *Histoire de la civilisation en France,* 2d ed. (Paris, 1840), vol. 1, pp. 251–252. To be sure, this warning did not prevent him from recognizing the problem. Speaking of a movement that he believed to be associated with "the introduction of the principle of equality," he noted: "From this it follows that in France today there is only the government on one side and citizens or individuals on the other. The public authority is the only real and powerful force. There remain virtually none of the intermediary and local powers that are created by aristocratic patronage or corporate ties or private privileges, powers that, by exercising avowed rights and a positive force within their jurisdiction, relieve the central government of part of the care necessary to maintain order everywhere"; speech of 3 May 1819, *A.P.,* 2d ser., vol. 24, p. 166.

24. Hercule de Serre, speech of 17 December 1816, *A.P.,* 2d ser., vol. 17, p. 716.

25. In his enthusiasm, de Serre went so far as to rehabilitate revolutionary associations! "At the height of our revolution," he said, "associations were formed, for criminal purposes to be sure, but their power is clear. I am far from calling for secret societies. They are vexing to governments. Their very zeal may compromise them. But if they offer no model, they do offer useful lessons. Make them public and general, and they will pose no threat"; ibid.

26. Charles de Coux, "Des associations patriotiques," *L'Avenir,* 21 March 1831, reproduced in *Articles de "L'Avenir"* (Louvain, 1831), vol. 3, p. 325.

27. It went through three printings in the 1820s.

28. "Rapport sur les travaux de la Société de la morale chrétienne pendant l'année 1822," *Journal de la Société de la morale chrétienne* 2, no. 11 (1823), 241.

29. Ibid., p. 247.

30. Publication commenced in 1832.

31. In his *Discours aux politiques* (1832), he held that only two political systems were possible: individualism and association. The latter was preferable because "society today is reaching the final stages of individualism and disassociation." See *Oeuvres de Pierre Leroux* (Paris, 1850), vol. 1, p. 196.

32. Ferdinand Béchard, *Essai sur la centralisation administrative,* vol. 1, p. 4. "The time has come to replace the destructive principle of individualism with the conservative law of sociability"; ibid., p. vi. On this very important author of the 1830s and 1840s, see H. Carpentier de Changy, *Le Parti légitimiste sous la monarchie de juillet,* 4 vols. (University of Paris XII, 1980).

33. On the opposition between "bachelor spirit" and "family spirit," see references in Matoré, *Le Vocabulaire et la société sous Louis-Philippe,* p. 22.

34. The law of 8 May 1816 reinstated divorce. Bonald had initiated the debate in 1801 by publishing *Du divorce, considéré au XIXe siècle relativement à l'état de la société.* See François Ronsin, "Indissolubilité du mariage ou divorce: Essai d'une chronologie des principaux arguments mis en avant par les par-

tisans et les adversaires de l'institution du divorce au cours de la période révolutionnaire," in *La Famille, la loi, l'état, de la Révolution au Code civil* (Paris: Imprimerie Nationale, 1989).

35. La Révellière-Lépeaux, *Réflexions sur le culte, sur les cérémonies civiles et sur les fêtes nationales* (Paris, Year V), p. 58.

36. Mona Ozouf, *Les Aveux du roman* (Paris: Fayard, 2001), pp. 302–303.

37. Pierre Leroux, "De l'individualisme et du socialisme," *Revue encyclopédique,* 1834, reprinted in *Oeuvres,* vol. 1, pp. 365–380. See what Leroux said about this neologism in *La Grève de Samarez* (1863), ed. Jean-Pierre Lacassagne (Paris: Klincksieck), vol. 1, p. 233. On the history of the word "socialism," see Gabriel Deville, "Origine des mots 'socialisme,' 'socialiste' et de quelques autres," *La Révolution française,* 54 (1908), which refers to occurrences as early as 1831 in the Protestant newspaper *Le Semeur;* Jacques Grandjonc, *Communisme/kommunisme/communism: Origine et développement interna- tional de la terminologie communautaire prémarxiste, des utopistes aux néo- babouvistes, 1785–1842,* vol. 1 (Trèves, 1989), chap. 2; Sonia Branca-Rosoff and Jacques Guilhaumou, "De 'société' à 'socialisme': L'invention néologique et son contexte discursif," *Langage et société,* nos. 83–84 (March–June 1998). The latter authors note that Sieyès, a great one for neologisms, had proposed in one of his unpublished youthful manuscripts writing a "Treatise on Social- ism." He did not use the term subsequently, however.

38. Quoted in Paul Bénichou, *Les Mages romantiques* (Paris: Gallimard, 1987), p. 51.

39. The expression can be found in his speech of 13 March 1834 on a bill con- cerning associations; Alphonse de Lamartine, *La France parlementaire (1834– 1851)* (Paris, 1864), vol. 1, p. 30.

40. In a letter to Anacharsis Combes, 29 March 1834, in *Correspondance d'Alphonse de Lamartine (1830–1867)* (Paris: Champion, 2000), vol. 2, p. 157.

41. Joseph de Villèle, speech of 13 December 1815, *A.P.,* 2d ser., vol. 15, p. 437. On the reception of this speech, see *Souvenirs du baron de Barante* (Paris, 1890– 1901), vol. 2, p. 219.

42. Letter to his father, 14 December 1815, in *Mémoires et correspondance du comte de Villèle* (Paris, 1888), vol. 1, p. 410.

43. Speech of 30 December 1816, *A.P.,* 2d ser., vol. 17, pp. 770–771.

44. Thus the theme of decentralization is prominent in Eugène d'Arnaud de Vitrolles's *Declaration de la majorité:* "We believe that the interests of subjects must be entrusted largely to local administrations, be they municipal, depart- mental, or provincial; that the centralization of all business and decision- making in Paris is abusive; and that it must cease, with the grant of more ex- tensive powers to senior agents delegated by the ministers. It is with these principles in mind that we call for revision of the administrative laws"; *Mémoires de Vitrolles,* new ed. (Paris, 1952), vol. 2, p. 304.

45. For a typical example of this nostalgia, see the pamphlet by Tocqueville's father, *De la charte provinciale* (Paris, 1829).

46. Speech to the Chamber of Deputies, 2 January 1822, quoted in Prosper de Barante, *La Vie politique de M. Royer-Collard*, vol. 2, p. 131.

47. *Appel au parti national.* See also, in the same vein, Honoré de Lourdoueix, *Appel à la France contre la division des opinions* (Paris, 1831), which contains a highly detailed "plan for municipal, departmental, and communal organization."

48. While awaiting a systematic synthesis of this vast topic, one can continue to use Henri Desroches et al., *Etudes sur la tradition française de l'association ouvrière* (Paris, 1955).

49. Prospectus of *L'Artisan, journal de la classe ouvrière,* 22 September 1830.

50. See the essential documentation collected in Octave Festy, *Le Mouvement ouvrier au début de la monarchie de juillet (1830–1834)* (Paris, 1908). See also the hundreds of workers' pamphlets from the period reproduced in *Les Révolutions du XIXe siècle (1830–1834),* 1st ser. (Paris: EDHIS, 1974), vols. 4–6 (birth of the workers' movement in Lyons and Paris).

51. See François-André Isambert, *Buchez, ou l'âge théologique de la sociologie* (Paris: Cujas, 1967).

52. Quoted in William Sewell, "La Confraternité des prolétaires: Conscience de classe sous la monarchie de Juillet," *Annales ESC,* July–August 1981, p. 660.

53. Jules Leroux, *Aux ouvriers typographes: De la nécessité de fonder une association ayant pour but de rendre les ouvriers propriétaires des instruments de travail* (Paris, 1833), p. 11.

54. Ibid., p. 9.

55. William H. Sewell, *Work and Revolution in France: The Language of Labor from the Old Regime to 1848* (Cambridge: Cambridge University Press, 1980).

56. See the collection of historical documents published by the Office du Travail, *Les Associations ouvrières professionnelles,* 4 vols. (Paris, 1894–1899).

57. *Le National,* 3 December 1833.

58. Published in 1861 in a series of "workers' pamphlets." In this text we read that "the organization of corporations is an essential condition of liberty." But this statement is accompanied by a crucial qualification: "What we are demanding is not the restoration of the old corporations with *jurandes* and *maîtrises* but the constitution of new corporations based on the suffrage of all their members" (p. 6). The pamphlet bears the signatures of a hundred authors, many of whom would also sign the *Manifeste des soixante* of 1864.

59. See Robert Brécy, *Le Mouvement syndical en France, 1871, 1921* (Paris: Editions du Signe, 1982) and *Congrès du monde ouvrier: France, 1870–1940* (Paris: CODHOS, 2002). A split within the CGTU led to abandonment of this vocabulary.

60. Maxime Leroy, *La Coutume ouvrière,* 2 vols. (Paris, 1913).

7. The Requirement of Liberty

1. Marc Marie René de Voyer d'Argenson, *Considérations sur le gouvernement ancien et présent de la France* (Amsterdam, 1764), p. 142.

2. Paul Henri d'Holbach, *Politique naturelle ou discours sur les vrais principes du gouvernment* (London, 1773), quoted in Denis Richet, "Autour des origines idéologiques lointaines de la Révolution française: Elites et despotisme," *Annales ESC*, January–February 1969.

3. On this point see the illuminating work of Catherine Secretan, *Les Privilèges, berceau de la liberté* (Paris: Vrin, 1990).

4. Joseph Fievée, "Développement de la 1re lettre," (21 May 1814), in *Correspondance politique et administrative* (Paris, 1815), p. 47. Another public intellectual characterized *communes* as "democratic corporations," stressing their character as intermediary bodies; see Conrad Malte-Brun, *Les Partis, esquisse morale et politique* (Paris, 1818), pp. 337–338.

5. Fievée, "Développement de la 1re lettre," p. 37. See also, by the same author in the same vein, *De la pairie, des libertés locales et de la liste civile* (Paris, 1831).

6. Balancing this judgment, he argued that "individualism is contrary to liberty." See Ferdinand Béchard, *Essai sur la centralisation administrative* (Paris, 1836), vol. 1, p. 7.

7. Cf. his comment: "In an aristocracy, the people are protected against the excesses of despotism, because organized forces prepared to resist the despot are always at hand. A democracy without provincial institutions possesses no guarantee against such evils"; Alexis de Tocqueville, *Democracy in America*, trans. Arthur Goldhammer (New York: Library of America, 2004), p. 108.

8. Ibid., p. 68.

9. Benjamin Constant, *De l'esprit de conquête et de l'usurpation*, 3d ed. (Paris, 1814), p. 48.

10. "What does despotism always require, notwithstanding the form in which it presents itself?" asked de Serre. "Ground so leveled that nothing escapes its gaze, a mass of peoples so pulverized that no common interest holds them together to limit its action"; letter to Lainé, December 1816, in *Correspondance du comte de Serre (1796–1824)* (Paris, 1876–77), vol. 2, p. 177.

11. Benjamin Constant, *Principes de politique* (Geneva: Droz, 1980), vol. 2, p. 389. See also the chapter "De l'uniformité," in *De l'esprit de conquête et de l'usurpation*, which includes similar statements.

12. Pierre Claude François Daunou, speech of 31 January 1831, *A.P.*, 2d ser., vol. 66, p. 437. "In a country as vast as France," he explained, "one of the first needs of government is to protect against the various ways in which its numerous and diverse agents may abuse its trust. And since, in order to guard against an eventual weakening or flagging of its power, it must seek a counterweight to the power that they exercise in its name so far from its eyes, I know

of none more authentic than the surveillance of the municipal councils elected by popular suffrage to express the wishes and, if need be, the complaints of citizens."

13. Charles de Rémusat, *Journal de la Société de la morale chrétienne,* 2 (1823), 247.

14. See, for example, Lerminier's important article "Science du droit" on Savigny's 1814 manifesto, "De la vocation de notre siècle pour la législation et la science du droit," *Le Globe,* 5 (18 August 1827), 3.

15. For a preliminary assessment of his work in this sense, see the papers in *Des libertés et des peines: Actes du Colloque Pellegrino Rossi organisé à Genève, les 23 et 24 novembre 1979* (Geneva: Georg, 1980).

16. Although the edict of 21 October 1790 theoretically allowed meetings and associations (not clearly distinguished at the time), coalitions of workers and popular societies were explicitly banned, as were various corporations suspected of constituting potential "states within the state" (like the congregations).

17. See Duvergier de Hauranne's two articles "Des associations," *Le Globe,* 6 (5 and 16 April 1828).

18. See for example the article "De l'association comme moyen de remédier à la misère des classes ouvrières," *L'Artisan, journal de la classe ouvrière,* no. 4 (17 October 1830).

19. See *L'Artisan,* no. 2 (5 October 1830). There was also a long commentary on this development in *Le Producteur.*

20. "Du droit de coalition," *L'Echo de la fabrique,* 8 December 1833 (the paper has been reproduced in a two-volume edition by Editions EDHIS, Paris, 1973).

21. "De l'association industrielle," *L'Echo de la fabrique,* 26 January 1834. See also the important article "De la nécessité pour tous les travailleurs de se rallier aux associations," ibid., 9 February 1834.

22. See the brochures reproduced in vols. 4–6 of the first series of *Les Révolutions du XIXe siècle (1830–1834)* (Paris: EDHIS, 1974). See also the pertinent remarks of Alain Faure, "Mouvements populaires et mouvement ouvrier à Paris (1830–1834)," *Le Mouvement social,* no. 88 (July–September 1974).

23. See, for example, "Sur la question des ouvriers de Lyon et sur la question des associations," 19 March 1833.

24. Félicité de Lamennais, "Des doctrines de 'L'Avenir,'" 7 December 1830, reproduced in *Mélanges catholiques: Extraits de "L'Avenir"* (Paris, 1831), vol. 1, p. 15.

25. The law increased the penalties for violation of Article 291 of the Penal Code and interpreted the "twenty-member" limit in a restrictive sense (to prevent camouflaging larger associations by dividing them into smaller "sections").

26. Odilon Barrot, 17 March 1834, *A.P.,* 2d ser., vol. 87, p. 530.

27. Pierre Antoine Berryer, 12 March 1834, ibid., p. 413.

28. On this point see "L'Ordre capacitaire," in Rosanvallon, *Le Sacre du citoyen: Histoire du suffrage universel en France* (Paris: Gallimard, 1992). The number of voters had increased fourfold by 1817 and eightfold by 1830.

29. Alexandre Pilenco, *Les Moeurs électorales en France: Régime censitaire* (Paris, 1928), p. 104.

30. There are also reports of committees formed for the elections of 1824.

31. For an early study of this society, see Charles Pouthas, *Guizot pendant la Restauration: Préparation de l'homme d'état (1814–1830)* (Paris, 1923); as well as Prosper Duvergier de Hauranne, *Histoire du gouvernement parlementaire en France*, vol. 9: *1814–1830* (Paris, 1869). See also documents collected in series Lb49(661–1260) of the Bibliothèque Nationale de France.

32. The popular societies of their Revolution also created networks of affiliated societies, but these had almost nothing to do with electoral activities. See Jean Boutier, Philippe Boutry, and Serge Bonin, *Les Sociétés politiques*, vol. 6 of *Atlas de la Révolution française* (Paris: Editions de l'EHESS, 1992).

33. See the description given in the Chamber of Deputies on 19 June 1819 by the deputy Jean Joseph Antoine Courvoisier, *A.P.*, 2d ser., vol. 25, p. 22: "Some talk of petitions and plots. One of the previous speakers asked for proof. I shall provide at least a presumption of truth. In Paris there is a head committee, and its relations with one of the principal cities of France take the following the form. A central committee of nine members corresponds with the head committee in Paris. It receives instructions, or, rather, orders. Each of its nine members seeks to form another committee, over which he presides. Then these subcommittees enter into correspondence with the rest of the *département*. This organization has been tried in other places. That is how petitions are solicited and obtained. (Vociferous and lengthy agitation in the chamber.)"

34. See [Ludovic Vitet,] *Aide-toi, le ciel t'aidera: Aux citoyens et aux électeurs* (Paris, 1827), pp. 4–5, which contains the statement that "the country is just beginning to learn when it comes to associations."

35. The law banned groups that met every day or on specifically scheduled days.

36. See the report by La Villegontier, 11 March 1828, *A.P.*, 2d ser., vol. 53, p. 27. During the debate, however, several peers raised the specter of a return of "clubs."

37. Benjamin Constant, speech of 29 March 1828, ibid., p. 184.

38. Circular of 21 October 1828, reproduced in Georges-Denis Weil, *Le Droit d'association et le droit de réunions devant les chambres et les tribunaux* (Paris, 1893), p. 65.

39. Félix Barthe, speech to the Chamber, 24 March 1834, *A.P.*, 2d ser., vol. 88, p. 17.

40. See *Le National*, 4 October 1846. All the documents I consulted on the repub-

lican committees of 1846 were provided by Stephen Sawyer, whom I thank for his assistance.

41. See André-Jean Tudesq, "Les Notables et les élections de 1846," in *Les Grands Notables en France (1840–1849)* (Paris, 1964), vol. 2.
42. See Raymond Huard, "Les Pratiques électorales en France en 1848," in *1848: Actes du colloque international du cent cinquantenaire, tenu à l'Assemblée nationale à Paris, les 23–25 février 1998* (Grâne: Créaphis, 2002).
43. See Alexandre Auguste Ledru-Rollin's circular of 12 March (*Bulletin de la République,* no. 1 [13 March 1848]) and the declaration of the provisional government (*Moniteur,* 19 March 1848).
44. Journal de Villefranche, 13 April 1848, quoted in René Lecour, La Révolution de 1848 dans le Beaujolais et la campagne lyonnaise (Lyons, 1954), p. 49.

8. Resistance and Reconfiguration

1. Louis Florent-Lefebvre, *De la décentralisation: Essai d'un système de centralisation politique et de décentralisation administrative* (Paris, 1849), p. 1.
2. For a history of the sudden abandonment of reform projects, see Rudolf Von Thadden, *La Centralisation contestée: L'administration napoléonienne, enjeu politique de la Restauration (1814–1830)* (Arles: Actes Sud, 1989); Stefano Mannoni, *Une et indivisible: Storia dell'accentramento amministrativo in Francia* (Milan: Giuffré, 1996), vol. 2; Charles Pouthas, "Les Projets de réforme administrative sous la Restauration," *Revue d'histoire moderne,* October–November 1926.
3. "Take care," he wrote. "The provincial and municipal system might well be today nothing more than a means of seizing at the source an authority that seems too difficult to acquire at the center of government"; Note IV to Frédéric Ancillon, *De la souveraineté et des formes de gouvernment* (Paris, 1816), p. 158.
4. Letter from Montlosier to Hercule de Serre, 17 March 1821, in *Correspondance du comte de Serre (1796–1824)* (Paris, 1876), vol. 4, p. 188.
5. Report of Jacques-Barthélemey Noaille, session of 16 February 1810, reproduced in Dalloz, "Associations illicites," in *Répertoire méthodique et alphabétique de législation, de doctrine et de jurisprudence* (Paris, 1846), vol. 5, p. 282.
6. The law of 10 April 1834 tightened restrictions on obtaining legal authorization to associate, particularly in regard to the interpretation of the twenty-member threshold. It broadened the definition of an association and blurred the boundary between an association and a simple meeting. Finally, it increased prison sentences and fines for violators.
7. Presentation of 25 February 1834, *A.P.,* 2d ser., vol. 86, pp. 690–692.

8. "I have always felt that this was not an individual right, like the exercise of individual freedom or freedom of the press or the right of petition; that it was a matter of transforming oneself, as it were, into a body within the state, of constituting a moral person having a civil existence distinct from the individual"; André Marie Jacques Dupin (known as Dupin Aîné), intervention of 21 March 1834, *A.P.*, 2d ser., vol. 87, p. 705.

9. Emile de Kératry, intervention of 11 March 1834, ibid., p. 365.

10. Ibid.

11. François Guizot, intervention of 12 March 1834, ibid., p. 409. In a similar vein, Kératry said that "the time has come when fathers must know, when they return home to their families every night, whether they will be allowed to relax in peace in their own homes or be called by the sound of drums to go put down the nightly riots staged by these associations"; ibid., p. 406.

12. Girod de l'Ain, 5 April 1834, *A.P.*, 2d ser., vol. 88, p. 304. Guizot noted that in his view the law "obviously is not aimed at literary or scientific associations." But in explaining why associations of these kinds should not be explicitly protected, he added: "We do not wish names to be used as masks to evade the law and to allow the political associations that the Chamber wishes to eliminate to reestablish themselves" (speech of 21 March 1834).

13. Guizot remarked that "this was a circumstantial law, which I remain convinced was necessary . . . but which should have been presented as an exceptional measure to remain in force for a limited period of time." See his *Mémoires pour servir à l'histoire de mon temps* (Paris, 1860), vol. 3, p. 230.

14. The concept of "minority" also needs to be understood in the context of property qualifications for voting.

15. See, in particular, the important law of 29 July 1848.

16. Another law of 27 November 1849 imposed even harsher sanctions for the crime of "coalition." These were removed only much later, in legislation passed in 1864 and 1884.

17. *Le Publiciste*, 30 Pluviôse, Year VIII (19 February 1800).

18. Adolphe Thiers, speech of 6 May 1833 on municipal prerogatives, *A.P.*, vol. 83, p. 399.

19. Ibid., p. 403.

20. Vital-Roux, *Rapport sur les jurandes et les maîtrises et sur un projet de statuts et règlements pour M. M. les marchands de vin* (Paris, 1805), p. 2.

21. Ibid., p. 42.

22. Ibid., pp. 102–103; emphasis added.

23. Ibid., p. 111.

24. Ibid., pp. 152 ff.

25. Ibid., pp. 176–177.

26. "The only real corporation," he wrote, "is the entire nation"; ibid., p. 47.

27. Ibid., p. 51. Similarly, he held that "no third-party arbitration" was possible

between the judge and the consumer (ibid., p. 139). "The authorities need no assistance from master tradesmen to ensure the public tranquility. Indeed, we believe that they would be ill served by intermediaries so inapt to serve as their organ" (p. 108).

28. Cf. pp. 130–131. The idea of an industrial code or manufacturing code was revived in an 1810 report by Louis-Guillaume Ternaux, published by the Conseil Général des Fabriques et Manufactures. See Paul Nourrisson, "Les Tentatives de restauration des corporations sous Napoléon Ier," *La Réforme sociale*, 1 August 1915, p. 151.

29. Louis-Antoine Macarel, *Cours de droit administratif* (Paris, 1846), vol. 4, p. 19. See the chapter "Des corporations d'arts et métiers," pp. 13–20.

30. See in particular Emile Vincens, *Exposition raisonnée de la législation commerciale* (Paris, 1819). On his thinking, see the interesting remarks in Jean-Pierre Hirsch, *Les Deux Rêves de commerce: Entreprise et institutions dans la région lilloise (1780–1860)* (Paris: Editions de l'EHESS, 1991), pp. 51–58.

31. Charles Dunoyer, *De la liberté du travail* (Paris, 1845), vol. 1, p. 172. This question was discussed at length in a lively debate involving Victor Cousin and others at the Académie des Sciences Morales et Politiques. See "Des limites de l'économie politique," in *Oeuvres de Charles Dunoyer* (Paris, 1870), vol. 3: *Notices d'économie sociale*, pp. 485–517.

32. Dunoyer, *De la liberté du travail*, vol. 1, p. 173.

33. Prosper de Barante, *Des communes et de l'aristocratie* (Paris, 1821). The work was regularly reprinted up to the 1860s.

34. Ibid., p. 66.

35. Rémusat's comments on one of the new editions of Barante's work are particularly eloquent in this respect: "M. de Barante has been particularly struck by two things: on the one hand, the difficulty, so often deplored by a certain school of writers and orators, of establishing a stable order and regular government in a nation without social hierarchy; and, on the other hand, the impossibility, too often ignored by the same men, of reviving class distinctions and corporations in a society in which events, opinions, and laws have conspired for more than a century to reduce everything to individuals." See *Le Globe*, 7 (28 February 1829), 131.

36. François Guizot, *Des moyens d'opposition et de gouvernement* (Paris, 1821), p. 164.

37. Idem, *Archives philosophiques, politiques et littéraires*, 3 (June 1818), 406.

38. Saint-Simon, *Essai sur l'organisation sociale* (1803), reproduced as an appendix to *Lettres d'un habitant de Genève à ses contemporains*, ed. Alfred Pereire (Paris, 1925), p. 93.

39. Auguste Comte, *Considérations sur le pouvoir spirituel* (1815), in *Opuscules de philosophie sociale (1819–1828)* (Paris, 1883), p. 272.

40. Félicité Robert de Lamennais, "Recension de la réponse aux quatre concor-

dats de M. de Pradi," *Le Conservateur,* 3, no. 36 (1819), 440. On Lamennais's search for a social-Christian order, see Jean-René Derré, *Lamennais, ses amis et le mouvement des idées à l'époque romantique: 1824–1834* (Paris, 1962).

41. Lamennais, "Recension de la réponse aux quatre concordats."

42. Saint-Simon, *Lettres d'un habitant de Genève,* pp. 66–67.

43. "Philosophy aspires to do what it has already done in other periods, namely, to bestow religious answers upon humanity and become a religion." See Pierre Leroux, "De la tendance nouvelle des idées," *Revue encyclopédique,* January 1832, p. 5.

44. Edgar Quinet, *Examen de la vie de Jésus* (1838), in *Premiers Travaux,* vol. 8 of *Oeuvres complètes* (Paris, Hachette, 1882), p. 211.

45. Jules Michelet, entry for 7 August 1831, *Journal* (Paris: Gallimard, 1959), vol. 1, p. 83. The key to the French character, he wrote, was that in it "the general dominates." With "beautiful centralization . . . spirit has triumphed over matter, and the general has triumphed over the particular"; *Histoire de France,* 2d ed. (Paris, 1852), vol. 2, pp. 117–124.

46. François Guizot, "Réflexions sur l'organisation municipale et sur les conseils généraux de département," *Archives philosophiques, politiques et littéraires,* 4, no. 16 (October 1818).

47. Ibid., pp. 428, 429.

48. Charles de Rémusat, *Mémoires de ma vie* (Paris, 1960), vol. 3, p. 327.

49. Adolphe Thiers, intervention of 6 May 1833, *A.P.,* vol. 83, p. 399.

50. Prosper de Barante, report to the Chamber of Peers, 4 April 1833, *A.P.,* vol. 82, p. 201.

51. Tocqueville disagreed, preferring to emphasize the new type of despotism to which generality, in the guise of conformism, gave rise in the modern world.

52. Guizot, "Réflexions sur l'organisation municipale," pp. 450–451.

53. In 1817 Joseph Louis Joachim Lainé, who was then minister of the interior, observed that "certain writers in favor, certain indiscreet petitions, certain positive votes by the general councils, and certain attacks on prefects are reminiscent of the provincial assemblies, landowners' committees, and the whole retinue of independent institutions that taxed the public's attention before 1790 and from their inception incited murmurs that were drowned out by the fracas of the Revolution. I have told the truth to my king, and, what is more difficult, I will tell it to the assemblies. To propose such institutions, when the Charter has created a broader, more central one to which all petitions are directed and from which all truth may emanate, is to attack that royal authority that must not be hindered if it is to offer the protection desired"; speech of 11 February 1817, *A.P.,* vol. 18, p. 734.

54. "France: Nécessité de donner la priorité à la loi départementale sur la loi municipale," *Le Globe,* 7 (14 February 1829), 97.

55. On this question see the next section of this chapter.

56. Report of Jean-Marie Pardessus concerning a decentralization bill presented to the Chamber of Deputies on 13 April 1821, *A.P.*, 2d ser., vol. 30, p. 755.

57. See Jean-Marie Duvergier de Hauranne, *Réflexions sur l'organisation municipale et sur les conseils généraux de département et les conseils d'arrondissement* (Paris, 1818).

58. For Thiers, the "necessary liberties" included freedom of the press, free exchange of opinions, free elections, national representation, and the right of the majority to control the government. These were liberties guaranteeing the ability of the central *institutions* of democracy to function, not liberties that increased the means of individuals to act directly. Speech included in *Discours parlementaires*, vol. 9: *Troisième partie (1850–1864)* (Paris, 1880).

59. On Dupont-White, see the informed and suggestive chapter in Sudhir Hazareesingh, *Intellectual Founders of the Republic: Five Studies in Nineteenth-Century French Political Thought* (Oxford: Oxford University Press, 2001).

60. Charles Dupont-White, *De la centralisation* (Paris, 1860), p. 248. Rémusat commented at length on this point in his review of the book in *Revue des deux mondes*, 15 October 1860.

61. Dupont-White, *De la centralisation*, p. 349.

62. Idem, *La liberté politique considérée dans ses rapports avec l'administration locale* (Paris, 1864), p. 102.

63. Ibid., p. 118.

64. Raymond-Théodore Troplong, *Du principe d'autorité depuis 1789, suivi de nouvelles considérations sur le même sujet* (Paris, 1853), p. 5.

65. Paul Leroy-Beaulieu, *L'Administration locale en France et en Angleterre* (Paris, 1872), p. 437.

66. Charles Forbes de Montalembert, speech to the National Assembly, 17 February 1849, *Le Moniteur universel*, 1st supp. to no. 49 (18 February 1849), 546.

67. Opinion of 24 April 1821, reproduced in *Délibérations des conseils généraux du commerce et des manufactures, établis auprès du Ministère de l'intérieur, sur le rétablissement demandé des corps de marchands et des communautés d'arts et métiers* (n.p., n.d. [1821]), p. 34.

68. Ibid., p. 31.

69. Deliberation of 18 May 1821, reproduced in Francis Demier, *Naissance des libertés économiques: Le décret d'Allarde et la loi Le Chapelier* (Paris: Institut d'Histoire de l'Industrie, 1993), p. 412.

70. For additional documentation on this controversy, see *Réponse des délégués des marchands en détail et des maîtres artisans de la ville de Paris aux rapports et délibérations des conseils généraux du commerce et des manufactures* (Paris, n.d. [1821]); and Antoine Levacher-Duplessis, *Réponse à la délibération prise*

par la Chambre de commerce de Paris, dans sa séance du 14 mars 1821 (Paris, n.d. [1821]).

71. See Rosanvallon, "La démocratie illibérale," in *La Démocratie inachevée* (Paris: Gallimard, 2000).

72. These expressions are taken from the indictment brought against the campaign committees by imperial prosecutors. See *Le Procès des treize en première instance* and *Le Procès des treize en appel* (Paris, 1864).

73. See Charles de Rémusat, *Mémoires de ma vie* (Paris, 1958), vol. 1, p. 383.

74. Saint-Roman, 11 March 1828, *A.P.*, 2d ser., vol. 53, p. 27.

75. These proposals came from the right and were also aimed at subduing and guiding voters under universal suffrage, which was still perceived as a threat.

76. Remarks of the minister of the interior in the debate in the Chamber of Deputies, 17 April 1837, reproduced in Jean-Marie Duvergier de Hauranne, *Lois, décrets, ordonnances, règlements* (1837) (cited hereafter as *Duvergier*), vol. 37, pp. 109–110.

77. Alexis de Tocquevillle, *Democracy in America,* trans. Arthur Goldhammer (New York: Library of America, 2004), p. 97. On this distinction and its limits, see "Décentralisation," in Maurice Block, *Dictionnaire politique* (Paris, 1874).

78. See the thesis of H. Carpentier de Changy, *Le Parti légitimiste sous la monarchie de juillet,* 4 vols. (University of Paris XII, 1980).

79. "De l'administration départementale et communale," *Le Globe,* 7 (3 January 1829), 1.

80. See his two articles "Centralisation et décentralisation," in *Le Réformateur,* 9 and 11 March 1835, reproduced in *Réformes sociales* (Paris, 1872), pp. 169–179.

81. In his "Discours sur la centralisation," which introduces the fifth edition of Marie-François de Cormenin, *Droit administratif* (Paris, 1840). Expanded in *De la centralisation* (Paris, 1842).

82. Louis Blanc, "De la commune" (1840), reprinted in *L'Etat et la Commune* (Brussels, 1866), p. 36. See also idem, *Histoire de dix ans,* vol. 2 (1842), in which he recounts the various debates on decentralization from 1830 on. He also speaks often of "true centralization" as opposed to "false centralization."

83. See the article "Centralisation," in Auguste Ott, *Dictionnaire des sciences morales et politiques* (Paris, 1854), vol. 1, cols. 969–970. After observing that centralization is "what distinguishes our nation from most other modern peoples," the author notes that "political centralization is the distinguishing feature of every state . . . It is a constant tendency in all governments." In other words, there is nothing distinctive about the trait.

84. Adolphe Thiers, intervention of 11 December 1834 in the Chamber of Peers, *A.P.*, vol. 91, p. 205. Thiers, who was then minister of the interior, had previ-

ously asserted that "municipal authority is above all an emanation of the central authority" (ibid.).

85. See Piero Craveri, *Genesi di una costituzione: Libertà e socialismo nel dibattito costituzionale del 1848 in Francia* (Naples: Guida Editori, 1985), p. 115.

86. See the almost identical formulations of the problem given by two individuals defending radically opposed views, Ferdinand Béchard and André Marie Jacques Dupin in the National Assembly on 18 April 1848, in *Moniteur universel*, 19 April 1848, pp. 2893–96.

87. See "Centralisation, concentration," in Francis Wey, *Dictionnaire démocratique* (Paris, 1848), pp. 248–249.

88. Decree of 25 March 1852. In 1850 Michel Chevalier offered the opinion that the first Napoleon "was in his person a striking protest against the excessive centralization that was his achievement." See "Les Questions politiques et sociales," *Revue des deux mondes*, 7 (1850), 337.

89. Buchez's definitions: "There are two terms to express the two opposite intellectual tendencies of our time: 'socialism' is the term for those who are far more concerned with society than with individuals . . . Its polar opposite is 'individualism,' the chief characteristic of which is that it regards society as the instrument of individual well-being." See "La Société et le socialisme," *L'Atelier*, 31 March 1843, p. 54.

90. See the end of his article "De l'individualisme et du socialisme," *Revue encyclopédique*, 1834, reprinted in *Oeuvres de Pierre Leroux* (Paris, 1850), vol. 1, pp. 365–380.

91. Ange Guépin, an important socialist from Nantes, wrote that "the workers' association is in my estimation merely the form that society will take on in the future. That society will be established in unity." See *Philosophie du socialisme* (Paris, 1850), p. 68.

92. It is worth recalling in this connection that Saint-Simon discussed the idea of a *national association*. "France has become a vast factory, a vast workshop," he wrote in *Du système industriel* (Paris, 1821).

93. Louis Blanc, *Organisation du travail* (Paris, 1840), p. 65. "Grafting association onto competition is a poor idea," he added, along with a wish that "the state place itself resolutely in charge of industry" (ibid., pp. 65–121).

94. François-Vincent Raspail, "Association," *Le Réformateur*, 27 (February 1835), reprinted in *Réformes sociales* (Paris, 1872), p. 142. In the same article he spoke of "the great association of the future."

95. Auguste Billiard, *De l'organisation de la République depuis Moïse jusqu'à nos jours* (Paris, 1846), pp. 88–89. In the same vein, see also his *Essai sur l'organisation démocratique de la France* (1837).

96. Elias Regnault, "Association," in Block, *Dictionnaire politique*, p. 116. The author adds: "Furthermore, with free discussion in the press, those associations

would make no sense and have no influence." The same article criticized political clubs on the grounds that "the National Assembly is the club of France," and asked the following question: "Outside this legitimate association, what is a private club composed of a group of citizens?"

97. "In the parliamentary monarchy, where everything is organized around antagonism and conflict, it would be an unjust blunder to prevent association"; ibid.

98. "Revue politique," *Revue républicaine*, 1 (1834), 152. "We are not among those who see in these associations the normal state of industry. We believe that a high social intervention is constantly necessary."

99. See Maurice Tournier, "Quand un mot en cache d'autres: Le vocabulaire de 'l'association' en 1848," *Cahiers pour l'analyse concrète*, nos. 39–40 (1998).

100. "Association, droit de réunion," in Wey, *Dictionnaire démocratique*, p. 451.

101. For a pioneering attempt to tackle the problem, see Michèle Sacquin, *Entre Bossuet et Maurras: L'antiprotestantisme en France de 1814 à 1870* (Paris: Ecole des Chartes, 1998).

102. The expression can be found in Joseph de Maistre, "Réflexions sur le protestantisme dans ses rapports avec la souveraineté" (1798), in *Oeuvres complètes de Joseph de Maistre* (Lyons, 1893), vol. 8, p. 97.

103. Félicité Robert de Lamennais, *Quelques Réflexions sur notre état présent* (1823), in *Nouveaux mélanges* (Paris, 1826), p. 332.

104. Idem, *Restauration de la science politique*, p. 464.

105. Prosper Enfantin, letter of June 1829, *Correspondance inédite d'Enfantin*, in *Oeuvres de Saint-Simon et d'Enfantin* (Paris, 1872), vol. 25, p. 212. Some liberals responded by attacking "the apostles of industrial Catholicism." See, for example, the important article of 30 January 1828 in *Le Globe*, 6, pp. 163–164.

106. "Sur l'éclectisme," preface to vol. 28 of P.-J.-B. Buchez and P.-C. Roux, *Histoire parlementaire de la Révolution française* (Paris, 1836), pp. ix, xiv.

107. Review of *Democracy in America* by Laurent Cerise in *L'Européen*, 25 December 1835, quoted in Françoise Mélonio, *Tocqueville et les Français* (Paris: Aubier, 1993), p. 67.

108. Conversely, Taine, a conservative liberal, would later convert to Protestantism because he was convinced that Catholicism and rationalism were the causes of France's woes.

9. The Great Turning Point

1. See Georges Bourgin and Hubert Bourgin, *Les Patrons, les ouvriers et l'état*, vol. 2 of *Le Régime de l'industrie en France de 1814 à 1830* (Paris, 1912), p. ix.

2. See the circular issued by Simon Pierre Joseph Montalivet, minister of the interior, on 31 October 1812, reproduced in Dalloz, *Répertoire méthodique et*

alphabétique de législation, de doctrine et de jurisprudence (Paris, 1846), vol. 5, p. 320. Under the Restoration, a circular issued by the prefect of police on 15 May 1819 observed that mutual aid societies were "backed and favored by the police." See "Associations," in P. Julien Alletz, *Dictionnaire de police moderne pour toute la France* (Paris, 1820), vol. 1, p. 68. These formulas were repeated verbatim by Charles de Rémusat in his famous circular to the prefects of 6 August 1840, quoted in Pierre Karila-Cohen, "L'Impossible Refondation: Charles de Rémusat, ministre de l'Intérieur (mars–octobre 1840)," master's thesis under the direction of Alain Corbin (University of Paris I, 1994), p. 273.

3. On this point, see the abundant documentation collected by Catherine Duprat, *Usage et pratiques de la philanthropie*, 2 vols. (Paris: Associations pour l'Etude de l'Histoire de la Sécurité Sociale, 1996). See also Octave Festy, "La Société philanthropique de Paris et les sociétés de secours mutuels (1800–1847)," *Revue d'histoire moderne et contemporaine*, 16 (September–October 1911).

4. François Guizot, intervention of 1 May 1829 at the society's general assembly, *Journal de la Société de la morale chrétienne*, 11 (1829), 100.

5. See Frédéric-Gaëtan de La Rochefoucauld–Liancourt, *Notice sur les associations des ouvriers de Paris* (March 1834). This was the son of the former chairman of the Constituent Assembly's committee on mendicancy, who was serving at the time as the head of the Société de la Morale Chrétienne.

6. See Tocqueville's speech of 12 September 1848 in *Le Droit au travail à l'Assemblée nationale: Recueil complet de tous les discours prononcés dans cette mémorable discussion* (Paris, 1848), pp. 99–113.

7. Ibid., p. 101.

8. Alexandre Auguste Ledru-Rollin, speech of 12 September 1848, ibid., p. 121. He also used the term "intelligent guide" to characterize the type of state he favored.

9. Antoine-Elisée Cherbuliez, *Etudes sur les causes de la misère tant morale que physique et sur les moyens d'y porter remède* (Paris, 1853), pp. 308–326.

10. The term *état-providence* was used for the first time in Emile Laurent, *Le Paupérisme et les associations de prévoyance. Nouvelles études sur les sociétés de secours mutuels: Histoire, économie, administration* (Paris, 1860). This work was awarded a prize by the Académie des Sciences Morales et Politiques. The author was a member of the prefectural corps who was well informed about the situation on the ground. In 1856, a few years before this book appeared, Tocqueville wrote in *L'Ancien Régime et la Révolution* that "when the government assumes the role of providence, it is to be expected that each individual will invoke his particular needs."

11. Ibid., 2d ed. (Paris, 1865), vol. 1, p. 68.

12. Emile Ollivier, *Rapport fait au nom de la commission chargée d'examiner le projet de loi relatif aux coalitions,* reproduced in *Commentaire de la loi du 25 mai 1864 sur les coalitions* (Paris, 1864), p. 52. Emile Ollivier raised the specter of the welfare state in this report, as the quotation shows.

13. See Rosanvallon, *Le Peuple introuvable* (Paris: Gallimard, 1998), pp. 67–99.

14. From 1853 to 1862 there were 749 prosecutions of workers' coalitions, compared with only 89 of employers' coalitions. See Emile Levasseur, *Histoire des classes ouvrières et de l'industrie en France de 1789 à 1870,* 2d ed. (Paris, 1904), vol. 2, p. 508.

15. The expression is that of Emile Ollivier, the rapporteur on the bill, in a speech to the Corps Législatif on 28 April 1864. "When a new invention transformed your industries, did the prospect of the woes that workers would endure prevent you from bringing the new machines into your factories?" he asked industrialists. "No! And you were right; you submitted to the fatal law of industrial progress, which you could not ignore without risk of perishing yourselves. Today we are asking you, in the name of the workers and their unanimous demands, to take your turn in enduring a fatal necessity." See *Annales du Sénat et du Corps législatif,* 1864, p. 169.

16. See, for example, *Procès des ouvriers travailleurs tailleurs (grève de mars–avril 1867)* (Paris, 1868). On the persistent problem of associations and coalitions, see the *Bulletin des arrêts de la Cour de cassation rendus en matière criminelle* for the years 1866 (no. 47) and 1868 (nos. 36 and 223).

17. See data in Michelle Perrot, *Les Ouvriers en grève: France 1870–1890,* 2 vols. (Paris: Mouton, 1974).

18. In 1888 *La Statistique annuelle de la France* published retrospective figures for strikes in the period 1874–1885. The Office du Travail began publishing annual strike statistics in 1892.

19. Letter of 4 August 1881 to the minister of agriculture, quoted in Francine Soubiran-Paillet, *L'Invention du syndicat (1791–1884): Itinéraire d'une catégorie juridique* (Paris: LGDJ, 1999), p. 115.

20. François Henri René Allain-Targé, report on behalf of the committee to examine the union bill, presented on 15 March 1881, *Annales de la Chambre des députés,* 1881 session, *Impressions,* no. 3420, vol. 49, p. 24.

21. Henri Tolain, report on behalf of the committee to examine the union bill, presented on 14 December 1883, *Annales du Sénat,* extraordinary session of 1883, *Impressions,* no. 112, vol. 1, p. 12.

22. Léon Gambetta, speech of 25 March 1881 before the Union des Chambres Syndicales du Commerce et de l'Industrie, in *Discours et Plaidoyers politiques de M. Gambetta* (Paris, 1883), vol. 9, pp. 170–171.

23. Paul Leroy-Beaulieu attacked English trade unions and their practices in *La Question ouvrière au XIXe siècle* (Paris, 1872).

24. In 1873 he also published *De la situation des ouvriers en Angleterre.*

25. Anthime Corbon, *Les Associations ouvrières en Angleterre* (Paris, 1869).

26. Quoted in Charles Brunot, *Commentaire de la loi de 1884* (Paris, 1884), p. 75.

27. Deposition of 23 November 1883 by delegates of the Union Nationale du Commerce et de l'Industrie appearing before the senatorial committee; ibid., p. 414.

28. See Pierre Marie René Waldeck-Rousseau, *Questions sociales* (Paris, 1900), pp. 304–305. "I regard associations as regulators, as agents in creating equilibrium among social forces," he told the Senate on 6 March 1883. See *Annales du Sénat,* ordinary session of 1883, vol. 1, p. 287.

29. Tolain argued that freeing the unions would rescue workers from "revolutionary influences" (28 January 1884, ibid., ordinary session of 1884, vol. 1, p. 225).

30. Félix Barthe, 31 July 1883, ibid., ordinary session of 1883, vol. 1, p. 1125.

31. Eugène Tallon, *La Vie morale et intellectuelle des ouvriers* (Paris, 1877), p. 452.

32. The expression is borrowed from Charles Benoist, *La Crise de l'état moderne* (Paris, 1905), p. 15, but the term was ubiquitous in politics from 1870 on.

33. Pierre Antoine Berryer, "Affaire des ouvriers typographes" (hearing of 27 September 1862), in *Oeuvres de Berryer,* vol. 4: *Plaidoyers* (Paris, 1878), p. 231.

34. Ollivier, *Rapport fait au nom de la commission chargée d'examiner le projet de loi relatif aux coalitions,* p. 52. "Out of this," Ollivier continued, "came the wicked laws on association, the strict decrees against investment companies, bond discounters, insurance companies, businesses, and factories. Out of this came the excesses of centralization, the limitless expansion of social rights, the exaggerations of socialist reformers. Out of this came Babeuf, the idea of the welfare state, and revolutionary despotism in all its forms"; ibid.

35. Alfred Darimon, 28 April 1864, *Annales du Sénat et du Corps législatif* (Paris, 1864), p. 162.

36. Bill filed by Edouard Lockroy on 4 July 1876, *Annales de la Chambre des députés,* session of 1876, *Impressions,* no. 270, vol. 4, p. 2.

37. Ibid., p. 3.

38. Henri Tolain, report of 14 December 1883 (Senate, extraordinary session of 1883, *Impressions,* vol. 1, p. 2).

39. Léon Gambetta, speech of 25 March 1831, in *Discours et plaidoyers de M. Gambetta,* vol. 9, p. 174.

40. François Henri René Allain-Targé, intervention of 17 May 1881, *Annales de la Chambre des députés,* ordinary session of 1881, *Débats,* vol. 2, p. 49.

41. Laurent, *Le Paupérisme et les Associations de prévoyance,* vol. 1, p. xiii: "Modern society is strong enough to combine individualism and sociability without danger."

42. He wrote: "What he [Le Chapelier] wanted to avoid was wage increases, and

he saw association in any form as reprehensible because he was so afraid that even a mutual aid society could serve as camouflage for workers seeking to improve their lot." See Paul Brousse and Henri Turot, *Histoire socialiste*, vol. 6: *Consulat et Empire* (Paris, n.d.), p. 562.

43. Jean Jaurès, *Histoire socialiste*, vol. 1: *La Constituante* (Paris, n.d.), p. 605. Jaurès was the first historian of the Revolution to attach such importance to the law of 14 June 1791; see pp. 605–608.

44. Karl Marx, *Capital*, book 1, chap. 28. In a letter to Engels on 30 January 1865, Marx described the law as "antiworker."

45. Inaugural lecture of his course in social science at Bordeaux (1888), in Emile Durkheim, *La Science sociale et l'action* (Paris: Presses Universitaires de France, 1970), p. 97.

46. On the 1815 generation, see Rosanvallon, *Le Moment Guizot* (Paris: Galli-mard, 1985). On the generation of 1870, see Claude Digeon, *La Crise alle-mande de la pensée française (1870–1914)* (Paris: Presses Universitaires de France, 1959). Espinas spoke at length of his perception of the situation and of the tasks facing his generation in a lecture given in April 1894 at the Faculty of Letters of the University of Paris, reprinted in *La Philosophie sociale du XVIIIe siècle et la Révolution* (Paris, 1898).

47. Durkheim lecture, in *La Science sociale et l'action*, p. 96.

48. The biological understanding of "organism" was profoundly different in this respect from the traditional conception of "organicism" (in medieval political theory, for example), which was based on a fixed, hierarchical division of the various parts of the "social body."

49. Alfred Espinas, "Les Etudes sociologiques en France," third article, *Revue philosophique*, 14 (1882), 513.

50. Idem, ibid., second article, p. 362.

51. Espinas, *La Philosophie sociale du XVIIIe siècle et la Révolution*, p. 196.

52. Ibid., p. 124.

53. Idem, "Introduction sur l'histoire de la sociologie en général," in *Sociétés animales*, 2d ed. (Paris, 1878), p. 128. "Society in the strict sense is only a special case of this universal law, the most complex and highest-order of all. Hence no being, social or otherwise, is absolute or indivisible; it is essentially relative and multiple. It is the point in which a range of forces converge, an unstable point in inorganic nature which becomes more stable as one moves higher up the scale of life, but always liable to resolve itself into multiple points if cohesion diminishes, or to attach itself to new centers if cohesion increases. Hence, strictly speaking, there are no beings in nature, only being at various degrees of concentration" (ibid.). In this perspective, associations and intermediary bodies are thus merely one of the forms of concentration of the social.

54. "We believe that the two ideas of social organism and social contract need to be combined in a more comprehensive idea, which we call the contractual organism." See Alfred Fouillée, *La Science sociale contemporaine* (Paris, 1880), p. 111. Later he argued that "if Kant was incomparably superior as a philosopher, Comte was superior as a sociologist"; *Le Mouvement positiviste et la conception sociologique du monde* (Paris, 1896), p. 230.

55. Fouillée, *La Science sociale contemporaine*, p. 179.

56. Ibid., p. 180.

57. Alfred Fouillée, *La Démocratie politique et sociale en France* (Paris, 1910), p. 164.

58. Ibid., p. 166.

59. Thomas Ferneuil, *Les Principes de 1789 et la science sociale* (Paris, 1889), p. 18. Ferneuil criticized Le Chapelier and his rejection of intermediary bodies at length (pp. 245–252).

60. Ibid., p. 17.

61. Emile Durkheim, "Les Principes de 1789 et la sociologie," *Revue internationale de l'enseignement,* 19 (1890), reprinted in *La Science sociale et l'action,* p. 215.

62. Ibid., p. 216.

63. Emile Durkheim, *De la division du travail social* (1893) (Paris: Presses Universitaires de France, 1967), p. 179. Durkheim criticized those economists and moralists who "reduce social science to mere ideological analysis. They start with the abstract concept of the individual in itself and develop its content." See Ferneuil, *Les Principes de 1789 et la science sociale,* p. 219.

64. The state, Durkheim argued in a well-known text, liberated the individual: "As the state gained strength, it emancipated individuals from the particular local groups that had tended to subsume them: family, city, corporation, etc. Individualism progressed historically along with statism. Not that the state cannot become despotic and oppressive. Like all forces of nature, it will, if not contained by some collective power, develop without limit and become in turn a threat to individual liberties. From this it follows that the social force in the state must be neutralized by other social forces acting as a counterweight. If secondary groups readily turn tyrannical when their action is not moderated by that of the state, conversely, the action of the state, if it is to remain within norms, also needs to be moderated. The way to achieve this result is to ensure that there exist in society, outside the state though subject to its influence, smaller groups (whether defined territorially or professionally is of no importance for now) powerful enough, and sufficiently individualized and autonomous, to resist the encroachments of the central power. What liberates the individual is not the elimination of all centers of regulation but their multiplication, provided that the resulting multiple centers form a coordi-

nated hierarchy"; *Une révision de l'idée socialiste* (1899), reprinted in Emile Durkheim, *Textes* (Paris: Editions de Minuit, 1975), vol. 3, p. 171.

65. Léon Duguit, "Un Séminaire de sociologie," *Revue internationale de sociologie,* 1 (May–June 1893).

66. Léon Duguit, "L'Election des sénateurs," *Revue politique et parlementaire,* September 1895, p. 463. "Individualism," he went on, "was ubiquitous in revolutionary legislation. Today, association is ubiquitous, in mores, aspirations, and laws. Things move quickly in France, and the time may not be far off when the all-out individualism born of the Revolution will be no more than a memory" (p. 473).

67. See Léon Duguit, "Le Droit constitutionnel et la sociologie," *Revue internationale de l'enseignement,* 18 (15 November 1889).

68. Some later works were quite influential: Guillaume-Léonce Duprat, *Science sociale et démocratie* (Paris, 1900); Gaston Richard, *La Question sociale et le mouvement philosophique au XIXe siècle* (Paris, 1914); Jean Baudeau, *Socialistes et sociologues* (Paris, 1905). The translated work of Léon Gumplowicz, *Sociologie et politique* (Paris, 1898) also came in for much comment. The impressive thesis of Henry Michel, *L'Idée de l'état: Essai critique sur l'histoire des théories politiques et sociales depuis la Révolution* (Paris, 1896), drew attention from a smaller group of readers but played an important role by presenting a full and subtle tableau of the various types of reaction against individualism.

10. The Trade Union Exception

1. Eugène Tallon, *La Vie morale et intellectuelle des ouvriers* (Paris, 1877), p. 439.

2. Pierre Jouin, intervention of 1 July 1882, *Annales du Sénat,* ordinary session of 1882, *Débats,* vol. 1, p. 825.

3. Joseph Brunet, ibid., p. 824.

4. Félix Cantagrel, intervention of 17 May 1881, *Annales de la Chambre des députés,* ordinary session of 1881, *Débats,* vol. 2, pp. 48–52.

5. Alexis Ribot, intervention of 17 May 1881, ibid., p. 55.

6. Edouard Lockroy, intervention of 16 June 1883, *Annales de la Chambre des députés,* ordinary session of 1883, *Débats,* vol. 2, p. 733.

7. Henri Tolain, intervention of 1 July 1882, *Annales du Sénat,* p. 826.

8. Lockroy, speech of 16 June 1883.

9. The 1798 edition of the *Dictionnaire de l'Académie française* defined the word *syndicat* as "the office or function of a syndic." Under the Old Regime *syndicat* also referred to the administrative responsibilities of a small rural community represented by a syndic. See Marcel Marion, *Dictionnaire des institutions de la France aux XVIIe et XVIIIe siècles* (Paris, 1923). Note that a law of 16 September 1807 used the word *syndicats* to refer to associations of *communes* or pri-

vate individuals charged with carrying out public works (such as building dikes, draining swamps, etc.). An important law of 24 June 1865 authorized the formation of syndical associations, meaning unions of land owners who agreed to undertake agricultural improvements in the public interest.

10. Henri Larousse, in his *Dictionnaire du XIXe siècle*, still defined *syndicat* as an "association of capitalists sharing common interests."

11. See Henri Tolain, *Quelques Vérités sur les élections de Paris* (31 May 1863).

12. See Office du Travail, *Les Associations professionnelles ouvrières*, vol. 2, p. 23. On the first unions, see also Maxime Leroy, *La Coutume ouvrière*, 2 vols. (Paris, 1913), vol. 1, pp. 44–47. The term *syndicat* did not come into common use until the early 1870s, however. See Jean Dubois, *Le Vocabulaire politique et social en France de 1869 à 1872* (Paris, 1962), p. 133.

13. See Denis Barbet, "Retour sur la loi de 1884: La production des frontières du syndical et du politique," *Genèses*, no. 3 (March 1991).

14. On this question, see the thesis of Monique Kieffer, *Aux origines de la législation du travail en France: La légalisation des syndicats et la démocratisation des conseils de prud'hommes* (University of Paris VIII, 1987), vol. 1, pp. 175–179.

15. Barbet, "Retour sur la loi de 1884," p. 22.

16. Quoted in "Chambres syndicales," in *Larousse du XIXe siècle* (1st supp.).

17. Cf. the terms used by Marcel Barthe, the rapporteur in the Senate. "Alongside the movement of workers toward the organization in each trade of an institution charged with defending corporate interests by legal means," he noted, "we find another quite different movement, the purpose of which is to provoke class division in society and to form within the great family of France a distinct class to be called the *workers' party* or *fourth estate*. This last denomination, which corresponds to nothing in our society of civil equality, is explained in the writing of the theorists who invented it. They deny the results of the French Revolution"; report to the Senate, session of 1882, appendix to the minutes of session of 24 June 1882, *Impressions du Sénat*, no. 296, vol. 3, pp. 12–13.

18. René Bérenger, intervention of 29 January–1 February 1884, *Annales du Sénat*, ordinary session of 1884, *Débats*, vol. 1, pp. 250–256.

19. Ibid., p. 235.

20. Emile Lenoël, ibid.

21. Cf. his arguments on this point in his important speech of 29 January 1884, reproduced in Pierre Marie René Waldeck-Rousseau, *Questions sociales* (Paris, 1900), pp. 218–237.

22. The argument had also been used by small employers. "Let [the unions] band together," their representative had argued, "and it is my firm hope that before long we will see regular or special general assemblies of these various permanent associations take the place of, or at any rate serve as a counterweight to,

the frequent meetings in which violent and theatrical harangues enjoy greater success than serious efforts"; deposition by M. Héliard, delegate of the Union Nationale du Commerce et de l'Industrie, before the senatorial commission, quoted in Charles Brunot, *Commentaire de la loi de 1884* (Paris, 1900), p. 417.

23. At the Rennes Congress of the Fédération des Travailleurs Socialistes in October 1884, for instance, the law was denounced as a "work of police and reaction." See the documentation collected in two theses: Pierre Bance, *Le Syndicalisme ouvrier français dans la genèse du droit du travail (1876–1902)* (University of Paris I, 1976); and Kieffer, *Aux origines de la législation du travail en France.*

24. Waldeck-Rousseau, *Questions sociales,* p. 128. Although the number of strikes increased, they became less violent. See Edward Shorter and Charles Tilly, "Le Déclin de la grève violente en France de 1890 à 1935," *Le Mouvement social,* no. 76 (July 1971).

25. See the "Proposition de loi relative à la création d'un Conseil supérieur du travail," presented on 30 January 1890 by Mesureur, Millerand, et al., *Annales de la Chambre des députés,* session of 1890, *Impressions,* no. 315, p. 3.

26. Ibid., p. 6.

27. The decree of 17 September 1900 was the occasion of numerous commentaries.

28. Alfred-Léon Gérault-Richard, *La Petite République,* 21 January 1900.

29. Jean Jaurès, "Le socialisme," *Revue socialiste,* 31 (March 1900), 265.

30. Paul Leroy-Beaulieu, "Un Nouveau Pas dans la voie du socialisme: Le syndicat obligatoire," *L'Economiste français,* 29 September 1900, p. 423.

31. Jules Epinay, "La Réforme de la législation des associations," in *Le Droit d'association: Etudes, notes et rapports* (Paris, 1899), p. 142.

32. Law of 12 March 1920. See Paul Nourrisson, *La Loi du 12 mars 1920 sur les syndicates professionnels et son extension nécessaire* (Paris, 1922).

33. See François Babinet, "Dit et non-dit du texte: Rapports sociaux et portée juridique de la loi du 21 mars 1884," in *Convergences: Etudes offertes à Marcel David* (Quimper: Calligrammes, 1991).

34. On this point, see the excellent comments by Jacques Le Goff, *Du silence à la parole: Droit du travail, société, état (1830–1985)* (Quimper: Calligrammes, 1985), pp. 108–116.

35. Henri Tolain, 21 February 1884, *Annales du Sénat,* ordinary session of 1884, *Débats,* vol. 1, p. 509.

36. On this point, see the stimulating though contestable article by Alain Cottereau, "Droit et bon droit: Un droit des ouvriers instauré, puis évincé par le droit du travail, France XIXe siècle," *Annales,* November–December 2002, which stands the usual argument on its head to the point of describing the late nineteenth century as a time when "the rights of workers were thrown out in favor of the right to work."

37. Charles Floquet, intervention of 21 May 1881, *Annales de la Chambre des députés,* ordinary session of 1881, vol. 2, p. 102.

38. Marc Sauzet, "Essai historique sur la législation industrielle de la France," *Revue d'économie politique,* 6 (1892), 923–924.

39. See Alain Cottereau, "Justice et injustice ordinaire sur les lieux de travail d'après les audiences prud'homales (1806–1866)," *Le Mouvement social,* no. 14 (October–December 1987); and Marcel David, "L'Evolution historique des conseils de prud'hommes en France," *Droit social,* February 1974.

40. Leroy, *La Coutume ouvrière,* vol. 2, pp. 664–665.

41. The exceptional existence of the collective is the reason for the centrality of "striker culture" in French revolutionary syndicalism.

42. On the establishment of these procedures and their results, see the dossier assembled by the Office du Travail, *De la conciliation et de l'arbitrage dans les conflits collectifs entre patrons et ouvriers* (Paris, 1891); and François Fagnot, "La Loi sur la conciliation et l'arbitrage," in Charles Gide et al., *Le Droit de grève* (Paris, 1909).

43. This bill was filed by a social Catholic, Abbé Lemire. See Isidore Finance, *Les Syndicats professionnels devant les tribunaux et le Parlement depuis 1884* (Paris, 1911).

44. André Rouast, *Essai sur la notion juridique de contrat collectif dans le droit des obligations* (Paris, 1909), p. 128.

45. Charles Gide, review of Barthélemy Raynaud, *Le Contrat collectif de travail,* in *Revue d'économie politique,* 17 (1903), 174.

46. See the *Bulletin de la société d'études législatives,* 3 (1904), 465–466. The issue was also treated in reports drafted in 1906 and 1908.

47. Raoul Jay, *Qu'est-ce que le contrat collectif de travail?* (Paris, 1908), p. 23.

48. Léon Duguit, *Les Transformations générales du droit privé depuis le Code Napoléon* (Paris, 1920), p. 135.

49. For a good overview, see Jacques Le Goff, "La Naissance des conventions collectives: Retour sur un débat doctrinal significatif (1890–1920)," *Droits,* no. 12 (1990); and Claude Didry, *Naissance de la convention collective: Débats juridiques et luttes sociales en France au début du XXe siècle* (Paris: Editions de l'EHESS, 2002). For contemporary views of this debate, see Gaëtan Pirou, *Les Conceptions juridiques successives du contrat collectif de travail en France* (Paris, 1909).

50. According to the law of 25 March 1919, "the collective labor agreement is a contract pertaining to working conditions concluded between the representatives of a trade union or any other group of employees on the one hand and the representatives of an employers' syndicate or any other group of one or more employers or even a single employer" (art. 31, sec. 1).

51. The phrase is that of the conservative republican Louis Barthou, *L'Action syndicale* (Paris, 1904), p. 303.

52. Alexandre Millerand, preface to Jules Huret, *Les Grèves* (Paris, 1901), p. 5.

53. Question from Paul Rogez, session of 22 November 1900, *Annales de la Chambre des députés*, extraordinary session of 1900, vol. 1, p. 349.

54. Millerand, ibid., p. 350.

55. See *Projet de loi sur le règlement amiable des différends relatifs aux conditions du travail*, filed on 15 November 1900 by Millerand and Waldeck-Rousseau.

56. For a summary of the various positions, see Huret, *Les Grèves*.

57. Quoted in Leroy, *La Coutume ouvrière*, vol. 2, p. 673.

58. See Rosanvallon, *La Question syndicale*, new ed. (Paris: Hachette-Pluriel, 1998), pp. 238–241.

59. Georges Scelle, *Précis élémentaire de législation industrielle* (Paris, 1927), pp. 319 ff.

60. Klotz was a Radical Socialist deputy from the Somme and founder of the Comité d'Action pour les Réformes Républicaines.

61. Alphonse Merrheim, "La Parliamentarisation du syndicalisme," *Mouvement socialiste*, April 1910, p. 244.

62. See "L'Avènement du syndicalisme," in Rosanvallon, *Le Peuple introuvable* (Paris: Gallimard, 1998).

63. Hubert Lagardelle, *L'Evolution des syndicats ouvriers en France: De l'interdiction à l'obligation* (Paris, 1901), p. 181. "The corporation of workers, ever more conscious of itself, is establishing itself more and more firmly as a collective organism with each passing day"; ibid., p. 1.

64. Ibid., p. 305.

65. "In the future," he said, "the Conseil Supérieur will be recruited by vote of the workers' corporations, but that will be achieved only when those corporations will have taken the trouble to make themselves known, to exist, and to represent if not all at least the vast majority of professional corporations"; Emile Mesureur, intervention of 17 February 1891, *Annales de la Chambre des députés*, ordinary session of 1891, *Débats*, vol. 1, pp. 441–442.

66. See Alexandre Millerand, *La Grève et l'organisation ouvrière* (Paris, 1906), pp. 23–24.

67. Though he added that these "new corporations" would be "inspired by the modern democratic spirit." See Raoul Jay, "L'organisation du travail par les syndicats professionnels," *Revue d'économie politique*, April 1894, p. 338.

68. Barthélemy Raynaud, *Le Contrat collectif de travail* (Paris, 1901), pp. 339–351.

69. Raymond Saleilles, "La Code civil et la méthode historique," in *Le Code civil: Livre du centenaire* (Paris, 1904), vol. 1, p. 117.

70. Ibid., p. 110.

71. See Raymond Saleilles, *Les Personnes juridiques dans le Code civil allemand* (Paris, 1902).

72. See, for a typical example, Henri Lorin, "Etudes sur les principes de l'organisation professionnelle," *L'Association catholique*, 15 July 1892.

11. Liberty and Institutions

1. Speaking of the revolutionary period, Tocqueville wrote: "Above the real society . . . an imaginary society was built piece by piece, an imaginary society in which everything seemed simple and coordinated, uniform, equitable, and consistent with reason"; *L'Ancien Régime et la Révolution* (Paris: Gallimard, 1952).
2. On the movements of this last period, see Philip Nord, *The Republican Moment: Struggles for Democracy in Nineteenth-Century France* (Cambridge, Mass.: Harvard University Press, 1995).
3. Confidential circular of 29 April 1834. The copy I examined came from the departmental archives of Finistère (4M40). I thank the chief conservator for obtaining it for me.
4. See Dalloz, "Associations illicites," in *Répertoire méthodique et alphabétique de législation, de doctrine et de jurisprudence* (Paris, 1846), vol. 5 (supp.), p. 282.
5. For numerous examples, see Jean-Luc Marais, *Les Sociétés d'hommes: Histoire d'une sociabilité du XVIIIe siècle à nos jours. Anjou, Maine, Touraine* (Vauchrétien: Ivan Davy, 1986).
6. Data in Sudhir Hazareesingh and Vincent Wright, "Le Second Empire," in Louis Fougère et al., eds., *Les Communes et le pouvoir de 1789 à nos jours* (Paris: Presses Universitaires de France, 2002), p. 273.
7. For a list of Agulhon's works on this topic, see the bibliography in *La France démocratique (combats, mentalités, symboles): Mélanges offerts à Maurice Agulhon* (Paris: Publications de la Sorbonne, 1998).
8. Maurice Agulhon, "La Sociabilité et la sociologie de l'histoire," *L'Arc*, no. 65 (1976).
9. See Philippe Gumplowicz, *Les Travaux d'Orphée: 150 ans de vie musicale amateur en France. Harmonies, chorales, fanfares* (Paris: Aubier, 1987).
10. See Pierre Arnaud, *Les Athlètes de la République: Gymnastique, sport et idéologie républicaine, 1870–1914* (Toulouse: Privat, 1987).
11. Statistics for the period 1853–1900 compiled by Pierre Arnaud, "La Trame et la chaîne: Le réseau des sociétés conscriptives (1870–1890)," *Sport histoire: Revue internationale des sports et des jeux*, no. 1 (1998).
12. *L'Orphéon*, 1 May 1867, quoted in Gumplowicz, *Les Travaux d'Orphée*, p. 177.
13. See "Compte rendu des réponses faites au questionnaire du Congrès," in *Le Droit d'association: Etudes, notes et rapports* (Paris, 1899).
14. Law of 16 September 1871, Article 9 of which stipulated that "as of 1 October 1871, subscribers to circles, societies, and meetings who pay dues shall pay a tax of 20 percent on said dues assessed to members and associates. This tax shall be collected by the officials, secretaries, or treasurers of said groups. Charitable and mutual aid societies are not subject to the tax, nor are societies

exclusively devoted to scientific, literary, agricultural, or musical purposes that do not meet on a daily basis."

15. Statistics compiled by the Direction Générale des Contributions Directes for fiscal year 1894: *Etat présentant, par département, le nombre de cercles, de billards, de vélocipèdes et de chiens imposés* (table 570). This statistic for 1894 indicates a total of 4,936 circles, a larger number than the Office du Travail estimate, a fact suggesting that the latter should be used with caution.

16. See, however, Annie Grange, *L'Apprentissage de l'association, 1850–1914: Naissance du secteur volontaire non lucratif dans l'arrondissement du Villefranche-sur-Saône* (Paris: Mutualité Française, 1993).

17. Jean Macé, intervention at Congress of Rouen, 28 April 1886, *Bulletin de la Ligue Française de l'enseignement*, no. 39 (May 1886), 166.

18. Report of Charles Bertauld, appendix to minutes of session of 28 March 1871, reproduced in *L'Avènement de la loi de 1901 sur le droit d'association: Genèse et évolution de la loi au fil des Journaux officiels* (Paris: Les Editions des Journaux Officiels, 2001), p. 11. This voluminous collection includes all bills and debates on the right of association from 1871 to 1901; hereafter cited as *L'Avènement de la loi*.

19. See the interventions in the parliamentary debate of 12–18 May 1872, ibid., pp. 17–50.

20. Albert de Broglie, *Le Concordat* (Paris, 1893), p. 28.

21. Paul Nourrisson, *Histoire de la liberté d'association en France depuis 1789* (Paris, 1920), vol. 2, p. 263.

22. *Le Droit d'association: Etudes, notes et rapports*, p. 54.

23. Jean-François Merlet, *Une Grande Loi de la IIIe République: La loi du 1er juillet 1901* (Paris: LGDJ, 2001), p. 8.

24. Ernest Vallé, report of 6 June 1901, in *L'Avènement de la loi*, p. 709.

25. This decree recognized a "right to assemble peacefully and to form free societies, provided that the laws governing all citizens are respected." It was ambiguous because numerous other texts contradicted it.

26. Ernest Vallé, motion on a bill filed on 14 May 1895 by Cunéo d'Ornano, in *L'Avènement de la loi*, p. 219.

27. Maurice Agulhon, "Associations et histoire sociale," *La Revue de l'économie sociale*, 14 (1988), 39. See also the arguments in "Les Associations depuis le début du XIXe siècle," in Maurice Agulhon and Maryvonne Bodiguel, *Les Associations au village* (Le Paradou: Actes Sud, 1981).

28. Jules Simon, intervention of 5 March 1883, in *L'Avènement de la loi*, p. 144. Recall that Simon, like Jules Armand Stanislas Dufaure, favored a single law of associations that did not treat the congregations as a special case. It was for this reason that his proposal failed.

29. Georges Trouillot, report of 8 June 1900, in *L'Avènement de la loi*, p. 247.

30. For example, he writes that "had it not been for the problem of the congregations, a law granting freedom of association would have passed along with laws on freedom of the press and assembly . . . as soon as the Republicans gained victory, in the 1880s." See Maurice Agulhon, "Vers une histoire des associations," *Esprit*, June 1978, p. 13.

31. Nourrisson, *Histoire de la liberté d'association*, vol. 2, p. 306.

32. Alfred Noël François Madier de Montjau, intervention in the Chamber on 16 March 1880, *Annales du Sénat et de la Chambre des députés*, ordinary session of 1880, vol. 4, p. 131. The statement was greeted with applause.

33. Pierre Marie René Waldeck-Rousseau, speech of 28 October 1900 in Toulouse, in Waldeck-Rousseau, *Associations et Congrégations* (Paris, 1901), pp. 37–42.

34. See Christian Sorrel, *La République contre les congrégations: Histoire d'une passion française (1899–1904)* (Paris: Editions du Cerf, 2003).

35. See Jacqueline-Lalouette and Jean-Pierre Machelon, eds., *Les Congrégations hors la loi? Autour de la loi du 1er juillet 1901* (Paris: Letouzey et Ané, 2002); Paul Nourrisson, *Histoire légale des congrégations religieuses en France depuis 1789*, 2 vols. (Paris, 1928); and Jean-Paul Durand, *La Liberté des congrégations religieuses en France*, 3 vols. (Paris: Editions du Cerf, 1999), vols. 1 and 2.

36. The expression is that of Raymond-Théodore Troplong, the great *civiliste* of the Second Empire, quoted in a decree of 15 December 1856 from the Cour de Cassation (Dalloz, *Jurisprudence générale*, year 1857, p. 97). Troplong added that the congregation touched "on everything that is gravest in the state" (ibid.).

37. Eugène Fournière, *L'Individu, l'association et l'état* (1907), pp. 46–47. I will have more to say later about this original thinker's analyses.

38. Jules Roche, *Proposition de loi tendant à la sécularisation des biens des congrégations religieuses*, Chamber of Deputies, session of 11 February 1882, in *L'Avènement de la loi*, p. 86. See also, in a similar vein, Pierre Marie René Waldeck-Rousseau, "Les Congrégations contre la République," speech delivered at Rennes on 6 September 1880, in *L'Etat et la Liberté*, 1st ser. (1879–1883) (Paris, 1906), pp. 11–18.

39. See chaps. 12, "Des congrégations et communautés religieuses," and 13, "De la société et compagnie de Jésus," in Jean-Marie Duvergier de Hauranne, *De l'ordre légal en France et des abus d'autorité* (Paris, 1826), vol. 1.

40. Adolphe Thiers, question concerning religious congregations in the Chamber of Deputies on 2 May 1845, in *Discours parlementaires de M. Thiers* (Paris, 1860), vol. 6, p. 625.

41. See his famous intervention of 3 May 1845, in *Oeuvres de Berryer: Discours parlementaires* (Paris, 1876), vol. 3. pp. 543–577. On the question of relations between the state and congregations in France at this time, see Jean-Michel

Leniaud, "Le Statut juridique des congrégations religieuses vers 1840," in Guy Bedouelle, ed., *Lacordaire, son pays, ses amis et la liberté des ordres religieux en France* (Paris: Editions du Cerf, 1991).

42. Georges Trouillot, intervention in the Chamber, 17 January 1901, in *L'Avènement de la loi*, p. 279. Trouillot also asserted that "this measure is nothing other than a reprise of the country's most ancient laws"; ibid., p. 276.

43. Ibid., p. 247.

44. Pierre Marie René Waldeck-Rousseau, intervention of 21 January 1901, in *L'Avènement de la loi*, p. 299. He repeated this assertion of "the supremacy of civil society" on several occasions.

45. It was of course vigorously debated and challenged.

46. Jules Simon, report of the committee charged with examining the Dufaure proposal, Senate, 27 June 1882, in *L'Avènement de la loi*, p. 114.

47. Pierre Marie René Waldeck-Rousseau, intervention of 7 March 1883 in the Senate, ibid., p. 159. "I regard associations as the regulator and in a sense the agent of equilibrium among the social forces," he added. "When a man by himself would be incapable of defending his interest, he goes and finds ten or a hundred of his fellow men. He combines his strength and exertion with theirs, and equilibrium is restored" (ibid.).

48. Idem, motion on a bill presented on 11 February 1882, ibid., p. 84.

49. Idem, intervention of 7 March 1883, ibid., p. 160.

50. Idem, intervention in the Chamber of Deputies, 22 January 1901, ibid., p. 300. "Associations," he had asserted decades earlier, "should not be seen as *sui generis*, as entirely distinct acts having nothing to do with all other acts accomplished by mutual consent" (bill filed on 23 October 1883, ibid., p. 173).

51. See Georges Trouillot and Fernand Chapsal, *Du contrat d'association: Commentaire de la loi du 1er juillet 1901* (Paris, 1902), p. ii.

52. "When we have in France a mass of Protestants animated by the spirit of free examination, this difficulty [of distinguishing between ordinary associations and congregations] will no longer exist," Jean-Jules Clamageran significantly observed; intervention of 7 March 1883 in the Senate, in *L'Avènement de la loi*, p. 153.

53. Waldeck-Rousseau put the point in these terms: "If the association is ended, each partner shall take away his share of the undivided whole. If a partner dies, each of his heirs can claim a share as part of his or her inheritance"; intervention of 21 January, ibid., p. 300.

54. The authoritative work on this subject is Merlet, *Une Grande Loi de la Troisième République*. See also the various papers collected in Claire Andrieu, Gilles Le Béguec, and Danielle Tartakowsky, eds., *Associations et champ politique: La loi de 1901 à l'épreuve du siècle* (Paris: Publications de la Sorbonne, 2001).

55. See, for example, Jacques Ion, "Le Modèle associatif entre l'idéal démocratique et la nostalgie des corps intermédiaires," *La Revue de l'économie sociale,* no. 14 (1988).

56. This is why firms do not exist as such in French law. They are covered by the intersection of separate legal regimes and various types of contract (the law of capital partnerships, labor, competition, etc.).

57. See Jacques Chevallier, "L'Association entre public et privé," *Revue de droit public,* July–August 1981.

58. Significantly, there is no article on mortmain in the great *Dictionnaire de l'économie politique,* ed. Charles Coquelin and Gilbert-Urbain Guillaumin (Paris, 1854), the authoritative reference in its day.

59. There is a long article on *mainmorte* in *Le Nouveau Dictionnaire d'économie politique* by Léon Say and Joseph Chailley, published in 1892.

60. Hubert-Valleroux, "Les Biens de mainmorte," *L'Economiste français,* 2d semester 1893, p. 709.

61. Georges Fonsegrive, "Le Fondement du droit d'association," in *Le Droit d'association: Etudes, notes et rapports,* p. 28.

62. See Félix Garcin, *La Mainmorte, le pouvoir et l'opinion de 1749 à 1901,* thesis (Grenoble, 1902); the chairman of the thesis jury was Léon Michoud, the leading theorist of moral personality.

63. See "La Vraie Mainmorte," *Le Correspondant,* 10 April 1901, which estimated that the congregations owned only 2 percent of property in mortmain at that time.

64. See P. Brochard, *La Mainmorte ouvrière,* thesis (Rennes, 1900).

65. Joseph Pierre André Massabuau, intervention in the Chamber of Deputies on 28 March 1901, in *L'Avènement de la loi,* p. 679.

66. Léon Say, "Lettre sur le budget" (concerning Brisson's proposal to tax mortmain), *Journal des économistes,* October 1890, p. 88.

67. Paul Leroy-Beaulieu, *La Question ouvrière au XIXe siècle,* 2d ed. (Paris, 1882); idem, *L'Etat moderne et ses fonctions,* 3d ed. (Paris, 1903); and idem, *Le Collectivisme: Examen critique du nouveau socialisme,* 4th ed. (Paris, 1903). See also Paul Hubert-Valleroux, "La Mainmorte et la charité en France," *Revue catholique des institutions et du droit,* 2d semester 1892.

68. Albert de Mun, intervention in the Chamber of Deputies, 21 January 1901, in *L'Avènement de la loi,* p. 289.

69. Brochard, *La Mainmorte ouvrière,* p. 254.

70. René Viviani, intervention in the Chamber of Deputies on 15 January 1901, in *L'Avènement de la loi,* p. 264.

71. Ibid., p. 270.

72. Among other things, he spoke of "hitting the congregations in the pocketbook" and regarded their elimination as a measure of "social hygiene";

Alexandre Zevaès, ibid., p. 488. The socialists, in an amendment proposed by Jules-Louis Breton, went so far as to suggest that congregationists be deprived of voting rights (session of 29 March 1901, ibid., pp. 694–697).

73. See Raoul Briquet, "Le Parti socialiste et la loi sur les associations," *Le Mouvement socialiste*, 1 August 1901.

74. Léon Gambetta, speech of 25 March 1881, in *Discours et Plaidoyers politiques de M. Gambetta* (Paris, 1883), vol. 9, p. 179.

75. For example, freedom of association was mentioned in only forty-six of the campaign platforms presented in the 1889 elections and ranked only twenty-ninth in order of importance. See Désiré Barodet, *Rapport fait au nom de la commission chargée de réunir et de publier le texte authentique des programmes électoraux*, Chamber of Deputies, session of 1890, *Impressions*, no. 493.

76. See the series of articles published under this title by the deputy Gustave-Louis-Edouard de Lamarzelle in *Le Correspondant* from 10 November 1900 to 25 January 1901. "Freedom of association," he wrote, "is not only a great liberty; it is *the* great liberty, the primordial liberty, the fundamental underpinning on which all other liberties rest" (p. 416).

77. Jules Ferry, speech of 14 August 1881, in *Discours et opinions de Jules Ferry* (Paris, 1897), vol. 6, p. 84.

78. Gustave-Louis-Edouard Lamarzelle, intervention of 11 June 1901 in the Senate, in *L'Avènement de la loi*, p. 729.

79. See Article 8 of the law of 1901. For a careful analysis of these differences, see Adolphe Pichon, *Des caractères distinctifs des associations soumises à la loi du 1er juillet 1901* (Paris, 1905). See also the thorough treatment in Edouard Clunet, *Les Associations au point de vue historique et juridique* (Paris, 1909), vol. 1 (the only volume published), pp. 232–287.

80. See Marie-Geneviève Dezès, "Les Patrons français: Association versus syndicat," in Andrieu, Le Béguec, and Tartakowsky, *Associations et champ politique*.

12. Polarized Democracy

1. See Jean-François Merlet, *Une Grande Loi de la IIIe République: La loi du 1er juillet 1901* (Paris: LGDJ, 2001). One important extension of the law, adopted in 1933, covered associations declared to be established solely for the purpose of assistance or charity.

2. Léon Duguit, *Traité de droit constitutionnel*, 2d ed. (Paris, 1925), vol. 5, p. 621.

3. Raymond Saleilles, "Rapport préliminaire sur le projet relatif aux fondations," *Bulletin de la Société d'études législatives*, 7 (1908), 359.

4. Idem, *De la personnalité juridique* (Paris, 1902), p. 30.

5. In 1902 new legal measures provided for stiff fines and prison terms for the

members of any congregation without official authorization. A law of 1904 envisioned the elimination of all teaching congregations within ten years.

6. Two laws adopted by the Vichy government (in 1940 and 1942) eliminated the crime of congregation along with the special disqualifications and fiscal penalties that had been imposed on the congregations but did not strike Title III of the law. These reforms remain in effect today.

7. Decision cited in Paul Pic, *Traité élémentaire de législation industrielle*, 4th ed. (Paris, 1912), vol. 1, p. 314.

8. See *Duvergier*, 1908, p. 303. See also the important law of 29 June 1907 on fraudulent practices in the wine trade. These laws were passed in response to the emergency created by an insurrection of wine growers in the south of France.

9. For an introduction to the debates on this issue, see Edouard Clunet, *Les Associations au point de vue juridique et historique* (Paris, 1909), pp. 292–338. See also the discussions in the *Bulletin de la Société d'études législatives* (1905), especially vol. 4; and the reports by Léon Michoud, Paul Hubert-Valleroux, and Gabriel de Vareilles-Sommières to the International Congress on Comparative Law in 1900, in *Procès-verbaux des séances et documents* (Paris, 1907), vol. 2, pp. 1–88.

10. Léon Michoud, *Le Théorie de la personne morale: Son application au droit français*, 2 vols. (Paris, 1906–1909); Raymond Saleilles, *De la personnalité juridique: Histoire et théories* (Paris, 1910).

11. On this point see the documentation in the thesis of Jean Escarra, *Etude sur la recevabilité des recours exercés par les syndicats et les groupements analogues* (Paris, 1907).

12. See Robert Brichet, *Association et syndicats*, 6th ed. (Paris: Litec, 1992).

13. Maxime Leroy, *Les Techniques nouvelles du syndicalisme* (Paris, 1921), p. 31.

14. Emile Eugène Gustave Mesureur, report of 5 November 1886, quoted in Fernand Pelloutier, *Histoire des bourses du travail* (1901) (Paris, 1946), pp. 111–112.

15. See *La Liberté d'association: Congrès des 25–26 janvier 1927* (Paris, 1927). This meeting may be compared with that of 1899, as both drew in part on the same groups. Paul Nourrisson served as secretary general of the organizing committee. The quotation from Duguit is taken from this volume (p. 5).

16. Auguste Rivet, "Réformes à apporter à la loi de 1901 quant à la capacité des associations," ibid., p. 117.

17. Ibid., p. 112.

18. Berthélemy, "De l'extension de la capacité des associations philanthropiques," *Revue politique et parlementaire*, August 1920, p. 20.

19. This has been the "official" doctrine of the administration since the Revolution. See the clarification issued in 1977 by the Ministry of the Interior, repro-

duced in Michel Pomey, *Traité des fondations d'utilité publique* (Paris: Presses Universitaires de France, 1980), pp. 403–404.

20. Between 1814 and 1914 fewer than 100 foundations were authorized.

21. Saleilles published a first "Report on Foundations" in the *Bulletin de la Société d'études législatives,* 5 (1906), 467 ff. Other reports on the same subject were published by the society in 1908, 1909, 1913, and 1919. In 1907 the *Bulletin* published an important exchange of letters on this subject between Gierke and Saleilles.

22. Joseph Paul-Boncour, *Le Fédéralisme économique, étude sur le syndicat obligatoire,* 2d ed. (Paris, 1901), p. 16. He envisioned an "economic and syndical federalism," noting that "we face the need to create an organization, to establish a sovereignty, hence we must begin at the beginning and first create very limited sovereignties, which by joining with others and integrating by stages will move toward ever more extensive sovereignty. That is the way a federative organization progresses" (p. 388).

23. Léon Bourgeois, *Solidarité* (Paris, 1896), p. 87.

24. Alfred Fouillée, *Le Socialisme et la sociologie réformiste* (Paris, 1909), p. 407.

25. Idem, *La Démocratie politique et sociale en France* (Paris, 1910), p. 62.

26. Léon Duguit, "Le syndicalisme," *Revue politique et parlementaire,* June 1908, p. 480.

27. Ibid., p. 479.

28. Thomas Ferneuil, "Le Syndicalisme: Réponse à M. L. Duguit," *Revue politique et parlementaire,* July 1908, p. 54.

29. See Caillaux's preface (written in 1923) to Emile Cazalis's *Syndicalisme ouvrier et évolution sociale* (Paris, 1925), p. xxix.

30. Ibid., p. xxviii.

31. Ibid., pp. xxxiii–xxxiv.

32. See Adhémar Esmein, *Eléments de droit constitutionnel français et comparé,* 2 vols., 8th ed. (Paris, 1927).

33. Napoleon III, speech at Limoges (1858), quoted in Brigitte Basdevant-Gaudement, *La Commission de décentralisation de 1870: Contribution à l'étude de la décentralisation en France au XIXe siècle* (Paris: Presses Universitaires de France, 1973), p. 24. Charles Auguste de Morny commented on this suggestion a short while later: "Let us imitate the English in seeking what we lack; let us derive strength from the spirit of association and not always call upon the government for support and assistance"; speech at the inaugural session of the Conseil Général of Puy-de-Dôme in 1859, quoted in Emile Laurent, *Le Paupérisme et les associations de prévoyance. Nouvelles études sur les sociétés de secours mutuels: Histoire, économie, administration* (Paris, 1860), vol. 1, p. 76.

34. Napoleon III, letter of 24 June 1863, reproduced in *Le Conseil d'Etat, son histoire à travers les documents d'époque: 1799–1974* (Paris: Editions du Centre

National de Recherche Scientifique, 1974), pp. 505–506. On the importance and consequences of this letter, see H. de Luçay, "La Lettre impériale du 24 juin 1863 et la décentralisation," *Revue critique de législation et de jurisprudence*, 29 (September 1866).

35. Edmond About, *Le Progrès* (Paris, 1864), p. 90.
36. Ibid., p. 91.
37. Emile Ollivier, *Commentaire de la loi du 15 mai 1864 sur les coalitions* (Paris, 1864), p. 52.
38. For an overview of the reform movement, see the *Compte général des travaux du Conseil d'Etat du 1er janvier 1861 au 31 décembre 1865* (Paris, 1866).
39. Reproduced in *Duvergier*, 1865, pp. 290–291.
40. Intervention of Napoleon at the Conseil d'Etat, 15 January 1807, quoted in Jean-Guillaume Locré, *Esprit du Code de commerce*, 2d ed. (Paris, 1829), vol. 1, p. 93.
41. See Anne Lefebvre-Teillard, "L'Intervention de l'état dans la constitution des sociétés anonymes (1807–1867)," *Revue historique de droit français et étranger*, July–September 1981.
42. See, for example, the intervention—much noted and commented on at the time—by Charles Coquelin, "Des sociétés commerciales en France et en Angleterre," *Revue des deux mondes*, 1 August 1843.
43. On the use of authorization in capitalist strategies of the period, see Anne Lefebvre Teillard, *La Société anonyme au XIXe siècle* (Paris: Presses Universitaires de France, 1985).
44. See Michel Chevalier, "L'Industrie moderne, ses progrès et les conditions de sa puissance," *Revue des deux mondes*, 1 November 1862; and Gustave de Molinari, "L'Association dans la sphère de l'économie politique," *Journal des économistes*, January 1867.
45. Report by Charles Godefroy Francisque Du Miral, *Duvergier*, 1863, p. 360.
46. Law of 24 July 1867. In addition to the previously cited works by Lefebvre-Teillard, see Charles E. Freedeman, "The Coming of Free Incorporation in France, 1850–1867," *Explorations in Entrepreneurial History*, 2d ser., 4 (Spring–Summer 1967).
47. Report of Du Miral, *Duvergier*, 1867, p. 247.
48. Ibid., p. 286.
49. Law of 5 April 1884. See also the circular of 15 May 1884. For an interesting discussion of local government under the Third Republic, see Jean-Pierre Machelon, in Louis Fougère et al., eds., *Les Communes et le pouvoir de 1789 à nos jours* (Paris: Presses Universitaires de France, 2002).
50. Quoted in Yvan Combeau, *Paris et les élections municipales sous la Troisième République* (Paris: L'Harmattan, 1998), p. 152.
51. A point stressed in A. Daniel, *L'Année politique 1884* (Paris, 1885), p. 51.

52. Louis Emile Gustave de Marcère, intervention of 30 June 1883, *Annales de la Chambre des députés,* ordinary session of 1883, *Débats,* vol. 2, p. 961.

53. See Christine Guionnet, *L'Apprentissage de la politique moderne: Les élections municipales sous la monarchie de juillet* (Paris: L'Harmattan, 1997).

54. Stephen Sawyer of the University of Chicago is preparing a dissertation on this subject. Louis Blanc, in his *Histoire de dix ans* (1840), did not dwell on these elections even though they offered the first experiences with a very broad direct vote.

55. Louis Emile Gustave de Marcère, report during the session of 19 December 1882, *Annales de la Chambre des députés,* extraordinary session of 1882, *Impressions,* no. 1547, vol. 21, p. 8.

56. Ibid., p. 10.

57. Ibid., pp. 10–11.

58. Ibid., p. 15.

59. Proposals backed by Sigismond Lacroix and Jean-Louis de Lanessan.

60. Antonin Dubost, intervention of 8 November 1883, *Annales de la Chambre des députés,* extraordinary session of 1883, vol. 3, p. 184.

61. Ibid.

62. Marcère developed this point at length in his intervention of 30 June 1883, cited above.

63. Today, a number of *communes* may be grouped together to form a *communauté urbaine,* and only the latter has the capacity to act in certain areas.

64. Law of 28 March 1882. See the debate of 5 March in the Chamber of Deputies, which concerned the history of the selection of mayors. On this point see the vast bibliography in Maurice Agulhon, Louis Girard, et al., *Les Maires en France, du Consulat à nos jours* (Paris: Publications de la Sorbonne, 1986).

65. On this point, see Rosanvallon, *Le Sacre du citoyen: Histoire du suffrage universel en France* (Paris: Gallimard, 1992).

66. See Article 42 of the law on municipal administration of 18 July 1837: "In towns with revenues of less than 100,000 francs, any discussion of special taxes or loans shall result in a summons to those paying the most taxes on the rolls of the town to participate in deliberations along with the municipal council, and the number of those summoned shall be equal to the number of council members. The leading taxpayers shall be summoned individually by the mayor at least ten days before the meeting."

67. The law of 7 April 1882 abolished the adjunction procedure. See the statistics given by Jules Labiche in his report to the Senate on the bill (reproduced in *Duvergier,* 1882, pp. 119–121).

68. The last of these restrictions was not lifted until 1975, in connection with the passage of a law on the rights of the handicapped.

69. In the late 1880s some mayors were suspended or dismissed for violation of this provision.

70. See André Mater, "Le Municipalisme et le Conseil d'Etat," *Revue d'économie politique*, 19 (April 1905).

71. Affaire Merlin, 29 June 1901, note in Maurice Hauriou, *Notes d'arrêts sur décisions du Conseil d'Etat et du tribunal des conflits, publiées au recueil Sirey de 1892 à 1928*, reprint (Paris: La Mémoire du Droit, 2000), vol. 2, pp. 223–225.

72. Ibid., p. 221.

73. Ibid.

74. Ibid., p. 226. Concerning another 1893 decision by the Conseil d'Etat, Hauriou noted: "Local administrations are not thrifty with the public's money. The increase in the debt owed by departments and towns over the past twenty years demonstrates this . . . This is clearly a serious problem, and the progress of democracy will only make it more serious"; ibid., p. 208.

75. Affaire Casanova, 29 March 1901, note in ibid., p. 229.

76. Ibid.

77. See especially André Mater, *Le Socialisme conservateur ou municipal* (Paris, 1909); and A. Veber, *Le Socialisme municipal* (Paris, 1908).

78. Hippolyte Taine, *Le Régime moderne* (1891), in *Les Origines de la France contemporaine* (Paris: Laffont, 1986), vol. 2, p. 587. "Today," he continued, "[state] interference is a boon, because if it did not intervene, the other power would become preponderant, and since that other power has belonged to the numerical majority, it has been nothing but a blind and brutish force."

79. Note, too, the purely economic character of the *syndicats de communes*, or associations of local governments, which constituted a singularly composite class.

80. On these experiments with municipal referenda, see Jacques Viguier, "Premières Expériences de 'référendum communal,'" *Revue française de droit administratif*, May–June 1996.

81. Conseil d'Etat, 7 April 1905, *commune* of Aigre, *Recueil des arrêts du Conseil d'Etat*, 1905, p. 345.

82. See Sudhir Hazareesingh, *From Subject to Citizen: The Second Empire and the Emergence of Modern French Democracy* (Princeton: Princeton University Press, 1998); and Sudhir Hazareesingh and Vincent Wright, "Le Second Empire," in Fougère et al., *Les Communes et le pouvoir*.

83. See Basdevant-Gaudement, *La Commission de décentralisation de 1870*.

84. See his typical speech on this subject of 18 September 1878 at Romans, in *Discours et plaidoyers politiques de M. Gambetta* (Paris, 1883), vol. 8, pp. 226–252. "I often groan at attacks on the state, which is France, which is universal

suffrage itself," he said (p. 236). "The administration is the steward of democracy," he added in 1881 (ibid., vol. 9, p. 374).

85. Gambetta, speech of 11 July 1876 on municipal organization, ibid., vol. 5, p. 304.

86. For a general overview, see the excellent work by Robert Elliot Kaplan, *Forgotten Crisis: The Fin-de-Siècle Crisis of Democracy in France* (Oxford: Berg Publishers, 1995).

87. See Paul Deschanel, *La Décentralisation* (Paris, 1895). Barrès's campaign in favor of decentralization was conducted in a series of articles published in the *Cocarde* between September 1894 and March 1895.

88. Decree of 16 February 1895, *Journal officiel*, 17 February 1895. In the same volume, see the report by the president of the Council, Alexis Ribot, which preceded the appointment of the commission.

89. The appointment of the commission came in the wake of a suggestion by two deputies, Louis Boudenoot and Camille Pelletan, who had strongly insisted on the need for simplification of public services (*Annales de la Chambre des députés*, extraordinary session of 1894, *Débats*, session of 8 December 1894, pp. 649–651). On the economic benefits expected from decentralization, see Georges Michel, "La Décentralisation administrative," *L'Economiste français*, 3 August 1895.

90. See especially Léon Aucoc, "Les Controverses sur la décentralisation administrative," *Revue politique et parlementaire*, April–May 1895. On this period, see also Jean-Patrick Bourdois, *La Réforme administrative dans la Revue générale d'administration, 1878–1928* (Paris: Presses Universitaires de France, 1975).

91. See Anne-Marie Thiesse, "L'Invention du régionalisme à la Belle Epoque," *Le Mouvement social*, July–September 1992.

92. Joseph Paul-Boncour, "La République et la décentralisation," in J. Paul-Boncour and Charles Maurras, *Un Débat nouveau sur la République et la décentralisation* (Paris, 1905), p. 16.

93. See Charles Maurras, "Que la République ne peut pas décentraliser," ibid.

94. Louis Emile Gustave de Marcère, "Lettre sur la décentralisation," *Revue politique et parlementaire*, 4 (April 1895), 1–2.

95. See the texts collected in Armand Charpentier, *Le Parti radical et radical-socialiste à travers ses congrès (1901–1911)* (Paris, 1913). See also Serge Berstein, "Le Parti radical et le problème du centralisme (1870–1939)," in Christian Gras and Georges Livet, *Régions et régionalisme en France du XVIIIe siècle à nos jours* (Paris: Presses Universitaires de France, 1977).

96. Georges Clemenceau, "La République et la décentralisation," in Boncour and Maurras, *Un Débat nouveau*, p. 114.

97. Ibid., p. 116.

98. Congress of Lyons, 1902, quoted in Charpentier, *Le Parti radical*, p. 363.

13. The Network State

1. Jules Michelet, lecture of 1 April 1848, in *Cours au Collège de France* (Paris: Gallimard, 1995), vol. 2, p. 393.
2. Mirabeau, *Travail sur l'éducation publique* (1791), in Bronislaw Baczko, ed., *Une Education pour la démocratie: Textes et projets de l'époque révolutionnaire* (Paris, 1982), p. 72.
3. See "Lettres d'un paysan d'Alsace à un sénateur sur l'instruction obligatoire" (December 1861), in Jean Macé, *Les Origines de la Ligue de l'enseignement (1861–1870)* (Paris, 1891) (quoted on p. 5 of the introduction). On the history of the Ligue, see Katherine Auspitz, *The Radical Bourgeoisie: The Ligue de l'Enseignement and the Origins of the Third Republic, 1866–1885* (Cambridge: Cambridge University Press, 1982); and especially Jean-Paul Martin, *La Ligue de l'enseignement et la République, des origines à 1914*, 2 vols., thesis of the Institut d'Etudes Politiques (Paris, 1992).
4. Eugène Spuller, "Démocratie et instruction du peuple," in *Education de la démocratie* (Paris, 1892), p. 4.
5. Ibid., p. 6.
6. Jean Macé, speech to the Ligue's Congress of Lille, 1885, *Bulletin de la Ligue française de l'enseignement*, no. 31 (June–August 1885), 196. "If we want to maintain the Republic . . . we ourselves must be with its governments," he said in a speech to the Congress of Rouen in 1886; ibid., no. 40 (June 1886), 213.
7. Idem, speech to the Congress of Reims, 1883, ibid., no. 19 (June 1883), 434. In this connection he even coined a new word: "omniarchy."
8. Jules Ferry, speech of 2 July 1880, quoted in Maurice Pellisson, *Les Oeuvres auxiliaires et complémentaires de l'école en France* (Paris, 1903), p. 127.
9. Idem, speech of 26 June 1892 to the pupils of the Association Philotechnique, in *Discours et opinions de Jules Ferry* (Paris, 1897), vol. 7, p. 392. On the role of this organization, see A. Pressard, *Histoire de l'Association philotechnique* (Paris, 1899).
10. Ferry, speech of 26 June 1892, p. 389.
11. Ibid., p. 390.
12. Macé used this expression. See his speech to the Congress of Lyons in 1888, *Bulletin de la Ligue française de l'enseignement*, no. 62 (April 1888), 104.
13. Macé, speech to the Congress of Rouen, pp. 213–214.
14. Jean Macé, *Les Idées de Jean-François*, vol. 4: *La Vérité du suffrage universel: Avant, pendant, et après* (Paris, 1872), p. 18.
15. Léon Bourgeois, speech to the 16th Congress of the Ligue de l'Enseignement (9 August 1896), in *L'Education de la démocratie française* (Paris, 1897), p. 231.
16. On the parallel that can be developed with the republican philosophy of scho-

lastic diversity, see Jean-François Chanet, *L'Ecole républicaine et les petites patries* (Paris: Aubier, 1996).

17. Léon Bourgeois, intervention in the Senate, 11 March 1892, in *L'Education de la démocratie*, p. 54.

18. See above, Chapter 2, on political immediacy.

19. Isaac-René-Guy Le Chapelier, intervention in the session of 14 June 1791, *A.P.*, vol. 27, p. 212.

20. Pierre-Louis Goudard, *Rapport sur la suppression des chambres de commerce, des inspecteurs des manufactures et de toute l'administration actuelle du commerce*, 27 September 1791, *A.P.*, vol. 31, p. 397. See also the *Rapport sur l'administration du commerce* by Lasnier de Vaussenay, *A.P.*, vol. 32, pp. 53–57.

21. "By entrusting the minister of the interior with the role of overseeing the general commerce of the kingdom, you have established a center to which all citizen petitions should be addressed, and you have directed administrative bodies to keep an eye on all aspects of our commerce. You have in a sense posted a vigilant sentinel, whose eye takes in all the various branches of French industry at a glance and thus maintains a constant watch over the sources of a great Empire's prosperity"; Goudard, *Rapport sur la suppression des Chambres de commerce*, vol. 31, p. 397.

22. Jean-Marie Roland de la Platière, letter of 28 April 1792, quoted in Paul Logie, *La Chambre de commerce d'Amiens, 1761–1961* (Amiens, 1964), p. 43.

23. See André Conquet, *Si les chambres de commerce m'étaient contées* (Lyons, 1976), vol. 2.

24. Jean-Claude Beugnot, letter of 24 Thermidor, Year IX (12 August 1801), reproduced in Jacques Delécluse, *Les Consuls de Rouen, marchands d'hier, entrepreneurs d'aujourd'hui: Histoire de la chambre de commerce et d'industrie de Rouen, des origines à nos jours* (Rouen, 1985), p. 125.

25. Decree of 14 Prairial, Year IX (3 June 1801).

26. This report is reproduced in André Conquet, *Le Rétablissement des chambres de commerce par Chaptal en 1802* (Paris: APCCI, 1983).

27. See Article 4 of the directive of 3 Nivôse, Year XI: "The functions attributed to the chambers of commerce are: to present views concerning ways of increasing the prosperity of commerce, to inform the government of factors impeding progress, to indicate resources that may be obtained, and to oversee the execution of public works pertaining to commerce."

28. The issue of correspondence had been central to the critique of popular societies ten years earlier.

29. Jean-Baptiste Champagny, letter of 31 March 1806, quoted in André Conquet, *Napoléon et les chambres de commerce* (Paris: APCCI, 1978), p. 34.

30. Letter from Chaptal to Beugnot, reproduced in Delécluse, *Les Consuls de Rouen*, p. 126. He argued further that the less "active power and influence [this institution] exerts over the administration, the less it will become the fo-

cal point of ambition and intrigue. This *type of isolation* will offer a guarantee of independence. It will be all the more useful if it is used only for its intelligence" (emphasis added).

31. Michel Regnault de Saint-Jean-d'Angély, report of 10 Germinal, Year XI (31 March 1803), to the Corps Législatif, reproduced in *Gazette nationale ou Le Moniteur universel,* 13 Germinal, Year XI, p. 870.

32. See the discussion in Jean-Claude Perrot, *L'Age d'or de la statistique régionale française (an IV–1804)* (Paris: Société des Etudes Robespierristes, 1977).

33. On the establishment of these institutions, see Chaptal's circular to his prefects of 12 Fructidor, Year XI (30 April 1803), reproduced in Conquet, *Napoléon et les chambres de commerce,* pp. 26–27. The designation of those eligible to vote for members of these chambers was left quite vague, and prefects were free to modify the constituency on a case-by-case basis as they saw fit.

34. See Claire Lemercier, *Un si discret pouvoir: Aux origines de la Chambre de commerce de Paris, 1803–1853* (Paris: La Découverte, 2003).

35. See Conquet, *Napoléon et les chambres de commerce.* The 1851 measure was a prelude to the omnibus law of 1898, which consecrated the roles of the chambers.

36. Léon Bourgeois, *La Politique de prévoyance sociale,* vol. 1: *La Doctrine et la méthode* (Paris, 1914), pp. 57–58.

37. See Léon Murard and Patrick Zylberman, *L'Hygiène dans la République: La santé publique en France, ou l'utopie contrariée (1870–1918)* (Paris: Fayard, 1996). For a more general overview of the redefinition of the state by way of development of its functions, see Christian Topalov, *Le Laboratoire du nouveau siècle: La nébuleuse réformatrice et ses réseaux en France, 1880–1914* (Paris: Editions de l'EHESS, 1999).

38. Bourgeois, *La Politique de prévoyance sociale,* vol. 1, pp. 180–181.

39. "Don't we feel an indispensable need to develop an ever broader conception of what tomorrow's state should be? Don't we think that the notion of state is too narrow, that it needs to be constantly adapted and extended so as to make room for the new elements and forces that daily grow more powerful and together contribute to the common interest?"; ibid., p. 181.

40. See Paul Nourrisson, *De la participation des particuliers à la poursuite des crimes et des délits* (Paris, 1894). Significantly, this work was awarded a prize by the Académie des Sciences Morales et Politiques.

41. See Edmond About, *Le Progrès* (Paris, 1864), pp. 91–95.

42. See, for example, Henry Joly, "Les Associations et l'état dans la lutte contre le crime," *Revue politique et parlementaire,* 5 (September 1895).

43. See the major work by Paul Nourrisson, *L'Association contre le crime* (Paris, 1901).

44. See Paul Nourrisson's paper "Les Associations auxiliaires de la justice," read at

the session of 9 May 1908 (*Séances et Travaux de l'Académie des sciences morales et politiques,* 1908, pp. 93–109). The question was also discussed at length by the Société Générale des Prisons (see the *Bulletin* of March–April 1896) and the Société de Législation Comparée (see the *Bulletin* of February–March 1903). Numerous comments on the issue can also be found in the *Revue pénitentiaire.*

45. See Alfred Fouillée, *La France au point de vue moral* (Paris, 1900).

46. See Jean Escarra, *Etude sur la recevabilité des recours exercés par les syndicats et les groupements analogues* (Paris, 1907).

47. See Robert Mothes, *L'Association et sa place dans l'état,* thesis (Paris, 1930).

48. The expression *corps législatif* also turned up in the Constitutions of 1793 and Year III.

49. See Ferdinand Brunot, *Histoire de la langue française des origines à 1900,* vol. 9: *La Révolution et l'Empire,* part 2, p. 1055.

50. Article 2 of the decree of 24 Messidor, Year XII (13 July 1804) concerning public ceremonies refers to *corps administratifs et judiciaires* and *corps de fonctionnaires publics* (*Duvergier,* vol. 4, pp. 42–43). The generic expression *grands corps d'état* was in common use by the middle of the nineteenth century.

51. See his interventions at the Conseil d'Etat in February and March 1806, reported in Pelet de La Lozère, *Opinions de Napoléon sur divers sujets de politique et d'administration* (Paris, 1833). For an overview of Napoleon's efforts in this area, see A. Aulard, *Napoléon Ier et le monopole universitaire* (Paris, 1911).

52. Napoleon, session of 20 February 1806, Conseil d'Etat, in Pelet de La Lozère, *Opinions de Napoléon,* p. 162.

53. Idem, session of 1 March 1806, ibid., p. 163.

54. Idem, session of 11 March 1806, ibid., p. 166.

55. "The great problem of modern societies," he often stressed, "is the government of minds." See the chapter with this title in Rosanvallon, *Le Moment Guizot* (Paris: Gallimard, 1985).

56. See chap. 6 of the *Essai.* Several conditions had to be met, he explained, in order for a *corps* of the type required to exist. "First, a certain degree of independence, which, by establishing its dignity, also establishes its power and credibility. By 'independence' I do not mean that the *corps* is isolated from the state, protected from all outside interference, and provided resources exempt from sovereign authority. I am deeply convinced that corporations of this kind are dangerous and invariably tend to degeneration. What I want instead is a teaching *corps* that belongs to the state, is sustained by the state, and receives its impetus and direction from royal authority . . . It is important to establish and strengthen these bonds between the teaching *corps* and the state. If this is done, the independence of which I speak poses no danger"; ibid., pp.

143–144. This theme was outlined earlier in Guizot's "Mémoire au roi sur l'instruction publique," January 1815, manuscript, Archives Nationales, 42 AP 28.

57. Guizot, *Essai*, p. 88.

58. On this point, see Guizot's intervention in the Chamber of Peers, 9 May 1844 (debate on secondary education), in François Guizot, *Histoire parlementaire de France* (Paris, 1863), vol. 4, pp. 333–337.

59. Idem, speech of 25 April to the Chamber of Peers, ibid., p. 325.

60. Idem, speech of 9 May, ibid., p. 332.

61. See his famous speech "Exposition du système de l'Université" (21 April 1844), in which he called for a teaching "*corps* having the power stemming from the *esprit de corps* but none of the dangers, and impervious to the vices that ruined the old corporations. This *corps* should have a purely civil power, emanating from the state and dependent on it. It should have its own life and its own forms of action, for otherwise it is not a *corps;* but it should also be under the permanent control of the higher power, which supervises all the *corps* of the state and makes sure that they remain within their proper limits"; *Oeuvres de M. Victor Cousin,* 5th ser., Instruction Publique (Paris, 1850), vol. 2, p. 47.

62. See Terry Shinn, "Des corps de l'état au secteur industriel: Genèse de la profession d'ingénieur (1750–1920)," *Revue française de sociologie,* 19 (1978); and A. Brunot and R. Coquand, *Le Corps des ponts et chaussées* (Paris: Editions du Centre National de Recherche Scientifique, 1982).

63. Intervention of 9 May 1838 in the Chamber of Deputies concerning the organization of the railroads, in Alphonse de Lamartine, *La France parlementaire (1834–1851)* (Paris, 1864), vol. 2, p. 120.

64. For an overview, see Marie-Christine Kessler, *Les Grands Corps de l'état* (Paris: Presses de la FNSP, 1986); and Dominique Chagnollaud, *Le Premier des ordres: Les hauts fonctionnaires, XVIIIe–XXe siècle* (Paris: Fayard, 1991).

65. See the report to the king preceding adoption of the ordinance of 18 September 1839 reforming the Conseil d'Etat; *Duvergier,* 1839, p. 287.

66. Bastiat's astonishing pamphlet *Baccalauréat et socialisme* came out in 1850.

67. On this key issue, which we cannot develop here, see H. S. Jones, *The French State in Question: Public Law and Political Argument in the Third Republic* (Cambridge: Cambridge University Press, 1993); and Jeanne Siwek-Poudesseau, *Le Syndicalisme des fonctionnaires jusqu'à la guerre froide, 1848–1948* (Lille: Presses Universitaires de Lille, 1989).

14. Differences and Repetitions

1. On the history of "balanced democracy," see Rosanvallon, *Le Peuple introuvable* (Paris: Gallimard, 1998). I should stress that this term implies no

value judgment. It is purely descriptive, and intended to characterize a form of political organization designed to do away with the constitutional instability that preceded the establishment of the Third Republic.

2. For further information, see Justinien Raymond, "Eugène Fournière," *L'Actualité de l'histoire*, no. 25 (October–December 1958). See also the chapter on Fournière in the thesis of Farid Lekeal, *Syndicalisme juridique, personnalisme et fédéralisme intégral* (Lille: University of Lille II, 1989), pp. 108–141.

3. Eugène Fournière, *La Sociocratie: Essai de politique positive* (Paris, 1910). Auguste Comte had used the term "sociocratic republic" half a century earlier; see his *Système de politique positive* (Paris, 1854), vol. 4, pp. 345–348.

4. Fournière, *La Sociocratie*, p. 102.

5. Fournière's political sociology deserves to be set alongside other classics of the period such as Roberto Michels, Moisei Ostrogorski, and Augustin Cochin.

6. Eugène Fournière, *L'Individu, l'Association et l'état* (1907), p. 177. On this theme, see also his article "Les Conditions de l'association moderne," *La Revue socialiste*, 47 (January 1908).

7. Idem, *L'Idéalisme social* (Paris, 1898), pp. 248–253.

8. See Géraud Poumarède, "Le Cercle Proudhon ou l'impossible synthèse," *Mil neuf cent*, no. 12 (1994).

9. Edited by the sociologist Célestin Bouglé, who was affiliated with the reform socialists; and Henri Moyasset, who ended up working for Pétain.

10. *Doctrine de Saint-Simon: Exposition, première année, 1829* (Paris, 1924).

11. Bouglé and Halévy use this expression in their preface, ibid., p. 68.

12. See Stéphane Rials, *Administration et organisation, 1910–1930: De l'organisation de la bataille à la bataille de l'organisation dans l'administration française* (Paris: Beauchesne, 1977).

13. Henri Chardon, *L'Organisation de la République pour la paix* (Paris, 1927), p. 1.

14. Published in 1924 in the new series of *Oeuvres complètes* mentioned above.

15. Leroy's two books on Saint-Simon were *Le Socialisme des producteurs: Henri de Saint-Simon* (1924) and *La Vie du comte de Saint-Simon, 1760–1825* (1925).

16. Maxime Leroy, *Pour gouverner* (Paris, 1918), p. 53.

17. Ibid., pp. 50–51.

18. Ibid., p. 333.

19. Gaëtan Pirou has calculated that 400 works dealing with corporatism were published between 1934 and 1943; reported by Steven Kaplan, "Un Laboratoire de la doctrine corporatiste sous le règne de Vichy: L'Institut d'études corporatives et sociales," *Le Mouvement social*, no. 195 (April–June 2001).

20. See Mihail Manoïlesco, *Le Siècle du corporatisme: Doctrine du corporatisme intégral et pur* (Paris, 1934).
21. See Georges Valois, *Oeuvre économique*, vol. 3 (Paris, 1927), which includes *L'Etat syndical et la représentation corporative*.
22. See Marcel Déat, "Corporatisme et liberté," *Archives de philosophie du droit et de sociologie juridique*, nos. 3–4 (1938).
23. See Claude Gautier, "Corporation, société et démocratie chez Durkheim," *Revue française de science politique*, October 1994; and Mike Hawkins, "Durkheim on Occupational Corporations: An Exegesis and Interpretation," *Journal of the History of Ideas*, 55 (July 1994).
24. See Auguste Detoeuf, "La Fin du libéralisme" (1936), in *X-Crise: De la récurrence des crises économiques* (Paris: Economica, 1982).
25. Quoted by Jean-Louis Loubet del Bayle, *Les Non-Conformistes des années 30* (Paris, 1969), p. 393.
26. Ibid., p. 355.
27. Many analysts of this period fail to distinguish sharply enough between the "sociological" corporatism of the late nineteenth and early twentieth centuries (in other words, from La Tour du Pin and Albert de Mun to Durkheim) and the "regulationist" corporatism of the 1930s. This criticism can be leveled at Matthew Elbow, *French Corporative Theory, 1789–1948* (New York: Columbia University Press, 1953); Isabel Boussard, "Les Corporatistes français du premier vingtième siècle: Leurs doctrines, leurs jugements," *Revue d'histoire moderne et contemporaine*, October–December 1993; Mike Hawkins, "Corporatism and Third Way Discourses in Inter-War France," *Journal of Political Ideologies*, October 2002.
28. On the uses and fortunes of "elastic words" of this sort in the 1930s, see the excellent remarks of Alain Chatriot, *La Démocratie sociale à la française: L'expérience du Conseil national économique, 1924–1940* (Paris: La Découverte, 2002), pp. 73–108. More broadly, this book is in an invaluable contribution to a better understanding of the transformation of the French model in the interwar period.
29. The literature is too abundant for a complete survey, but let me single out the work of Gaëtan Pirou, François Perroux, Maurice Bouvier-Ajam, and Jean Brèthe de La Gressaye.
30. This theme is well developed in Richard Kuisel, *Capitalism and the State in Modern France: Renovation and Economic Management in the Twentieth Century* (Cambridge: Cambridge University Press, 1981).
31. See Henri Michel and Boris Mirkine-Guetzévitch, *Les Idées politiques et sociales de la Résistance* (Paris, 1954); as well as the texts collected by Jean-Eric Callon, *Les Projets constitutionnels de la Résistance* (Paris: La Documentation Française, 1998).

32. Even though attempts to establish a corporatist regime were in fact far from successful.

33. See the theses of Michel Lascome, *Les Ordres professionnels* (Strasbourg: University of Strasbourg III, 1987); and Michel Bazex, *Corporatisme et Droit administratif: Le statut administratif des organismes professionnels* (Toulouse: University of Toulouse, 1967).

34. See Jean-Pierre Le Crom, *Syndicats nous voilà! Vichy et le corporatisme* (Paris: Editions de l'Atelier, 1995).

35. See Richard Kuisel, "Vichy et les origines de la planification économique (1940–1946)," *Le Mouvement social,* no. 98 (January–March 1977).

36. A largely formal distinction between taxes and "social dues" was invoked to justify the granting of power over certain sectors of public action to the so-called social partners. On the institutionalization of the trade unions after 1945, see Rosanvallon, *La Question syndicale.*

37. See the statement of motives accompanying the ordinance of 3 March 1945: "In the law of 1884, the working classes found an opportunity to demonstrate their strength and contribute to the social life of the nation in the most active fashion. Now that the restoration of liberty has once again accorded workers a broad range of opportunities to express their interests through their professional organizations, the moment seems ripe to outline, in the same atmosphere of liberty, the construction of a *corps familial* that would serve as the government's staunchest support in the courageous effort of demographic restoration that it has decided to undertake"; *Journal Officiel,* 4 March 1945, p. 1137. See also René Théry, "Le Corps familial de l'ordonnance du 3 mars 1945," *Droit social,* June–October 1951 (three articles).

38. Article 6 of the ordinance.

39. The decision of the Conseil Constitutionnel on 16 July 1971 invalidated the provisions of the Marcellin bill allowing the administration in certain cases to withhold issuance of receipts for declarations of association deemed to include objectives contrary to law.

40. See Pierre Grémion, "Les Associations et le pouvoir local," *Esprit,* June 1978.

41. This characterization was suggested by Jean-Paul Négrin, "L'Utilisation par l'administration des associations de la loi de 1901," *Revue française d'administration publique,* July–September 1977, p. 115.

42. François Bloch-Lainé, *L'Emploi des loisirs ouvriers et l'éducation populaire,* thesis (Paris, 1936), pp. 286–290.

43. For a preliminary study of the question, see Jean-Marie Garrigou-Lagrange, *Recherches sur les rapports des associations avec les pouvoirs publics* (Paris: LGDJ, 1970).

44. See François Bloch-Lainé, "Le Mouvement associatif et le droit public," *L'Actualité juridique: Droit administratif,* March 1980, p. 117.

45. See Jean-Paul Négrin, "Les Associations administratives," ibid. He defines them as "associations declared, founded, and run by the authorities or by agents of one or more public persons and financed exclusively or primarily by subsidies provided by said public persons for the purpose of discharging a responsibility normally attributed to them" (p. 129).

46. See the lengthy and very well-documented discussions of "dismemberment of the bureaucracy" in the *Rapport au président de la République* by the Cour des Comptes for the years 1960 and 1961 (pp. 42–51). The court objected in particular to a "distortion of the notion of public service" (p. 50).

47. See René Théry, "L'Octroi d'un monopole à une association," *Droit social*, July–August 1969.

48. This figure is taken from Raphaël Hadas-Lebel, "Considérations générales: Les associations et la loi de 1901, cent ans après," in Conseil d'Etat, *Rapport public 2000* (Paris: La Documentation Française, 2001). The equivalent shares were 64 percent in Germany, 47 percent in the United Kingdom, and 31 percent in the United States.

49. See Edith Archambault, "Le Secteur sans but lucratif: Situation du secteur associatif en France et perspective internationale," in *A but non lucratif: 1901–2001, cent ans de liberté d'association* (Paris: Fischbacher, 2001).

50. Commissariat Général au Plan, *Rapport de la Commission aménagement du territoire et cadre de vie,* VIIe Plan (Paris: La Documentation Française, March 1975). The text spoke of "broadening the field of action open to associations" and called for their further development in order to involve citizens more directly in public life and to encourage social experimentation (pp. 35–36).

51. *Rapport sur l'orientation préliminaire du VIIe Plan* (Paris: La Documentation Française, June 1975). The report called on the authorities to consult systematically with associations dealing with living conditions and consumer issues (pp. 24–25).

52. René Lenoir, "Associations, démocratie et vie quotidienne," *Le Monde,* 17 June 1975. Lenoir also announced various measures of material support for associations. See idem, "La Participation des citoyens à la vie sociale," *Projet,* July–August 1976.

53. *Rapport sur la participation des Français à l'amélioration de leur cadre de vie* (Paris, January 1976). This report, which was never distributed, can be consulted today at the Centre de Documentation of the Commissariat Général au Plan. A presentation of its recommendations can be found in *Correspondance municipale,* no. 175 (February 1977). The report includes Valéry Giscard d'Estaing's letter to Jacques Chirac dated 25 February 1975, as well as Chirac's mission statement to Pierre Delmon.

54. *Rapport sur la participation,* p. 7.

55. Giscard, in his letter of 25 January, expressed the hope that procedures might

be found so that user groups would not be led "to remain wedded to a negative attitude." The *Rapport de la Commission vie sociale* on Plan VII (Paris: La
Documentation Française, 1976) also called for "encouraging associative life"
without excluding associations that "cause disruption" (p. 27).

56. See the Barre Report on the financing of housing (1976), the Nora Report on
renovation of older housing (December 1975), and the Guichard Report
on the development of local responsibilities (January 1977). On this crucial
point, see Bernard Roudet, "Le Discours de l'état sur les associations," in Guy
Saez, ed., *Les Associations entre l'état et la société civile* (Paris: Association pour
la Diffusion de la Recherche sur l'Action Culturelle, May 1980).

57. See Pierre Rosanvallon, *L'Age de l'autogestion* (Paris: Editions du Seuil, 1976);
and, with Patrick Viveret, *Pour une nouvelle culture politique* (Paris: Editions
du Seuil, 1977).

58. The conditions under which universal suffrage was achieved offer a good example of *productive ambiguity* of this sort.

59. Perhaps for want of an institutional vision to support the proposals for an alternative. On this point, see the history of the municipal action groups in
Michèle Sellier, "Les Groupes d'action municipale," *Sociologie du travail*, January–March 1977.

60. See François Bloch-Lainé, "Elus, techniciens et militants," *Le Monde*, 21 May
1976.

61. On these changes, see Jacques Chevallier, "L'Association entre public et privé,"
Revue du droit public, July–August 1981, pp. 904–906. In this connection, one
should analyze the decree of 7 July 1977 specifying the conditions for soliciting the consent of associations concerned with living conditions (seniority of
three years, "sufficient" number of members, etc.), which were similar to
those imposed on nonconfederated trade unions.

62. On this point, which cannot be developed here, see the seminal works of
Alessandro Pizzorno and Philip Schmitter.

63. See the excellent overview by John Keeler, *The Politics of Neocorporatism in
France: Farmers, the State, and Agricultural Policy-Making in the Fifth Republic*
(Oxford: Oxford University Press, 1987).

64. The Conseil National, which reported to the prime minister (in the classic
mold of other "Superior Councils"), was a consultative organ charged with
proposing reforms and conducting research into how associative life might be
expanded, as well as submitting an annual assessment of how associations
were doing (decree of 25 February 1983).

65. A detailed account of how these bills became bogged down in the bureaucracy can be found in Jean-Paul Durand, *La Liberté des congrégations religieuses* (Paris: Editions du Cerf, 1999), vol. 3, pp. 62–80.

66. See Jean-Pierre Loisel, *Les Français et la vie associative* (Paris: CREDOC Re-

port Collection no. 201, July 1999); Viviane Tchernonog, *Le Monde associatif aujourd'hui* (Paris: Conseil Economique et Social, 21 June 2001); and *Bilan de la vie associative, 2000–2002,* published by the Conseil National de la Vie Associative (Paris: La Documentation Française, 2003).

67. At this meeting Lionel Jospin stressed that associations were "one of the pillars of the Republic" and proposed a series of fiscal and financial measures to benefit them. See *Le Monde,* 23 February 1999.

68. Signed on 1 July by the prime minister and the Conférence Permanente des Coordinations Associatives (an organization formed in 1999 and recognized by the government as "representative"). The charter affirmed "the importance of the associative contribution to the general interest." Associations were encouraged to "deepen democratic life and the civic and social dialogue."

69. See *Elus locaux et Associations: Visions croisées,* a report on a qualitative study carried out on behalf of the Interministerial Mission for the Celebration of the Centennial of the Law of 1901, published in *La Gazette des communes, des départements, des régions,* 30 July 2001 (cahier no. 2).

70. See Martine Barthélemy, *Associations: Un nouvel âge de participation?* (Paris: Presses de Sciences-Po, 2000), pp. 19–35. More broadly, this work offers a good overview of associative practices and the debates connected to them since the late 1960s.

71. See the masterful work of Pierre Grémion, *Le Pouvoir périphérique: Bureaucraties et notables dans le système politique français* (Paris: Editions du Seuil, 1976).

72. Jean-Pierre Worms, "Le Préfet et ses notables," *Sociologie du travail,* July–September 1966.

73. The expression "rationalizing corporatist state" sums up the analyses of Pierre Grémion in *Le Pouvoir périphérique.*

74. Pierre Richard, quoted in Marc Abelès, "Les Chemins de la décentralisation," *Les Temps modernes,* February 1985, p. 1403.

75. On the changes of the 1980s, see Vivien Schmidt, *Democratizing France: The Political and Administrative History of Decentralization* (Cambridge: Cambridge University Press, 1990).

76. To borrow the title of Jonah Levy's book, *Tocqueville's Revenge: State Society, and Economy in Contemporary France* (Cambridge, Mass.: Harvard University Press, 1999). This book explains how centralization and *dirigisme,* still the dominant approaches to economic intervention in the 1960s, subsequently receded, but without making room for a truly compensatory dynamism stemming from civil society.

77. See Jacques Capdevielle, *Modernité du corporatisme* (Paris: Presses de Sciences-Po, 2001).

78. Evidence for this can be seen in the vast literature that has grown up in the English-speaking countries since 1990 around the question of civil society. Interest in the subject in these countries has nothing to do with the critique of Jacobinism, which does not exist there. It stems from more fundamental questions about how to strengthen democracy and citizenship at a time when both seem to be in some danger of decline.

Index

341

Freedom or right *(continued)*
    42; to form free societies, 45; to assembly,
    45–46, 48, 191; political, 46; Burke on,
    64; and modernity, 72; of commerce, 80;
    debate over, 94; Guizot on, 131–132; to
    work, 151–152, 176; of labor, 154; of
    speech and action, 191; of choice, 196; of
    exit, 196. *See also* Liberty
French Alliance for the Education of the
    People, 256
French Revolution: and generality, 4; and
    hatred of corporations, 13–16; and clubs
    and popular societies, 35, 36, 37; Burke
    on, 64; and continuity with Old Regime,
    66–67, 68, 70; Hegel on, 69, 70, 71;
    disincorporation of social in, 73; and
    corporations, 79; essence of, 86;
    sociological effects of, 86; as totalizing,
    109; and Le Chapelier Law, 158, 159, 160;
    changing views of, 161; Ferneuil on, 165–
    166; and trade unions, 175–176; and
    associations, 234; and chambers of
    commerce, 236, 237
Freppel, Monseigneur, 161
Friendly Societies, 156
Friendship and fraternity, 5, 24, 25–26, 27

Gambetta, Léon, 143, 155, 160, 164, 191,
    194, 205, 227
Ganil, 126
Gazette nationale, La, 103
General interest, 1–2, 8, 15, 16, 26
Generality: and Jacobinism, 4, 63; and
    individual, 5; utopian, 6, 119, 137;
    meaning of, 14–15; and particularity, 21,
    68–71; intermediary bodies as obstacles
    to, 28; and democracy, 35; and
    immediate democracy, 41; and law, 50,
    55–57, 73; and self-evidence, 52; origins
    of, 63; in Portalis, 65; and absolutism, 67;
    power's claim to, 74; de Serre on, 99; and
    liberalism, 109; and right of association,
    116; broadened definition of, 119, 127–
    131; Vital-Roux's theory of, 126; and new
    aristocracy, 128; and representation, 132;
    and civil society, 140; and trade unions,
    174; and associations, 202; and
    individual-state relationship, 219
Generality, political: inception of, 4; and

Jacobinism, 4; as regulatory procedure, 4,
    5–6; as social form, 4–5, 56, 189; and
    intermediary bodies, 5; challenges to, 7;
    and women, 31; and abstraction, 65; and
    unity, 118; and absolutism, 122; and
    ambiguity, 140–146; and centralization,
    142; and associations, 234
General will: and rejection of intermediary
    bodies, 5; and law, 6, 53; and friendship,
    26; and fraternity, 27; and property, 29;
    and intermediary political bodies, 38;
    immediate expression of, 42; in
    Lanthenas, 42; in Rousseau, 56; and
    campaign committees, 139
Gerando, Joseph-Marie de, 150
German historical school, 109
Germany, 68, 175, 261
Gide, Charles, 179
Gierke, Otto von, 165
Girardin, René-Louis de, 40
Giscardians, 259
Glaneuse, La, 113
Globe, Le, 97, 103, 109, 132, 141
Goudard, Pierre-Louis, 235, 236
Gournay, Vincent de, 126
Great Britain: and women, 32; House of
    Commons, 43; and liberalism, 52, 53, 70;
    and Burke, 64; democracy in, 68; Hegel
    on, 69, 70, 71; corporations in, 73;
    pragmatism in, 75; privilege in, 108; right
    of coalition in, 111; rights in, 136; trade
    unions in, 155, 156, 168, 170, 175
Great Depression, 251
Great whole *(un grand tout),* 7, 13, 21, 24,
    27–28, 30, 32, 86–87, 96. *See also* Unity
Grémion, Pierre, 262
Guesde, Jules, 203, 248
Guilds, 14, 16, 79, 81, 160
Guiraudet, Toussaint, 14, 15, 32–33
Guizot, François: *Histoire de la civilisation
    en Europe,* 66; on corporations, 90; on
    society, 96, 98; and Daunou, 109; and
    electoral process, 114; and
    decentralization, 120, 131–132, 133, 134;
    on associations, 121–122; and political
    economy, 127; and aristocracy, 128; on
    intermediary bodies, 131–132, 133, 134,
    244–245; modernity in, 133; and Billiard,
    144; mutual aid societies in, 150; on